A Life in Balance?

Edited by Catherine Krull and
Justyna Sempruch

A Life in Balance?
Reopening the Family-Work Debate

UBCPress · Vancouver · Toronto

21 20 19 18 17 16 15 14 13 12 11   5 4 3 2 1

Printed in Canada on FSC-certified ancient-forest-free paper
(100% post-consumer recycled) that is processed chlorine- and acid-free.

Library and Archives Canada Cataloguing in Publication

A life in balance? : reopening the family-work debate /
edited by Catherine Krull and Justyna Sempruch.

Includes bibliographical references and index.
ISBN 978-0-7748-1967-1 (cloth); 978-0-7748-1968-8 (pbk.)

1. Work and family – Canada. 2. Caregivers – Family relationships – Canada.
3. Women – Employment – Canada. 4. Women – Canada – Social conditions.
I. Krull, Catherine II. Sempruch, Justyna

HD4904.25.L53 2011	306.3'6	C2010-906817-3

e-book ISBNs: 978-0-7748-1969-5 (pdf); 978-0-7748-1970-1 (epub)

Canadä

UBC Press gratefully acknowledges the financial support for our publishing program of the Government of Canada (through the Canada Book Fund), the Canada Council for the Arts, and the British Columbia Arts Council.

This book has been published with the help of a grant from the Canadian Federation for the Humanities and Social Sciences, through the Aid to Scholarly Publications Program, using funds provided by the Social Sciences and Humanities Research Council of Canada.

Printed and bound in Canada by Friesens
Set in Stone by Artegraphica Design Co. Ltd.
Copy editor: Judy Phillips
Proofreader: Lesley Erickson
Indexer: Lillian Ashworth

UBC Press
The University of British Columbia
2029 West Mall
Vancouver, BC V6T 1Z2
www.ubcpress.ca

Contents

Acknowledgments / vii

Introduction
Diversifying the Model, Demystifying the Approach:
The Work-Family Debate Reopened / 1
Catherine Krull and Justyna Sempruch

Part 1: Transcending the Prevailing Myths

1 Destabilizing the Nuclear Family Ideal: Thinking beyond Essentialisms,
Universalism, and Binaries / 11
Catherine Krull

2 Intergenerational Care Work: Mothering, Grandmothering,
and Eldercare / 30
Nancy Mandell and Sue Wilson

3 Maternal Employment, Childcare, and Public Policy / 47
Maureen Baker

Part 2: Integrating Family and Work

4 Work, Care, Resistance, and Mothering: An Indigenous Perspective / 67
Donna Baines and Bonnie Freeman

5 "I Am the Patient and Compassionate Cashier": Learning through
Unpaid Household Work for Paid Work / 81
Margrit Eichler

6 Employment in the New Economy and the Impact on Canadian
Families / 98
Ann Duffy and Norene Pupo

7 What Impedes Fathers' Participation in Care Work?
Theorizing the Community as an Institutional Arena / 115
Andrea Doucet

8 Addressing the Interlocking Complexity of Paid Work and Care:
Lessons from Changing Family Policy in Quebec / 130
Patrizia Albanese

Part 3: Feminist-Informed Family Initiatives and Family Visions

9 Beyond the "Cultural" Landscape of Care: Queering Childcare,
Caregiver, and Work / 147
Justyna Sempruch

10 Working-Time Regimes, Flexibility, and Work-Life Balance:
Gender Equality and Families / 170
Judy Fudge

11 The Increasing Invisibility of Mothering / 194
Margaret Hillyard Little

Epilogue
A Feminist Vision for Caring-Employment Integration in Canada / 206
Susan A. McDaniel

References / 219

List of Contributors / 251

Index / 257

Acknowledgements

Justyna and I are grateful to a number of people who assisted and supported us in this endeavour. We want to especially thank Janelle Hippe and Sylvia Bawa for their careful reading of and insightful comments on various parts of this book. The support, assistance, and never-ending patience of Wendy Schuler in the Sociology office at Queen's University were of considerable importance to this project. We also appreciate the support we have received from the editorial staff at UBC Press, and are especially grateful to Emily Andrew, senior editor, and Anna Eberhard Friedlander, production editor, for their continuous encouragement and sage advice. We are also indebted to our families, whose support and words of encouragement helped to move this project forward.

   As with most families, mine is in constant flux – some family members leave us, willingly or reluctantly, and new ones materialize. I lovingly dedicate this book to the memory of my father, Brian Scott, who recently left us but who will always be part of who I am; to the memory of my dear Cuban friend and mentor Sonia Enjamio, who challenged me to imagine "other" ways of knowing; and to my new granddaughter, Maria, who has changed my world completely.

Catherine Krull
September 2010

A Life in Balance?

Diversifying the Model, Demystifying the Approach: The Work-Family Debate Reopened

Catherine Krull and Justyna Sempruch

Several years ago we worked at the same university and, as it happens, were introduced to each other at one of the interdepartmental meetings. That day we ended up evaluating some reports on mothering and academia, which turned out to be a trigger for exchanging our shared frustrations that centred on the failing mainstream practices of balancing work and family. As full-time working mothers with children, grandchildren, and aging parents to care for, we found ourselves bemoaning how little the state has done to resolve social and economic changes that affect families. Our conversation led then to a number of more constructive discussions at the kitchen table. The clearly dominating question was why does the workplace and home life continue to be viewed as two different and conflicting spheres? And more precisely, why does the unquestioned belief persist that these two spheres are in need of balance?

With the exception of some feminist-informed academic work, the majority of contemporary research across sociology, psychology, politics, and law continues to analyze the "conflict" as if the public and private spheres do not cross and overlap in many different ways, as if work does not indicate or involve our families and can be measured only in wages. Moreover, mainstream Canadian debates, the media, and politicians often assume an incompatibility between work and family without simultaneously considering numerous external factors such as consumerism, exposure to competition, and shrinking public support that accumulates new pressures. Even at our own universities, children have tended to be viewed as briefly visiting bodies that need to be under immediate parental supervision – and then only in emergency situations when there are no alternative caregivers. Even in the Department of Women's Studies, mothering was not necessarily a fashion.

Mothering and work have also been slowly disappearing from many Canadian research agendas, giving the false impression that women-specific family tensions are resolved. Drawing on our own lives as feminist academics, and as mothers who work at home and at the university, we have thought to reflect otherwise. The gendered family-work divide has never left us but, rather, has simply become less visible and certainly less discussed. This realization concerned us and, therefore, one of the prevailing reasons for this endeavour was to revisit feminist understandings of this complex dynamic and to address a missing focus on positive research and policy outcomes, especially those deriving from a model based on the diversity of care needs.

Our starting point was to address contemporary research that overwhelmingly centres on the act of "reconciling" family and work and on "striking a balance" between these two incompatible spheres. Despite numerous feminist studies about the decline of the employment norm and the contract between genders (that is, the male breadwinner–dependent female caregiver exchange), the normative heterosexual family model continues to be the reference point in current mainstream thinking and policy making. Self-help books line the shelves of Canadian bookstores, advising readers, especially women, on how to achieve a healthy "balance" between employment and family. Paid work (employment) and unpaid work (caregiving and household work) are set against each other, as if they are components of a zero-sum game. Moreover, household duties and looking after children or other dependent family members are primarily depicted as emotional and spontaneous acts of caring, cast as an altruistic sacrifice that we make out of love and concern for our families. Although these acts of caring remain important, "actual" work is rarely thought to take place in the family. Thus, allowing family pressures to interfere with one's employment is assumed to be costly for the employer, and it communicates incompetence on the part of the employee. Conversely, reducing our time at these tasks because of paid-work responsibilities is often construed as cheating our families – and ourselves.

Following these thoughts, we aimed to address the artificiality of such thinking in the context of Canadian societal structures that perpetuate erroneous assumptions about work, as well as about its neo-liberal functions at the beginning of the twenty-first century. Eventually, we collected enough material to come up with the book's objective: to expose dichotomous thinking about family and work by the systematic demystification of the divide. By no means did we hope to be all-inclusive but, rather, our intention from the onset has been to reopen the work-family debate from a new philosophical angle. Therefore, this book aims to fill the interstice in critical literature on the so-called reconciliation agenda and to define a common theoretical ground on which to discuss the interdependence of paid work and family life. Ultimately, we formulated specific objectives, the first of which was to re-examine the persistent ways in which the dichotomy of family and work is perpetuated by the assumed contradiction. Our second objective was to critically assess why current approaches to the family and work balance are inadequate and fail to meet the diverse needs of caregivers. The third objective was to examine new ways in which various approaches to family and work, including Quebec's agenda, can be instructive in building a national childcare policy. Our final objective was to provide a feminist-informed discussion on how family care-work integration can be achieved.

Early in our discussions, we also understood that our work would have to involve theoretically diverse positions and, hence, it would need to become a collection of chapters by specialists in the field. We carefully selected eminent Canadian scholars to expand on the debates from a care-centred approach. This we felt would provide the policy framework through which to address the interdependence of work and family, while reflecting the diversity found in both. Care work in our collection has therefore become a combined issue of the continuous alterations in family arrangements and the changing norms of employment that create new challenges for the workplace. Clearly, then, such diversified care-centrism required the involvement of a meaningful interdisciplinary exchange, which was subsequently classified into three specific yet interrelated sections of this book.

Many concepts found in the family and work literature – reconciliation, balance, conflict, integration – originate with the notion of a division that is in need of resolution. We begin the book with a chapter written by Catherine Krull that illuminates this paradox, destabilizes the nuclear family concept and other related binaries, and discusses possible consequences for Canadian policy making. It is an apt place to commence demystifying the family-work contradiction. The chapter targets the underlying but clearly outdated middle-class assumption that one contributes to family life either through paid work outside the home or through unpaid family care. The necessity to opt for one or the other part of the equation speaks to two issues: the problem that one is simply made to *choose* between family and professional employment, and a subsequent long-familiar frustration that one cannot do both. The concept of choice also implies or assumes equality, which renders socially generated inequality invisible. Despite the diversities clearly experienced across families, workplaces, and political institutions today, the postwar model continues to be supported by current policy research, which typically discusses "reconciliation" and "conflict," reinforcing socio-cultural significations of the separate family and work spheres. All this might explain why current feminist critiques incessantly focus on the negative policy outcomes of work and family reconciliation. In the absence of profound shifts in public policy regarding the nexus between family life and the economy of the labour market, the qualities based on the nuclear family model in Canada are clearly decreasing.

In this theoretical vein, Part 1, "Transcending the Prevailing Myths," addresses the need for developing barometers of change across Canadian communities. Such a move requires that we abandon discussions that posit the gender contract as an economic institution of family wage – as has been the case since the Second World War. In the Canadian past, as in those of other Western societies, the gender contract was the reason why informal care was not considered work as opposed to formal and less formal caregiving jobs. The gender contract structured the division between paid "productive" labour and unpaid domestic work. As presumed by postwar policy makers, the labour market has been based on the vast majority of men being in secure, full-time wage employment and on economically "inactive" women taking care of households or, otherwise, being in the labour market as supplementary workers. In contradistinction to such a clearly upper-middle-class-oriented model, single-parent households or culturally different family scenarios have been neglected. Today, the gender contract is only superficially maintained by numerous change-resistant mainstream beliefs. Examples of such beliefs are that the family as a basic social form is in decline, or that family time is in short supply as employed mothers neglect their children. The same presumptions maintain that women are natural caregivers, whereas other care models, often utilized by immigrant, ethnic, or racialized families, are somehow inferior.

Consequently, the co-written chapter by Nancy Mandell and Sue Wilson and the chapter by Maureen Baker discuss the complexities and transformations of family and work. As this new research suggests, studying family life is not about examining decline; it is about understanding the various meanings of diversity and liberalization, as well as the inevitable adjustments governed by the free market economy. What is certainly declining is the norm of the nuclear family modelled on a white, middle-class, heterosexual couple with children. Although many mothers have already begun to shift the boundaries of domestic work, grandparents and other family members have usually been excluded and continue not to be acknowledged for their participation in the private sphere. An increasing number of middle-aged women provide simultaneous care for their children, their grandchildren, and their step-grandchildren.

With this picture in mind, the central part of the book, Part 2, "Integrating Family and Work," is dedicated to the ongoing challenges and diversification of family dilemmas. To understand the vulnerability with which many Canadian families live today, we begin with a chapter focused on rebuilding communities. Donna Baines and Bonnie Freeman reflect on the impact of colonialism and the collective trauma of the First Nations with respect to indigenous meanings of care. In the context of cultural healing, sustenance, and connection, care transcends the typical family models and becomes a natural continuum between home and community. Margrit Eichler's exegesis follows a similar mode of continuum, which she applies to learning opportunities that derive from household and care work – often indispensable in paid work. A significant body of literature demonstrates that the performance of unpaid work has a deleterious effect on paid work; Eichler's research questions these results by examining the very skills learned through unpaid work at home that are transferable to the marketplace. Worldwide, very few studies have involved such analysis, and one might conclude with the question of why such substantial knowledge acquisition has not been widely acknowledged in the employment sector.

Indeed, the expectation of overtime, mobility, and general work flexibility, so typical for care work at home, has become characteristic of many career trajectories. Yet neither opportunity for mobility and flexible time nor actual access to paid employment is equal for all parents. The blanket approach for Canadian working parents, resulting from the over-reliance on general and often deregulated rights, is not only gender-blind but also seriously incapable of integrating and harmonizing the dynamics of work and family. In particular, there is a fair amount of discontinuity between the changing structure of employment and actual women's employment patterns. Census data and the observations of our own immediate environment equally confirm that women contribute the lion's share of unpaid work, along with non-standard work, contract work, telecommuting, and multiple job holding.

Drawing on these economic transformations and the fast-forward growth of information technology, Ann Duffy and Norene Pupo's chapter focuses on the shifting norms and deregulation of employment in the Canadian labour market. What their research reveals is that Canadian families increasingly experience a wide diversity of employment forms that are often characterized by insecurity, discontinuity, and intensification of demands – already reflected in the long processes of attaining formal education and in the unpredictable daily hours at paid employment.

Another interesting transformation in Canadian families in the past four decades has been the rising number of stay-at-home fathers and the increasing role of women as primary breadwinners. As Andrea Doucet's chapter reveals, policy supports, community programs, and ideological conceptions that support fathers' participation in caregiving are in high demand. In some significant ways, of course, other ideological conceptions based on the supposed universality of the male breadwinner hinder such participation. Meeting the demands of paid and unpaid work is particularly interesting in the context of Quebec's approach to policy, known as the most child- and family-friendly policy in Canada. Drawing on lessons the rest of Canada might take from Quebec, Patrizia Albanese's work analyzes major difficulties in balancing the demands of a free market economy, childcare, and other family obligations.

Following these intersections of theory and research, we ultimately arrive at the question of how we can learn from all these findings and propositions. In other words, where can we go from here? The final part of this book attempts to set possible directions, and it concerns specifically feminist-informed family initiatives and family visions that draw on the ethics of care and politics, as well as on the philosophy of diversity and difference. The chapters therein reflect on the key theoretical tensions that arise for scholars conducting research on mothers, fathers, and care within families. Justyna Sempruch's chapter, grounded distinctively in the philosophy of care, discusses gender subjectivity as crucial to feminist critiques of care practice. As she argues, masculinity and femininity do not necessarily imply any exclusiveness of actual gender. Rather, the simultaneity of gender positions no longer privileges women as those with exclusionary access to reproduction, nor men as those in control of the "productive" economy, allowing for an argument that fathers can also be constructed as marginal to the symbolic order. So long as care work policies do not include formulated gender flexibility, caregivers will continue to battle against exclusion carried out informally where formal restrictions are now illegal and specific policy actions in favour of care are required. In fact, as Justyna Sempruch concludes, gender flexibility recognizes and redistributes value across the public and private spheres, refusing the caregivers' exclusion from economic and political relevance.

The extent to which concepts such as flexibility and gender simultaneity have been adopted by the present working culture needs our attention on several fronts. Judy Fudge reveals that although we have more work flexibility than ever before, working parents, mostly mothers, continue to experience serious time pressures. The double burden and time crunches have certainly not disappeared from Canadian households. One of the key elements, to follow Judy Fudge, is to develop a more equitable distribution of paid and unpaid labour while shifting paid working-time norms in a direction that better accommodates and values care work. Revising hours of work, especially overtime, is as important as revising occupational exclusions, part-time work, and flexibility itself.

Finally, one must not forget that traditional cultural values and normative assumptions about caregiving as unpaid labour most profoundly affect single mothers. Margaret Hillyard Little's chapter informs, in this respect, with the theme of the increasing invisibility of mothering dilemmas. Competing policy agendas and current labour practices have often counteracted recent Canadian programs promoting maternal employment. Although political discourse today focuses on children as a "future resource," politicians continue to encourage low-wage work without ensuring high-quality care for employees' children. Likewise, the growing gap between the income of poor single mothers and the state's expectations reveals that neo-liberal welfare regulations do not aim at decentralizing the normative practice. Margaret Little's research concludes that discussions of child poverty are both erroneous and unethical, for it is the parents who are and remain poor. The only ethical turn is to ask why a large number of Canadian parents are poor and why most of them tend to be female. Consequently, feminist examinations of the legal regulation of working-time and working practices in Canada are instrumental in evaluating the regulatory regime and its contribution to various work-family conflicts.

Our concluding perspective presents, therefore, a feminist vision for the integration of family and work, based on a political ethic of care and allowing for a clear picture of where we should go from here with responsibilities for care work. If gender, in its full complexity, is to be understood as a set of social relations that shape access to variously defined citizenship rights in their sexual, socio-cultural, and political dimensions, then all three aspects must be targeted simultaneously. Consequently, it is not care work alone but, foremost, its complex intermingling with market work that we believe is providing fodder for the national and provincial governments and their policy agendas. A pivotal proposal initiated by this book is, therefore, a call for a renewed understanding of social citizenship that politically embodies and promotes equality without sacrificing the health and stability of Canadian society. These aspirations, integrated in Susan McDaniel's epilogue, are neither mutually exclusive nor impossible to attain. Addressing them as such necessitates, however, a culturally integrative and cross-societal positioning that until now has not been sufficiently researched. With this book, we have demonstrated this necessity.

Part 1
Transcending the Prevailing Myths

1

Destabilizing the Nuclear Family Ideal: Thinking beyond Essentialisms, Universalism, and Binaries

Catherine Krull

The nuclear family, composed of a heterosexual husband and wife and their biological children, has long been thought to be the ideal family structure in Canada. Nowhere is this more evident than in our various social resources and policies – government benefits, public policies, laws, national censuses, the structuring of employment and schools, access to contraception and reproductive technologies, pensions, and more – all of which have been fashioned on the assumption that the nuclear family structure is not only ideal but also representative of most Canadian families. Implementation of these social resources and policies in turn reinforces the normative nuclear family ideology. Despite growing family diversity in Canada, this hegemonic family form has permeated our collective understanding of the ideal family. According to a national survey, most Canadians view the traditional nuclear family as "the most recognizable and most preferred family form" (Bibby 2004, 10). As a normative ruler, all non-nuclear family forms become conceptualized as "special" or "other." Terminology such as "broken families," "blended families," and "reconstituted families" makes sense only if such forms are understood in reference to the ideal, namely, the normative nuclear family.

Idealizing the nuclear family form, centred on the male breadwinner–dependent wife caregiver binary, has meant that even after decades of feminism, family care work – domesticity – and paid market work remain bifurcated and deeply gendered. As such, these two types of work have emerged in the public imaginary as distinct, incompatible, and in need of careful balance; as a consequence of seeking this balance, women's and men's full participation in both family care work and paid work has been impeded. Mothers in particular often feel conflicted in trying to achieve the neo-liberal image of the ideal worker while struggling to measure up to the normative nuclear family ideology of good motherhood. Many women therefore continue to be marginalized in the workforce, and their family care work is rendered invisible. Contemporary fathers, on the other hand, experience difficulties living up to the masculine breadwinner ideal – often feeling conflicted between time spent at their employment and time spent with family members.

Such gender ideologies have sustained the private-public binaries of work. Narratives of men's and women's disparate yet complementary experiences within the private-public domains are essentialist in that they are linked to the "confines of the nature, essence or biology of the two sexes" (Grosz 1995, 49; see also Grosz 2005). The sexual division of social roles has therefore been rendered natural, necessary, and politically justified. Essentialist approaches to family life disregard diverse and fluid understandings of family and work across ethnicity, geographic location, class, sexuality, and generations. In assuming that women's experiences within families are more or less similar, family experts have typically failed to take into account that "gender is different as lived and imagined by different social groups" (Williams 2000, 145). Moreover, essentialist rationalizations persist despite feminists repeatedly pointing out that women's subordination is not because of biological differences but, rather, because of the meanings that are attributed to those differences (J. Butler 1993). As Cornell (2005, 35) argues, it is the capacity to give life that "is used to justify our treatment as lesser beings, not truly worthy of personhood."

This chapter focuses on the complex legacy of the normative nuclear family model, an apt place to begin this book on demystifying the family-work contradiction. The first section outlines important changes that have contributed to increased family diversity in Canada over the past few decades. A discussion then ensues over the often heated and contradictory interpretations of these transformations in family life. The chapter concludes with a discussion of how the socially constructed family-work binary might be overcome by formulating new understandings of family and work. A necessary step toward this end is to destabilize the nuclear family concept by exposing, examining, and challenging its underlying assumptions and the implications they have on performing family care work and paid market work. In this way, the legitimacy of the gendered family work-market binary and ideas of family and work as irreconcilable entities to be balanced can be exposed and challenged.

Changing Family Trends

Although the majority of Canadians – about 84 percent – still prefer to live as families, significant changes have been taking place in the forms that these families take (Lewis 2003). The traditional nuclear family is certainly not as prevalent as it once was; only 17 percent of all census families were classified as nuclear families in 2006 (Milan, Vezina, and Wells 2007).[1] According to Clarence Lockhead, executive director of the Vanier Institute of the Family, "Even when you look at families today, who may on the surface have the appearance of looking like those stereotypical, traditional families of the past, there's probably many, many ways in which those families are quite different" (Canadian Press 2007).

Marriage's popularity has also been waning. Although married-couple families remain the most common type of family, the proportion of such families relative to other family types has been decreasing for the past twenty years. In 1986, married-couple families accounted for 80 percent of all Canadian families; today, they account for 69 percent. Crude marriage rates have hit record lows; there are now only 4.7 marriages for every 1,000 people across the country, except for Quebec, where the rate is even lower – 2.8 marriages for every 1,000 people (Milan, Vezina, and Wells 2007). And marriages are less enduring – approximately 38 percent of marriages are expected to end in divorce by the thirtieth wedding anniversary (Statistics Canada 2005a). Consequently, an ever-increasing number of Canadian children do not live with both parents in the same household. Between 1986 and 2006, the percentage of children under age fourteen who lived with married parents decreased from approximately 81 percent to about 66 percent. Likewise, between 2001 and 2006, the percentage of lone-parent families in Canada increased from 13 to 16 percent, and the majority of these families were headed by women (Milan, Vezina, and Wells 2007). Moreover, the percentage of repeat divorces, involving persons previously divorced at least once, has tripled in the past three decades (Statistics Canada 2005a).

Although the popularity of marriage has waned, the appeal of cohabitation has grown: between 1986 and 2006, the percentage of common-law-couple families increased from 7 to 15.5 percent (Milan, Vezina, and Wells 2007). Cohabitation rates are particularly high in Quebec, where almost 30 percent of all couples live common law, compared with 12 percent in the rest of Canada (ibid.). There is also greater social acceptance of unmarried women having children – the number of lone parents never legally married increased from 1.5 percent in 1950 to 29.5 percent in 2006 (ibid.). The total fertility rate, however, remains well below replacement level, hovering at 1.5 children per woman. Unprecedented in Canada, there are now more census families composed of couples without children than those with children – 43 and 41 percent, respectively. On the other hand, the number of adult children who are living in the parental home – often well into their twenties – has increased dramatically, and the transition to adulthood is taking longer to complete (Clark 2007). Because young people now tend to leave home for less secure reasons – to attend university or to live on their own, rather than to get married or to take on employment – approximately one-third will return home within five years (Mahoney 2006). According to Turcotte (2006, 2), the number of adults between the ages of twenty and twenty-four who live with their parents increased from 40 percent in 1981 to almost 60 percent twenty years later.

Family diversity has also been enhanced because of the incredible change in the ways that individuals can become parents, including in vitro fertilization, surrogacy, sperm banks, transnational and transracial adoption, and implanting frozen embryos. Although there appears to be a multitude of reproductive choices, accessibility tends to be regulated along gender, class, sexuality, and racial lines (Bartholet 2005; Fogg-Davis 2005; Haslanger and Witt 2005; Roberts 2005; Davis 2001).

Another epic change contributing to family diversity in Canada is the legalization of same-sex marriages. After several years of public debate, the Civil Marriage Act (Bill C-38) was passed in Canada on 20 July 2005, making Canada the fourth country in the world to legalize same-sex marriage.[2] The 2006 Canadian Census reported that 45,300 same-sex couples lived in Canada and, of these, approximately 7,500 (16.5 percent) were married and 37,900 (83.5 percent) were common law. Between 2001 and 2006, the number of same-sex couples increased by about 33 percent, more than five times the growth observed for opposite-sex couples, and in 2006, approximately 9 percent reported that they had children (Milan, Vezina, and Wells 2007). The first divorce of a same-sex married couple took place in September 2004. Interestingly, the initial divorce application was denied because the federal Divorce Act defines a spouse as "either of a man or a woman who are married to each other." Eventually, the Ontario Superior Court ruled that the federal definition of "spouse" in the Divorce Act was unconstitutional.

Family diversity is also significantly enhanced by the cultural and ethnic composition of immigrant families coming to Canada. Since the beginning of the twentieth century, the number of ethnic groups has grown from approximately twenty-five to more than two hundred (Statistics Canada 2006c). There are about 6.2 million foreign-born people currently living in Canada, an increase of more than 13 percent since 2001 (Milan, Vezina, and Wells 2007). This means that about one in five (19.8 percent) of the total population is foreign born, the highest proportion reported in seventy-five years (Statistics Canada 2008b). Moreover, since the 1960s, when the Canadian government removed race and place of origin from immigration criteria, there has been a striking shift in the countries of origin of new Canadians, accounting for a significant increase in the number of individuals belonging to visible minorities.[3] Between 2001 and 2006, the percentage of visible minority Canadians increased five times faster than the general population. Today, more than 5 million people, approximately 16 percent of the Canadian population, belong to the visible minority population, a significant increase from 1981, when 1 million people (4.7 percent of the population) were considered visible minorities. The majority of recent immigrants (84 percent) were born in non-European countries, and almost 60 percent originated from Asia – including the Middle East – a high figure compared with the period before 1960, when only 2.4 percent of newcomers came from this region but almost 90 percent came from Europe. There have also been substantial increases in immigrants from Africa, the Caribbean, and South America (Statistics Canada 2008a). More than 70 percent of the foreign-born population report a language other than English or French as their mother tongue (Statistics Canada 2008b). Canada's family diversity is also enhanced by approximately 300,000 interracial marriages or common-law relationships, which is nearly 30 percent more than in 2001 (Weeks 2008).

Of course, changes in market work have had a significant impact on Canadian families. This has been particularly the case for women, who no longer typically leave their employment when they begin to have children. The male breadwinner and family wage model of work – forty-eight hours for forty-eight weeks of forty-eight years – has ceased to characterize most paid market work (Siltanen and Doucet 2008, 98). So-called non-standard forms of employment have become more widespread, including part-time work, temporary employment, and self-employment, all typically characterized by low wages, lack of job security, and little access to employment benefits. In fact, a large portion of these jobs have been filled by women: "In 2002, women accounted for more than six in ten of those employed in part-time temporary jobs or part-time self-employment, and for nearly three-quarters of part-time permanent employees" (ibid.). Although women's labour force participation has increased enormously – almost 60 percent of women age fifteen and older are employed – the types of jobs in which they are overrepresented have not changed; they continue to have fewer opportunities but more constraints in the workforce, and they continue to earn less than men. In terms of an average hourly wage, women receive less than men in all occupations (ibid., 105), and women also continue to do most of the unpaid household and family care work (Daly 2004a, 2004b; Baker 2001; Benzanson 2006).

Globalization has also had a decided impact on family structures. With increased international trade and exchange, national boundaries have become increasingly fluid. Numerous men and women regularly cross borders to live and work as easily as they once travelled to different cities in the same country (Krull 2006b). Consequently, transnational families have become commonplace, although their experiences vary by ethnicity, gender, country of origin, and occupational class.[4] For example, based on interviews of transnational families in Vancouver, British Columbia, Waters (2002, 118) found that they exemplify "the ways in which social relationships can operate over significant distance, spanning national borders, and reducing the importance of face-to-face context in personal interaction." But whereas migration tends to be empowering for men, women tend to view it as a necessary sacrifice for their children rather than as a way to improve their own life chances (Dreby 2006; Lan 2003).

Global market demands for low-wage female domestic and service labour have resulted in women from developing countries leaving their own children and spouses to take on domestic work in another country. This trend in transnational mothering has disrupted the notion of family in one place: "Transnational mothers are improvising new mothering arrangements that are borne out of women's financial struggles, played out in a new global arena, to provide the best future for themselves and their children" (Hondagneu-Sotelo and Avila 1997, 567).[5] Globalization might have increased flexibility in the labour markets and, in eroding the material conditions for the male-breadwinner system, produced greater equality between professional men and women, but it has also created new forms of marginality (Dreby 2006; Krull 2006b; Lan 2003; Young 2001) and an international division of gendered reproductive labour (Hondagneu-Sotelo 2007; Salazar Parreñas 2001, 2005, 2008).

Interpreting Changing Family Trends

There is intense debate over how to interpret these changes in Canadian families. As Vincent (1966, 31) recognized in the mid-1960s, "Since the earliest writing available, changes occurring in the institution of the family have been used and interpreted to support either an optimistic or a pessimistic premise concerning social change, and the pessimists have consistently outnumbered the optimists." Whereas some view the contemporary transformation in Canadian families as requisite change in a move toward equity and greater tolerance of family diversity, others regard it as an indication of family decline.

Proponents of the family-in-decline perspective argue that increases in the number of divorces, single parents, and absent fathers, along with the legalization of same-sex marriages, are indicative of the eroding institution of marriage and the two-parent heterosexual nuclear family. Accordingly, increasing individualism, the rise of feminism, and a weakening in religiosity and moral consciousness are held accountable for the breakdown in family values, which have placed children at greater risk of experiencing behavioural problems. As Walker (2003, 407) reasons, "Political debates about marriage and divorce are at their most intense when effects on children are discussed, and deeply held moral, religious, and political views tend to dominate the agenda. Thus, children are viewed as the innocent victims of their parents' selfish behavior."

Neo-conservative narratives advocating for a return to traditional family values have infused Canadian politics for some time. Dave Quist, executive director of the Institute of Marriage and Family Canada, insists that "a first priority [of the federal Conservative government led by Stephen Harper] should be to change the tax rules so only married couples – not those living common law – are allowed to split their incomes, thereby reducing their tax hit" (Greenaway 2007). And in the 2007 Ontario provincial election, the Family Coalition Party ran a record number of candidates in eighty-three electoral districts. Its platform was based on strengthening nuclear families and the traditional values of marriage (see its website for a description of party family policies); election results indicated that more than thirty-five thousand Ontario residents agreed with them (FCPO 2010; Diebel 2007). Likewise, Ted Morton, a former University of Calgary political science professor and now Alberta's minister of finance and enterprise maintained: "After years of producing research that helped to weaken civil society, social scientists are finally recognizing the social and economic value of the traditional family and the moral infrastructure that it helps to sustain" (Morton 1998). Recently, Morton proposed Bill 208, which would have legislated that "information about G/L/B/T [gays, lesbians, bisexuals, transsexuals] not be allowed in schools; marriage commissionaires could opt out of performing same-sex marriages; and, a person expressing their opinions and ideas about homosexuality could not have a claim of discrimination brought against them" (Cournoyer 2006). The then Alberta premier, Ralph Klein, supported the bill and justified his position by asserting that Bill 208 was simply an "extension of existing government policies" (Klein 2006).

And although assisted reproductive technologies allow the possibility of transcending the state-informed heterosexual, nuclear, monogamous family (Satz 2007; Spar 2006; Cornell 2005; Haslanger 2005; Throsby and Gill 2004), new technologies have primarily been used to reproduce normative understandings of family. Baker (2005), for example, found in her study on infertility that despite the potential of reproductive technologies to radicalize families, they have often been used by middle-class couples for the purpose of creating nuclear families. And, reflecting the high value that is placed on children who are genetically related, there is a booming industry in reproductive services, whereas adoption continues to be viewed as "a clearly inferior way of forming a family" (Satz 2007, 525).

Given the increasing family diversity in Canada, the nuclear family exists more as an ideal than an actuality (Fox 2009; Ranson 2010). And as an ideal, deviations become indicative of "family decline," their very difference justifying public scrutiny and surveillance (Little and Marks 2010). As such, they are regarded as being in need of resocialization to conform to the normative form (ibid. 1999). However, the argument that families and family values are in decline rests primarily on three flawed assumptions: (1) the normative nuclear family model is superior to all other family forms, (2) families were more stable in the past, and (3) families are declining in importance to Canadians.

Outcomes of Privileging the Nuclear Family

Despite research indicating that marriage, mothering, fathering, domesticity, and work have very different meanings for different communities and, therefore, are highly contested categories (Baines 2004a, 2004b; Collins 1990,

2000; Das Gupta 2000; Smith 1987), the normative nuclear form is privileged in Canada. Even in non-normative families, such as single-mother families, the nuclear family ideal can have a powerful impact in shaping interactions and expectations among family members (Nelson 2006b).

Not replicating the hegemonic family structure has had devastating consequences for many marginalized communities in Canada (see Baines 2004a, 2004b; Das Gupta 2000; Dua 1999; Walmsley 2006). Residential schools for Aboriginal children, the Sixties Scoop, and foster care are cases in point. The primary objective of earlier government policies was to purge Aboriginal children of all traditional cultural identifiers. And they were successful – of fifty distinct Aboriginal languages once spoken in Canada, only three are now considered secure: Cree, Inuktitut, and Ojibwa. And despite decades of documented atrocities committed against Aboriginal children at residential schools – mental, physical, and sexual abuse – the federal government did not close the last residential school until 1996 (Krull 2006b, 2010; Das Gupta 2000). Aboriginal children continue to constitute the largest percentage of children in foster care in Canada – approximately 40 percent – which means that about 5 percent of all Aboriginal children are still being removed from their homes (Canadian Press 2008).

The result of Canadian federal policies has been a legacy of trauma with which First Nations people are still trying to cope. In addition to generations of family breakdown caused by the residential school system and forced adoption, many Aboriginal communities suffer the lowest living standard of any other family group in the country and have suicide rates two to seven times that of the national population (Beaujot and Kerr 2004; Beavon and Cooke 2003). And it took until June 2008 for the federal government, under Prime Minister Harper, to properly acknowledge and apologize for federal policies that devastated the families of Aboriginal peoples: "We now recognize that, in separating children from their families, we undermined the ability of many to adequately parent their own children and sowed the seeds for generations to follow ... The government of Canada sincerely apologizes and asks the forgiveness of aboriginal peoples for failing them so badly" (Curry and Galloway 2008).

In privileging the nuclear family, the growing importance of multi-generational bonds (Bengtson 2001) and created family bonds (Cherlin 1999; Stacey 1996; Collins 2004) are disregarded. The value of the extended family in terms of social identity, economic support, and psychological nurturing for many immigrant and Aboriginal families cannot be overstated. Kin networks of First Nations people are twice as extensive as those of other Canadians (Fiske and Johnny 2003; Strain and Chappell 1989), and it is not unusual for First Nations people to identify over fifty different familial relationships among people living with them (Buchignani and Armstrong-Esther 1999). Many black families include multi-generational relatives, as well as members of the community. Black communities have historically distin-guished between the fluid meanings of a blood mother (the biological mother of a child) and other mothers (women in the family and community who share the mothering responsibilities of a child). Bell hooks (2000, 144) also points out that other mothering "is revolutionary in this society because it takes place in opposition to the ideas that parents, especially mothers, should be the only childrearers." However, the subordination of blacks in Canada has often been rationalized and reinforced by their portrayal as promiscuous and less deserving of parenthood (Calliste 2003). Multi-generational bonds have also been important to many minority immigrant groups in Canada. Yet, despite liberal changes to immigration policy, minority immigrant groups continue to face barriers to their participation in family life. Canada's im-migration policies continue to privilege the nuclear family form by restricting which immigrants count as family members.

Indeed, Bengtson (2001, 5) argues that for many families in North America, "multigenerational bonds are becoming more important than nuclear family ties for well-being and support over the course of their lives." And because of changing family demographics, like high divorce rates and increased lon-gevity, a significant number of grandparents have become primary caregivers for their grandchildren, a phenomenon known as skip-generation households. In Canada, over 56,000 grandparents are raising their grandchildren on their own, and two-thirds of these grandparents are women (Statistics Canada 2004a). Bengtson (2001, 12, 14) concludes that there is little evidence to support the family-in-decline argument: "Families continue to perform their socialization function across successive generations, transmitting aspirations, values and self-esteem, even when parents are divorced ... the increasing prevalence and importance of multigenerational bonds represents a valuable new resource for families in the 21st century." This conclusion echoes the research of Levin (2004) and Roseneil and Budgeon (2004) on partners who are not living together, Pahl and Spencer's work (2004) on "personal com-munities," Stacey's study (2004) on creative "families of choice," and Mc-Daniel's work (2004, 2008) on intergenerational transfers.

An additional outcome of idealizing nuclear families is that inequities within these families are often rendered invisible. Depending on gender and age, there tends to be significant differences among members of nuclear families in terms of power and access to resources. Le Bourdais, Lapierre-Adamcyk, and Lapierre-Adamcyk (2004, 940) assert: "Families remain, to this day, the last places where equality between men and women does not seem to be fully recognized" (see also Eichler 1997a, 2008). This disparity is particularly salient within power differentials associated with paid work (men's domain) and household-care work (women's domain). According to Butler (2004, 43), "A restrictive discourse on gender that insists on the binary of man and woman as the exclusive way to understand the gender field performs a regulatory operation of power that naturalizes the hegemonic instance and forecloses the thinkability of its disruption." Naturalizing the gendered distribution of power and resources renders the disparity necessary and justifies it politically.

Power differentials between family members can spill over into family violence (Sev'er 2010; Gelles 1987, 1994; Strauss and Gelles 1990; Strauss, Gelles, and Steinmetz 1986). It has often been assumed that women and children within middle- and upper-class nuclear families are more insulated from family violence, since they are less likely to experience the stress factors that plague working-class and single-parent families. However, these assumptions have been challenged by feminist scholars showing that the ostensible prevalence of family violence in poor non-nuclear families is partly due to their higher surveillance, and that the invisibility of violence in largely middle- and upper-class nuclear families has been largely due to romanticizing the nuclear family as a place of loving and supportive relationships between equals. Research indicates that women in traditional marriages who are economically dependent on their husbands are more likely to be victims of spousal assault than wives who are more independent (Baker 2010). More prosaically, rather than an outcome of family form, family resources, or other stress factors, family violence is the outcome of an inequitable distribution of power and access to resources (Sev'er 2010; Le Bourdais, Lapierre-Adamcyk, and Lapierre-Adamcyk 2004; Baker 2010; Eichler 1997a; Pence and Paymar 1993; Mackinnon 1982; O'Brien 1981).

Idealizing the nuclear family reinforces the fallacy that it operates as an independent, self-contained unit that satisfies the needs of its members and is ideally suited for raising children. But as Hansen (2005, 3) points out, this supposition ignores today's reality that both parents within the household are likely to be employed and that they "consciously and creatively construct networks of interdependence" that include having people outside their immediate families care for their children. Moreover, in presuming that the nuclear family is a self-contained unit, the contribution of domestic workers (usually women of colour) in maintaining privileged nuclear families is ignored (Iacovetta 2006; Salazar Parreñas 2008; Williams 2000). Marriage is also becoming less common and, therefore no longer provides a guarantee of stability (Le Bourdais, Lapierre-Adamcyk, and Lapierre-Adamcyk 2004, 937-38). As research indicates, children are resilient and can in most cases adapt to changes within their families, including divorce (Strohschein 2007; Walker 2003; Smart and Neale 1999).

The "Golden Age" of Family?

To believe that family values are in decline presupposes a golden age of family life, a time when "the family" was more vital, stable, and efficient than it is today. In North America, the 1950s is often considered to be such a time (Beaujot 2004; Smart and Neale 1999). At this time, Canadian families lived more than ever as nuclear family households – most children lived in a two-parent breadwinner-homemaker home (Milan 2000, 5), and about 20 percent lived with at least five brothers or sisters (Saccoccio 2007). For the first time in North America, nuclear family emotional bonds became valued over those of other relationships (Coontz 1997, 37; see also Coontz 1992). Accordingly, the 1950s nuclear family is thought of as the "traditional" family because it has been "discursively constructed as the way the family was before change began" – in other words, the impression has been created that "once upon a time, the family did not change" (Smart and Neale 1999, 28).

Even though the 1950s might have been more stable than preceding or following decades, it nonetheless did not constitute a golden age of family life. As Canadian historian Doug Owram (1999, 8) explains:

> The post-war family is surrounded by popular myths ... the ideal nuclear family with working father, understanding mother and lively but loving children. There is also a darker story however that descends from the second wave of feminism and from critics of the suburban wasteland. It is the story of isolated housewives and commuting husbands surrounded by tick-tacky houses and an ethic of competitive consumerism.

Three ideals became reinforced in this era – the nuclear family form, companionate marriage whereby wives and husbands are each other's best friend, and the veneration of motherhood that viewed stay-at-home mothers as best suited to raise children and maintain domestic life – all of which contributed to a framework that disguised gross gender inequities in the distribution of power and allocation of resources and disregarded class and ethnic differences (Luxton and Corman 2001, 40). Middle-class women became increasingly economically dependent on their husbands as post-Second World War government efforts purged many married women from the paid workforce by closing government-sponsored daycares and generating "propaganda claiming maternal care was the most appropriate care for children" (Luxton and Corman 2001, 48). Age of marriage decreased by approximately two years for both men and women, though women married at a younger age than men – "more than four out of every ten women were married by the age of 22" (Owram 1999, 11). An unprecedented baby boom ensued and, by 1959, women were having on average 3.9 children (Ambert 2006b, 9). Accordingly, the gap in the educational attainment of middle-class men and women significantly increased (Milan 2000; Owram 1999). With divorce difficult, divorce rates remained low – only about one in twenty marriages ended this way. As Owram (1999) spells out, divorce reform was improbable at a time when society believed that divorce psychologically damaged children. Moreover, women who worked typically earned half of men's average salary (Lowe 2006) – low employment rates meant that many women were isolated from most of the adult world.

But probably most damaging to women's equity was a cult-like transformation of domesticity, whereby women's worth and identity became exclusively linked to their domestic skills – the 1950s modern woman was fundamentally a wife and mother (Spencer 2006, 226; Baker 2001, 92). This assumption was reinforced by academics who exalted the gendered division of labour as progressive, inevitable, and ideal. One of the more influential scholars in this regard was sociologist Talcott Parsons, who asserted: "The importance of the family and its function for society constitutes the primary set of reasons why there is a social as distinguished from purely reproductive differentiation of sex roles ... the male adult will play the role of instrumental leader and the female adult will play the role of expressive leader" (Parsons and Bales 1955, 315, 341). According to Bradbury (2000, 216), historians contributed in constructing nuclear families as "normal" while marginalizing and even rendering invisible single-parent families. Not surprising, less than 5 percent of Canadians believed that it was acceptable for mothers to be employed outside the home (Owram 1999).

Given the family's new ascendancy, women were also bombarded with advice and even admonished by so-called family experts in the media. *Chatelaine* magazine, for example, advised women that they could be whatever they chose to be as long as their primary roles remained that of housewife and mother:

> It is important for a woman to cultivate, with ever-increasing perfections, elegance and beauty as well as the various household arts which, in our daily lives, carry on the finest French traditions ... the accomplished woman should also know a little about everything, since her destiny and that of her children are tied to the fate of the world. (Cited in Clio Collective 1987, 303; see also Spencer 2006)

Television was also culpable for reinforcing the idea of the happy well-adjusted 1950s family in which fathers were successful breadwinners and mothers were content in their self-sacrificing role as family care worker. Nowhere was this romanticized ideal better exemplified than in the fictional Cleaver family in the 1950s American television sitcom *Leave It to Beaver*, which was also popular in Canada. Ward Cleaver went to work every day after eating a wholesome breakfast prepared by his always smiling, empathetic, and well-dressed wife, June; when he returned at the end of the day, he found the house clean, dinner ready, the boys – Wally and Beaver – quietly occupied; indeed, the minute he walked through the door, his still-smiling wife would offer him his slippers and pipe, all problems of the day sorted out (Canadian Press 2007). As nonsensical as this sounds, *Leave It to Beaver* and other similar television programs reinforced an ideal family form that persists today.

As the expressive leader in the home, mothers became liable for any and all family dysfunctions. For example, in addressing concerns over what was perceived to be a diminishing nationalism among Canadians in the immediate post-Second World War period, women were implicated by the media for not having instilled adequate national pride in their children (Spencer 2006, 237). Women's active role as nation builders during the war years was superseded by their more passive roles as mothers and wives. For Thurer (1994, 251), "It was as if the New Woman, Rosie the Riveter, and the women's suffrage had never happened." And little tolerance existed for those who defied normative gender role expectations: "Childless couples were considered selfish, single persons were seen as deviants, working mothers were considered to be harming their children, and single women who became pregnant were expected either to marry or to give up the child for adoption" (Beaujot 2004, 7). Given this context, it is not surprising that the 1950s gave way to a resurgence of antifeminism (Cancian 2004).

The new-found prosperity, optimism, domesticity, and consumerism of the 1950s characterized primarily white, middle-class families. Discrimination against gays, non-Christians, and visible minorities was endemic throughout North America (Coontz 1997; Thurer 1994), and family diversity among these groups was often attributed to their inferior status (Luxton and Corman 2001, 40). Therefore, problems within working-class and marginalized families were rendered invisible. But problems experienced within white, middle-class nuclear families were also obscured because of the acute belief that these families were somehow exempt from such difficulties. Exasperating this was the indubitable conviction that family matters were private, even though "alcoholism, substance abuse, spousal abuse, child abuse, poverty, mental illness, stress and marital problems were all certainly present. But, at the time ... airing dirty laundry was considered shameful" (Lowe 2006). Tending to be isolated in their homes, women were rendered particularly vulnerable by this code of silence; it cut them off from any potential support from friends or community members, and victims of violence and abuse had little recourse (Beaujot 2004).

As Baker (2010) and others have pointed out, family forms were as diverse in the 1950s as they are today and just as vulnerable to family problems. Still, politicians, the media, and others who lament the demise of "the family" continue to make references to a golden age of the family – idealized and hegemonic – despite evidence to the contrary. As Luxton (1997, 11) writes, "During a period of social insecurity and disruption, arguments supporting plurality can easily appear to promise chaos while those calling for a return to a golden age of the 'traditional family,' however mythical it may be, appear to promise stability and security." And since rhetoric echoing fears that "the family" is in decline escalates at times of social stress, it is not surprising that this current economic crisis in North America has brought about a resurgence of defenders of "family values."

The Importance of Families Today

A third neo-conservative argument that the family is in decline pertains to the assumption that family life is diminishing in importance to Canadians. Such arguments are often tied to women's public participation. Accordingly, fertility rates and marriage rates have plummeted while divorce rates have rocketed as women "choose" the pursuit of education and their own career aspirations over prioritizing and sacrificing for their families. But as many feminists have long argued, this idea of paid work as a choice is not only incredibly sexist – men need to work, women choose to work – but it totally disregards women's lived reality, since most women also need to work. It is also telling that despite women's labour force participation, they remain primarily responsible for household work. But in spite of such evidence, the rhetoric of choice continues.

Conceiving women's paid work as a choice facilitates the myth that women must balance their responsibilities in the home with those at their place of employment if they are to be successful in both. Investing too much in one form of work would constitute losses or failures in the other. Family work and employment are thus treated as irreconcilable entities that are in need of careful balance – an approach that reinforces gendered work and negates the need for social policies that work at integrating household-care work and paid work. As Susan McDaniel points out in the Epilogue, work and family have historically been thought to be indivisible and not separate entities in need of balance: "People work and have families. The two are inextricably linked and dependent one on the other."

The argument that in doing paid work, women are valuing their careers over family life is incongruous. Regardless of family form, family life continues to be highly valued by both women and men. Indeed, between 2001 and 2006, the number of census families increased by 6.3 percent (Milan, Vezina, and Wells 2007). Citing results from an Angus Reid opinion survey that indicated that two-thirds of Canadians over age eighteen identified their families as the source of their greatest joy in life, Milan (2000, 5) insists that "Canadians remain fiercely loyal to the idea of family." She also points to the fact that the majority of young Canadians plan to marry, have children, and remain married to the same spouse. And in his recent comprehensive survey of 2,100 Canadians, Bibby (2004) found that the majority of Canadians aspire to fairly traditional family ideals – that most Canadians want to marry, stay married, and have children – and the majority of Canadians "are convinced that families are essential to both personal and social well-being, contributing to healthy communities and a healthy nation" (7). Almost 60 percent of respondents stated that the traditional nuclear family was ideal, and 80 percent indicated that getting married was either "very important" or "somewhat important," whereas less than 10 percent indicated that marriage was "not important at all." When asked why they want to marry, especially at a time when divorce and cohabitation rates are high, Canadians regardless of gender or age cited three reasons: marriage signifies commitment, marriage is morally the right thing to do, and children should have married parents.[6] Bibby concludes that Canadians do indeed aspire to an ideal family structure and that the future of marriage is not in doubt. Obviously, family is not in decline; people today simply have more choices in terms of how they arrange themselves as families. Young Canadians may be rejecting marriage, especially those living in Quebec, but the increasing incidence of common-law unions indicates that the majority of young people continue to want to live as couples.

Avowing that paid work and family work are incompatible and that women who value their families should stay at home reinforces domesticity and divides women against themselves, each trying to live up to either the role of the ideal worker or the full-time caregiver. This has sparked what has been dubbed "the mommy wars," whereby women extol the benefits of either staying at home or of being employed, adamantly arguing that they are doing what is best for their families (Steiner 2007). Full-time working mothers continue to be characterized as "uninvolved, absentee parents ... full-time homemakers, [as] nonintellectual, hovering, and provincial ... the women in each group have nothing in common with the women in the other; they share no values" (Peskowitz 2005, 20). This depiction fails to consider the significant number of mothers who work part-time, and it treats each group of women as fixed, ignoring that most women move in and out of the workforce over the course of their lives. Moreover, mothers are often put in the position of having to justify their choice to continue or discontinue working (Peskowitz 2005; Gerson 2002).

Primarily directed at women, but not precluding men, the family-work balance narrative is based on gendered and incongruent conceptions of the family. For Litt and Zimmerman (2003, 156-63), the "constructs of public and private spheres constitute a false dichotomy that serves only to obscure the more fundamental mechanisms perpetuating gender." Women do not need guidance on how to balance work and family: they need options that increase their choices so they are not put in a position of having to choose between family care work and paid work. Policies that help parents integrate family and work are essential. Such policies could assist parents who want to be at home full-time raising their children, or working either full-time or part-time in the paid market. The failure of the current Conservative federal government to implement its Liberal predecessor's proposal for universal childcare reflects the state's unwillingness to assist parents with such integration.

Conclusion: Performing Family and Market Work

The nuclear family continues to prevail in the public imaginary as the ideal family form despite growing diversity in how Canadians choose to live as families, the concomitant deinstitutionalization of marriage (Amato 2004b; Cherlin 2004), the tendency of Canadians to move in and out of different family forms throughout their lifetime (Baker 2010), and an abundance of research that clearly indicates that the links between traditional and non-traditional family forms are fluid, not closed (Coontz 1997, 3). Clearly, this gendered heterosexual family model needs to be decentred in our intellectual imagination if we are to develop a more integrative understanding of care work and market work. However, the key to decentring lies not in adopting more pluralistic descriptions of family – that is, adding "ies" to "family" – since past efforts of family researchers to pluralize "the family" have simply emphasized "the 'still alive-ness' of the category" (Budgeon and Roseneil 2004, 127). Instead, it calls for destabilizing the normative assumptions about family and reconceptualizing intimate relations and care work.

Margrit Eichler (1981, 1988, 1997b, 2001, 2008) has spent most of her career admonishing family researchers about the dangers of assuming a monolithic family. This assumption results in conjectures of congruence that lead to biases in data collection and the negation of the incidence of non-congruence. Consequently, genuine problems in large numbers of families are overlooked, and the work of family practitioners and policy makers is rendered ineffective. Eichler (1997b) promotes the social responsibility model of family characterized by a concerted effort to minimize stratification based on sex. Legal marriage is an option rather than a privilege over other types of relationships, and marital status, residency, gender, and sexuality are not requisites for parental responsibilities. All individuals are entitled to equal state benefits, and care for dependent children is a parental and societal duty. Similarly, Simonen (1991, in Litt and Zimmerman 2003, 158) advocates "social mothering" – the state-funded occupation of municipal homemakers, which allows the state to share and adjudicate private household divisions of labour. Stacey (1996) favours "the postmodern family condition," a pluralistic, fluid space where diverse and even unorthodox "families of choice" can be constructively created. She points to the choice in understanding contemporary families:

> Either we can come to grips with the postmodern family condition by accepting the end of a singular ideal family and begin to promote better living and spiritual conditions for the diverse array of real families we actually

inhabit and desire. Or we can continue to engage in denial, resistance, displacement, and bad faith, by cleaving to a moralistic ideology of *the family* at the same time that we fail to provide social and economic conditions that make life for the modern family or any other kind of family viable, let alone dignified and secure. (1996, 11, emphasis in original)

In demonstrating that sex, gender, and sexuality are discursive constructions, several feminists have laid the groundwork for destabilizing concepts such as family, mother, father, wife, and husband and for deconstructing the forms of work normatively linked to each (see, for example, Fausto-Sterling 1999, 2000, 2003; Butler 1990, 1993; Wittig 1992). Judith Butler's concept of performativity is particularly useful here. Performativity, she argues, is "not a singular act, but a repetition and a ritual, which achieves its effects through its naturalization in the context of a body, understood in part, as a culturally sustained temporal duration ... it is that reiterative power of discourse to produce the phenomena that it regulates and constrains" (Butler 2004, 94). Performance is a crucial part of performativity – within families, the "act that one does, the act that one performs, is, in a sense, an act that has been going on before one arrived on the scene" (Butler 1990, 272). Thus, performances are conditioned by the social norms and ideologies within one's culture – by "what other practices are and by what practices are legitimating" (Butler 2004, 345). In effect, individuals perform cultural norms.

Understanding work and family as performative acts that are constrained by norms opens up possibilities to destabilize the nuclear family ideal and, hence, a gendered private-public binary. In *Gender Trouble* (1990), Butler demonstrates how "doing gender" involves shared structures of imitation. Performing family can be understood in a similar fashion. In performing gender, males and females also enact the fabricated roles of family. Through "a sustained set of acts" that we "anticipate and produce through certain bodily acts," we come to understand ourselves and others not only as man (male) or woman (female) but by extension also as mother, father, husband, wife, son, or daughter (xv). And it is in producing and reproducing a specific set of behaviours that men and women become anchored within the household-market work continuum, coagulating the material embodiment of family roles. Accordingly, the private-public binary is a fiction created to sustain the status quo.

In this important sense, families emerge as something we do, not what we are. However, even though conceptualizing family as performance allows for incredible diversity in how we do family, it can only do so if gender is displaced. Otherwise, a hierarchical placement of family performances results that privileges masculine performances over feminine performances. We need to approach domesticity as Butler approaches feminine gender display, not with a pre-emptory demand for its immediate abandonment but with the goal of gender bending, of focusing attention on the contingent and stitched-together quality of our performances, thereby opening up ways to bend the elements of domesticity into new configurations. Suppleness and a sense of open-ended play are important weapons if the goal is domesticity in drag (Williams 2000, 198).

Conceptualizing family work and market work as performances challenges the family's ontological status and raises possibilities for more diverse, complex, and fluid ways of "doing" family. In one view, doing family is a perspective that "emphasizes interactional work and activities that create and sustain family ties, define family boundaries, as well as specify appropriate behaviors for difference family members" (Sarkisian 2006, 804). It is the process that comes about as people perform family life within both structural and ideological constraints. For example, there is a multitude of ways that single mothers doing family are shaped by cultural normative ideals and structural material forces (Nelson 2005, 2006a, 2006b). These and other families are continually being created, dismantled, and recreated. Nelson (2006b, 790) contends that it is possible to "do several types of families simultaneously and in motion," something Hertz (2006, 799) maintains "captures a new dynamic of the multiple families in which women and their children live and function simultaneously and over time." Indeed, Nelson is lauded for demonstrating how single mothers "are not reconstructing a dated, diseased North American model that ensures male domination" but, rather, "are seeking newer, decidedly less 'standard' models that promise a more balanced reciprocity and offer companionship and emotional closeness" (Cherlin 2006, 803). Research on gay and lesbian families have also highlighted how families can be creatively constructed (Naples 2001).

Frameworks such as "doing family" are decisively central to the process of destabilizing the nuclear family ideal and, therefore, the family-work binary. "Doing family" opens up possibilities for understanding families as networks of love, support, and work, regardless of gender, blood, or marriage ties. Whom we call family will come to be defined by the type of interactive performances that individuals engage in, rather than in terms of gender or how they are related to us. With such networks of support and coinciding family policies that reflect the diverse needs of Canadian families, women will have the possibility of performing both family and paid market work in an integrative manner and will thus be freed from the fruitless pursuit of balance.

Notes

1 Statistics Canada (2010) defines a census family as being composed of "a married couple and the children, if any, of either or both spouses; a couple living common law and the children, if any, of either or both partners; or, a lone parent of any marital status with at

least one child living in the same dwelling and that child or those children. All members of a particular census family live in the same dwelling. A couple may be of opposite or same sex. Children may be children by birth, marriage or adoption regardless of their age or marital status as long as they live in the dwelling and do not have their own spouse or child living in the dwelling. Grandchildren living with their grandparent(s) but with no parents present also constitute a census family."

2 The passing of Bill C-38 in 2005 allowed same-sex couples to marry across the country, but several provinces allowed same-sex marriages prior to Bill C-38 (Ontario and British Columbia since 2003; Quebec, Yukon, Manitoba, Nova Scotia, Saskatchewan, and Newfoundland since 2004; New Brunswick since 2005).

3 Canada has a long history of implementing racist policies that not only prevented certain people from immigrating here but also prevented family reunification for those already living in the country (Beaujot and Kerr 2004; Harrison and Friesen 2004; Das Gupta 2000). Aboriginal people were particularly vulnerable to racist Canadian policies designed to strip them of their culture, language, and religion. Residential schools and the 1960s adoption sweep are cases in point in which families were torn apart based on beliefs of their inferiority (Castellano 2002; Emberley 2001; Das Gupta 2000).

4 According to Bryceson and Vuorela (2002, 3), transnational families are those "that live some or most of the time separated from each other, yet hold together and create something that can be seen as a feeling of collective welfare and unity, namely 'familyhood,' even across national borders."

5 Researchers such as Salazar Parreñas (2001) also point to the more harmful impact that mothering from a distance can have for families in the country of origin.

6 Significantly fewer Quebecers believed that it was important for children to have married parents (Quebec: 61 percent; rest of Canada: 81 percent).

2
Intergenerational Care Work: Mothering, Grandmothering, and Eldercare

Nancy Mandell and Sue Wilson

Care work is a complex, contested concept that refers to a range of diverse social, emotional, and physical expectations and activities that take place over the life course and involve individuals and groups engaged in both its delivery and acceptance (Ronning 2002). Care work is socially constructed around cultural ideas of care, about who in society needs care, what type of care, how much, and from whom. As a normative ideal, care work involves different sets of standards at different stages of the life course that guide our expectations about what we should desire and hope for as givers and receivers of care. As a set of practices, care work represents everyday ways of acting in which help and support are distributed and obtained. As both a cultural norm and a social practice, care work represents a fundamental undertaking in which individual subjectivities and social identities are constituted (Twigg 2004).

Using an intersectional perspective, our purpose is to reveal three types of care work – mothering, grandmothering, and eldercare – as both reproducing cultural meanings and subjectively producing gendered, raced, and classed subjects. At the centre of our approach is a social understanding of care as a relationship-based activity involving reciprocal interactions of dependence, independence, and interdependence (Fine and Glendinning 2005). As a relationship, care work is subject to the social and material conditions under which it occurs. Identities are embedded in social relationships and social processes that, taken together, constitute socially determinative structures. Care work is thus shaped by the structures within which it occurs. Care work is also a dynamic concept in that its meanings shift over the life course as needs and involvement alter. By looking across the life span at three types of care work, we see how it is serial, discursively produced, and embodied.

Care work is gendered, raced, and classed in its norms and expectations, in its involvement and intensity, in the relationship of caregivers to care recipients, and in its effects on individuals and social arrangements. Within age groups, individuals become involved in diverse mothering, grandmothering, and eldercare experiences. This diversity reveals the intersectional nature of care work and the power of social location. Racial, classed, and gendered advantages and disadvantages accrue through the life course, leaving some marginalized individuals and groups with limited care work options (Hooyman and Gonyea 1999, 152). The exploitation of women in the context of care work reinforces a system of coerced care. By caring for younger generations, old women and other mothers may ensure the survival of racial ethnic communities, but by taking up these caring subject positions, they simultaneously reproduce interlocking systems of marginality (Zajicek et al. 2006).

Our focus is on family or "informal" care. Informal care includes the help and care provided to family members of all ages who may or may not live in the same household. Informal care involves physical and emotional components and is measured as both an instrumental and an emotional activity that takes place throughout the life course for both short and long periods. As a narrow set of tasks, care work can be measured, organized, and, if necessary, commodified. As emotional work, it is difficult to operationalize. As racialized work, caregiving often is taken up by people of colour, especially women, some of whom migrate to other countries to take up paid care work for others (Zajicek et al. 2006). Ehrenreich and Hochschild (2003) suggest that there is a global care chain characterized by a series of personal links between people across the globe based on their paid and unpaid care work.

Instrumentally, family duties in the form of hours rendered and tasks completed are measured by the number of weekly hours a person performs tasks for others. Duties include those taking place within the home, such as preparing meals, doing housework, financial management, and personal care – bathing, dressing, toileting – as well as tasks that take place outside the home, including yardwork, house repairs, transportation, and financial maintenance.

As an emotional engagement, care work is much talked about, as providers and receivers discuss its positive and negative impact. Carol Smart (1999) talks about caring as nurturing a psychological connection between individuals, for example, providing emotional support, keeping up someone's spirits, providing reassurance and encouragement, and checking up on someone either by visiting or telephoning to ensure his or her well-being. Caring about others implies affection and perhaps psychological responsibility (Hooyman and Gonyea 1999, 151). Fine and Glendinning (2005) talk about care work as involving connection (building intimacy and trust or sustaining ties between intimates) and concern (giving expression to the ties of affection that sustain the connection). By all accounts, delivering and accepting care places individuals in structurally induced positions of ambivalence in which they experience care work as both gratifying and disappointing (Mandell, Wilson, and Duffy 2008; Connidis and McMullin 2002).

Relations of social inequality frame both types of informal care work – instrumental and affective. Broad structural forces have an impact on how care work is executed and experienced (Chappell and Penning 2005). Racialized women and poor women provide direct care for familial others in a variety of roles, and they spend more time doing it over their lifetime than do men. In their child-bearing years, all women are more likely to be high-intensity care workers compared with men, while men of the same age are more than twice as likely to work longer hours at paid employment. Men are increasingly taking on care work, but there are differences in the type and amount of care work performed because of class and racial privilege. Findings about race and ethnic care work are less clearly articulated than those concerning gender, making it difficult to discern whether economic difference, cultural difference, or racism accounts for the differential distribution of care work across groups (ibid.). Over a lifetime, however, gender, race, and class differences seem to add up to distinctly different and unequal portraits of care work for individuals and groups.

Postmodern Mothering Discourses

Since the 1960s, we have witnessed the emergence of postmodern mothering. Both mothers' employment (which has tripled in the past thirty years) and the rise of mothers as primary wage earners (now one-quarter of all dual-earner couples) are trends that have precipitated a "seismic shift" (Greaves et al. 2002, 5) in how we think and act toward mothering. Hegemonic, intensive mothering discourses have been disrupted, giving rise to multiple, contradictory, and heterogeneous ideologies of mothering (Kaplan 1992). Traditional perspectives coexist in uneasy tension with more egalitarian, collaborative views on mothering, even though the former are increasingly decried as essentialist and out-of-date (Carroll and Campbell 2008).

Normatively, intensive mothering discourses view mothers as "special and crucial" to their children (Greaves et al. 2002, 5). Practically, they proscribe a set of childcare practices that are exclusively female, child-centred, labour intensive, emotionally absorbing, and expertly guided activities (Hays 1996; Braverman 1989). Traditional mothering is presumed to be a full-time job with constant responsibilities. A motherhood mandate presupposes a psychological bond between mother and child in which children's needs are prioritized and mothers' needs are seen as synonymous with those of the child (Dillaway 2006).

In contrast, conscious collaboration discourses of mothering (Cowdery and Knudson-Martin 2005) urge adoption of more nuanced understandings of care work that shift responsibility for childcare work to both parents and other mothers (ibid.; Schwartz 2004; Elvin-Nowak and Thomsson 2001). In "postgender" couples, biology is separated from culture by freeing discussions of mothering and employment from discourses of maternal morality and gendered caring (Cowdery and Knudson-Martin 2005). Fathers take on tasks without mothers' instructions and are open to learning, and mothers neither monitor nor intervene in fathers' care work. When fathers take responsibility for childcare work, they report a sense of satisfaction and emotional closeness that deepens their connections with children and encourages them to stay involved throughout their children's lives (ibid.).

Katherine Marshall (2006) notes that gendered divisions of labour among Canadian men and women have diminished in the last two decades. Women have increased both their income and their time spent on paid labour. As women's job attachment has increased, men's involvement in housework and childcare has also increased. Although gender differences persist in the division of labour, they are steadily diminishing. One in ten fathers now takes a formal employment leave to be home with their newborn, which is a statistically and socially significant change (Marshall 2006). The proportion of some men doing some housework daily, be it making sandwiches for lunch, vacuuming, or taking out the garbage, increased from 72 percent in 1986 to 79 percent in 2005 (ibid.). Changes in the daily participation rate for core housework (meal preparation, meal cleanup, indoor cleaning, and laundry) are the most noticeable – 40 to 59 percent for men and 88 to 85 percent for women. Despite these significant trends, in all family types, daily participation rates for housework continue to be significantly higher for women than for men (Sussman and Bonnell 2004).

Money disrupts the balance of power within households. High personal income, for either sex, is associated with spending more time at a job and less on housework. When wives have an income of $100,000 or more, the division of paid labour and housework between partners is more likely to be split equally. The higher a wife's education, the higher is her husband's share of housework. Partners with relatively high education and income have more power to get out of doing housework by buying domestic help. In addition, there has been a fairly recent rise in the number of wives who earn more than their husbands. In 2003, about 1.4 million couples or one in four dual-earner couples had wives as the primary breadwinner (Sussman and Bonnell 2004). Primary-earner wives are slightly older and more educated than secondary-earner wives and primary-earner husbands. They are more likely to be employed in managerial and professional occupations (40 percent versus 26 percent), to work more hours per week, and to have had more years of experience than their secondary-earner counterparts (ibid.).

Despite high levels of female labour force participation, many Canadians believe that home and children take precedence over working for pay in women's lives. Expectations remain for women, even when employed, to maintain primary responsibility for home and family. In 1995, 46 percent of both men and women agreed or strongly agreed that "while a job is all right, what most women really want is a home and family" (Ghalam 1997, 16). In the past decade, women have increased the time they spend in paid employment without a significant corresponding decrease in the time they spend on domestic labour and childcare. In 1997, of all women in two-parent families, 62 percent of women with children under the age of sixteen were employed (Hunsley 2006). In 1998, employed mothers with children under the age of five spent double the amount of time on personal childcare activities than men: ninety-one minutes per day for mothers compared with forty-seven minutes per day for fathers (ibid.).

Canadians have taken up multiple, postmodern mothering mandates. Families with dependent children manage multiple cultural discourses and hold contradictory ideologies related to parenting and care work: they desire equal parenting but simultaneously hold on to ideologies of motherhood as a gendered talent. Unless couples work hard to fight against hegemonic discourses of traditional mothering, what they seem to end up with are contentious and significant compromises in childcare work. Cowdery and Knudson-Martin (2005, 343) label these compromises as "gender legacy" mothering discourses, which seem to be critical sources of marital stress as well as perpetuating gendered and raced inequities in care work (Blume and Blume 2003; Blaisure and Koivunen 2000).

Racialized Care Work
White middle- and upper-class mothers' employment is often made possible by the labour of women of colour who provide necessary childcare and domestic services (Arendell 2000). Within Canada, there exists a racial division of mothering, with women of colour doing the hard "mother" work for women of privilege. Because they lack choices in life, these women may have to put aside their responsibilities of caring for their own children while caring for the children of others (Bryceson and Vuorela 2002). Nannies and au pairs "manufacture motherhood" through their care work (Macdonald 1998), leaving unchallenged both the gender-stratified order in which women have primary responsibility for children and home and racialized systems of labour (Collins 1994; Glenn 1994).

Prioritizing childcare work over employment is neither possible nor idealized by many Canadian women. Traditional discourses of intensive mothering have always been primarily white, economically secure, ablest ones that have never matched the realities of working-class, dis/abled, or ethnic racial women. Economically insecure and racial ethnic mothers have always worked longer hours at lower-paying jobs than white mothers overall (Arendell 2000). Providing economically for children is more commonly understood among some minority groups to be an intrinsic aspect of a woman's mothering role (Bryceson and Vuorela 2002; Collins 1994; Glenn 1994).

Struggling to ensure economic survival involves racial ethnic mothers in what Reyes (2002, 3) calls "postcolonial mothering," namely, allowing other mothers close and far – grandmothers, aunts, sisters, neighbourhood women – to fulfill the mothering role. "Other mothering" practices including patterns of circular migration (sending children off to extended family members in the home country for a period and then retrieving them, bringing them back to Canada), co-residing with their own mothers who perform the care work, using community members as mothers, and "mothering from afar" (leaving their children in their host countries for most of their childhood) (Arendell 2000; Farrar and Gyant 1998). In the later case, mothers are often separated from their children for long periods but see themselves as successful because they are economic providers for the children and sometimes entire families. Their labour extends their families' living standards. Postcolonial mothering practices seem to break down traditional gender roles. Through their creation of matrilineal diasporas and postcolonial care work practices, ethnic and racialized mothers are less likely to socialize their daughters into proscribed roles as subordinates (Reyes 2002).

Mid-Life Care Work
Ideologies of mothering continue to shape care work expectations and activities for women in the middle and later stages of their lives. Mothering is usually associated with young children but, as Dillaway (2006) reminds us, care work never wanes. Serial engagement in care work represents one of the defining characteristics of mothering and, increasingly, of fathering. Spitze and Logan (1992) report that help from parents to children is common throughout the life course. Adults help children more than adult children help their parents (Keefe and Fancey 2002; Spitze and Logan 1992). Help peaks in the child's late twenties and early thirties and falls off after age thirty-five. The proportion of giving and receiving help between parents and children is not equal until parents are in their seventies and adult children are in their mid-forties.

Mid-life (aged forty-five to sixty-four years) care work has intensified with the lengthening of adolescence and the corresponding delay in independence for young adult children. In 2001 in Canada, 57 percent of twenty to twenty-four year olds were living with their parents (Turcotte 2006). Reasons for this pattern include employment or relationship uncertainty, high housing costs, and post-secondary educational costs. One-quarter of these are boomerang kids, adult children who leave and return home several times before they create separate households of their own (Beaupré, Turcotte, and Milan 2006). Because the "revolving door" (Dennerstein, Dudley, and Guthrie 2002) pattern has become common, there is little stigma associated with young adults living with their parents (Beaupré, Turcotte, and Milan 2006).

Care work for adolescents and young adults differs from that provided to young children. Boomerang kids typically receive three types of help: instrumental, financial, and emotional. Mothers may continue to do their adult children's cooking and laundry (Beaupré, Turcotte, and Milan 2006). Parents may continue to provide financial assistance, such as paying for post-secondary education, living costs, and leisure pursuits. Class affects financial help, for parents with greater educational and financial resources tend to provide young adult children with more money than parents with fewer economic resources. Interestingly, financial help does not result in adult children providing greater instrumental, emotional, or social support to parents (Grundy 2005).

Even when adult children establish their own homes, parents continue to provide help and support. When adult children are in their twenties and thirties, parental assistance consists mainly of actual assistance with childcare, services, and giving advice (Cooney and Uhlenberg 1992). As adult children reach their forties and fifties, parental help takes on the form of potential assistance, for instance, having someone to call on for help in case of emergencies, helping in financial or emotional crises, and providing advice only when asked. According to Eggbeen and Hogan (1990) in their study of over thirteen thousand families who responded to the American National Survey of Families and Households in 1987-89, 42 percent of parents gave advice, 33 percent gave money, 29 percent received advice, and 29 percent gave childcare. Intergenerational help is so common that mid-life parents who simultaneously provide care work both for adult but still partly dependent children and for elderly parents are now called the "pivot generation" (Attias-Donfut 1995).

Women in mid-life continue to identify primarily as mothers, drawing on intensive mothering discourses as guides for nurturing relationships with adult children. They commit considerable time, energy, and affection to their adult children, following the dictate that children's needs and interests take priority over those of the mother. Mid-life mothers tend to minimize their past contributions to adult children and go to extreme measures to remain independent from their children by not complaining about certain matters (Dillaway 2006). They tend to prioritize their children's topics of conversation and make conscious efforts to bury personal concerns when interacting with children. By centring conversations on their children, they avoid the stereotype of being a "bad" mother who talks only about herself (ibid.).

Structures of race and class privilege continue to shape mid-life care work. Adult children receive more help from parents if they are white, female, have fewer siblings, and live closer to their parents. More help is received from parents by non-Hispanic whites, those with more education, those who live close by, and those with more frequent contact. If there are grandchildren and both parents are healthy, even more parental care work takes place. Mid-life parents with good health become regular sources of assistance for adult children, rather than becoming additional responsibilities (Zajicek et al. 2006).

African-Americans are only 48 percent as likely as white Americans to give or to be "high exchangers" with parents. They are only 67 percent as likely to receive support from their parents and only 57 percent as likely to give advice to their parents (ibid.).

If boomerang kids return home with offspring of their own, the care burden for mid-life mothers is increased. Grandparenting represents a growing form of care work undertaken by mid-life mothers. Nearly two-thirds of Canadian women aged fifty-five to sixty-four were grandparents in 2001, with an average of 4.5 grandchildren per woman (Milan and Hamm 2003, 3). Even though half are retired, more than 30 percent of grandparents continue to work for pay. For this group, care work demands continue to cut into their leisure time, making a mockery of the notion of mid-life leisure. For ethnic racial, poor, and disabled women, grandmothering may represent a form of domestic oppression as difficult as that experienced by younger married women attempting to juggle paid and unpaid work (Zajicek et al. 2006; Chappell and Penning 2005).

Typically, grandparent care work takes two forms: skip-generation support and the provision of daily care (Conway-Turner 1999). According to the 2001 Canadian census, nearly half a million grandparents live with their grandchildren. Fewer Canadian children (3.3 percent) live in skip-generation households, compared with the United States, where 6.1 percent of all children live in grandparent-headed households. Goodman (2007) calls these "grandfamilies" in which grandparents raise grandchildren alone.

In Canada, 4 percent of households are multi-generational, making co-residence a growing trend among Canadian families. In one-third of three-generation homes, the middle generation has a lone parent – and in 10 percent of these cases, the grandparent is forty-five years of age or under, suggesting perhaps a very young parent, possibly a pregnant teen mother (Milan and Hamm 2003, 4). In these households, in both countries, grandparents are surrogate parents because their own children are unable or unwilling to support their offspring. They may be incarcerated, ill, suffering from mental illness, or living with a drug or alcohol dependency. They may simply have abandoned their children. Grandparents thus provide emotional – and financial – security for these presumably vulnerable children but may sacrifice their own leisure and financial security in doing so.

Culture and class shape co-residency. Minority groups and lower socio-economic status families report higher rates of co-residence (Keefe, Rosenthal, and Béland 2000). Globalization has not brought the economic prosperity expected by middle-age generations, who increasingly rely on families to help out. Half of contemporary three-generation households are headed by immigrants or Aboriginal families (Milan and Hamm 2003; Che-Alford and Hamm 1999). Parents born in Asia and Central and South America are far more likely to live with their adult children than are some other ethnic groups (Turcotte 2006).

A recent study of British, Chinese, and Indo-Canadians living in the Greater Vancouver area found that 7 to 10 percent of adult children share a home with an elderly parent (Mitchell 2003). Co-residence reflects what Mitchell (2003) calls a collectivist orientation to family formation shaped by norms emphasizing close family ties, family obligation, co-operation, respect, piety, honour of the elderly, and a responsibility to take care of aging parents. The strongest predictor of positive attitudes toward sharing a home with an aging parent is not ethnic background but, rather, a child's relationship with his or her mother (ibid.). Minority women rarely use formal services, preferring instead to call upon extended family networks (Chappell and Penning 2005). Families with disabled members are sometimes forced to co-reside. Over half of three-generation households include a person with an activity limitation (40 percent) or a disability (13 percent). Given increased longevity and continuing levels of immigration, the number of three-generation households in Canada may increase.

In situations in which grandparents do not live with their grandchildren, grandparents provide a range of support, from surrogate parenting to financial support and occasional babysitting, all of which props up extended families (Calasanti and Slevin 2001). In a British study analyzing intergenerational relationships, participants were categorized according to the degree of exchange among adult children, parents, and elderly parents. Although only one-quarter to one-third of families can be characterized as "high exchangers" or "tight knit," if intergenerational exchange takes place, it is far more likely to be parents to children than parents to elders. The proportion in both the United Kingdom and the United States that helps a child is far greater than the proportion that helps a parent or parent-in-law (Grundy and Henretta 2006). About one-third of families provide help to both parents and children, and their level of help bears no connection to social class, income, marital status, health, or family characteristics.

Some grandmothers provide daily childcare so that the mother can work for pay, even if they are poor and in ill health (Zajicek et al. 2006). Rather than being a drain on the economy, being able to count on the care work of grandparents, especially grandmothers, frees younger women to engage in paid employment (Keefe and Fancey 2002). Some 40 percent of American adult children who have their own children under the age of five receive babysitting help from parents (Spitze and Logan 1992). In Canada, in 1996, about 54 percent of grandparents in three-generation households helped out with household finances (Che-Alford and Hamm 1999).

Of the 5.7 million Canadians who are grandparents, most describe their care work with grandchildren to be a source of delight and companionship (Milan and Hamm 2003). Mandell, Wilson, and Duffy's study (2008) describes how care for adult children and their offspring may well be experienced by mid-life Canadian mothers as affectionate and sustaining as well as coercive and disempowering. Given the association of worth with productivity, mid-life women report feeling compelled to offer whatever resources they have available. Certainly, the support grandparents provide explains why, in turn, both grandchildren and adult parents generously provide eldercare to grandparents when it becomes necessary.

Eldercare
Neither the care provided by adult grandchildren for their grandparents nor the care provided by seniors for their spouses has received extensive research attention. Both are largely invisible.

As we have argued, care work is lifelong. Some middle-aged Canadians care for children and aging parents at the same time. These are the "sandwich generation." Studies from Canada, the United States, and Great Britain indicate that about one-third of women are "sandwiched." Nevertheless, this proportion is expected to rise substantially in the next few decades. By 2010, there will be only 5.6 persons aged forty to sixty-four for every person aged seventy-five and over, and this number will decrease to 3.2 by 2030 (Hunsley 2006). Over 700,000 Canadians in their forties, fifties, or sixties have children under twenty-five living at home and provide some kind of eldercare for at least one senior.

Over 1.7 million Canadian middle-aged men and women – 16 percent of those forty-five to sixty-four years old – provide informal care to almost 2.3 million seniors with a long-term disability or physical limitation (Stobert and Cranswick 2004).[1] As expected, most (67 percent) are providing care for their own parents, while a significant minority are looking after their spouse's parents (24 percent) or close friends or neighbours (24 percent) (ibid.). Approximately equal numbers of men and women provide care, but more women are high-intensity caregivers (Pyper 2006, 12). At mid-life, male caregivers spend an average of 16 hours a month compared with women, who spend about 28 hours. Among senior caregivers, men provide 20.9 hours compared with 32.9 for women (Stobert and Cranswick 2004). Meanwhile, "among Canadians ages 80 and over, 39 percent of women and 46 percent of men are cared for entirely by friends and family" (Fast 2005, 5).

Although both men and women care for parents or partners, it is frequently noted in caregiving studies that they provide different types – as well as different amounts – of care. For example, Stobert and Cranswick (2004) and Habtu and Popovic (2006, 27) find that informal care by Canadian mid-life women includes more personal care (bathing, dressing, and feeding) and inside work, whereas mid-life men do more outside work and provide transportation. Older male caregivers do more inside work. Generally, it is argued that men's care work is more instrumental. Men and women approach the challenges of spousal caregiving differently. Husbands adopt a problem-solving and skill-building approach. Wives, in contrast, draw on their lifelong experience as nurturers (Calasanti 2006).

Two-thirds of Canadian mid-life women and half of men combine work and caregiving. In this group, more men are low-intensity caregivers and more women are high-intensity caregivers (Pyper 2006). The impact on paid work is greater for women than for men. Women are more likely to change work patterns because of care responsibilities and are more likely than men to reduce hours of work (Habtu and Popovic 2006, 30). On a day-to-day basis, 55 percent of employed women and 45 percent of employed men state that caregiving duties affect their work, citing instances of coming to work late or leaving early, or having to miss at least one day of work (34 percent of women and 24 percent of men), and 44 percent say they have incurred extra expenses because of their responsibilities (Cranswick 1997). Those who do the most caregiving (in terms of hours spent) feel the greatest caregiving burden. One in five working women report that their sleep and health are affected by caregiving. Women are more likely to change their social activities (33.0 percent versus 27.8 percent for men) as well as their holiday plans (28.3 percent versus 10.9 percent) to accommodate caregiving responsibilities.

Recently, more attention has been paid to parental care provided by mid-life men. Campbell and Carroll (2007) talked with male caregivers in Ontario. Their findings suggest that when male caregivers are solely responsible, they engage in much the same care behaviour as women, though they continue to believe that women are more suited to caregiving and better at it. As a result of their findings, Carroll and Campbell (2008) argue against assuming that all care work is traditionally gendered. There has also been little investigation of the role of grandchildren caring for their grandparents, though there is reason to believe that adult grandchildren are an increasingly important group in the care of elder family members (Fruhauf, Jarrott, and Allen 2006). The grandchildren in Fruhauf, Jarrott, and Allen's study (2006) who were in their twenties reported caregiving experiences resembling those of their parents or grandparents.

The care that seniors provide to one another is almost invisible largely because it is considered to be an extension of household work. Husbands and wives see their roles as caregivers as reciprocal and as flowing "naturally" from the marital relationship. They may in fact perform the duties of caregiver for a long time before they begin to identify themselves as such. Caregivers in a Canadian study accept the identification of caregiver in response to deterioration in the health of their partners or when it is "assigned" to them by a health care provider or support group member (O'Conner 2007). Since women still typically marry older men and since men may reasonably expect to live into old age, many women spend a portion of their lives caring for ailing partners. The average older caregiver in Canada is seventy-three years old and is generally looking after a spouse, close friend, or neighbour (Stobert and Cranswick 2004).

The Benefit and Burden of Caregiving

For many years, care responsibilities were described in the literature as more onerous than not, focusing on the emotional, physical, and economic costs to caregivers (Moen, Robison, and Dempster-McClain 1995). A life-course approach, in contrast, sees the care receiver–caregiver relationship as more fluid and more complex than either burden or benefit and as including a certain degree of reciprocity. This should not imply that caregiving is burden-free. Indeed, caregivers experience both objective burden (the actual demands they experience as caregivers) and subjective burden (feelings of worry, sadness, resentment, anger, or guilt) (Hooyman and Gonyea 1999). Statistical evidence indicates that for both men and women, caring eats away at their time, energy, and money.

As a culture, we do not typically acknowledge how taxing it is for women to try to manage paid employment, housework, childcare, or eldercare. Nor do we acknowledge the cumulative effect. As is apparent in the popular media, tension is part of the taken-for-granted reality of Canadian women's lives. Because we accept that stress is an individual's responsibility to manage, there are few structural supports to relieve it. We therefore try as individuals to deal with our own pressure through counselling, support groups, and myriad individual coping strategies. Survey results confirm the endemic nature of stress. Constant worry was the most frequently mentioned health problem in Walters and Denton's study (1997) of Canadian women. Williams (2003b, 9) found that the most significant source of job stress was "too many demands or too many hours." Mid-life women experienced the greatest strain in this regard. According to Statistics Canada, one-quarter of Canadians describe their days as "quite" or "extremely" stressful (Shields 2004, 9). When we add in the hassle of dealing with racial and ableist discrimination, we can see how burdened some groups really are.

Emotionally, care work is seen as a burden because it disrupts one's life and places restrictions on one's activities. Yet studies reveal considerably more positive then negative emotional components of caring. Mothers and fathers of young children report caring for children the most meaningful aspect of their lives. Middle-aged adults report more positive than negative feelings about caring, even when it involves caring for someone with a long-term illness. Cranswick (1997) reports that, when providing help to someone with a long-term health problem, the majority of caregivers (64 percent) said their relationship was strengthened with the care receiver, and 63 percent said they rarely wished that someone else would take over the caregiving tasks. The emotional aspects of caring require, therefore, a more nuanced understanding of caring as a positive, meaningful, and supportive interpersonal exchange, albeit one that takes up a lot of individual resources and is frequently frustrating and conflictual.

Over the past quarter century, the burden of family caregiving has increased because of changes in family structure and dramatic increases in women's labour force participation. Chappell and Penning (2005) argue that changes in the public support of health care have also had an impact on family caregiving. For example, over the past two decades, Canadians have seen a decreased supply of acute- and extended-care beds, decreased hospital admissions and lengths of stay, and shifts in surgical treatment to outpatient settings. As well, community-care services appear to be declining despite increased spending, because the intensity of service has increased. As Chappell and Penning (2005, 457) note, "Home care is providing more medical support and less social care." This intensifies the personal and family responsibility for health care and, in so doing, reinforces and amplifies "existing structural inequalities of gender, ethnicity, race and class" (461).

When asked to evaluate their experiences in the 2002 Canadian General Social Survey, both middle-aged and senior caregivers rated their eldercare positively. Between 80 and 90 percent felt that helping others strengthened their relationships with care receivers and repaid some of what they themselves had received from others and from life (Stobert and Cranswick 2004). The majority of Canadian caregivers report that they have, overall, received more positive than negative emotional consequences from providing care (Williams 2005).

Because they invest more emotionally and instrumentally, women experience more burden and distress than men (Marks 1998). Sons are less stressed than daughters, more task-centred, and assume a more businesslike approach, similar to husbands caring for their wives and as opposed to daughters, who are more concerned about the emotional needs and well-being of their mothers (Arber and Ginn 1991). Reasonably, most daughters caring for their mothers find the experience both rewarding and trying, and experience a degree of ambivalence (Connidis and McMullin 2002) as they negotiate this terrain.

According to McGraw and Walker (2004, S324), women are "both burdened and enriched" by family care as they struggle to find a balance between connection and autonomy. Further, Lee and Porteous (2002, 90) find that some Australian women who are involved in eldercare internalized an ethic of care while others perceived it as being imposed. Some women in the Australian study refer to their valuable but unappreciated contribution to the country's health care system. Although they recognize the way care is gendered, many women see no choice – regardless of the cost to them. Some accept or are resigned to their situations. Others are angry about the compromises they are required to make. Whether "true believers" or resentful skeptics, these women still accept their obligation to provide care.

Grandchildren too describe feelings of reciprocity as grounding their decisions to become caregivers (Fruhauf, Jarrott, and Allen 2006). They speak positively of the personal benefits and voice concerns about the impact on their time, social lives, and careers. We highlight, therefore, the experience of family care as multidirectional, reciprocal, and dynamic.

Little research exists on how it feels to be a recipient of care. To avoid conflict, aging parents report the need to maintain a position of deference with their caregiving children, to "back down" from conflict, and to carefully consider their children's wishes and interests when making decisions (McGraw and Walker 2004). Spitze and Gallant (2006) conducted focus groups with older parents who live independently but receive help from their children. These parents use numerous strategies to cope with the ambivalence they feel about receiving care. One of these strategies is to emphasize the reciprocal nature of exchanges with children. Another is to use friends rather than family as confidants, and to simply avoid giving children information about their health status, eating habits, and plans.

Implications for Policy and Practice
Three factors – demography, economics, and gendered-racialized care practices – make it necessary to rethink care work policies. Demographically, families have changed dramatically in the last two generations. People now marry later, have smaller families later in life, and live longer, healthier lives. The implications are clear in terms of caregiving as proportionately more seniors seek support from fewer family members. Thus, we have seen more grandparents providing primary care for grandchildren, grandchildren providing primary care for grandparents, and men caring for parents, grandparents, and spouses. Given the potential shortage of caregivers in the future, public policies need to expand care work by rewarding those who provide care. One material enticement could take the form of tax incentives for those providing either sole or major responsibility for care.

Policies also need to expand networks of care providers. Young adults often experience difficulty finding part-time work and in establishing work credentials while continuing their schooling. Perhaps networks of young adults, supervised by both mid-life adults and seniors, need to be established in neighbourhoods in order to provide in-home care work in the same way that home care is now provided. In teams or alone, young adults could regularly perform care work for those requiring regular supervised help.

Economically, care work continues to represent a largely underpaid enterprise that requires considerable material sacrifices from its providers. Social scientists have begun to write about a "second work family incompatibility" (Perrig-Chiello and Hopflinger 2005, 185) that describes the conflicting demands of later-stage career with caring responsibilities for aging parents. The first family-work incompatibility was, of course, between paid work and the care of young children. But this term implies that care work is intermittent and takes place in two large time periods when, in fact, care work is ongoing throughout the life course. One of its key distinguishing features is its unremitting nature. Although it never ceases, it does have periods of high and low intensity.

Public policies have never grappled sufficiently with the intensity, necessity, and unequal distribution of unpaid care work within the life course, within families, or within society. Just as mothers of young children are culturally and materially seen as responsible for managing care work, adult women caring for their ailing parents are required to invoke personally negotiated strategies in order to manage their responsibilities. Depending on the nature of the burden, some will reduce working hours or retire; others will hire professional care or try to solicit help from other relatives (Perrig-Chiello and Hopflinger 2005). Yet, at the same time, economic uncertainty and financial turmoil put pressure on our shrinking base of working-age people to remain in the labour force in order to support the bulging superstructure of older people in Canada (Conference Board of Canada 2006; Hallamore 2007).

Reflecting the demographic changes in marriage, fertility, and longevity, it is expected that labour force shortages will follow the retirement of baby boomers. Because each following cohort is significantly smaller than the baby boomers, their retirement will leave a labour skill gap that will be difficult to fill. Employers are now realizing that it will be important to find ways to keep baby boomers actively employed beyond normal retirement years. Those same baby boomers will also be called on to help support aging parents, so it is incumbent on employers to follow the lead of some European countries in designing flexible work options for the future.

The growing income gap between the economically secure and the economically insecure has major implications for pensions and income security in old age. Studies have pointed out the gendered and racialized nature of this gap. Economic restructuring has disproportionately affected poorly paid sectors of the labour market, especially recent immigrants, so much so that Galabuzi (2006) characterizes the increasing polarization of the labour market and the consequent racialization of poverty as a form of "economic apartheid" (in Creese 2007, 200). Presumably, an aging population combined with possible government deficits and financial turmoil will harden racialized and gendered divisions in the labour market in the future, creating an even more polarized economy (ibid.). We require accurate and detailed statistical analysis of economic security patterns of the near-retirees and their care work in order to develop strong policy initiatives to curb the effects of an increasingly gendered-racialized labour market in which the social construction of skill and experience (ibid.) remains characterized by a lack of correspondence between educational credentials, employment, and income levels.

Political pressure is mounting from community agencies and social policy organizations across the country calling for state action. The Conference Board of Canada (2006) wants policies to increase employment opportunities for older workers – for instance, job subsidies or lower taxes that would increase the demand for and supply of jobs for low-paid older workers. The House of Commons Standing Committee on the Status of Women (Ratansi 2007) suggests employment recommendations aimed at alleviating poverty among seniors, especially among immigrant women, and expanding care work provision.

Finally, old modernist theoretical models have largely ignored intersectionality and life-course perspectives. Understanding the interplay between gender and race allows us to parse out similarities and differences among racialized groups, thus creating more effective community action. Life-course theoretical models allow us to understand the relationship among the interdependence of life spheres (work, marriage, family, community), linked lives (family-work interactions), contextual embeddedness (individual responsibilities and involvement in employment and family), and the timing and sequencing of events (interrupted careers, unpaid work responsibilities, immigration) (Szinovacz 2006). Intersectional analysis allows us to promote social policy based on a holistic awareness of life-course trajectories and care work. For example, if unpaid work duties force individuals to retire early, an intersectional approach may help identify which members of certain groups are most likely to do so. Who will have the opportunity to remain at work or return to it? Who will have the responsibility to provide care, and who will be able to pay for care help? In short, policy designed to keep seniors in the labour force may end up simply extending the gendered-racialized workplace through to death. Providing more nuanced and detailed statistical analysis of contemporary trends of care work will help stimulate more informed public discourse around aging.

Conclusion

In this chapter we have looked at the raced, gendered, and classed dynamics of three types of care work: mothering, grandmothering, and eldercare. Much of care work is invisible and some of it is coerced, largely because it is normalized in ideologies of mothering and partnering. Through adherence to the norms of care work and by undertaking the work of caring, individuals take up raced, gendered, and classed social positions. In so doing, traditional mothering discourses are destabilized as more varied and fluid postmodern and postcolonial discourses emerge, thus taking into account wide variations in economics, ethnicity, and ability. Social inequality shapes care work. In amount, intensity, and effect, care work is unequally distributed across ability, class, and ethnic racial lines. Using an intersectional perspective, we see how cumulative advantages and disadvantages pile up, making things worse for certain individuals and groups over time, not better (Calasanti and Slevin 2006).

Understanding care work as a relationship-based activity allows us to appreciate the serial nature of care work. We see that women assume a lifelong task of providing care work, often while trying to balance paid employment with other family responsibilities. Although men now contribute more time to both child rearing and housework, the responsibilities are not shared. As young families grow older, different care dynamics emerge. Adult children do not require the intensity of care needed by young children, and their relationships with their parents, especially in the case of mothers and daughters, begin to be marked by reciprocity as well as ambivalence. Similarly, as mid-life women begin to care for their aging parents, relationships of dependence and independence shift as mid-life adults begin to receive, as well as continue to provide, care. Grandparenting is also multidirectional, as grandparents care for grandchildren and support their children – financially and emotionally – and in turn receive care from adult grandchildren and middle-aged children.

Researchers have addressed key areas of concern in this growing field, but much work remains to be done to make visible inequities in the provision and receipt of care, and to continue to push for increased public support at the community and societal levels to ensure that, as the need increases, the burden on individual family members does not. The accumulated burden of care is stressful. Overwork, tension, and lack of sleep are the consequences of a lifetime of seeking but failing to find balance between paid and unpaid work and the intense emotional work of caring. Until we have institutionalized supports that allow increased flexibility for men and women at work, better social supports for dependent family members, and more community-based supports for caring family members, we cannot expect the situation to change.

Note

1 In Canada, estimates of the extent of informal caregiving and the nature of the associated responsibilities come from Statistics Canada's General Social Survey on Aging and Social Support (GSS). The 2002 GSS asked questions about informal care provided to Canadians aged sixty-five and older.

3
Maternal Employment, Childcare, and Public Policy
Maureen Baker

This chapter discusses the ways that employment patterns are shaped by gender, parenthood, and social policies, focusing on the liberal welfare states that have relied largely on private earnings to ensure well-being and provided targeted benefits for those in need (Esping-Andersen 1990).[1] Within these states, I show that there are two broad models of state support for childcare. Some countries, including Australia, New Zealand, and the United Kingdom, have provided more support for maternal childcare at home, whereas others, such as Canada and the United States, have encouraged maternal employment. Although these countries now pressure low-income mothers to seek paid work, state support for maternal employment continues to vary cross-nationally, influenced by the strength of local interest groups, employment conditions, living costs, and cultural attitudes about mothering.

Historically, the liberal welfare states have viewed maternal employment and childcare as private matters of little concern to either governments or employers (Baker 2006; Timpson 2001). Early in the twentieth century, however, the state began to provide tax relief to male-breadwinner families to help support maternal childcare at home, and later developed universal child allowances and targeted income support programs for the temporarily unemployed and mothers without male earners (Hantrais 2004; McClure 1998; Gauthier 1996; Baker 1995; Bolderson and Mabbett 1991).[2] By the 1970s and 1980s, childcare advocacy groups had successfully pressured governments, especially in North America, to view the accessibility and affordability of childcare as a social policy issue that influences women's employment equity as well as children's early development.

Some governments provide strong public support for earning and caring, but others *say* that they are enhancing and "strengthening families" while restructuring income-support programs and deregulating the labour market. However, most states have made significant policy trade-offs in recent years, reducing family support in certain areas but improving it in others (Baker 2006). These trade-offs have been influenced by pressure from politicians, interest groups, and the general population. Childcare – one area of recent policy enhancement – forms the focus of this chapter, in which I argue that recent reforms have strengthened public discourse about the importance of paid work for economic well-being and have improved childcare services in some jurisdictions. However, although more mothers are now employed, many remain part of the "working poor" and cannot support their families solely on their employment earnings. Drawing on cross-national comparisons, I show how employment and earnings are influenced by social policies, cultural ideas about family responsibilities, and gendered family practices.

Changing Labour Markets and "Dependency"

Before the Second World War, the male-breadwinner family was imbedded in social policy in the form of the family wage, especially in Australia and New Zealand. With trade union support, governments allowed married men to gain priority to many paid jobs, and these men were expected to be paid enough to support themselves and their so-called dependants. Married men had a moral duty to become good family providers, which typically gave them privileged positions in their families, with few responsibilities for household work. Women were expected to marry, procreate, and care for their household, but married women gained indirect access to male wages and benefits. By the end of the 1930s, widowed and deserted mothers with low incomes were also given a small state pension to care for their children at home (Baker and Tippin 1999).

The family wage policy meant that earners were divided implicitly into two groups – those who supported dependants and those who were supported by others (or were likely to be in the future). Unmarried working women were in the latter category, but so also were some partnered women and lone mothers whose wages were regarded by policy makers as little more than supplemental income (Webb, Kemp, and Millar 1996). Furthermore, in Australia, among other countries, the family wage policy permitted governments and trade unions to exclude married women from certain segments of the workforce until well into the 1960s. Yet the family wage did not always meet financial needs, which was a source of continuing political debate and trade union protest (Baker and Tippin 1999). During the expansionary years of liberal welfare states, from the 1940s to the 1970s, policy development and labour negotiations focused on the social rights of the worker-citizen and unemployment-related benefits (Orloff 1993).

The idea of basing wages on gender and family circumstances became viewed as unjust by the 1960s, and women's groups and unions fought for women's access to certain jobs and equal pay with men. However, labour markets also became more competitive and international, and employers sought new ways to control labour costs and enhance profits. The development of the service sector of the economy and of part-time work formed part of this strategy and, along with rising costs, encouraged more mothers into employment. However, labour protections were gradually eroded from many jobs, and labour markets became polarized into "good" jobs and "bad" jobs, based on their security, hours of work, pay, and working conditions.

Women's employment rates have increased substantially in most OECD countries in recent decades (OECD 2007b, 56). Rising living costs, marriage instability, ideologies of gender equality, revised notions of human rights, and reformed government policies have all encouraged women to gain more qualifications and contribute financially to their households. Despite the improvements in women's qualifications, they are still more likely than men to work in jobs that are temporary, part-time, and low paid, especially when they become parents (73). Although these positions are usually considered to be "bad" jobs, many mothers find that they suit their interests because they enable them to combine earning and caring. This suggests that gendered understandings about work and family still permeate our culture (Baker 2006).

Whereas men tend to work longer hours after marriage and parenthood, many mothers reduce their hours and work in positions that are closer to home, with less responsibility but lower pay and fewer fringe benefits. In addition, the paid work that women typically do is influenced by financial need as well as by personal and social perceptions of domestic responsibilities. Studies from many countries indicate that who cares for children and the household often coincides with conventional ideas about "doing gender," along with interpersonal negotiations, household resources, and the availability of public childcare services. In moderate-income and lower-income families, women continue to do most of the care work and routine indoor housework, while men do occasional care work, outside maintenance, and repairs (Ranson 2009; Baxter, Hewitt, and Haynes 2008; Johnson and Johnson 2008; Lindsay 2008). In higher-income families, couples often contract outsiders for housework and repairs, send their young children to high-quality preschools, or hire nannies or housekeepers to live in their homes. However, even these couples usually retain a gendered division of household labour for other household tasks. When women enter paid work, their jobs often relate to traditional female roles: caring for others or providing services and support.

Despite the gendered nature of paid and unpaid work, policy makers have urged low-income parents to avoid "dependency" and earn their own living. They talk about employment status as though it were an indicator of moral worth and the main solution to family poverty. However, class differences in maternal employment expectations offer mixed messages about the importance of caring work. Low-income lone mothers are expected to support themselves through paid work, whereas middle-class partnered mothers are sometimes praised for their decision to care for children at home. This is especially the case in Australia. In the liberal states, both categories of mothers are expected to closely monitor their children's behaviour with minimal state support.

Feminist scholars continue to argue that the concept of dependency makes the false assumption that all wage-earning citizens as well as their home-making wives are independent, whereas all those relying on state income support are dependent. Neither academics nor policy makers can ignore the extent of unpaid caring work normally done by wives, mothers, and daughters or the value of this work to the nation (as well as to men and children). Feminist scholars also demonstrate that lingering domestic responsibilities often impede women's attempts to become self-supporting through employment or to rise through the ranks (Baker 2004; Leira 2002; O'Connor, Orloff, and Shaver 1999). Furthermore, both homemakers and employed women can easily become impoverished through marital separation or lack of a male earner in the household.

Gendered Patterns of Work

Explanations for women's lower contributions to household income focus on the type of jobs they accept, their lower wages, their shorter working hours than men's, and the priority they often give to childcare and other unpaid household work. Research on marriage patterns also indicates that brides are typically younger than grooms, and the discrepancy between their earned incomes grows larger over time. Furthermore, Canadian women with the highest earning capacity are less likely than other women to marry, to stay married, and to reproduce (Baker 2010; Beaujot 2000). For women who become mothers, paid work seldom leads to economic prosperity, especially if they become self-supporting. In fact, lone mothers receiving state benefits generally improve their income through finding paid work, but they are likely to improve their economic status even more through repartnering with a male breadwinner (Hunsley 1997).

Researchers in Canada and the United States have suggested that employed women suffer from a "motherhood penalty." One indicator is that potential job applicants or actual employees who are pregnant or mothers are perceived as less qualified, competent, and committed to the job, both in experimental situations and by real employers (Correll, Benard, and Paik 2007). Another indicator is that the earnings gap between mothers and childless women is substantial and rises with women's age, education, job experience, time outside the labour force, and the number of children she has. For Canadian and American women under age thirty-five, the earnings gap between mothers and childless women is larger than between men and women (Zhang 2009; Crittenden 2001).

Mothers often make employment concessions for children (and male partners), especially when their children are very young, but this varies

Table 3.1

Percentage of employees working part-time, by gender and presence of children, 2000

Country	Women without children	Mothers of one child	Mothers of two or more children	Total women	Men without children	Fathers	Total men
Australia*	40.8	54.1	63.1	41.8	8.0	5.5	6.9
Canada	17.0	22.9	30.7	21.4	5.2	3.2	4.3
Denmark	18.5	13.3	16.2	16.6	–	–	3.7
New Zealand	20.6	37.6	50.8	32.4	5.9	5.3	5.6
Norway	24.7	33.5	41.1	31.8	5.0	–	5.0
Sweden	14.6	16.6	22.2	17.9	5.2	3.4	4.3
United Kingdom	23.7	46.6	62.8	38.6	4.1	3.2	3.7
United States	10.1	15.8	23.6	14.6	3.5	1.8	2.7
OECD average	18.7	28.7	36.6	23.2	4.2	2.9	3.6

* Australia uses a different definition of part-time work than the other countries (thirty-five hours per week or less compared with thirty hours in the other countries).

Source: Extracted from OECD 2002, 78.

cross-nationally. Among mothers with children under three years old, only 43.2 percent of New Zealanders were employed, compared with 58.7 percent of Canadians and 72.9 percent of Swedes (OECD 2005, 41). This suggests that it is more difficult and expensive (or considered less desirable) for mothers with young children to be employed in countries such as New Zealand. Full-time employment rates for mothers also vary cross-nationally as well as among the Canadian provinces (Roy 2006), but these rates remain higher in Canada and the United States (and many Nordic countries) than in Australia, New Zealand, and the United Kingdom (OECD 2002, 78).

Mothers with two or more children are less likely than other women to be employed full-time, whereas fathers with large families seldom work part-time and tend to work longer hours than childless men (OECD 2007b, 57). Table 3.1 shows that part-time work for parents also varies considerably by country as well as family size. For mothers with two or more children, part-time employment rates in Australia are more than double the rates in Canada and the United States, and nearly four times higher than in Denmark.[3] Although the Australian government supports part-time work through the income tax system, research indicates that women who work part-time over their lifetime seldom see any increase in pay or seniority, though full-time female workers show substantial increases over their lifetime (Chalmers and Hill 2005). These cross-national differences in part-time work can be explained by variations in the taxation of part-time earnings, the financial need for more than one household income, the cultural concept of a "good mother," local employment policies and practices, and state support for families (Hantrais 2004; Leira 2002).

Women's lower employment earnings are influenced by the nature of their jobs, their qualifications relative to men, and their working hours. In many families and jurisdictions, mothers are seen as secondary workers, who shape their employment around family responsibilities. In 2006, the gender wage gap varied considerably by country, even within the liberal states, from 10 percent in New Zealand, 17 percent in Australia, and 19 percent in the United States to 21 percent in Canada and the United Kingdom, compared with 11 percent in Denmark and 15 percent in Sweden (OECD 2008a, 358).[4] The relatively low gender gap in New Zealand reflects a labour force that contains a high percentage of educated women as well as a high percentage of low-wage (mainly Polynesian) males. In addition, both Australia and New Zealand have historical legacies of high unionization rates and centralized bargaining, which kept wages high, though these have eroded since the 1990s (Baker 2009; Baker and Tippin 1999). The gender gap is apparent in hourly earnings but persists for full-time employees and all workers, reflecting gendered differences in type and hours of work but also discrimination. Daly and Rake (2003) argue that men's jobs tend to receive higher remuneration *regardless* of qualifications or skills required.

Women also tend to earn less than their male partners, who are often older and work longer hours for pay (Baker 2010; Beaujot 2000). If women live with men who earn adequate wages, their lower earnings may be less consequential to household income, but the differential may alter spousal power relations (Potuchek 1997). The financial consequences of lower female incomes are particularly apparent when mothers raise children without a male partner in the household, as these households have the highest poverty rates (OECD 2007a).

The employment rates of lone parents (mainly mothers) have increased over past decades but continue to vary cross-nationally, with half employed in Australia but over 80 percent in Denmark and Sweden, as Table 3.2 indicates. The table also shows that having a job does not guarantee that lone parents escape from poverty, which is measured in this table as 50 percent of median income after taxes and transfers and adjusted for family size. About one-third of children with an employed lone parent live in poverty in Canada and New Zealand but only 4 percent do in Denmark, where incomes are higher and more state services and benefits are universal. In the case of lone unemployed parents (usually on income support), 89 percent of their children are poor in Canada and 92 percent in the United States, but only 18 percent are poor in Denmark (OECD 2008b, 138). This suggests that cross-national variations exist in levels of state income support, tax benefits, and wage levels, as well as the social pressures and opportunities to become self-supporting.

Table 3.2

Employment and poverty rates in one-parent households

Country	Percentage of sole parents employed	Child poverty rate with employed parent	Child poverty rate with non-employed parent
Australia	49.9	6	68
Canada	67.6	32	89
Denmark	82.0	4	20
France	70.1	12	46
New Zealand	53.2	30	48
Sweden	81.9	6	18
United Kingdom	56.2	7	39
United States	73.8	36	92
OECD average	–	21	54

Sources: OECD 2007a, Table 1.1; OECD 2008b, 138.

Paid employment certainly improves household income, even for lone mothers, but it also reduces the need for state income support. For this reason, governments have encouraged beneficiaries or welfare recipients to seek employment, and social assistance programs now require most categories of recipients to move into paid work or training earlier than in previous decades (Baker 2006). However, the effectiveness of welfare-to-work programs varies with the type of beneficiary; their qualifications, wages, and employment benefits; the strength of the local economy; and the generosity of state income support and social services. Participants who have the daily care of children or no recent job experience have limited opportunities to develop skills and move to higher-paid jobs, although savings are apparent for governments (Vosko 2002; Shragge 1997). This suggests that many mothers still need state income support and affordable childcare services to effectively combine paid work and raising children.

State Support for Earning and Caring

Members of the OECD have adopted at least two broad policy approaches to help families integrate earning and caring (Baker 2006). The first views the "normal" family as one in which the husband/father earns household income and the wife/mother retains primary responsibility for the home and children, though she may also earn money. Within this model, the state might provide tax benefits for the family breadwinner and his "dependants," while the female caregiver might be given a small caring allowance if the household income is low. However, the state makes only a gesture toward the needs of employed mothers, such as subsidizing childcare for low-income households, though some mothers manage to find high-paid employment and private childcare. Until recently, Australia, New Zealand, and the United Kingdom could be classified in the first category because interest groups fought harder for programs for mothering at home than for employed mothers.[5]

The second approach assumes that both husbands and wives are employees capable of self-support and that both are responsible for supporting any children they produce. This family model offers varying degrees of public support for childcare, parental benefits, and employment leave for family responsibilities but does not usually assume that adult partners are depend-ants or that gender roles are substantially different. This approach can be further divided into two subcategories: jurisdictions that expect mothers to become workers but provide few public supports, and those that offer more generous statutory benefits and services for employed mothers. The United States and parts of Canada (such as Alberta) fit into the first subcategory, whereas Sweden, Finland, Denmark, France, and Quebec fit into the second (Baker 2006; Christopher 2002).

Countries that view women primarily as housewives and mothers and/or accept a residual role for the state in social provision tend to offer few public supports to help parents combine child rearing with full-time employment. In these countries, at least three structural barriers have made it difficult for employed mothers to maintain paid work: ungenerous or no statutory maternity or parental benefits, the shortage of affordable childcare facilities, and persistent cultural attitudes that children are somehow damaged by non-maternal care (Baker 2006).

In New Zealand, for example, all three barriers existed until recently. Most social programs assumed that families had a male breadwinner and female caregiver, even though women's educational levels were high and maternal employment rates had increased (Baker 2001). The childcare subsidy for low-income families did not cover full-time working hours until 2003, despite the focus on paid work and self-sufficiency in welfare-to-work programs established in 1997 by the conservative National government. This subsidy still remains targeted to low-income families rather than to all families re-quiring childcare services, and there is no significant tax deduction for employment-related childcare. However, the previous Labour government introduced twenty hours a week of "free" educational care for employed parents in 2007 (Baker 2008). In addition, New Zealand offered only unpaid maternity leave to female employees until 2002, when twelve weeks of paid parental benefits were introduced for those with one-year continuous em-ployment with the same employer, though this was raised to fourteen weeks in 2005 (Baker 2006).[6] In the past, many employed women quit their jobs at childbirth, returning when all their children were in school.

Canadian social programs have generally supported maternal employment more effectively than similar programs in New Zealand, Australia, and the

Table 3.3

Effective paid parental leave, 2008 (duration of statutory leave multiplied by proportion of salary paid)

Country	Effective parental leave (weeks)
Australia	0
Canada	29
Denmark	53
France	103
New Zealand	7
Norway	116
Sweden	48
United Kingdom	23
United States	0

Source: UNICEF 2008, 16.

United Kingdom (Baker 2006). Canadian maternity benefits were first paid in 1971 to eligible female employees for fifteen weeks through the federal Unemployment Insurance program. In 1990, ten weeks of parental benefits were added and later expanded to thirty-five weeks, making a total of fifty weeks paid leave available to eligible mothers (or thirty-five weeks to fathers).[7] In contrast, the duration of parental benefits is fourteen weeks in New Zealand and eighteen weeks in the United Kingdom. There are still no statutory benefits in the United States, but the Australian (Labor) government has recently announced that eighteen weeks of paid leave will be introduced in 2011 (*Sydney Morning Herald* 2009). Table 3.3 shows the effective parental leave in 2008, which was calculated as the duration of statutory leave measured in days multiplied by amount of the benefit available to the employee. This table shows that parental benefits were the most generous at that time in Norway and France but that Canada compared favourably with the other liberal states. Wide variations are also apparent in the way parental benefits are delivered. Some are provided at a flat rate similar to a welfare benefit (such as in New Zealand), which usually means that a high percentage of pregnant women are entitled to these payments. Others are paid as social insurance and as a percentage of previous earnings (as in Canada), which means that entitlement relates to labour force attachment and previous earnings.

Childcare Costs
Reducing childcare costs has been found to increase maternal employment (Roy 2006; Christopher 2002), but different jurisdictions focus their support on different kinds of households. Canada offers a more substantial income tax deduction for the childcare expenses of employed parents, though this deduction has been criticized for providing greater benefits to moderate and

Table 3.4

Childcare costs as a percent of net income for working couples and lone parents

Country	Two-earner families (both with average wages and two children)	Two-earner families (one with average wage, one with low wage, and two children)	Lone parent (one average wage and two children)
Australia	22	19	17
Canada	18	29	27
Denmark	9	10	9
Ireland	29	34	53
New Zealand	21	26	42
Norway	11	12	4
Sweden	6	7	5
United Kingdom	26	27	9
United States	19	23	38
OECD average	15	17	17

Source: OECD 2007b, 59.

higher-income households (Baker 2006, 193). As Table 3.4 indicates, childcare costs for lone parents with average earnings have been especially high in Ireland and New Zealand, where those with two young children were spending 53 and 42 percent of their household earnings, compared with 4 to 5 percent in Norway and Sweden (OECD 2007b, 59).

Recently, many jurisdictions have reduced specific childcare costs to enhance the employability of mothers. For example, Quebec heavily subsidizes childcare to all parents who need it, regardless of employment status, for a maximum price of $7 per day (Albanese 2006). The other Canadian provinces are less generous. In 2010, the Ontario Liberal government announced the introduction of full-day kindergarten for four to five year olds (Babbage 2010). The New Zealand Labour-led government initiated free childcare for twenty hours a week for three to four year olds in educational care in 2007, though state transfers to childcare centres fall short of the operating expenses of some centres (Baker 2008). Australia increased the tax rebate for childcare expenses but also extended subsidies to commercial providers, which restricted government opportunities to improve the quality of care (Brennan 2007). Consequently, many Australian childcare services were jeopardized when the largest provider (ABC Learning Centres) experienced financial difficulties in 2008. The Labour government in the United Kingdom substantially reduced childcare costs for lone parents (OECD 2007b, 59).

The provision of more generous childcare subsidies to a broader category of providers or parents has been a controversial issue in all the liberal states for several reasons. Some people doubt that paid carers or educators can provide better early childhood education than biological mothers and are concerned that all-day care by "strangers" will somehow harm children. Others believe that the upfront cost of establishing high-quality public childcare services, expanding public kindergartens, or offering more generous childcare tax benefits is too high. Encouraging more private childcare services might be less expensive but could give the government less control over quality of care and childcare standards. Furthermore, using taxpayers' money to fund for-profit care has been resisted by many childcare advocates. Pushing more mothers into the workforce could increase the overall unemployment rate while aggravating "time poverty" and stress levels for mothers. However, reducing childcare costs does seem to encourage maternal employment.

The impact of more affordable childcare is apparent in recent Canadian statistics. From 1992 to 2004, the number of supervised daycare spaces increased over 310 percent in Quebec and over 100 percent in all of Canada but decreased by 7 percent in Alberta (Roy 2006). During the same period, the employment rate for mothers with children under the age of six years increased substantially in Quebec but declined in Alberta, even though labour force participation rates were similar in 1999. By 2005, the employment rate was 76 percent of mothers with preschool children in Quebec compared with 65 percent in Alberta (ibid.). This change suggests that the availability and cost of childcare services directly influences mothers' employment decisions.

Long childcare waiting lists, rising fees, and provincial variations in accessibility and affordability have been political issues in Canada for years, but childcare falls under provincial jurisdiction, and the federal government has been unable to encourage the provinces to agree on a national strategy. Before the 2006 election, the federal Liberals promised to increase childcare funding and build a national early learning system, but the subsequent Conservative government continues to rely on tax incentives as well as small payments to parents requiring services (Bailey 2007). Some provincial governments have gone ahead and introduced costly improvements to early childhood education, such as junior kindergartens. In Ontario, for example, the full-day kindergarten programs for four and five year olds in the public schools, announced to begin in September 2010, will be optional. However, they will require considerable administrative coordination because early childhood education has been shared by kindergarten teachers and childcare workers (Babbage 2010).

New Zealand pays neither subsidies nor substantial tax deductions for the childcare expenses of middle-income parents. As part of the Working for

Families program, the Childcare Subsidy for preschool children in low-income households was extended in 2006 from a maximum of thirty to fifty hours per week and the Out of School Care and Recreation Subsidy is now paid for up to twenty hours for school-aged children (New Zealand 2006). The hourly subsidy depends on parental income but covers only a fraction of the actual cost.[8] Beginning in July 2007, the New Zealand Labour-led government claimed to eliminate parental childcare fees for children aged three to four years old in early childhood development programs. However, the subsidy falls below the actual cost of many centres and covers only six hours a day to a maximum of twenty hours per week, rather than full-time working hours.[9] Furthermore, New Zealand employees are not entitled to sick leave until they have worked for the same employer for six months, which means that dealing with childhood illness is problematic, especially for employed sole mothers (Baker 2008).

The quality and affordability of childcare remain contentious issues, as does the availability of care services for the children of workers with non-standard hours, for those living in rural areas, and for children with special needs (Baker 2006; Cleveland and Krashinsky 2001a; Jenson and Sineau 2001). Canadian benefits for employed mothers were won after years of lobbying by groups such as the Child Care Advocacy Association of Canada. Politicians were forced to listen to these interest groups because maternal employment rates had increased earlier and faster in Canada than in New Zealand and Australia, and high-quality childcare was considered to be crucial to women's employment equity as well as to early child development (Baker and Tippin 1999). In Australia and New Zealand, the women's movement tended to focus on gender differences and pensions for mothers caring for children at home.

Reforms to Other Family Benefits

Recent reforms have also been made to child benefits, income support, and family services, often using the discourse of "fighting child poverty" and "taking children off welfare" (Baker 2006). Several governments have made promises before the United Nations and their own parliaments to abolish or reduce child poverty by a certain date (ibid.). The Canadian government has been talking about "investing in children," a policy paradigm that enhances child benefits and subsidies for public childcare services, creates children's advocates, and develops more effective child protection services. However, provinces with neo-liberal governments (especially Alberta) have been less accepting of the investing-in-children discourse and have been reluctant to reform policies for early childhood education and care (Jenson 2004c).

Most of the liberal states, however, have reduced certain types of income support for particular types of families (Baker 2006). For example, they used

Table 3.5

Social spending on families* as a percent of gross domestic product, 2003

Country	Cash	Services	Family-related tax breaks	Total
Australia	2.6	0.7	0.0	3.3
Canada	0.9	0.2	0.1	1.2
Denmark	1.6	2.3	0.0	3.9
New Zealand	1.9	0.4	0.0	2.3
Norway	1.9	1.5	0.1	3.5
Sweden	1.6	1.9	0.0	3.5
United Kingdom	2.2	0.8	0.4	3.4
United States	0.1	0.6	0.7	1.4
OECD average	1.3	0.9	0.2	2.4

* Includes child payments and allowances, parental leave benefits, and childcare support.
Source: OECD 2007a, Chart 4.1.

to provide universal family allowances for parents with children, designed to promote "horizontal equity" between households with and without children. They also offered income tax deductions for all taxpayers with "dependants," which were particularly beneficial to higher-income taxpayers. In the late 1980s and early 1990s, Canada, Australia, and New Zealand replaced their universal child allowances with targeted child tax benefits, raising the value of the benefit sporadically since then. Canada and Australia now target child benefits to moderate- and low-income families; New Zealand directs this payment to lower-income families (ibid.).

Canada and New Zealand have also tied the level of children's benefits to their parents' working status as well as to their income (St. John 2008; Baker 2010). Targeting child benefits to parents who earn moderate or low incomes saves public money while conveying the message that governments expect parents to support their children through employment. However, children's needs do not depend on their parents' earning activities, and anti-poverty groups view paying a lower child benefit to parents receiving social benefits as unjustifiable because these households have the lowest incomes. The level of child benefits is not always indexed to the consumer price index (as are old-age benefits in Canada and New Zealand), and targeting child benefits has especially reduced entitlement for New Zealand families.

Social spending has traditionally been seen as an indicator of welfare state generosity. Table 3.5 shows how countries apportion their social spending on families, which includes child payments and allowances, paid parental benefits, and childcare support. The table reveals that the Nordic countries had the highest level of social spending in 2003 and that most of their spending related to cash payments and family services rather than tax breaks.

In Australia, New Zealand, and the United Kingdom, cash benefits were also relatively high, reflecting the payments for care. These benefits are currently paid to low-income lone parents to care for their children at home for a much longer duration and at a higher rate than most similar programs in North America. In Canada, social spending is among the lowest of the countries listed in the table.[10]

Vast disparities in income support are also apparent among the Canadian provinces. Although the child benefit and maternity and parental benefits are federal jurisdiction, childcare provision and welfare payments fall under provincial jurisdiction. The total welfare income for a lone parent with one child living in Alberta is only 65 percent of the poverty line (using the absolute measure of the market basket of goods), compared with 100 percent in Quebec and 102 percent in Newfoundland (Sauvé 2009). Clearly, some provincial governments in Canada provide more support than others to low-income families.

Paid work has been promoted as the route to family well-being, especially in North America. Although wages vary by jurisdiction, some of the liberal states have paid less attention to ensuring that incomes match living costs. The United States and Canada in particular have high proportions of low-paid workers but have downplayed the need to pay income support to parents deemed employable, though definitions have varied considerably. The liberal states have also placed less emphasis on enforcing pay equity for women, dealing with rising household debt, and providing social housing for the growing number of families that cannot afford market rents. In contrast, some European countries – for instance, Sweden, Finland, and Belgium – have made considerable public investments in health and social services for families, including universal child benefits, family-related employment leave, heavily subsidized childcare services, social housing for low-income families, and other forms of income support (UNICEF 2005; Hantrais 2004; Gauthier 1996). Social programs in France and Sweden more effectively support employed mothers than any of the liberal states (Jenson and Sineau 2001; Kamerman and Kahn 2001).

In the European Union (EU), women have become a strong political constituency and consequently pressured the European Parliament to adopt various measures to help parents reconcile work and family life (Hantrais 2000, 114). EU employment guidelines now contain measures to help workers better integrate paid work and family life, including leave for family responsibilities, part-time work with comparable wages and pro-rated benefits, parental leave, more flexible hours, childcare services, and policies to facilitate the return to paid work. Cross-national research clearly illustrates that maternal employment and economic well-being can be influenced by government and supra-government policies, even under the prevailing economic and political conditions (Baker 2006).

Conclusion: Maternal Employment and the Low-Wage Economy

Few liberal states are now willing to encourage prolonged maternal childcare at home if it also requires state income support, though middle-class women are still praised for choosing to care for their children at home. Canada and the United States in particular have chosen to pay time-limited benefits to low-income mothers caring for very young children, but these mothers are expected soon to become self-supporting through paid work. However, few social supports have been provided to assist mothers to find work, retain their jobs, and gain promotion through the ranks. Encouraging the employment of mothers with preschoolers continues to be resisted in New Zealand, Australia, and the United Kingdom, where women's groups argue that maternal employment may slightly improve the incomes of low-income households but also causes myriad other problems with childcare and time management, especially in lone-parent households (Baker 2004, 2006). Nevertheless, mothers with paid jobs receive higher incomes on average than those relying exclusively on social benefits (OECD 2005). The desire to escape the social stigma of welfare, exit from poverty, and contribute to the household income as well as the larger society has motivated many low-income mothers to make serious efforts to become self-supporting. Yet many employed mothers with young children also report feeling stressed by the demands of their paid work and domestic responsibilities.

With the decline in marriage stability and the transformation of labour markets and taxpayer expectations, public discourse about maternal employment has shifted. In the 1940s, when universal family allowances were first developed, male breadwinners were expected to support their families while mothers cared for their children, husbands, and homes. However, men were also paid higher wages than youths and female workers and were granted income tax deductions for their dependants. States later guaranteed income support to mothers without male breadwinners as well as others in financial need. In the 1960s and early 1970s, when domestic labour markets expanded, governments helped create jobs, developed new social programs to prevent poverty, and promoted gender equity in the family and labour market.

Since the 1980s, many governments have signed freer trade agreements that encourage global markets and the deregulation of segments of the labour market, under strong pressure from employers and investors. Politicians now urge their citizens to increase productivity, to improve national competitiveness, and to develop an educated and skilled workforce. At the same time, they talk about children as a "future resource" and stress the importance of "good parenting" while urging parents to support their children and provide good role models for their children's future employment. However, many employees now work in highly competitive labour markets that favour low wages and long hours, though some professional and managerial employees and entrepreneurs are earning high incomes.

In the current economic climate, many employers minimize payroll costs by hiring part-time or casual workers. Part-time jobs might enable students to further their education and mothers to retain their domestic responsibilities, but these jobs seldom pay enough to support both parents and children. In Canada and the other liberal welfare states, full-time, high-paying jobs are becoming harder to find. At the same time, state income-support programs are being restructured to shorten the period that beneficiaries can receive payments, and case managers have heightened expectations that former beneficiaries can earn their way out of poverty.

Social programs in the liberal states generally provide a social safety net, but policy makers do not always fully acknowledge that paid and unpaid work is often gendered. Furthermore, the incomes associated with many current jobs fail to pay enough to enable parents to support their children, especially in North America. Many mothers accept responsibility for most of the caring work at home, and non-family childcare services are not always accessible, culturally appropriate, high-quality, or affordable. In addition, the transition from welfare to work can be risky for low-income mothers who forfeit income security and social services when they move into employment. If former beneficiaries lose their new-found jobs and also experience delays re-enrolling for social benefits, they may be worse off than if they had remained on income support. For political reasons, however, the state needs to ensure that services for beneficiaries of income support are not more generous than those for low-wage workers (Baker 2006).

Cross-national research indicates that some governments (especially in Nordic countries) regulate wages and working conditions, develop tax systems and government transfers that stabilize and supplement earnings, keep poverty rates low for families with children, and provide high-quality childcare services with low parental fees (Baker 2006; OECD 2005; UNICEF 2005; Hantrais 2004; Bradshaw and Finch 2002). Canada and the liberal welfare states offer various programs to assist employed parents, but fathers still earn considerably more than mothers, women still perform more unpaid household work than men, most children remain with their mothers after parental separation, and welfare programs tend to push beneficiaries into low-paid jobs. In the liberal welfare states, government strategies to assist employed parents are often insufficient to enable women to support their children without a male breadwinner in the household. Furthermore, when these policies focus on maternal employment or propose to increase public expenditure, they are typically viewed as controversial political issues to be debated at length. Nevertheless, the cross-national comparisons in this chapter underline the importance of national and regional politics, effective advocacy, and a gendered model of family in the development of social policy.

Notes

1 The liberal welfare states are Australia, Canada, New Zealand, the United Kingdom, and the United States.
2 Of the states that developed universal child allowances, the United States is the exception.
3 Definitions of part-time work vary.
4 The gender wage gap is the difference between the median earnings of men and women relative to the median earnings of men.
5 Since 1973, both Australia and New Zealand have paid income support to lone parents with low incomes.
6 The 2002 legislation originated as a private member's bill from a female member of the (left-leaning) Alliance Party but was implemented by the Labour-led government and its female prime minister (Helen Clark).
7 In recent years, the percentage of paid workers eligible for Employment Insurance has declined considerably.
8 For example, parents with moderately low incomes had their subsidies raised in 2006 from $1.10 to $1.28 (an increase of only 18 cents an hour).
9 The average cost of childcare in New Zealand at the time was between $200 and $300 per week (Hann and Thomas 2007).
10 Several countries in the original OECD table have been omitted here.

Part 2
Integrating Family and Work

4

Work, Care, Resistance, and Mothering: An Indigenous Perspective

Donna Baines and Bonnie Freeman

> More than a hundred native women including powerful clan
> mothers locked arms in a human chain to block a police arresting
> party ... More than 200 people had gathered at the entrance of the
> Douglas Creek Estates [Caledonia, Ontario] ... natives from other
> parts of Canada and the United States responded to a judge's court
> order last week which ordered protestors to leave the site by 2 p.m.
> If they didn't go on their own, they were told they'd be arrested for
> contempt of court and face a possible 30-day jail sentence. About
> half an hour after the deadline passed with no sign of police
> intervention, the group started to relax and disperse. After holding
> their position at the front of the line for almost 45 minutes, the
> women unlocked their arms for the first time. (Legall 2006)

> *Akhwa:tsire* ["family" in the Mohawk language]

The epigraph that opens this chapter refers to an important moment in a
lengthy Aboriginal struggle over land rights and government promises. It
highlights the leadership role and consistency provided by Haudenosaunee
women (Thomas 1994) within the traditional Haudenosaunee clan structure
and in leading resistance to injustices perpetrated by non-Native society.
Resistance and social activism have been part of the lives of Native women,
families, and communities since European contact, yet this socially important
and life-sustaining activity is rarely classified as work or understood to be a
core focus of family life, mothering, or the activities of women.

Categories commonly used to examine family and work life are of little
use in understanding many of the activities of mothers and families from
particular racial-cultural groups, such as Native families (Das Gupta 2000;
Collins 1990, 2000). Rather than discrete, tightly self-contained categories,
activities such as mothering, family life, resistance, and work interweave in

continuous ways through women's identities, endeavours, and relationships (Baines 2004a, 2004c; Smith 1987). In this chapter, we argue that starkly decontextualized, demarcated categories circumvent an in-depth understanding of Haudenosaunee women's sustaining activities and relationships in traditional and contemporary Indigenous contexts. Defence of the land and Indigenous culture, mutual and multidirectional care, *Akhwa:tsire* or extended blood- and non-blood-related family ties and obligations, and Indigenous community building are rarely included in studies of work, mothering, or family life. This chapter disrupts the widely held notion that families are best understood as nuclear and apolitical with little or no connection to struggles for continuities of culture, defence of the land for future generations, social and political leadership, and governance. We present "family care" not as a private activity involving unbounded female sacrifice but as a politically and socially important public activity involving myriad mutually beneficial, community-sustaining activities and endeavours. Similarly, resistance cannot be separated from social caring, and both span the spheres of home, paid and unpaid "work," politics, and our relationship to and use of the land. Finally, we assert that although multi-generational community activism and sustenance arise from the social, historical positioning of Aboriginal people vis-à-vis colonialism, it is something that many other populations on the margins of consumer society also display, and from which all "families" can draw lessons and inspiration.

Indigenous mothers and families, and the work they do, are products of the history of colonization and resistance to it. The Haudenosaunee possess one of the world's oldest democracies, known as the Haudenosaunee Confederacy, in which women played central roles in co-governance, leadership, and collective rule and were pivotal to the production of goods and services necessary to survival (Shenandoah 1992; Lyons 1984). Indigenous society and Indigenous women's social, political, and economic roles did not fit with the European model of authoritarian monarchical rule, waged labour, or the patriarchal family (Bourgeault 1988). Extensive measures were taken to compel Indigenous people into new roles in relation to their land, production, governance, and activities that sustain human life. Foremost among these measures was the acquisition of Indigenous lands and the imposition of waged labour. The European model of wage labour required the devaluation of unpaid social and familial care work undertaken by women, concomitant with the valorization of men's paid work outside the extended family group, female dependence on the male wage, and the stripping of female authority within and outside the home. The imposition of Indian agents and elected "band councils" displaced the consensual democracy of Native confederacies, dismissing women's public role in governance and peacekeeping.

The forced removal of children and disruption of family ties during the traumatic years of residential schools (1880s to 1960s) and the Sixties Scoop further undermined Indigenous women's status as competent mothers. Coupled with the displacement and marginalization of elders and the rupturing of extended blood and non-blood family ties, this situation could have remade the Indigenous family in the image of a white, male breadwinner–dependent wife nuclear family. At times bubbling to the surface and other times dormant, Native people's resistance to colonial rule kept traditional practices alive and nurtured hope for a better future. As exemplified in the epigraph, protection of the land, self-determination, and women's leadership in sustaining Indigenous knowledge were central to this resistance.

Through an analysis of the socially meaningful and sustaining activities of Indigenous women, particularly those involved in defending Indigenous lands and culture, we highlight in this chapter inadequacies in our current understandings of work and family as distinct, self-contained spheres with little or no overlap, integration, or connection to resistance, activism, and political struggle. We also introduce a range of activities, not usually thought of as work, that nevertheless sustain communities and individuals to provide for their continuity. We suggest that our current understandings of care, mothering, and the role of families depoliticize and demobilize the potential of families to care for one another within and through struggles for social justice and a sustainable future.

Language is always a force in political struggles, and the struggle for First Nations self-determination and governance has used language and labels in important and strategic ways to gain public awareness, to name "problems" and their "solutions," and to reclaim sovereignty. Several terms are used in this chapter to describe First Nations people. Reflecting the diversity of terms used in the wider world and among the five hundred Indigenous groups in Canada, we use terms such as "Indigenous," "Native," "First Nations," and "Aboriginal" interchangeably. Reflecting the rights of groups to name themselves, we also use the term "Haudenosaunee" to designate the People of the Longhouse, known in English and French Canada as Iroquois.

Non-Native Approaches to Family, Work, and Mothering

Is the provision of care within a family a form of work or something else? And if it is work, how does it fit with the notion of work and family as two separate spheres? What if the family was conceived of as both immediate and extended blood and non-blood ties, and care work in all its many forms had the same status as other forms of work? What if work was conceived of as meaningful, sustaining activities rather than as wage labour – how would this change the evaluation of women's contributions to society? These questions form the backdrop to the investigation undertaken here. Although the generalist, feminist, and critical literatures provide useful insights into these questions, none provides a complete answer. Generalist perspectives on the family tend to view it as the "basic unit" of society or social institution through which values, traditions, and roles are transmitted (Ambert 2006a; Beaujot 2000). Feminists are often in agreement with Marxist-critical perspectives that view the family as a basic economic and social unit of society in which labour is reproduced, or refreshed daily, so that workers are available and will supply their labour power to the capitalist system of production (Armstrong and Armstrong 1990; Connelly 1978). Simultaneously, feminist perspectives have viewed the family as a socially constructed patriarchal unit of society in which unequal gender relations are transmitted, practised, and reproduced (Eichler 1997a; Luxton 1997).

Mainstream thinking on families tends to focus on the nuclear family or households composed of two generations (adults and their children). Family forms that do not fall into the nuclear family model are often termed "pre-capitalist" or "extended," and although not always denigrated, they are rarely thought to provide inspiration or road maps to the future. Government policies and practices have done much to erode extended kinship relations among Native people, yet this model continues to be central to Native communities, the "cornerstone of self-determination," a powerful, enduring, and hopeful idea "etched" in the Native psyche (Castellano 2002, 16; see also Fiske and Johnny 2003; Anderson 2000; Weaver and White 1997). Generalist literature has little to offer debates concerning inequitable divisions of labour and the impact of the larger socio-economic system, accepting wage labour as an unquestioned norm of contemporary society. It tends to restrict its focus of inquiry to how family units (mostly nuclear) and family members negotiate the challenges of both socialization and care of children (Beaujot 2000). Feminist literature is interested in the roles women are compelled or choose to play within nuclear families and the broader economy, as well as how a range of policies and practices make paid and unpaid work more or less accessible, equitable, rewarding, and meaningful (Eichler 2001; Fox and Luxton 2001). Although great diversity exists within Canadian families (Krull 2006b), within the nuclear family, men generally assume the role of major breadwinner, ultimate authority, and secondary parent, whereas women take on roles such as homemaker, primary consumer, primary parent, and secondary wage earner (Ambert 2006a). Women are much more likely than men to take on unpaid care roles in the community, extended family, and voluntary organizations (Reitsma-Street and Neysmith 2000). This work often includes social activism or other measures to extend dignity and care to those in difficulty (Abrahams 1996; Weeks 1994). Studies involving Aboriginal women show that unpaid care, including social activism, is socially necessary work, though it is rarely recognized, measured, or rewarded (Baines 2004c).

Capitalist production pivots on wage labour, a system in which people who do not own ways of producing goods or services are placed in a position in which they must sell their capacity to perform work in order to receive wages and, thus, purchase the means to survive (Tucker 1972). Wage labour was not part of pre- and non-capitalist formations, such as those found in Indigenous societies prior to white contact (Bourgeault 1988). Instead, these societies operated on the basis of productive labour, wherein one's labour power was used to directly produce the goods and services needed in everyday life or to produce goods and services that were bartered, traded, or sold.[1] The wage labour model elevates paid employment, concomitantly devaluing other ways of sustaining individuals and society. This offers a partial explanation for the degradation and eclipsing of unpaid care work in the home and community, as it has no direct tie to wage labour, though at times it may supplant or supplement it. It also highlights why political activism and resistance are not seen as work, as they too have no direct tie to wage labour and may, at times, challenge, disrupt, or supplant it.

Various theorizations attempt to explain the gendered division of paid and unpaid care and work in our society. Generalist theories link these divisions to traditional and cultural practices, noting that they are changing as society changes (Walsh 2003; Beaujot 2000). Marxists use the notion of reproductive and productive work to analyze the differences between socially necessary but unpaid work in the home and paid work outside the home (Armstrong and Armstrong 1990).[2] More orthodox interpretations emphasize the notion of work and home as separate spheres of activity characterized by very different relationships. The former relationships are thought to be alienating and oppressive, whereas the latter are thought to be where genuine human care and emotion can be displayed. Feminists criticize this characterization, pointing out that for too many women and children, home is a place of violence, alienation, and oppression (Proffitt 2000; Walker 1990). Marxist approaches advocate women's full involvement in the labour force as a way to provide them with a status equal to men (Fraser 1997). Although women's participation in paid labour is currently at record-high levels in Canada, rather than full social and economic equity, this has resulted in double and triple days for many women as they struggle to balance the demands of home, work, and community (Baines 2004a; Armstrong and Armstrong 1990). Feminist approaches have argued for a retheorization of labour to include paid and unpaid work, community involvement, social activism, and other forms of care and service to others (Abrahams 1996; Weeks 1994; Naples 1992). In tandem, some feminists have suggested concepts such as a continuum of work, particularly care work, to explain the interweaving of tasks, skills, mindsets, and values involved in women's paid, unpaid, and activist work (Baines 2004c; Baines, Evans, and Neysmith 1998). Concepts such as activist mothering (Naples 1992) and family activism

(Verberg 2006) capture the multi-generational and community-wide integration of family life, work, and efforts to bring about social change in the lives of women.

Similar to Bettina Aptheker's notion (1989) that women's resistance occurs within the context in which they work and live, theorizations of work, family, and mothering need to start with women's everyday experience to understand the overlay of work, care, and resistance. Since women's lives are often focused on providing care to family and community, their resistance also focuses on building dignity, social connections, and endurance in and among the people for whom they care. As Aptheker (1989, 180) puts it: "In the context of a society in which the quality of daily life is continually undermined and in which connections between people are continually threatened, such strategies, which form the sinew of life, are strategies of resistance."

Colonization and the Remaking of Women's Roles

Records such as Kayanaren'kó:wa – the Great Law of Peace – and Kaswehntha – the Two Row Wampum – are agreements recorded on wampum belts of the Iroquois or Haudenosaunee Confederacy revealing that peace among the member nations operated on the basis of mutual love, charity, and equality, and that all participants were fully self-determining (R. Hill 1992; Mitchell 1984). Within Haudenosaunee societies, it was the role of women to foster and protect the capacity for fair and inclusive self-determination, to defend and care for the land, and to ensure connection to the land for future generations (Anderson 2000; Wagner 1992; Mitchell 1984). Europeans were initially welcomed to the area now known as Canada on the understanding that they would operate within the same framework. However, as discussed in further detail below, for European colonialism to be successful, Indigenous people's connection to the land and self-determination, as well as their forms of work, gender relations, and the family, had to be supplanted by processes and relationships more compatible with capitalist production and accumulation. Although self-determination and the family were attacked and undermined through myriad policies and practices, Native people, and in particular women, kept traditional practices and values alive. It is the continuity of these practices, values, and roles that can be seen today in both the protests at Caledonia and the assertion of women's political and spiritual leadership in the ongoing struggle for the self-determination of Native people.

Roles for women varied across Indigenous societies. Pre-European Native societies ranged from patrilineal, patriarchal groups, such as the Blackfoot Confederacy in what is now western Canada, to matrilineal societies such as the Haudenosaunee Confederacy in what is now central Canada (Krull 2006a). Although gendered divisions of labour were present in both types of Aboriginal society, neither gender was restricted from performing other kinds of work, nor was all work seen as essential to the functioning of society (Bourgeault 1988). Women played major roles in government and policy making within matrilineal societies, including control of decision-making processes, selection of chiefs, and protection of the land (Noel 2006; Anderson 2000; Wagner 1992). The rights and roles of women within matrilineal Indigenous societies far surpassed those in Europe at the time and for some centuries to come. The central role of Haudenosaunee women in governance, leadership, and policy development strongly influenced the struggle for women's suffrage in the United States and Canada (Wagner 2001). As Sally Roesch Wagner (2001, 48-49) argues, in the late nineteenth century, Haudenosaunee women possessed rights unknown to European society – "control of their own bodies, custody of the children they bore, the power to initiate divorce, choice in the type of work they did, and the enjoyment of a home life free of violence." In 1893, Matilda Gage, a non-Native woman, observed that "family relations among the Iroquois demonstrate women's superiority in power" (cited in Wagner 2001, 72). Haudenosaunee women's connection to the land and its use was also observed by Gage, who wrote that "no sale of land was valid without consent of the squaws and among the State Archives at Albany, New York, treaties were preserved signed by the 'Sachems and Principal Women of the Six Nations'" (10). Similarly, Alice Fletcher, another non-Native woman, noted in 1888 that in the late nineteenth century, Haudenosaunee women could overturn decisions made by chiefs and took a very serious view of their role of protecting the resources and lands for their children and future generations:

> In olden times, the women claimed the land. In the early treaties and negotiations for the sale of land, the women had their voice, and the famous Chief Cornplanter was obliged to retreat from his bargains because the women forbade, they being the landholders, and not the men. With the century, our custom of ignoring women in public transactions has had its reflex influence upon Indian customs. (Cited in Wagner 2001, 91)

In the passage above, Fletcher notes the erosion of Haudenosaunee women's social participation and leadership as they bend to the practices of the dominate society. Circular intergenerational families, interconnected by blood and non-blood ties, formed the basic unit of Indigenous societies in earlier times and formed interconnected networks of relations and mutual obligation (Red Horse 1980). Unlike European societies, children, not men, formed the core of the society, offering promise for the future and carrying forward knowledge and traditions (Anderson 2000). Elders assumed the next most central role, entrusted with "maintaining the spiritual, social and culture life ways of the nation" (158). Women were seen as the third layer of society – the strength of the community, aware of what all groups were doing and focused on the support and sustainability of the entire community. Men formed the outside circle of matrilineal Indigenous societies; as the providers and protectors, they were inextricably integrated within the projects and responsibilities of the other layers of society (Freeman 2007). The flow and integration of this extended family system provided strength and stability to Indigenous society, which became something that non-Native policy makers would try to reorganize and dismantle.

The introduction of wage labour and displacement of extended family relations would not have been possible without the purchase and surrender of Indigenous lands (Shewell 2004). This loss left Indigenous people with no means of support within a suddenly alien and often hostile system (Bourgeault 1988). Deprived of their land and unable to continue the practices of pre-European Native life, many Native people found paid work as farm workers, loggers, and fishers (men) and domestics (women). Residential schools reinforced this positioning within the low-wage, low-skill workforce, training Aboriginal children in farm work and domestic duties (Milloy 1999; Fournier and Crey 1998). The introduction of residential schools was a deliberate strategy to assimilate Indigenous children; inculcate them with the values, language, and religion of white society; and groom them to take on low-wage positions within the mainstream economy (Shewell 2004; Fournier and Crey 1998). Residential schools disrupted Native families in numerous ways (Hill 2002; Milloy 1999; Weaver and White 1997). Parents, elders, and children experienced deep loss and dislocation when children were forcibly taken away from everything they knew or loved. The children had to adapt to a new paradigm emphasizing Christian values, wage labour, and individual responsibility, while being taught to despise the language, values, spiritual beliefs, and practices of their communities (Bourgeault 1988). They were also raised in the absence of family, emerging from school with very little knowledge of how to raise children, build relationships, or sustain family ties. Many of the children were abused in the schools and traumatized by their experience. As Grant (1996, 224-25) notes:

> At sixteen the children returned to their home communities – angry, contemptuous, superior, rebellious children ... Healing attempts were almost impossible because the language of the children had been destroyed. Bewilderment gripped the communities, often before any resolution could be reached, the returned children themselves became parents and their children were doomed to repeat the same cycle which worsened with every generation. As the parents themselves were products of the Residential schools, they were less and less inclined to question the system which had broken their spirits and destroyed their identities as Indian people.

Problems such as poverty, abuse of alcohol and drugs, violence, and neglect grew rapidly and, in what became known as the Sixties Scoop, child welfare agencies began apprehending Native children in unprecedented numbers, fostering or adopting them out to non-Native families, thereby expanding the number of Native children growing up outside Native influence and care (Milloy 1999). White society adopted the image of Native women as neglectful and addicted – rather than as the nurturers and defenders of the community – and Aboriginal families as pathologically flawed (Weaver and White 1997). Chrisjohn and Young (1997) assert that the cumulative impact of government policies – the theft of land and removal of Native people's economic base; the destruction of the extended family, including the role of elders and blood and non-blood ties; and the transplanting of children into a foreign, racist system – constitutes genocidal intentions directed at Indigenous people.

Increasingly, the experiences described above are coming to be known as historical trauma or the "collective compounding emotional and psychic wounding both over the life span and across generations" (Brave Heart 2000, 258; on this see also Freeman 2007; Hill 2002; Warry 2000; Lederman 1999; Duran et al. 1998). Unresolved, this trauma contributes to mental health problems, addictions, violence, social disruption, and struggling communities (Brave Heart 2000; Duran et al. 1998). Revitalizing and extending traditional practices that were banned in many parts of Canada, Indigenous people have developing ceremonial, spiritual, and social processes to heal and fortify their communities (Freeman 2007; Hill 2002; Kulchyski, McCaskill, and Newhouse 1999). Although these practices have strong spiritual and psychological dimensions, they also focus on strengthening the individual so that he or she can rebuild and defend *the community*. A sense of responsibility for the land and the people is woven into healing ceremonies and practices, and taking up this responsibility is part of any healing journey.

Warning that even traditional practices can be used to exclude and exploit women, mirroring rather than displacing colonial relations (Anderson 2000), several authors have called upon Native women to lead the struggle for community revival and self-determination (Noel 2006; Anderson 2000; Harjo and Bird 1997). Placing women at the head of this collective struggle for land and justice rebuilds Indigenous women's traditional political and social roles in matrilineal societies, helping to restore extended family ties and obligations and drawing on the knowledge and strength of elders returned to their rightful place alongside children within the concentric, overlapping circles of Indigenous society. Within this model, there is no "work" that is more important than the continuity, self-determination, and overall revitalization of Indigenous society. There is no division between this work and family life and care of the broader community – it is an indivisible whole, feeding continuously back into itself with a porosity and vitality all its own. The leadership work and role undertaken by Indigenous women can take many forms, ranging from soup lunches with neighbours or fellow students (Freeman 2007) to the arm-linked human defence of stolen land described in the epigraph that opens this chapter.

Four Hundred Years of Resistance and the Struggle for Self-Determination

Despite unrelenting oppression, Indigenous society has a history of continuous resistance and struggle for self-determination. In the aforementioned genocidal and assimilationist context, mere survival became a form of resistance. However, First Nations people survived not just as individuals but also as social and cultural units with distinct practices, values, and beliefs. Self-determination, or the duty and responsibility to defend the land and sustain the people, as set out in the creation story and Kayanaren'kó:wa, forms the central core of this resistance. Indeed, First Nations people are more likely to view this "work" as duty and mutual obligation rather than as resistance, though this duty certainly fits within Aptheker's framing (1989) of resistance as everyday, incremental activities that sustain life and extend dignity.

The distinct role played within Haudenosaunee society combines caring with governance, resistance, political activism, and leadership. Non-Native models of the nuclear family individualize and depoliticize most things within and outside the family. In contrast, the mutual obligation of extended blood and non-blood ties to each other and to the larger community compels "family" members to politicize relationships within and beyond the family, community, and larger society. Although many First Nations people view the imperative to defend the land and self-determination as a spiritual duty rather than a political activity, it is generally seen by First Nations people as both. Concentrating on socialization of the young, generalist models of the family eclipse our understanding of the often political nature of the nurturing and resistance "work" that families perform.

Rather than a break with past tradition or a sudden resurgence of activity, modern-day actions such as challenges to the Indian Act through Bill C-31 – the latter passed by the Canadian Parliament in June 1985 to bring the Indian Act into line with the provisions of the Canadian Charter of Rights and Freedoms – and the protests at Kanesatake and Caledonia represent a continuity of resistance and an assertion of women's spiritual and leadership role within that resistance. For example, it was women's activism around Bill C-31 that changed the Indian Act and permitted the legal reinstatement of the matrilineality central to many Native societies (Silman 1988). Although the Indian Act dismissed the importance and duty of women's roles and duties, reinforcing "Indian" status through the father's lineage, many Native groups maintained matrilineal values and beliefs (Monture-Okanee 1992). Aboriginal women's activism around Bill C-31 focused on gender equity as well as the need to nurture and defend those at the centre of Native society – children, especially children deprived of "Indian" status when their mothers married non-Native men. Reinstatement of "Indian" status under Bill C-31 provided an injection of energy to Native women's struggle against Eurocentrism and assimilation to non-Native life and served as an impetus for many bands to redouble their efforts for self-determination.

Similarly, during the struggles at Kanesatake and Caledonia, Haudenosaunee women assumed full political and spiritual leadership roles and have been consistently seen at the forefront of barricades: assuming the role of spokespeople for the media; acting as central negotiators with government officials, police, and security forces; and acting as leaders within Native forums and strategic debates.[3] While non-Native residents of Caledonia and Châteauguay worried about how to get past the barricades to get to their paid work, Haudenosaunee people under the leadership of Haudenosaunee women took on the unwaged but highly important sacred "work" of defending the land on behalf of past and future generations, sustaining those directly involved in the standoff, and caring for the Native communities impacted by the blockades and the often violent reactions within non-Native society.

Indeed, it was the inconvenience experienced by commuting suburbanites around Châteauguay and Caledonia that sparked some of the most appalling acts of violence and racial hatred against Native people during the Kanesatake-Oka and Six Nations Reclamation struggles. A major clash of paradigms involving notions of the role of land, women, family, community, and "work" could be seen in the intense frustration and non-comprehension among suburban commuters. The imperative of white wage labourers collided head-on with the spiritual duty of Native people to protect the land, sustain the community, and practise self-determination. Those operating within the wage labour paradigm had no framework from which to understand the activism–social care paradigm of the Haudenosaunee people, while Haudenosaunee people had the benefit of understanding, but selectively rejecting, aspects of the wage labour paradigm embraced by their non-Native neighbours. The wage labour paradigm requires a split between home and work life, disciplining people to leave the more pleasurable and meaningful realm of home and go to work each day. Without paid work, most people cannot afford the realm of home and family. Failure to participate in paid work means that one will lose respect and legitimacy in the larger community, as well as most of what people enjoy in the way of home and hearth. Within the paradigm of Native self-determination, meaning and pleasure are derived from the activities and tasks associated with fulfilling one's duty to extend self-determination and sustain those within the concentric circles of Native society. Work and non-work, care and relationship are not so easily separated. The realm of paid work does not exclusively sustain the realm of love and home; instead, these realms are saturated with caring, resistance, and politics in ways that are mutually reinforcing and inseparable.

Patricia Hill Collins (1990) uses the term "othermothering" to describe the role that Black women often play as community mothers in their inter-action and response to hostile and political surroundings. Black academics and educators have used this term to describe the relationships between Black students and their teachers within predominantly white institutions (Guiffrida 2005; Loder 2005). In the context of struggles against land de-velopers, governments, and police forces, Haudenosaunee women undertake othermothering of the broader Native community, providing leadership, role models, credibility, and care. As mothers, aunts, grandmothers, and neighbours, they also undertake activist mothering (Naples 1992), an inter-locking of political activism, mothering, community work, and paid labour. Naples argues that activist mothering goes beyond kinship to dynamic re-lationships where family-based work such as caring and activities that promote the betterment of the community become blurred. For both Collins and Naples, the lines between care and resistance, duty and political action, and paid and unpaid work are not hardened: they are permeable, easily disturbed, and require careful retheorizing.

Conclusion

Rather than providing illumination, the starkly polarized categories of work and family obscure many of the activities, values, and obligations expressed in the everyday resistance and activism of Aboriginal women within their families and communities. Mainstream categories make it hard to view life other than as paid work (which must not be jeopardized) and family-home life, where we hide from the rigors of paid work and recreate ourselves for another day of paid work. Mainstream categories also strip political content from the overlapping realms of family and work, remaking them into benign areas of uncontested wage production and familial-individual reproduction. These frameworks fail to provide a way to understand Aboriginal women's ongoing commitments to change the world for themselves and their ex-tended, overlapping families; to defend the land for past and future genera-tions; and, in doing so, to care for the well-being of their communities and their families within those revitalized communities. In failing to provide a way to understand the uninterrupted flow of family, mothering, caring, working, and activism, mainstream analytic categories erase these activities and relationships from the social and academic landscape, and they permit studies of the family to proceed as if they do not exist or are of only marginal interest when and if they happen to surface.

Although Aboriginal women have a particularly noteworthy history of mothering, caring for family, resistance, and work, they are not the only group for whom this model, or parts of it, is central to everyday life. Many other groups at the margins of capitalist society also find themselves involved in community care-activism aimed at the survival of themselves and their communities. Others choose to act in solidarity with these groups, seeking ways to inject deeper meaning and social sustenance into lives increasingly dominated by consumerism and the private market. The depoliticization and erasure of this kind of continuous resistance-caring-work depoliticizes the experience of many women as they struggle to hold families together, generate sufficient income, provide care to extended family and across communities, resist various kinds of oppression, and inject meaning and dignity into everyday life. Like the Aboriginal model, community-sustaining/social justice-directed activities must be embedded in notions of defending the land and culture for *all future generations,* rather than for the narrow self-interest of one group over another. Otherwise, we risk valorizing NIMBY-ism or groups that short-sightedly defend their privilege while depriving others of dignity, belonging, and participation. Using community-sustaining activities/resistance/social care as an entry point to studies of families highlights the complete interdependence of families and work, as well as the much broader array of social and political activities associated with both.

Although they provide some of the most enduring models of family resilience and dignity, concepts that reflect the community-activist-sustaining experiences are largely beyond our language, obscured and repressed within the conceptual parameters of mainstream models of analysis. Instead of clearly defined concepts, we are compelled to resort to strings of words and ideas such as family/mothering/care/resistance/work. Within the activism and decolonizing activities discussed above, tasks, values, skills, and mutual responsibilities *spill* or *leak* into one another in permeable ways. It seems likely that the *spilling* is what holds this model of family/mothering/care/resistance/work together. Rather than an examination of discrete activities such as paid work or unpaid domestic duties, the Aboriginal model embodies a caring and nurturing community as central to the care of one's family. This family-community-care-resistance pivots on self-determination and defence of the land for future and past generations. Paid work outside the home, though necessary for survival, comes secondary to the core task of caring for and defending the land, the community, and the concentric circles of family life. Thus, the interweaving or *spilling* is a more appropriate entry point for analysis than is an exploration of discrete activities within the presumably separate spheres of work and family. Studies of interweaving/

spilling provide a way to describe and analyze activities and relationships without having to resort to long strings of words such as mothering-community care-extended family care-self-determination-work-resistance-survival, and they may help repoliticize these realms by pointing to policy and practice changes that start with the realities of women's lives rather than categories that depoliticize and demobilize.

Notes

1   Unlike the wage labour system, goods were not sold or exchanged in order to accumulate wealth and build up productive enterprises and technologies (capital) in which others would work and be paid a wage (wage labour) and from which profits would be drawn (surplus).
2   Feminists have used Marxist concepts such as the reserve army of labour to explain why women are sometimes drawn into the paid labour force in great numbers (as during the First and Second World Wars) and then pushed back into unpaid care work in the home and community (Armstrong and Armstrong 1990; Connelly 1978). This tenuous status as a labour force always in reserve means that women's contributions to home life and the workforce are valued differently from men's, and that their position in both realms can easily be undermined and degraded.
3   The struggles at Kanesatake and Caledonia were disputes over land ownership and use. In both cases, the Mohawk women assumed their traditional leadership role in governance and spirituality. For fuller accounts see http://sisis.nativeweb.org/actionalert/background. html; http://www.kanesatake.com/heritage/crisis/events/html; http://www.reclamationinfo. com/.

5

"I Am the Patient and Compassionate Cashier": Learning through Unpaid Household Work for Paid Work

Margrit Eichler

The usual assumption of an irreconcilable contradiction between paid work and the family is one-sided. This assumption, I argue, blinds us to recognizing potential positive synergies between the two. I demonstrate one such synergy by focusing on what can be learned through the performance of household work, and how this can be useful for the performance of paid work.

The interaction between unpaid household work and paid work has been studied from multiple angles by sociologists. The most basic fact is that unpaid household work provides the biological and social reproduction of the labour force (see Delphy 1984 for an excellent overview; also Waring 1999). The paid labour force, therefore, rests squarely on the unpaid labour that maintains it. Beyond that, for those who actually perform the unpaid household work, this is usually seen as detracting from their paid work. There is much evidence that women – who continue to do most of the unpaid household work – may leave the paid labour force to care for one or more family members: a baby or a sick or disabled child, spouse, parent, or other relative. Alternatively, they may reduce their paid work from full-time to part-time. In either case, this has many negative consequences for them, including reduced pensions and difficulty reintegrating into the paid labour force when they are able to return to full-time paid work (MacDonald, Phipps, and Lethbridge 2005; Ginn 2001), and it is also cited as a reason for the continuing lower pay and access to lower-level paid jobs for women. There is evidence too that housework leads to loss of self-esteem (Grana et al. 1993); however, Caplan and Schooler (2006, 898) demonstrate that "doing substantively complex household work generally had positive effects on self-esteem for women and negative effects for men."

When women are members of the full-time labour force, they still perform most of the household work. This has been identified as "the second shift" (Hochschild 1989) that leads to a "time crunch" (Sayer 2005, 298). Although all kinds of care work and housework are likely to increase the "time stress" for women, this is particularly true for eldercare and housework (MacDonald, Phipps, and Lethbridge 2005, 89). Doing housework full-time is bad for one's health: women who work in the home report a lower level of health than women who participate in the paid labour force (Borrell et al. 2004, 1883; Grana et al. 1993). Although I am not questioning the accuracy of these studies, I have always wondered whether that is the whole story, or whether we tend to ignore other aspects of household work that relieve this bleak picture. I remember one of my high school teachers challenging us to tell her how we would behave in the following situation: An important guest is arriving in exactly forty minutes, and we need to have an attractive meal and a nicely set table ready for his arrival.[1] In what order would we do what? How would we manage it so that the potatoes, meat, and vegetables are ready to be served at the same time?

It is a classic example that shows that besides cooking skills, household work requires multi-tasking and time management. Obviously, this question must have made an impression on me, since I remember it long after I have forgotten almost everything else I was taught. My belief that there are things to be learned from performing household tasks therefore goes back to my childhood. So when I was offered the opportunity to participate in a study on work and lifelong learning, with a specific focus on unpaid household work and lifelong learning, I jumped at it. This chapter is one of the reports stemming from this study (described further below). The study deals with all types of learning, but for this chapter I draw out only those aspects directly relevant to learning that may be useful for paid work.

Of course, as soon as I asked what can be learned through unpaid housework that is useful for paid work, problems in the literature emerged.

Setting the Framework

There are two obvious literatures relevant in this context: sociological research on household work and the literature on lifelong learning. The literature on housework and care work, which together make up household work, is voluminous and has been reviewed elsewhere (Eichler and Albanese 2007; Eichler and Matthews 2005, 2007). One problem is particularly relevant in this context: the prevailing definition of household work. In most empirical studies of housework, no definition is provided; instead, it is operationalized through a list of activities, such as doing dishes, cleaning, doing laundry, cooking, and more.[2] Most of the specified tasks tend to be seen as repetitive, physical, and rather low level. When we asked people in our study what type of household work they had done in the previous week, we usually received a similar list of chores.[3] Only occasionally would someone spontaneously mention planning, arranging events, doing emotion work, and providing care other than childcare. The popular understanding of housework therefore reflects its prevailing definition in the sociological literature. The consequence of this is, of course, that if the task is defined as simple, it is unlikely that we will find evidence óf complex learning.

The literature on lifelong learning is similarly voluminous. In its definition it does embrace unpaid household work but, in effect, the literature ignores it (Eichler 2005; Gouthro 2000, 2002, 2005). Altogether, I found only four empirical studies that deal with learning and unpaid household work.[4] In the oldest study, by Hasselkus and Ray (1988), fifteen family caregivers were interviewed in their homes in a Midwestern community. They were people who provided daily personal and/or instrumental care to family members and did not receive monetary reimbursement for their work. All care recipients were sixty years of age or older. Their providers learned through their care work about a sense of self, of managing, of the future, of fear or risk, and of change in customary relationships. No connection to paid work is made in this study. Livingstone (2000) has demonstrated that housework is a significant source of learning in Canada – those involved in household work (about 80 percent of his respondents) averaged about five hours in informal learning related to their household work. This figure derives from answers to a structured interview schedule – the appropriate means of collecting data with a large sample. The drawback of this method is, of course, that people can answer only the questions posed to them. In this instance, all the questions related to specific skills rather than general skills. He found that "(1) over 60 percent were involved in learning about home renovations and gardening; (2) nearly 60 percent were learning home cooking; and (3) over half were learning home maintenance" (Livingstone 2000, 19). Even more stunning is his conclusion that "it appears that Canadians are now devoting about as much aggregate time to informal learning related to housework as to paid employment" (Livingstone 2005, 983). Clearly, we are dealing with an important social phenomenon that is severely understudied.

A very interesting study from Britain (L. Butler 1993) specifically examined the acquisition and transferability of competencies acquired through unpaid work in the home and the paid labour force. One of the stumbling blocks is that the women who do perform household work are "competence-blind," since housework is subject to two contradictory preconceptions. On the one hand, it is most readily understood by women and men as a limited set of functions such as cooking, cleaning, washing, and ironing, which are common to all homemakers, whether male or female, and which are stereotypically perceived to be low skilled. On the other hand, there is a long-standing body of research and educational practice that attempts to differentiate and upgrade the functions of housework, often by pointing to the apparent relationship between the management of the home and business management (ibid., 68).

Participants thus needed to be made aware of the actual range of activities in which they engaged in the course of their unpaid work. An intricate set of workshops raised their awareness and clarified the relevance of their activities for much paid work. They then empirically developed a set of nine key roles:

1   Develop and manage systems to meet routine and non-routine needs.
2   Optimize the acquisition and use of material and financial resources.
3   Obtain, record, and provide information to others.
4   Support and care for adults.
5   Care for and supervise children.
6   Maintain the health and safety of household members.
7   Provide services to household members.
8   Maintain the interior and the exterior of the home.
9   Contribute to the national and local community.

They concluded that unpaid home work should be seen "as a domain in which the full range of levels [of competence] can be discerned. The level will vary from function to function, from individual to individual, at different points in time, just as it does in paid occupations. There should be no assumption that the levels of competence are low" (L. Butler 1993, 77-78). Linda Butler notes that "women cannot attempt to claim credit or reward for competence which they do not even know they possess" (80) – but even if they do know it, employers are likely to be skeptical.

The latest study comes from the European Union, which organized a research project on the competencies acquired through family work (Gerzer-Sass 2004). The aim of the study was to create individualized profiles of competencies that had been acquired through family work. Like in Linda Butler's (and our own study), the first step was to create an avenue to make people aware of the range of functions they perform for their family work; the second was to find a means of translating these functions into terms useful for the paid labour market. In this case, a life history approach was taken, and then participants were advised, using the example of the sudden illness of a child, what competencies are required in coping with such a situation and how this compares to responsibilities in a corporate setting. Following this, participants were provided with a set of skills required in a corporate setting, and they then rated themselves on these same skills in terms of their family work. By the end of the exercise, based on their self-assessment, participants had a profile of their competencies that they judged were acquired through family work. Supraprofessional skills included reliable execution and completion of tasks; approaching other people and establishing contacts; contributing one's own interest and strengths to the team;

willingness to compromise in favour of team-friendly solutions; and ability to cope with various requirements simultaneously (ibid.).

Beyond these four studies, I have so far found no other studies that address the issue directly; however, I surprisingly found an interesting set of studies in the management literature. The interaction between unpaid family work and paid work has long been of interest to management studies. Early studies focused primarily on family-work conflict, particularly for women, but a more recent emphasis is on positive and negative family-work and work-family spillover, which tends to be discussed under the heading of "family-work facilitation." This latter term refers to "the extent to which individuals' participation in one life domain (for example, work) is made easier by the skills, experiences, and opportunities gained by their participating in another domain (for example, family)" (Grzywacz and Butler 2005, 97). These studies are usually theoretically located in role theory and are not oriented toward learning or learning theory. Their language is problematic for a sociologist – family work is regularly called "non-work" (for example, Sumer and Knight 2001; Cohen and Kirchmeyer 1995; Kirchmeyer 1992a, 1992b), and "work" refers to paid work only. Nor is "family" synonymous with household work as we have defined it. Nevertheless, these studies are intriguing and suggestive for our topic.

The studies demonstrate that both positive and negative spillover from work to family and from family to work are common for both women and men. Here, however, I concentrate only on positive spillover from family to work. Positive spillover depends on the nature of the job, for instance, a managerial job (Kirchmeyer 1995) versus nurses (Cohen and Kirchmeyer 1995) versus a large sample of employees (E. Hill 2005) show different patterns. The same is true of family work, such as parent care (Stephens, Franks, and Atienza 1997) versus childcare (Ruderman et al. 2002). Gender (Hill 2005; Rothbard 2001) and age (Grzywacz, Almeida, and McDonald 2002) are obviously important. Likewise, the personality of the individuals affects the nature of the spillover (Wayne, Musisca, and Fleeson 2004; Sumer and Knight 2001), as does the response of the employer (Kirchmeyer 1995). It is not my intent to provide a summary of this literature (see Greenhaus and Powell 2006 for an excellent overview) but instead to explore to what degree these studies allow one to infer that learning is taking place in the homeplace. Fortunately, a few of the authors provide the wording of the questions they addressed to respondents, rather than just summary measures (for example, "positive spillover").

Looking at just those few studies that provide this type of detailed information, I am here teasing out only those strands relevant to learning. I am thus not representing the actual emphasis of the studies, which was quite different, nor reporting on all of their results, since I am here focusing only on positive spillover from family to paid work. It needs to be kept in mind that there is also negative spillover and that spillover also happens in the opposite direction (from paid work to family), both positively and negatively. Keeping these restrictions in mind, then, we find that there are a slew of potential positive benefits from playing multiple roles (what I call here engaging in household work). Ruderman and colleagues (2002, 373) identify the following:

1 opportunities to enrich interpersonal skills: understanding, motivating, respecting, and developing others
2 psychological benefits
3 emotional support and advice
4 handling multiple tasks
5 personal interests and background
6 leadership.

Most of these benefits involve learning skills on the part of the respondent that would be transferable to anyone in a management position: inter-personal skills, a mature perspective, multi-tasking, priority setting, planning capacity, and leadership skills. With respect to emotional advice and support, the authors go on to explain that friends in similar positions "coached one another in how to deal with problems with no easy solutions" (Ruderman et al. 2002, 374). They quote one of their respondents at some length, who states that "my planning skills have improved tenfold since becoming a parent" (ibid.). Similarly, Kirchmeyer (1992a, 788) states: "It was more time spent in parenting and community work, and not less time, that was associ-ated with greater organizational commitment and greater job satisfaction." In another paper, she provides coping strategies that women and men employ in their family work. Freely translated, these include capacity to concentrate, prioritizing, delegating, team work, multi-tasking, gaining perspective, ac-curate self-assessment (Kirchmeyer 1993, 538). In an earlier article, she provides the items with which she measured the positive spillover from family to work (Kirchmeyer 1992b, 238).

Although I have used this literature for a purpose for which it was origin-ally not intended, it seems to demonstrate that significant learning can happen through household work, with direct beneficial effects for paid work. I now turn to our own study.

The Household Work and Lifelong Learning Study

This study is part of a large-scale set of Canadian studies on work and lifelong learning (WALL).[5] The overall study consists of a large-scale national survey (*n*=9,063) and twelve case studies. Ours is one of only two case studies in the larger WALL study that looks at unpaid work.[6] We structured our research into four distinct phases of data collection. Each phase is built on the foregoing one.[7]

Phase one involved a mailed questionnaire to members of Canadian women's groups, asking them what housework and care work they perform and what they learn from it: 815 surveys were mailed out, and 254 were completed and returned (a 31 percent response rate). In the case of Mothers Are Women (MAW), our community partner, we asked members to give their partners a copy of the questionnaire. In addition, for female MAW members only, we added an extra sheet in which we asked specifically whether the skills they use in their unpaid family work are transferable to their paid work. This chapter provides, among other things, an analysis of this extra sheet. Like Linda Butler (1993) and Gerzer-Sass (2004), we wanted to assess to what degree respondents were actually aware of the range of household activities they engaged in. We therefore asked a series of open-ended questions about the nature of the housework and care work that people performed. As we expected, and again similar to Butler and Gerzer-Sass, the majority of respondents responded with a limited range of activities that are commonly assumed to require low skills, though some provided evidence of mental and emotion work (Eichler and Albanese 2007).

In phase two, the intent was to make respondents aware of a broader range of activities. To examine this, we held eleven focus groups: nine with women, two with men, a total of sixty-six participants – fifty-seven women and nine men – in three Canadian cities. Three groups consisted of white women only, diverse in age and socio-economic status; two of black women; one of Aboriginal women; one of white disabled women; one of disabled women of colour (except for one participant who was not disabled); one of Chinese women who had recently immigrated to Canada; and two of men, all of whom were white except for one Chinese man. In addition, there was an online focus group. We started out by asking people, as an icebreaker, what housework they had done in the past week and got the usual list of mainly physical tasks – with the exception of the group of Aboriginal women, who spontaneously listed all of the activities we asked about later. We then asked participants if they performed any of the following tasks:

1 Provide emotional support to someone (comfort, console, counsel, give advice, listen to).
2 Organize, plan, manage, or arrange matters (for example, organize family events or schedules; arrange repair people, tutors, play dates for children).
3 Deal with crises.
4 Maintain contact with family members or friends through telephoning, writing letters, or visiting.
5 Take care of oneself.
6 Resolve conflicts.

Uniformly, people agreed that they did these things. In other words, they perform a much larger range of household work than they are usually aware of.

Phase three shifted the focus to learning and followed up with seventy people who were part of the large national WALL survey.[8] We chose respondents who had experienced a major life change within the past five years, assuming that such a change would result in changes in their unpaid housework and care work and, hence, require new learning. The respondents had all indicated in the prior WALL survey that they had either lost a partner, found a new partner, lost a job, found a new job, were disabled, or had immigrated from China within the past five years. We focused on whether they had learned anything new in their household work and presented them with a list of how people learn that was derived from the answers in phases one and two.[9] One of the questions asked directly whether what they had learned from their unpaid household work was useful for their paid work. I draw on those data as well in this chapter.

On the basis of the data we obtained, we arrived at a new definition of household work: *Household work consists of the sum of all physical, mental, emotional, and spiritual tasks that are performed for one's own or someone else's household and that maintain the daily life of those for whom one has responsibility*. This definition is considerably broader than those that usually underlie research on housework: it includes housework as well as care work, and within care work, both childcare and care for adults – not only for parents and spouses but also for adult children, siblings, or friends – a factor that is usually excluded. It recognizes four dimensions of household work: physical, mental, emotional, and spiritual. It includes household work that may be performed in someone else's household, and there is an implicit dynamic aspect to it through the formulation "those one has responsibility for" – since that is an aspect that changes regularly as people move into and out of households, age, fall sick, develop new needs, and so on.

Having an adequate understanding of the nature of household work is crucial for assessing the learning that may take place through the performance of this work. If the work is conceptualized as primarily consisting of repetitive, low-skill tasks, then obviously all that can be learned is equally at a relatively low level. However, if we take into account the myriad mental, emotional, and spiritual tasks that confront people within their own households, we are talking about organizational, interpersonal, and spiritual skills that can be transferred to many types of paid work.

Results

Of the MAW women, fifty-nine filled out the supplementary sheet in phase one. Of these, forty-eight held a job and eleven were not working for pay but expected to be back in the labour market at some time. We asked respondents: "In what way do the skills you use in your unpaid family work transfer to your paid work?" In answer to this question, we find two distinct types of responses. The majority simply list the skills they have acquired. The following are typical examples:

The childcare skills obviously totally transferred from my unpaid work to the paid work. I can work independently, [am] efficient, [have] good time-management skills, and I can handle new situations that occur unexpectedly – all because of my unpaid work. I also value my time with my family and time spent doing other things like volunteering – I *know* there's more to life than making *money*. [Emphasis in original]

I feel that my "mother-work" has made a huge contribution to my skills and competencies: time-management, organization, patience, perspective, conflict-resolution, organizational behaviour, budget and financial management, leadership and, best of all, humour.

I am able to juggle more demands than I did pre-family. I am better organized, more definite in my decision making.

In everything that I do, I use patience, compassion, leadership, organization, motivation/motivating, teaching/training, good communication, social responsibility, environmental awareness.

Many ways! Managing my home and family has given me experience in organization, prioritizing, budgeting, patience and diplomacy, management, social skills, time management, resourcefulness, listening and speaking skills, teaching skills.

Two non-typical responses tie the skills learned through household work to a job that is not obviously similar to running a household:

Directly and completely. I am the person I am with these skills *because* of my family work. As I am a physio-occupational/therapist assistant, my potential "job" of training people to become physically and emotionally healthy independent people through programmed activities is what being a wife and mother is all about.

I have learned patience and compassion. You could say I am the Patient and Compassionate Cashier!

All of the skills listed are summarized in Table 5.1.

Table 5.1

Skills acquired through household work that are transferable to paid work

Skill	Times mentioned	Skill	Times mentioned
Organization	25	Decision making	1
Multi-tasking	14	Charity	1
Time management	13	Concentration	1
Communication	10	Coping with stress	1
Working with people	10	Diplomacy	1
Patience	9	Environmental awareness	1
Perspective	5	Faith	1
Compassion	4	Following one's dreams	1
General management	4	Humour	1
Negotiating	4	Life experience	1
Teaching	4	Nurturing	1
Understanding people better	4	Perseverance	1
Creativity	3	Price comparing	1
Financial management	3	Providing safe environment	1
Leadership/coordination	3	Recognizing/dealing with problems	1
Planning/prioritizing	3	Resourcefulness	1
Adaptability	2	Responsibility	1
Assertiveness	2	Self-knowledge	1
Child development	2	Social responsibility	1
Conflict management	2	Staying calm under pressure	1
Efficiency	2	Thinking quickly	1
Motivating others	2	Warmth/empathy	1
Administration	1	Working independently	1
Attention to detail	1		

What is remarkable about this list is that these skills could be categorized under human relations skills, organizational skills, and management of self/work ethic. With the exception of "price comparing," none of them is task specific, and no one mentioned learning specific skills such as cooking or home maintenance and repair. In other words, the majority of respondents see the most important skills as those that are clearly general and transferable from one set of circumstances – or type of work – to another. The second set of responses, much less frequently adopted, is by women who hold a paid job in which the specific skills acquired through household work are *directly* of use in their paid work, because their paid work deals with children or families in some capacity. This was true for teachers, foster parents, a family-life educator, a family sociologist, and a writer who concentrates on women's or family issues. Here are three examples:

Directly! I parent at home and teach workshops and seminars of "parenting skills"!

There is a *direct* transfer of skills from home and community work to my paid work. I am a family educator and I design and deliver programs to parents at children's birth to ... ?

Highly applicable – I teach sociology courses on the Canadian family. Also general efficiency/delegation/behaviour management skills.

In phase two, we did not ask directly whether the things the respondents learned through performing their household work also helped them in the performance of their paid work. However, the skills we asked for – for instance, managerial and organizational skills, dealing with crises, conflict resolution – would be useful in many types of jobs. All of the focus groups provided an enormous richness of detail about these skills. Occasionally, the connection to paid work was explicit. Even though in this phase we did not ask about the connection to paid work, it was occasionally made specific, as in the focus group with Aboriginal women, three of whom worked together in the same organization:[10]

> *Cheryl:* And the three of us work together a lot, on the same things ... and no offence to the male coworkers, but they're responsible sometimes for planning and organizing things and everything, and it looks like they do it, but they don't. If it wasn't for Sarah, a lot of times, and Doralee and myself to pull things together, lots of things would get missed ... just as an example, okay, let's take a trip to Disney World. That's the big plan ... the decision's been made, and everything's going to happen. Who's going to pack the clothes, who's going to ... take care of all of the arrangements? ... It's all the details in organizing, planning, and managing that actually are done by us.
> *Me:* Would you say you're able to do this because you do it at home?
> *Cheryl:* Because we automatically know what's missing, okay, this didn't get done, that didn't get done ... You know what kinds of consequences are going to happen if those details get missed. Your trip to Disney World, well you're going to be stuck in a broken-down motel for a couple of days because you didn't check the oil before you left.

In phase three, we posed the question of what skills people developed in their unpaid housework and care work that were useful in paid work. What is most interesting in this instance is the difficulty people had in answering this question – even though it came at the end of an interview that had asked about what they had learned about household work following on an important change in their life circumstances. Thirty-four percent expressed some difficulty with answering the question. This difficulty took various forms. Two respondents simply said that they did not learn anything from their unpaid household work that was useful for their paid work. A few people answered at length but with irrelevant information – recounting things they had learned from unpaid community work or talking about other issues. Some misunderstood the gist of the question, talking instead about what they could do with specific skills such as washing, cleaning, or caring for people, if that was relevant for the jobs they held, with the implication being that it was not relevant for their jobs. On the other hand, some did hold jobs where such skills were, indeed, part of their job, and they did identify these skills as having been learned during unpaid household work and having transferred them directly to their job.

It becomes interesting in the next set of instances that I coded, in which respondents expressed difficulty in answering the question but nevertheless ended up identifying skills they had learned. There are two ways in which this happened. In the first situation, a male respondent first rejects the possibility that anything he did for unpaid work might be relevant, and then talks himself into identifying some skills. For instance, Fox replied spontaneously: "Where do these obscure questions come from! Oh. My immediate reaction is one of impatience and absolutely not." But as he muses on the question, without any interruption from the interviewer, he recounts that he from time to time relieved his wife in taking care of his mother-in-law:

> And I guess that I learned patience, which I thought I had a lot of and I think is really, really important in dealing with others, in every way, whether you are giving care to them or not. But having patience and understanding are things that are key in almost every walk of life, and so those two things, I guess, were heightened in my awareness over the past ... five months, let's say. And yes, I would use those – you know, patience and understanding ... to a greater degree in my next consulting job than I would've in my last one.

Another set of answers that I coded as expressing difficulty but which ended by identifying very tangible skills were instances in which the interviewer prompted a respondent by referring back to earlier answers. I employed a total of six interviewers and, despite intensive training, the transcripts reveal significant differences in the degree to which each interviewer prompted his or her respondents. This particular interviewer asked: "So, it's interesting because I think that a lot of the skills you've developed, professional development skills, seem, as you said, [to] flow into your personal life. I'm wondering if there are any skills that you've developed in your unpaid housework and care work that would be useful in paid work?"

Jane: Hmm.

Interviewer: The other direction.

Jane: The other direction, yeah, yeah. [*coughing*] I wish I could think of a really good example 'cause it's a great question, but, [*laughs*] but, um [*silence*]. Hmm. I don't think I know.

Interviewer: In a way, ... when you were talking about organizing things in your own apartment and managing that, I'm just thinking that perhaps that could also be relevant to that question. Because, you can sort of answer two questions in one go?

Jane: Uh-hmm.

Interviewer: And I might put those two together because it also might have helped you learn to organize a vast amount of testing materials and resources you know, trying to figure out a system?

Jane: Yes.

Interviewer: To work out of the trunk of your car. Would you say that's true?

Jane: I would say so for sure. Um, yeah, that was certainly bi-directional learning, yeah, just around organization – and – also organization of time. I would say was bidirectional, like, 'cause those changed at the same time, or occurred at the same time where I had to organize an entirely different job and then also a home, like manage my home by myself with nobody else and all that kind of stuff – so they both developed at the same time. So I think that the things that I've learned have gone across.

This is the most explicit example of an interviewer prompting a respondent, and it shows an interesting progression in which the respondent seems reluctant at first, until, in the last paragraph, she picks up steam and identifies another skill (time management). This excerpt is also a good instance of a very real problem that was mentioned by several people and that I coded as expressing a difficulty in answering: the directionality of learning. It is, indeed, difficult to sort out where particular skills are learned – through paid or unpaid work.[11] Regardless of the difficulties that a minority of respondents had in answering this question, the majority provided a clear answer that they had learned skills through their unpaid household work that were useful for their paid work. For instance, a woman who worked in the hospitality industry replied:

Holy cow! Skills! I think just being able to prioritize. Ah, being able to recognize, um, what needs to be done. Seeing the big picture. Um, timeliness, and being organized well enough, or just sticking to a schedule, that sort of thing, so – prioritizing, time frames, and being realistic about time frames. Um, doing things well. That comes from personal pride of mine to do well. Ah, [*long pause*] resourcefulness. Um ... I think that is a skill that people already have, that they can develop even greater. Um, resourcefulness and creativity.

The most frequently mentioned skill was organization, including time management and prioritizing. People skills were next, including communication, team work, listening skills, compassion, dealing with parents, and understanding and getting along with people. Numerous people mentioned specific skills such as cleanliness, computer skills, resourcefulness, and creativity; several prominently mentioned patience and aspects of their work habits: increased thoroughness, seeking advice, flexibility, and efficiency. As we can see, there is considerable overlap in the few studies that have looked at skills that can be acquired through unpaid household work and that are useful for paid work. They fall basically into the categories of organizing/management skills; people skills; self-knowledge and self-management skills, such as patience; and flexibility, adaptability, and creativity.

Discussion

The major aim of this chapter is to present an argument that unpaid household work and learning is an understudied area that deserves considerably more attention than it has been awarded so far and, specifically, that learning obtained through the performance of unpaid household work may be beneficial for one's capacity to perform paid work. This runs counter to the prevailing dominant view that sees unpaid household labour as simply detracting from paid work. On the other hand, there is no question that unpaid household labour may and often does interfere with paid work – witness the many women (and the few men) who leave the paid labour market or who reduce their involvement because of demands to care for family members. The learning becomes relevant for paid work when people wish to re-enter or re-intensify their participation in the labour market.

At this stage, we are dealing with three problems: the lack of recognition of the skills acquired by the job seekers themselves, the lack of recognition of these skills on the part of employers, and the sparseness of research that deals with these issues. There are methodological consequences to the low levels of consciousness that people bring to the nature of the unpaid work they perform in their households. The transcripts for phase two, which involved focus groups – that is, group interviews – reveal that participants were inspired by the other members reexamine the work they do and the learning that occurs through it. Discussion was always lively and usually so enjoyable for the participants that we had to exercise considerable tact and determination to conclude the sessions. One person would say something, and the others would join in to concur, disagree, or shed a different light on the issue. The groups were maximally different in terms of race and ethnic membership, disability status, age, socio-economic status, and immigrant status, but all groups ended up identifying significant learning they had gained through household work – and for most, this was a new insight.

In comparison, the transcripts of the individual interviews we conducted in phase three read more laboured, and the connection between work performed and the learning that took place is somewhat more tenuous. I believe that had we asked the question about the applicability of the learning for paid work in phase two, which for various good reasons we did not do, participants would have experienced fewer difficulties in making the connection. What was missing in phase three was the group process that resulted in a changed vision of the nature and importance of the work and learning that occurred through unpaid household work. As one of our focus group participants said: "It's that unnamed stuff ... I remember when I was young and I had children, there was no words for it." This raises the question of why it was possible to get such good results from the extra sheets in phase one, which consisted of a mail-in survey – that is, there was no preceding group interaction, and there was not even the social presence of an interviewer who could point out connections between what was said earlier and its applicability in another context, as manifested in the interview with Jane.

The answer in this instance lies, I believe, in the nature of the group. Mothers Are Women was a feminist organization whose goal was specifically to fight for recognition of the value of unpaid motherwork.[12] Members would have been involved in group discussions and would have been exposed to literature that made the same points before answering our questionnaire. Future research, thus, would need to integrate a collective consciousness-raising process, as Linda Butler (1993) and Gerzer-Sass (2004) reported in their studies, before trying to examine the learning that takes place through unpaid household work.

In terms of a policy effect, making household workers themselves aware of skills they may possess is only one aspect of a broader issue. Employers, particularly those in positions directly involved in hiring people, not only need to be aware of the skills that may be acquired through unpaid household work but also need to have tools with which to assess them – and research that provides evidence of when and under what circumstances people learn transferable skills through their household work would be helpful. A series of German studies, summarized by Frey (2004), suggests that women who have combined a full-time job with children and marriage demonstrate a particularly high degree of flexibility, adaptability, and capacity to optimize their work, and that this can be directly related to their discontinuous and non-straightforward career development.

Conclusion

In this chapter, I demonstrate that skills acquired through unpaid household work may be directly transferable to paid work and should be recognized as such. Much more research is needed in this area, especially to address the issue of the directionality of learning, what conditions encourage or discourage learning, and how to assess the skills acquired. Nevertheless, it seems safe to conclude that this has been a largely neglected area of study that, if taken up, promises rich returns.

Notes

1 At the time, an important visitor was synonymous with being male.
2 I use "housework" when referring to the literature that uses this term. In this concept, care work, with the exception of childcare, is usually excluded. I use "household work" when referring to both housework and care work.
3 I alternate between using "I" and "we" deliberately. I use "we" when talking about tasks that were performed not only by me, or opinions or definitions that were developed by the research team.
4 We engaged in multiple computer searches, interviews with experts, and so on to find relevant literature but, at the design stage of our study, were able to locate only the Livingstone study. The other references came to light over three more years of diligent searching, using multiple sources of information. Some of the literature was published only after our own study was already under way.
5 The data reported on here were gathered as part of the research network on the Changing Nature of Work and Lifelong Learning (WALL) funded by the Social Sciences and Humanities Research Council (SSHRC) from 2002 through 2007 as a Collaborative Research Initiative on the New Economy (Project No. 512-2002-1011). This network is composed of a large national survey and twelve case study projects. For further information, see the network website at http://www.wallnetwork.ca. I thank David Livingstone for inviting me to take part in the study. Many students were involved in our project at various points as coders, interviewers, transcribers, data analysts, and collaborators in a broader sense. I want to thank them cordially for the contributions they made. They are Robyn Bourgeois, Alexia Dyer, Lingqin Feng, Susan Ferguson, Young-Hwa Hong, Willa Lichun Liu, Gada Mahrouse, Carly Manion, Ann Matthews, Tracey Matthews, Gayle McIntyre, Thara Mohanathas, Sam Rahimi, Susan Stowe, Carole Trainor, and Natalie ZurNedden. Willa Lichun Liu and Ann Matthews are both writing their PhD theses on this project, and their contribution is consequently considerably more substantial than that of other students who were involved for shorter periods. Susan Ferguson coded forty of the interviews of phase three and thus contributed substantially to the analysis. Patrizia Albanese is co-investigator of the project.
6 The other case study examines unpaid community work.
7 More details about this study can be found in Eichler and Albanese (2007).
8 We added seven Chinese immigrants through snowball sampling, since there were not enough Chinese people who had immigrated within the past five years in the WALL sample within our geographic area; see Liu (2007).
9 Phase four involved interviews with ten female housecleaners and ten nannies who do similar work for pay and without pay. They were asked if and how the work – and therefore the learning – shifts when it is performed with or without pay. I am not drawing on this phase of the research in this paper.

10 All names have been changed to preserve anonymity.
11 Because of the variance in probing between interviewers, I have not included numbers of responses to this question. My assumption is that the degree of learning through unpaid work for paid work is probably under-acknowledged.
12 I am using the past tense because, since the start of the project, the organization has, unfortunately, formally dissolved.

6

Employment in the New Economy and the Impact on Canadian Families

Ann Duffy and Norene Pupo

> I am stunned by how many citizens in our nation feel lost, feel
> bereft of a sense of direction, feel as though they cannot see where
> our journeys lead, that they cannot know whether they are going
> ... What they know, what they have is a sense of crisis, of impend-
> ing doom. Even the old, the elders ... say life is different in this
> time ... [there is] a wilderness of spirit. (hooks 2009, 1)

In the past decade, social commentators, working from diverse perspectives,
have devoted increasing attention to the "troubles" in our personal lives,
families, and communities. Much of this commentary has focused on the
marked decline in the quality of personal lives and social relationships.
Singular among these profiles was Robert Putnam's *Bowling Alone* (2000),
which argued that there had been a dramatic decline in civic engagement,
particularly since the mid-1960s. His work resonated through other social
analyses, for example, the individuation theory of contemporary family life
(Smart 2007). As with Putnam's perspective, families were understood from
the individuation viewpoint to be disintegrating under the pressure of current social conditions. Although Putnam's work and the individualization
theory have tended to capture the popular as well as the academic imagination, what is missing from this literature is a clear causal link. For example,
Putnam (2000, 284) argues that generational change (followed by urban
sprawl, changes in work, the television generation, and an enigmatic "other"
category) is at the root of the general social malaise – an explanation that
invites the question, where did this generational change come from?[1] Ultimately, Putnam (2000) appears to argue that the Second World War galvan-
ized its generation, and the absence (until recently) of a "palpable national
crisis, like war or depression or natural disaster" has allowed subsequent
generations of Americans to drift into an increasingly atomistic society.
Other analysts argue that the economic pressures of globalization and/or

the invasion of technology into private lives have produced a social order in which individuals are increasingly "fragmented, isolated, and unknowing of, or hostile to, one another" (Childs 2003, 7).

In the following discussion, we offer a meta-analysis proposing that it is changes in the nature of paid employment (as generated by the new economy) that have produced the deficits experienced at the level of individuals, their families, and their communities. Since the 1970s, the emergent economic realities have been inclined to generate quite specific types of work and work experiences in Canada, as well as throughout the industrialized world. Embedded in these new work patterns has been a profound challenge to extant patterns of social interaction and connection. For many individuals, the old social contract in which hard work translated into relative economic and social security, opportunities to belong and participate in local communities, and a predictable personal life has been steadily dismantled (Rubin and Brody 2005), and in its place a new economic order is emerging that has profoundly altered both the labour force and the labour force experience and, by extension, personal, familial, and community lives.

As discussed in detail below, work in the new economy is increasingly characterized by "bad jobs," by the intensification and diversification of paid work, and by the dramatic expansion of service sector jobs. "Bad jobs" refers to work that is, in relative terms, poorly paid and with few if any paid benefits and that is realistically perceived to be insecure or short term. As workers, especially young workers seeking entry to paid employment, increasingly face primarily only these work options, the very structure of their employment tends to propel them by circumstance and structure, rather than by choice, into unsatisfying personal lives and limited social relationships.

Socio-Historical Background to Work Change

The factors implicated in the emergence of the new economy are so complexly interwoven and mutually supportive that it is not possible to succinctly summarize the process. Certainly, the concentration of economic power, which was well advanced by the 1980s, was important to the new developments in the economic order (Carroll 2004). The increasingly concentrated power of national and, more typically, international corporations has meant a massive capital base that could finance the application of advanced technologies in ever-expanding areas of employment, as well as in diverse geographic spaces. The application of these advances provided for the dramatically increased consolidation of corporate, financial, and political power in the hands of a few. Corporate consolidation, in turn, translated into rapidly deployed political support for a more intense phase in the globalization of corporate production and corporate markets (Childs 2003). The corporate marketplace increased exponentially, not only internationally but also particularly in the "minority world" as consumer products permeated the public and private lives of individuals. Finally, advances in the depth and intensity of corporate power translated into the promotion of a political agenda that advanced corporate interests and demanded reductions in state spending (Shaw 2004). Neo-liberalism, in its various manifestations, was a corporate agenda – one that vigorously fought the role of organized labour and challenged the role of the welfare state in mitigating societal inequalities.[2] In short, dramatic increases in corporate power and "huge and growing systems of economic domination" – complexly intersecting with the successful deployment of a pro-corporate, neo-liberal political agenda throughout much of the world and with dramatic advances in technological advances and applications – all may be seen as foundational to the creation of new kinds of employment in the modernizing economy.

The Decline in "Good" Jobs

The most dramatic feature of employment in the new economy has been the decreased availability of good jobs.[3] Although variously characterized by analysts, "good" work is typically seen as involving some combination of job security, good wages, good benefits, opportunities for both education (training) and advancement, control over the scheduling of working hours, workplace control, and stimulating or interesting work. It is this type of employment that has been in decline in the new economy and that has been steadily replaced by poorly paid and benefitted, insecure, dead-end, non-standard, intensely controlled, and tedious forms of employment.[4] For example, between 1997 and 2004 in Canada, the occupations with above-average employment growth rates were cashiers, salespersons, and food and beverage servers – positions notorious for their poor work conditions (Usalcas 2005).

Several decades ago, employment analysts often differentiated the labour force into core and periphery, with core positions being synonymous with good jobs and frequently involving advanced education and technological expertise and the larger periphery referring to those workers who, to varying degrees, were engaged in bad jobs that offered little in the way of rewards while expecting little in the way of skills (Wood 1989, 5). As the characteristics of paid work have shifted, this distinction has become increasingly anachronistic. The line between the rarefied core sphere of employment and the proletarian periphery has been blurred, particularly around issues of employment permanency and job security. The bursting of the high-tech bubble, for example, meant layoffs for many workers with sophisticated technological training, and the recent dismissal of tens of thousands of skilled financial workers underscores the fact that few workers in the new economy can rely on their employment position.

Nowhere has the erosion of good jobs been more evident than in the dramatic decline in manufacturing and resource extraction employment in Canada (and elsewhere). Between 1988 and 2002, 110,000 Canadian workers aged twenty-five to sixty-four lost their jobs through firm closure or mass layoffs (Morissette, Zhang, and Frenette 2007). In the midst of these losses were 35,000 auto jobs – work that pays $65,000 per year on average (Stanford 2008). In an increasingly globalized labour market, much of this work has been relocated (or offshored) to lower-waged, often non-unionized, workers in the majority world. Advances in technology have facilitated this process by supporting the compartmentalization and fragmentation of the production process. In addition, technology has supported the robotization of many production lines and resource extraction processes, further reducing the numbers of traditional good jobs. Although very far from idyllic, these industrial and resource extraction jobs were often characterized by good wages, job security, and workplace control. In particular, much of this employment in Canada and the United States was in strongly unionized jobs. The large unions offered these workers a sense of control over their employment and its future. Further, these jobs did not typically demand extensive prior education or training. In the 1960s, workers could easily transition from high school into a well-paying job at General Motors, Inco, or Westinghouse – a job that was sufficiently secure and financially rewarding enough that it was possible to quite adequately support a family (Luxton 1980).

Despite strong protests from the labour movement, throughout the last two decades, these jobs have been steadily replaced by growing numbers of jobs with poor job characteristics.[5] These new jobs, for example, are often precarious. In 1989, full-time permanent employment was held by 71 percent of employed males; by 2001, this figure had dropped to 66 percent. Among employed women, permanent full-time work declined from 63 to 60 percent, and during the same time period there were increases for both men and women in full-time temporary, part-time temporary, and self-employment in Canada (Morissette and Picot 2005, 11). In 2004, 21 percent of newly hired workers in the private sector held temporary jobs, and only 63 percent of Canadian workers held full-time permanent jobs, leaving 37 percent in self-employed, part-time, or temporary (contingent) jobs (Cruikshank 2007). Cobbling together several part-time or contract positions in order to generate a living wage may not only be inconvenient and costly but also impossible. Not surprisingly, many workers in these non-standard jobs, the majority of whom are women or young workers, tend to earn significantly lower incomes than average (Cranford, Vosko, and Zukewich 2006, 110; Vosko 2007). In short, the types of work that have become increasingly generated since the 1980s – part-time, temporary, non-standard – are precisely the kinds of work that generate minimum wage or low wages while providing little in the way of job security (Sussman 2006; Morissette and Picot 2005).

The growth in bad jobs is also reflected in the fact that many new jobs, notably in the expanding service sector of the economy, are characterized by tedious, highly controlled, and standardized work. These features are epitomized, for example, in the burgeoning field of call centre work – where communication is dictated by computerized scripts, bathroom breaks are timed, key strokes are counted, and work performance is continuously monitored (Buchanan 2006; Head 2003). In this context, it is not surprising to find that a significant minority of workers (8.6 percent), especially young (eighteen to twenty-four years old) workers (more than one in seven), explicitly indicate that they are not satisfied with their work. Again, predictably, these unhappy workers are more likely to be found in sales or service occupations and in processing, manufacturing, or utilities work and low-income work (Shields 2000, 2006).

This general tendency of the emergent economy to generate jobs with bad traits is also reflected in the dramatic rise in the numbers of overqualified workers stuck in jobs for which they are overeducated. Between 1993 and 2001, the number of university-educated workers who were overqualified for their jobs increased by nearly one-third (increasing to 331,100 workers). In 2001, nearly 20 percent of workers who had a university education were working (at some point) a job that required at most high school education. This mismatch between education and employment may also contribute to the failure of wages to reflect education in recent years. In the past five years, the average weekly earnings of young men with a high school diploma rose by 5 percent, whereas they dropped by 3 percent for those with university education (Chung 2006, 9). Predictably, young workers and immigrants were particularly susceptible to the problems of overqualification (Li, Gervais, and Duval 2006).

Embedded in the above deployment of bad jobs is a gendered subtext. Many of the good jobs that have been lost have been primarily held by men (though women had made some advances moving into manufacturing, industrial, and resource extraction work prior to the declines in these employment sectors), and the bad jobs that have grown have often been characterized as women's work. The shifts in employment described above have, necessarily, been reflected in a long-term decline in male employment and a similar increase in the employment of women, particularly wives and mothers. Between 1980 and 2000, full-time employment rates declined for men (regardless of age or educational attainment), and there has been a continued decline in the full-time rate for men through to 2005, but mostly among young workers with a university degree, whose full-time employment rate dropped 2.5 percentage points during this period to 75.7 percent. As discussed in more detail below, women have been drawn increasingly into paid employment but often into bad jobs in the service sector of the economy. Meanwhile, many men have lost their niche in the full-time paid labour force.

Intensification and Diversification of Paid Employment

The rise in bad jobs is complexly intertwined with a second major characteristic of employment in the new economy – time intensification and schedule diversification. The work that has emerged in recent decades is frequently characterized by a new time intensity along with a diversification of scheduled hours. Facilitated by advances in computerization as well as the availability of a compliant workforce, it is now possible to run many services and industries 24/7/365 or to sculpt employment to the ebb and flow of consumer demand. This is reflected, for example, in the proliferation of part-time and contract jobs – jobs that allow the employer to moderate its workforce in terms of specific times of the day, month, or year and thus reduce workforce costs. Many part-time workers have little control over their employment hours as employers reduce overhead by constructing a just-in-time workforce. For example, in the retail sector, employers such as Overwaitea are demanding that shifts be reduced from four to two hours in order to maximize the flexibility of its labour force (Lorinc 2008). The net result has been a steady reduction in the numbers of workers who are employed for the traditional forty-hour, nine-to-five pattern. Whereas in 1978 47.4 percent of Canadian workers worked between thirty-five and forty hours per week, by 2000 only 39.4 percent did (Heisz and LaRochelle-Côté 2006).

At the same time, many workers find themselves working longer hours (more than 2,400 hours per year). Between 1978 and 2000, workers employed for longer hours increased from 23.0 to 26.4 percent. Predictably, the self-reported incidence of stress is highest among this group (Heisz and LaRochelle-Côté 2006). This over-employment issue is a widespread problem in post-Fordist economies. Even men and women who are employed part-time may find themselves working more hours than they prefer, and yet employment in less time-greedy workplaces is difficult to obtain (van Echtelt, Glebbeek, and Lindenberg 2006).

Recent research documents that this generalized trend toward spending longer hours each day in paid work (working-time intensification) is a particularly significant feature of the new economy. Between 1986 and 2005, the average daily time spent in paid work increased from 4.7 hours per day to 5.4 hours. For men, the increase was from 6.1 hours to 6.3 hours daily, and for women, indicative of ongoing increases in their labour force participation as well as a general movement toward full-year full-time employment, from 3.3 to 4.4 hours per day (Marshall 2006; Heisz and LaRochelle-Côté 2006).

Further, as noted above, these longer hours are increasingly structured around non-standard and/or unstable working hours. For example, between 1997 and 2001, only about one in three employees worked "always standard" hours. Over 43 percent consistently worked fewer than 1,750 hours, with substantial variability from one year to the next, and 7.8 percent were employed for highly variable work hours (an annual variation of more than 420 hours of work) – a pattern that is related to both low income and reports of higher levels of stress and bad health (Heisz and LaRochelle-Côté 2006).

Working-time obligations, of course, extend beyond the time spent in an office, store, or factory. Travel to and from employment is also part of the compulsory time most workers must devote to employment. In Canada, drivers average 59 minutes in their daily commute, and public transit users average 105 minutes (Kopun 2006). Not surprisingly, increased urbanization, along with inadequate transportation infrastructures, means that numerous workers commuting in congested urban areas report both longer and more stressful commutes.[6] In the Greater Toronto Area, for example, commuters averaged 79 minutes in transit in 2005 (up from 68 minutes in 1992), and 36 percent indicated they disliked the commute to work (ibid.; Kalinowski 2007).

Finally, not only has the working day become longer as well as more unpredictable for many workers, it is experienced as obligatory. A recent survey of 1,594 Canadian adults found that 83 percent reported having shown up for work while sick and exhausted; more than one in ten (12 percent) had engaged in this presenteeism (physically at work and mentally absent) more than ten times in the past year. These workers indicated that they had deadlines to meet (61 percent) or that they didn't want their work to pile up (55 percent) (Grant and Immen 2008). Other research supports the view that workers' sense of working-time obligation is intensifying in the new economy. A recent poll found that 29 percent of Canadians (up from 28 percent in 2007) had not used all their vacation entitlement in the past year, and 31 percent felt guilty about taking time off. Yet 33 percent of respondents considered themselves vacation-deprived. It appears that time pressures in the new economy are related not only to increased working time and a growth in unpredictable and insecure working hours but also to intensification in workers' sense of time obligations.

The nature and causes of these shifts in the time structure of paid work are complex and are tied in part to the growing application of computer technology to the workplace. Almost half (48 percent) of the Canadians in the vacation poll mentioned above indicated that technology made it difficult to get away from work while on vacation. However, in the midst of growing economic insecurities and intensified global competition, even questioning working hours or insisting on "real" vacations may seem unwise. Some analysts suggest that in the context of good job scarcity, downsizing, and layoffs, and few, if any, union protections, time-demanding organizational cultures are able to thrive. It is increasingly the norm in various corporate structures and professional settings to demand long hours, regarded as an indicator of employees' commitment and loyalty to the organization (Rubin and Brody 2005). Of course, advances in communication technology have facilitated the invasion of the workplace into all facets of workers' lives; cellphones, laptops, computer networks, and so on all ensure that many workers are never completely away from work.[7]

The Expansion of Service Sector Work

Very much entwined with the changes in work triggered by the new economy is the rapid expansion in service sector employment. Work within the services is extremely diverse and encompasses some very well-paid, standard, and secure forms of employment. However, the new economy has become synonymous with the dramatic expansion of service work in general and low-wage service sector jobs in particular – the so-called McJobs (Osberg, Wien, and Grude 1995). Between 1984 and 1997, employment in the service sector grew by 30 percent, in contrast to only 6 percent in goods sector employment. The net result was that the service sector grew to encompass from 69 to 73 percent of Canada's jobs (Little 1999). Employment growth patterns between 2003 and 2007 simply attenuated these trends, with a 10 percent growth in employment in services and an approximately 7 percent increase in all industries. Almost all of this industrial growth was situated in dramatic expansion in employment in mining, oil and gas, and construction. This increase was sufficient to offset the more than 10 percent decline in manufacturing employment and more than 5 percent decline in agricultural employment. In the meantime, virtually all services (outside the "other services" category) witnessed at least a 5 percent surge in employment, with particularly strong (10 to 15 percent employment growth) activity in finance, insurance, and real estate services and in educational services (Macdonald 2007, 9).

In short, the new economy tends to grow service jobs – a pattern that is likely to be attenuated as the population ages.[8] Fewer and fewer workers are working in factories and at machines, and more and more are engaged in activities that require some contact with and provision of service to customers. This is particularly significant given that much of this interpersonal work has been traditionally identified with greater emotional stress and burnout. The 2005 National Survey of the Work and Health of Nurses in Canada reveals the ways patterns of non-standard work, neo-liberal reductions in state funding for public services, gendered work roles, and job strain intertwine. Although 84 percent of Canadian nurses are in permanent jobs, fewer than two-thirds have full-time employment, and almost half (49 percent) report working unpaid overtime. More than two-thirds reported they had too much work for one person to complete, and almost two-thirds worked through their breaks to complete their work. Predictably, this pattern of employment generated difficulties – almost one-third (31 percent) were classified as experiencing high job strain (Shields and Wilkins 2006). A more recent survey of all health care providers reiterates these results, reporting that nearly half carried a high degree of work stress. Almost half (45 percent) of these workers indicated that most workdays they found to be quite or extremely stressful (in contrast with 31 percent of all employed persons) (Statistics Canada 2007b).

The Impact of New Economy Work on Workers and Their Families
The growth of low-wage bad jobs, particularly in the midst of a burgeoning consumer economy, has had a profound and readily apparent impact on family life. The absence of employment that generates a secure "family wage" has necessitated the deployment of increasing numbers of family members. Not only have wives and mothers steadily entered paid employment but so too have teens. The cumulative effect of these and other changes appears to be a generalized increase in the time intensity of many family relationships, along with heightened personal and familial stress and a decrease in time available for family activities, including household work. As a result, for example, many families with young children have externalized some portion of child care by making use of formal or informal paid child care arrangements. These shifts in the patterning and content of families' lives are particularly acute among socially and economically vulnerable populations – young families, families of recent immigrants, single-parent families, and so on. Further, these trends have been exacerbated by major changes in the larger societal context – the rapid urbanization of the Canadian population, the aging population, and the ongoing consolidation of corporate and neo-liberal governance. In many respects, the overall result has been a decline in the quality of family life, in particular, parental involvement with children. Although the outcome of this reduced parenting time continues to be debated, some researchers suggest there is evidence that new patterns of paid employment may have a negative impact on children and on family relations (Han 2008; Lewis, Noden, and Saree 2008; Presser 2000, 2007).

Certainly, history suggests that certain family forms are facilitated by specific economic and employment arrangements. The successful drive for a family wage in the economic boom after the Second World War meant that for the first time in history one wage earner (overwhelming male) could adequately support a spouse and children. Despite the many personal negatives attached to these arrangements, the prevailing patterns of wage rates and job security meant that a single-earner, male-headed family was possible. In contrast, employment in the new economy has necessitated "a duality of male/female public-sphere-generated income as well as work around the domestic sphere" (Weis 2006, 265). In short, the new economy in many respects necessitates new families.

Admittedly, a small contingent of these new families has benefitted enormously from current economic arrangements. The top 5 percent of Canadian families in 2004 received an average annual income of $296,000 and have seen their share of the income pie increase by 25 percent between 1992 and 2004 (whereas the bottom 95 percent of Canadian families saw their share of the total Canadian income pie decrease) (Murphy, Roberts, and Wolfson 2007). These wealthy families are winners in the new economy and, as a result, are often insulated from negative family implications of the new world of work. In this privileged context, family income permits access to the outpourings of the consumer economy, including advances in technology. Employment-related time pressures may be addressed in a diversity of ways. Time scarcity can be responded to through the employment of nannies, household cleaners, and specialized workers (catering to the specific needs of the household). As children grow older, pricey private schools – many of which provide extended study hours and meal service – can provide further backup. Other caregiving responsibilities are similarly amenable to marketplace solutions (Atkinson 2006, 47).

In contrast, most middle- and working-class families will find themselves in a "daily struggle ... as they try to manage time at work, at home and in the community within a task oriented working culture" (Williams, Pocock, and Skinner 2008, 745). Repeatedly, research documents the conflict experienced between the temporal demands of the workplace and the needs of family members (Maher, Lindsay, and Franzway 2008). Although a minority of families may be sufficiently affluent to avoid these contradictions, and some may be lucky enough to obtain excellent working conditions, such as permanent part-time work or job sharing, it is clear that such families are the exception. Many family members find there is not enough time in the day to juggle the demands of paid employment and personal relationships. However, increasing numbers of families have no alternative but to maintain their current employment pattern. Although there are few good jobs available, opting out of employment or reducing working hours is not financially viable.

Since the emergence of the new economy, the gap between privileged styles of family living and that of the remainder of the population has widened significantly. After remaining stable through the 1980s, after-tax income inequality among families rose throughout the 1990s. The gap between high- and low-income families grew significantly, and the share enjoyed by middle-class families declined (Heisz 2007). Not surprisingly, the proliferation of low-wage, insecure employment coupled with the loss of well-paid jobs (and exacerbated by increased costs of housing) has undermined the financial stability of many Canadian families, particularly recent immigrant families, lone parents, young families, and low-income families. Between 1999 and 2005 alone, the median debt load for family units rose 37.8 percent. In 2005, Canadians averaged an estimated $13.52 in debt for every $100 in assets, and debt load was much higher for lone parents ($28.32 per $100) and young families ($39.40 for every $100) (Statistics Canada 2006b).[9] When men aged twenty to twenty-four are averaging $12.48 per hour in 2004 and women $11.28, and these young workers are averaging thirty-five hours a week (men) and thirty hours a week (women), it is not surprising that debt load is a concern for young families and lone parents (Usalcas 2005, 10).

Finally, much of the work in the new economy results in earnings instability (the short-term up-and-down movements of family earnings). Changing work schedules, especially among part-time workers, contract or temporary work, and so on are all likely to result in fluctuations in income. Among young lone parents, earnings instability increased by almost 25 percent between 1984 and 2004, and among young families (husbands aged twenty-five to thirty-four) by about 13 percent, while it went unchanged in dual-earner families. Clearly, families relying on one income earner and/or on young income earners must struggle not only with earnings inadequacies but also with instability (Morissette and Ostrovsky 2006).[10]

Families Respond to the New Economy

In this employment context, it is not surprising that many Canadians rethink their personal lives, their family commitments, and their community involvement. It makes sense to postpone family formation, to turn to alternative family forms such as common-law relationships or single parenthood, and to delay or reject parenthood (Milan, Vezina, and Wells 2007; Beaujot 2004). In some respects, these shifts in the Canadian family are a strategic response to increased economic and employment insecurities. Similarly, the well-established mobilization of wives, mothers, and teens into paid employment addresses income concerns and the lack of good jobs by providing the family with a multi-earner foundation (Usalcas 2005). Further, the intensification of women's labour force involvement – the steady move from part-time to full-time work involvement, along with increases in hours of work – has been useful in maintaining the economic stability of the family: a fact testified to by the dramatic increase in the numbers of women (29 percent in 2005) who are now the primary earner in dual-earner couples (Sussman and Bonnell 2006).

Further, confronted with the dearth of good jobs in the new economy, it is to be expected that parents are responding by investing much more in the education of their children, while often engaging in continued education themselves. Statistics Canada documents that between 1980 and 2000 there have been dramatic sustained increases in post-secondary education

(2005b). There is certainly the widespread perception that any hope for success in the new economy hinges, however precariously, on educational qualifications, and research does suggest a widening gap between the earnings of young workers who are well educated and those who are not (Chung 2006). Even traditionally marginalized populations such as lone mothers have sought to improve their educational position. In 1981, 46 percent of lone mothers had not completed high school; by 2001, this figure had fallen by more than half to 22 percent (Galarneau, Maynard, and Lee 2005, 5).

Not unrelated to the prolonging of education among next-generation workers has been the extension of parental responsibilities into adulthood. The dramatic growth in adult children living at home is reflective of many of the economic realities in the new economy and has direct impacts on family and personal life for both adult children and their parents. By 2006, more than two-fifths (43.5 percent) of young adults aged twenty to twenty-nine had either stayed in the parental home or moved back in – up from one-third (32.1 percent) in 1986 (Milan, Vezina, and Wells 2007, 28).[11] This familial pattern – adult children living at home – provides a strategy for responding to the expanding time requirements of education, the lack of well-paid secure work being generated by the economy, and the staggering costs of housing in our increasingly urbanized communities.

Finally, entirely compatible with the consumer society are efforts by the family to respond to the new economy by buying goods and services. There is a considerable literature detailing the ways in which unpaid household labour has been commodified and sold back to families in the form of either paid services or products (Pupo and Duffy 2007). Numerous examples might be cited, but certainly the purchasing of childcare responds to families' need for multiple income earners. Between 1993 and 1996, 60 percent of women returned to work within six months of childbirth and 90 percent within one year. In the absence of friends or relatives who will volunteer to provide childcare, families must turn to the marketplace. As a result, in 1999, 13 percent of Canadian households reported paying for childcare services at some point, and between 1975 and 1996, the number of licensed childcare spaces increased sixfold (Stafford 2002).

Struggling Families in the New Economy
Despite strategic changes in personal and familial lives in recent decades, considerable evidence suggests that many Canadian families continue to be plagued by stresses associated with working in the new economy: economic insecurities and instability and an intensification of the time conflicts between work and home.[12] These pressures will vary depending on the specific family formation and the moment in the life course, though it appears that young families, recent immigrant families, low-income families, and mother-headed (and to some degree, father-headed) lone-parent families

are particularly likely to struggle and that women when they have young children and when they face combined care work for children and aging parents are particularly likely to feel overwhelmed (Sauvé 2002).

Indeed, some research suggests that familial responses to the new economy have often attenuated problems. The movement of teens into paid labour, for example, has meant Canadian teens are now engaged in various obligatory activities for long hours (7.1 hours) each day (including weekends).[13] Indeed, teens spend the same number of hours daily on paid and unpaid work that adult Canadians spend (7.2 hours). The net result is that almost 50 percent of older teen girls (eighteen to nineteen years old) indicate they feel constant pressure to accomplish more than they can handle (Marshall 2007). It is likely that the task of providing emotional care work for stressed-out teens and helping to organize and schedule family life to mesh with their hectic schedules does little to improve the quality of family life.[14]

Similarly, prolonged education may appear to be a reasonable solution to the demands of an increasingly technological workplace, but the presence of adult children who remain in the home in order to afford their schooling may increase familial stress. Their presence may mean additional household costs, increased household work obligations, and a loss of time for the parents. Interestingly, among parents of boomerang kids (adult children who returned to live at home), only 57 percent of parents strongly agreed with the statement "having children has made me a happier person," in contrast to 68 percent of parents whose adult children were living elsewhere (Turcotte 2006, 7-8). Further, if adult children remain in the home to pursue education, they may, particularly if they are children in low-income families, have to rely on increased personal indebtedness (student loans) to finance their education. Finally, the sacrifices and stresses involved in allowing adult children to continue to live at home in order to pursue their education may not pay off in terms of long-term good employment. The sharp increase (more than doubling) in permanent layoffs among highly educated tech workers in 2001 suggests that no sector of the new economy is safe from employment insecurities (Frenette 2007).

Given the problems attached to these and other changes in families, it is not surprising that parents continue to indicate that they feel high and increasing levels of stress. Between 1992 and 1998, for example, reported stress rates increased to the level that 26 percent of married employed fathers, 38 percent of married employed mothers, and 38 percent of single employed mothers (all aged twenty-five to forty-four) reported experiencing severe time stress in their daily lives. Significantly, it is the presence of children in the home that triggers the highest levels of the time crunch (Daly 2000). A similar note of desperation was sounded by Ontario mothers polled by Ipsos Reid, which reported that 77 percent of respondents felt they were "starved for energy" and 49 percent didn't feel they got enough sleep most nights (Ipsos Reid 2006a).

Indeed, there is a variety of evidence suggesting that workers in the new economy frequently experience parent-child relationships as problematic. A recent Ipsos Reid survey of 1,600 parents in Manitoba, Saskatchewan, Alberta, and British Columbia found that 61 percent of parents worry that they don't spend enough quality time with their children, and 76 percent said if there was one thing they could change about their life, it would be that they be able to spend more time with their child (Ipsos Reid 2006b).[15] Yet research suggests that many workers confront a profound contradiction between any hopes for success in their employment and meeting the needs of their family. A survey of employees at Eli Lilly found that only 36 percent thought it was possible to get ahead (at work) and still devote sufficient time to families (Atkinson 2006). Many parents try to manage by multi-tasking. A recent study found that when dual-earner parents are with their children, the parents are frequently involved in some form of household work (shopping, cleaning, household maintenance) (Sussman and Bonnell 2006, 14). Finally, the Carnegie Council on Adolescent Research concludes that, from the perspective of the child, there is indeed a problem: "In survey after survey, young adolescents from all ethnic and economic backgrounds lament their lack of parental attention and guidance" (cited in Atkinson 2006, 47).

Yet it is to be expected that parents employed in jobs that are some combination of poorly paid, highly routinized, heavily monitored, intensely demanding, and insecure will find it tremendously difficult to manage the demands of family relationships, especially child rearing.[16] This is particularly the case if they are fearful about their ability to simply continue to financially support their families. Even in 2000, when the economy had rebounded from the economic doldrums and unemployment was decreasing, more than one in ten (13 percent) of Canadian workers indicated that they were stressed by their fear of job loss or layoff, and 40 percent of these individuals felt it was likely or very likely that they would indeed be laid off or become unemployed in the coming year (Williams 2003a). Certainly, analysts suggest that workers confronting work insecurity – whether the university lecturer on a one-year contract or the recent immigrant employed as a casual clerk – will be at increased risk of both stress-related diseases and problems in their non-work relationships (Monsebraaten 2007).

The Future of the New Economy

The trajectories of workers and their families, and by extension their communities, in the new economy are not unequivocally negative. Several analysts are now commenting on the trend toward gender convergence in both paid and unpaid work and the breakdown of traditional gendered inequalities in family life. Not only are women shouldering more of the economic obligations, but men are slowly increasing their contributions to household and care work, including childcare. From 1986 to 2005, men increased their participation rate in daily household work from 54 to 69 percent and in primary childcare from 57 to 73 percent (Marshall 2006, 7). Particularly noteworthy is that more than one in ten fathers now take paid parental leave to stay home with their newborn children (11).

The traditional patriarchal male – the boss, the breadwinner, the head of the household – will likely find it difficult to fit in to either the new economy or the emergent families and communities. The linkages between masculinities and industrial work are being ruptured, and there is little societal space for the traditional male outside the military and professional sports. In Lois Weis's intriguing examination (2006) of masculinity in the new economy, she argues, based on her research, that the new economy increasingly demands a more feminized male – one willing to associate with traditionally female activities such as schooling and willing to share breadwinning as well as homemaking responsibilities. In a similar vein, Valerie Preston and colleagues' (2000) research into the impact of the new economy on working-class families reveals signs of gender rapprochement. When, in response to new economy pressures, pulp-and-paper workers were faced with not only increasingly precarious employment but also a shift toward twelve-hour shifts, it was primarily the women who made accommodations in their lives – by dropping out of the labour force, keeping children quiet while their husbands slept during the day, and so on. However, the 24/7/365 operation of the mills and the resultant shift work also meant husbands were at home for longer periods and, as a result, actually became more involved in childcare (Preston et al. 2000, 18). Clearly, such gender change may benefit both the individual and his family relationships and the larger community.

Of course, there are other, less sanguine indications. Numerous analysts are arguing that the new economy is creating or demanding certain human traits. Richard Sennett (2006), for example, suggests that workers who successfully adapt to the new economy will be self-oriented to the short term, focused on potential ability, and willing to abandon past experience. In a similar vein, George Morgan (2006, 149-51) proposes that the worker who is a "good citizen of the new economy [will express] the 'one step ahead of the game' individualism that is so valued; she will be focused on working on and developing herself, conceiving of herself as human capital." Clearly, such ego-driven individuals do not present themselves as ideal parenting material and, not surprisingly, both analysts suggest that the emergence of this dominant type of worker is unlikely since, at some point, as Morgan puts it, "the narrative of individualism gives way to more collective impulses and sociological understandings of the processes they have been through" (149). Beth Rubin and Charles Brody (2005, 858) take this position further and propose that younger workers who live with employment and financial insecurities may lessen their commitment to any organization – including their employer – focus more firmly on their family, and reject demands that they sacrifice their family.[17] Certainly, the current economic crisis will provide an invaluable test of the possibilities for workers to step aside from the strictures of employment and focus on self, family, and community.

Notes

1 The following discussion challenges Putnam's conclusions that changes in paid work (relating to time and money) are key to the transformation of personal, familial, and community lives.

2 "Neo-liberalism" refers to a wide-ranging renegotiation of the social responsibilities of the state and a strenuous campaign to retrench state services. For example, as a result of reductions in the benefit period and significant decreases in the numbers of eligible employment insurance applicants in Canada, from 1990 to 2007, the percentage of unemployed Canadians covered has dropped from 80 to just over 40 percent. Further, changes in the system have had particularly negative effects on part-time workers, many of whom are women, youth, new immigrants, and low-income workers (*Toronto Star* 2007). At the same time, there has also been a reduction in social welfare provisions in many Canadian provinces, along with the introduction of workfare programs (National Council of Welfare 2006). The net effect is that many workers have been simply compelled to take on the bad jobs that are spun off by the new economy.

3 Quite rightly, some analysts object to the overly simplified distinction between good and bad jobs. Clearly, jobs may entail a complex and changing array of positive and negative characteristics. The good-bad distinction is used here to draw attention to the overall qualities of certain types of employment.

4 Here the reference is to non-standard schedules of work.

5 The extensively documented efforts to undermine organized labour throughout Canada and the United States have increasingly pushed workers' unions into a defensive posture (Gindin and Stanford 2006). Declines in union ranks and in union density, despite important advances in public sector unionization and the unionization of traditional female employment enclaves, mean that unions have been severely disadvantaged in any attempts to challenge McJobs and the Walmartization of the economy (Akyeampong 2006). This detoothing of the workers' traditional advocate is nowhere more apparent than in the recent signing of a no-strike agreement between the CAW (the Canadian Auto Workers' union) and Magna International or the demand that UAW (the United Auto Workers' union) workers accept a no-strike agreement in return for a bail out of General Motors.

6 The trajectories of the new economy are also intertwined with the generalized trends toward urbanization. For example, the rapid increases in housing costs that are related to urban concentration have helped stimulate the movement of wives and mothers into paid employment. At the same time, increasing numbers of workers are facing lengthy commutes to work, with the net effect that urbanization tends to contribute to the overall intensification of labour market-related activities (Bookman 2003).

7 A recent US study titled *The National Study of the Changing Workforce* reports that one-third of the two-thirds of employees who used computers daily at work, particularly managerial and professional employees, also used computers at home to do employment-related work (as cited in Rubin and Brody 2005, 850). Clearly, the deployment of technology by the new economy has blurred both the spatial and temporal boundaries of work.

8 The aging population has resulted not only in social policies demanding rapid increases in the numbers of immigrant workers to Canada (most of whom contribute to urbanization by locating in large urban centres) but also in increased demands for personal service workers (many of whom are recent immigrants) to care for the elderly (Lyon 2006).

9 Young families are defined here as couples headed by someone under thirty-five years of age.

10 The financial strain and instability is also reflected in the boom in fringe banking. Outlets offering short-term payday loans charge between 335 and 650 percent interest rates. However, young families (in which the major income recipient was aged fifteen to twenty-four) were three times more likely to have recourse to payday loans than other families (Pyper 2007).
11 Adult children living at home is particularly common among certain immigrant groups and clearly reflects a complex mix of economic, social, and personal factors.
12 As indicated throughout this discussion, certain families – lone-parent, young, low-income, and recent immigrant families – are all more likely to struggle with issues related to precarious, low- or minimum-wage work.
13 These activities include household work, schooling, homework, and paid employment.
14 As Eichler and Albanese (2007) point out, providing emotional care work to these teens and adult children in the family may be more intense than the provision of care for very young children.
15 Given rates of employment, it is likely that the majority of these parents were employed.
16 It is likely that teens and adult children experience similar difficulties negotiating the new workplace and family life.
17 Some support for this argument may be provided by the fact that both employed mothers and fathers are increasing their "direct involvement" time with their children. However, rather than rejecting workplace demands, it appears that there is reduced attention to household work (Marshall 2006, 11).

7

What Impedes Fathers' Participation in Care Work? Theorizing the Community as an Institutional Arena

Andrea Doucet

> There's a lot of networks for moms and yet there isn't a network for guys, and I think a huge part of that is it isn't as easy for a guy. I've been out to the library and I've seen a guy pushing a baby carriage. But it's just not so easy for a guy to go up to another guy and say, "Hey, how old is she? Do you want to be friends?"
>
> – Martin, stay-at-home father of one for two years

> For the most part, there is a sense that if a man stays home there is something wrong with him, he's lost his job or he's a little off-kilter. It's not their job. They shouldn't be there.
>
> – Archie, stay-at-home father of two for seven years

Martin and Archie are stay-at-home dads, a family form – often referred to by the acronym SAHD – that has grown slowly but incrementally in many Western countries, including Canada, the United States, and the United Kingdom.[1] Their statements that open this chapter highlight the varied ways in which men point to the importance of community settings and how social networks and community assumptions and judgments of gender, caring, and earning act to facilitate or impede the daily work of caring and, ultimately, the taking on of domestic responsibility. Stay-at-home fathers provide a useful case study that illuminates some of the key issues that arise when men attempt to take on more family work and to share in the juggling acts that women have typically balanced in their hands.

I interviewed Martin and Archie and sixty-eight other stay-at-home fathers at the beginning of this new millennium as part of a larger study of Canadian fathers who identify themselves as primary caregivers (see Doucet 2006a, 2006b). One of the central aims of this research was to understand or solve a widely recognized gendered puzzle about the responsibility for domestic life. More specifically, a recurring question in the work of scholars who study gendered paid and unpaid work is: Why it is that, across class, ethnicity, and culture, it is overwhelmingly women who take on the domestic responsibility for housework and childcare? Across time, countries, and cultures, it is overwhelmingly mothers who organize, plan, orchestrate, and worry. This responsibility and what Susan Walzer (1998) has termed "thinking about the baby" carries into thinking and worrying about children and teenagers; it is also a principal reason for women facing ongoing struggles and stress over the balance between paid work and home, as well as for fatigue, burnout, and sometimes the economic consequences of switching from full-time to part-time work or giving up paid work altogether.

A multitude of social explanations exist for continued gender differences in the responsibilities for care work. Most of these factors are related to the interconnections of the social institutions of paid work, the state, and family. Thus, for example, many authors have pointed to gender differences in workplace commitments, pressures, and tensions between work and family (Dowd 2000; Deutsch 1999; Pleck 1985); to the propensity of women rather than men to take parental leave; and to the difficulties they may face as they attempt to fully balance their workplace commitments and their parental responsibilities (Doucet 2006a; Coltrane 2004; Dowd 2000; Marsiglio et al. 2000). In relation to family-based influences on gender differences in care work and responsibilities, researchers have highlighted co-constructed processes of "doing gender" by both mothers and fathers (Risman 1998; Coltrane 1989, 1996; West and Zimmerman 1987; Fenstermaker Berk 1985), gender ideologies (Deutsch 1999; Hochschild 1989) and distinct discourses of motherhood and fatherhood (Mandell 2002; Dienhart 1998; Lupton and Barclay 1997), and maternal gatekeeping from wives or female partners (Allen and Hawkins 1999; Parke 1996; Pleck 1985).

All of the above-noted factors are critical for understanding continuing differences and inequities in women's and men's positioning within, and contributions to, paid and unpaid work. In this chapter, however, I argue that outside of the oft-cited call for connections between work and family, there is another social site that matters greatly for the ways in which domestic responsibility and gender divisions of labour occur. This site is that of the *community as an institutional arena*. This chapter is thus premised on a close interrelationship between the community and domestic responsibility and the adoption of a wide definition of domestic responsibility as community based, inter-institutional, and spatially located between households, as well as between households and other social institutions. This conceptualization of what I have termed "community responsibility" (see Doucet 2006a, 2006b, 2001a, 2001b) opens up theoretical room for thinking about the community as a site and as a social institution that links with current research ideas about the underlying gender contract that frames women's and men's opportunities in contemporary Canadian society (see Introduction).

Theoretical and Methodological Background

Methodology and Canadian Context

As with the other chapters in this book, the principal location for the research described herein is Canada, where the social terrain is characterized by the rising labour force participation of mothers of young children, a dramatic increase in households with mothers as primary breadwinners, a growing social institution of single fatherhood – either through joint or sole custody – and gradual increases in the numbers of stay-at-home fathers. The larger social landscape is one where the social institutions and everyday experiences of mothering and fathering have been radically altered by changing state policies on balancing employment and child rearing, shifting labour market configurations in relation to gender – for example, full-time and part-time work, flexible working – diverse ideologies, and by mothers' and fathers' varied choices in relation to all of these factors.

The Canadian study that informs this chapter is based on an in-depth qualitative study, conducted between 2000 and 2004, of seventy stay-at-home fathers with a wide range of diversity across class and ethnicity, mainly in Ontario but with some representation across the country.[2] In-depth interviews were conducted with two-thirds of the fathers; the remaining one-third was interviewed in focus groups, by telephone, or through an online open-ended survey. Twenty fathers were interviewed several times over the course of the project, and fourteen couples – with a stay-at-home father and with some diversity along the lines of income, social class, and ethnicity – were interviewed to include some mothers' and couples' views in the study.[3]

Social Networks and Domestic Responsibility

There are many different kinds of responsibility that occur within households with dependent children. My own work on domestic responsibilities has focused on defining them as existing in several distinct forms, including financial, "moral," emotional, and community responsibilities (see Doucet 2004, 2006a, 2006b). The focus of this chapter is on the latter form. By "community responsibility," I mean the extra-domestic, community-based quality of the work of being responsible for children. This conception recognizes that responsibility for domestic life and for children involves relationships between households as well as between the social institutions of families/households, schools, the state, the workplace, and the community. Within and between households and other social institutions, parents share the responsibility for their children with others who take on caring practices – caregivers, other parents, teachers, school principals, neighbours, kin, childcare experts, nurses and doctors, librarians, music teachers, soccer coaches, and so on. Community responsibility thus implies close relationships between parents and others to meet children's diverse social needs. It is very much akin to the description of caring as evinced by political theorist Selma Sevenhuijsen. She writes that the concept of care is much more than the meeting of children's needs; it is also the "ability to 'see' or 'hear' needs, to take responsibility for them, negotiate if and how they should be met and by whom" (Sevenhuijsen 1998, 15).

This conceptualization of domestic responsibility calls for a broader way of thinking about the communities within which care work is undertaken. One particularly useful way of theorizing the community is to argue that the community is an *institutional arena* within which families/households, inter-household relations, community-based social networks, and a wide array of community activities occur (see Doucet 2000). As argued by Anne Marie Goetz in her edited book *Getting Institutions Right for Women in Development* (1997), social and societal processes occur within three main institutional arenas: (1) the *state,* as "the larger institutional environment of the public service administration"; (2) the *market,* as "the framework for organization such as firms, producers' cooperatives, and financial intermediaries"; and (3) *the community,* which is "the context for the organization of families or households, kin and lineage systems, local patron-client relationships, village tribunals or other organizations presiding over customary law," as well as "NGOs [non-governmental organizations], women's organizations and civic organizations" (Goetz 1997, 8). Goetz's work is set in Third World communities, but her analysis, in my view, is relevant to Western settings. In Canada, the community as an institutional arena could, for example, include all of the non-state and non-market institutions that contribute to the functioning of communities and to the raising of young children, as well as caring relationships more generally – for instance, for the elderly and the disabled. Included here are playgroups; community parenting networks; informal inter-household arrangements for childcare, along with other kinds of care; the organizing of events that bridge households (for example, birthday parties) and community youth groups (for example, Brownies, Scouts, Girl Guides, the YMCA); community fundraising activities; and a broad range of athletic and social activities that are run on a volunteer basis for the social, physical, and creative development of children and teens.

The conceptualization of community as laid out above calls, in turn, for a broader way of understanding domestic responsibilities. A point that arises from the above discussion is defining and theorizing the linkages between the community as an institutional arena and the responsibility for domestic life. Although the responsibility for care is often conceived as intra-domestic work centred on the management and organization of housework and childcare, the focus here calls for a conception of community responsibility that involves relationships among households as well as between the household and the social institutions of schools, health institutions, and other community institutions.

This concept of community responsibility appears in varied guises and with differing names in a wide body of feminist work on families and households. Concepts such as kin work (Di Leonardo 1987; Stack 1974), servicing work (Balbo 1987), motherwork (Collins 1990), and household service work (Sharma 1986) each describe in assorted ways domestic responsibilities that go beyond the more commonly identified spheres of housework and childcare. These authors, and many more (for example, Hansen 2005; Doucet 2000, 2001a, 2001b; Hertz and Ferguson 1998; Walzer 1998; McMahon 1995; Bell and Ribbens 1994; Mederer 1993; Hessing 1993a, 1993b; Balbo 1987) have argued that across class, ethnicity, sexuality, and cultural lines, this level of care work and responsibility has remained persistently in the hands of women. This argument raises the question of what might enable men to become more involved in taking on this responsibility, particularly when they are in situations of being primary – or shared primary – caregivers of children? Given the community-based and relational quality assigned to this aspect of domestic labour, it follows that if men are to take on, or share in, the responsibility for children, the ways in which they create and maintain social networks and inter-institutional community relationships will become particularly significant.

Findings on Fathers, Social Networks, and Obstacles to Fathering Involvement

As indicated above, much international research has confirmed that both the responsibility for children and the broader work of building bridges and social support between families and households is still overwhelmingly taken on by women. But what about fathers who take on the primary care of children? Do fathers create and maintain social networks around their children? Do they coordinate and orchestrate the work that goes on between households, schools, and health institutions and the wide variety of social and development activities that children partake in throughout their varied stages of growing up?

A diversity of patterns relating to community responsibility emerges from my research on stay-at-home fathers (see Doucet 2006a, 2006b). Nevertheless, across varied patterns of paternal care, the overall picture is one in which women, even when they are primary breadwinners, are still the main actors in creating and maintaining social networks around children. In short, mothers remain overwhelmingly responsible for community responsibility. What also emerges from my study is that both men's limited propensity to form and maintain community and parenting networks and their concurrent developing social acceptability as carers within communities figure into understanding the slow pace of change for men taking on domestic responsibility. Six such processes are explored below.

Networking around Kids: "It's Just Not Easy for a Guy to Go Up to Another Guy."

From my study of stay-at-home fathers – across class and ethnicity and rural and urban areas – the overwhelming majority of fathers commented that the patterns of friendships and connection necessitated by the daily work of care were often beyond the scope of their own experience. They pointed to residual effects from having grown up as boys engaging in traditional patterns of boy and male friendship patterns, as well as their consistent belief that men and women simply form friendships differently. For example, in the quotation that opens this chapter, Martin points to the potential misfit between traditional avenues for male friendships and newly evolving male practices of caring. His simple rendering of this difficulty is well captured in his snapshot of himself and another father entering the library to participate in a children's program: "It's just not so easy for a guy to go up to another guy and say, 'Hey, how old is she? Do you want to be friends?'"

At home for five years, Peter makes this point about men milling about on the social scenes of parenting but never really connecting with one another in a meaningful way:

> There are men around that I see, but I have not struck up a bunch of close friendships. Like, the men don't do the same thing; they don't network in the same way. We're all just acquaintances. We know each other from the schoolyard. But we have not formed a support group of men in a minority who are doing this job.

In a similar way, Derek, a stay-at-home father of two and a part-time driving instructor, points to how men "don't network at all":

> I don't think men network at all. Guys do not get together. The only guy that I used to get together with was a school teacher. He'd be off in the summers, and we'd get together after supper. We'd put our children on the back of the bikes and go to the parks. We never really got together in our houses, it was totally different. We might meet there and go from there.

These fathers' statements resonate with some of the research on men's friendships (Seidler 1992, 1997; K. Walker 1994; Oliker 1989; Rubin 1985). Such research highlights how they are relatively sparse in comparison to those of women and are built largely around sports, employment, or hobbies. In the main, these primary caregiving fathers do not challenge some of the key research findings on men's friendships from the past few decades, which have argued that men have significantly fewer friends than women, especially close friendships or "best friends." What is notable in these fathers' narratives is that children are not readily regarded as an obvious basis on which to form friendships with other men. Moreover, the literature underlines how men's friendships are framed by a fear of intimacy with other men and by homophobia (Kaufman 1999). In speaking about their social networks with other fathers, the men in my study are narrating, in clear and articulate voices, some of the dimensions of hegemonic masculinity (Connell 2000, 1987).

Hegemonic Masculinity and Men's Friendships: "One-Liners" and "Zingers"

Hegemonic masculinity plays out in fathers' relationships with other fathers. Defined as different and superior to cultural symbols and practices of femininity, hegemonic masculinity can illuminate how men are keen to differentiate their friendships from those of women, which are often viewed as more open and intimate. Moreover, in relation to the discussion above on men's friendships, hegemonic masculinity includes qualities of exclusive heterosexuality, homophobia, emotional detachment, and competitiveness (Connell 2000, 1987). What characterizes fathers' narratives as they speak both about community responsibility and friendships with other fathers is a combination of needing to be autonomous and self-reliant and to evade intimacy with other men. Martin, for example, alluded to one of the reasons why men do not make the effort to form networks with other men – that they are afraid of being seen as inferior:

> It really is a guy thing ... They make friendships in a different way. I think it takes a lot more time and it usually ... almost has to be the right circumstances ... it almost lets you look inferior if you're out there looking for a friend.

Related to the issue of looking inferior is the strong belief espoused by many of the men that they are self-reliant and autonomous individuals. Eduardo, for example, a Latino father who works in international development and was home with his infant son for one year, points to the awkwardness men experience when they go to parent-toddler groups; he reflects that this has something to do with internalized male notions of self-reliance and independence:

Perhaps men in this society have been taught to be independent, to be self-reliant, to be – "Oh, I can do this by myself." I think mothers are more open. In the playgroup, there was immediately a connection between women. It happened naturally.

Several men mentioned this issue, and one father, Dean, spoke about these issues eloquently and at length. Formerly a stay-at-home father and now a joint-custody father of three daughters, he was in a men's group for several years. His interview with me provided an analysis of men's friendships that came out of his years of speaking about these issues with other men, highlighting the need for keeping a "respectful distance," the "danger of closeness," and the need for constant "zingers" and "one-liners" to connect men with one another. He says: "It has got to do with intimacy. In terms of men, we equate intimacy with sex, so if I'm getting close to this guy, then sex must be just around the corner, and no thank you. With men, then, we've got the homophobic line." While avoiding the "danger of closeness" with men, heterosexual fathers find themselves equally wary of the "danger of closeness" with women.

Cross-Gender Friendships: "There Always Is a Bit of a Limit"
The female-dominated character of parenting networks can cause some tension for men and may further reinforce men's feelings of isolation within these same networks. Many fathers make a point of saying that they have to tread carefully into, and through, this world. Archie, Theo, and Vincent referred to "estrogen-rich" or "high estrogen" environments, and Aaron pointed to the challenges involved in his working "in a female world." Owen, at home for ten years, says: "I would go to other women's houses. But I was always conscious of how it would be read." Alexander, who took two parental leaves and is now a joint-custody father, observed: "I am more connected with the mothers. But cross-gender friendships always have a complicated dimension."

Many stay-at-home fathers readily offer their observations on the possible tensions involved with meeting in other women's homes; they see this as a strain both for themselves and their mothering friends, as well for each of the spouses involved. Aaron, a stay-at-home father of two boys, brings up such worries without being prodded with a specific question:

You had to make friends with two people. You had to make friends with them and their husbands, because it was threatening to a lot of the relationships with the women. Their husbands were not comfortable with it. It is one thing to say, "I am having Liz over for coffee this morning, and the kids will play." It is another thing to say, "Hey, I am having Aaron over for breakfast." So it is a different reaction.

Archie notes how the community cast a suspicious eye when he went on kids' outings or socialized with one other mother, Lisa: "I think some people raised their eyebrows and wondered, and quite frankly are still wondering. And for the record, *nothing happened!*"

In their joint interview, one couple, Linda and Peter, acknowledge the difficulties for Peter being at home. Peter says that although he is "sort of plugged in for the practical purposes, making the play dates or arrangements or whatever," his situation as a male parent is still "not the same as it would be for the mothers." He admits that although he does "know a lot of people because it's been several years" that he has been home with the kids, nevertheless "that's it, I just *know* them." Linda agrees with this assessment of the situation but tells Peter: "You *do* get along with some of the moms, but *there is always a bit of a limit*" (Linda's emphasis). Peter and Linda also make this point about the importance of numbers. "It could also be numbers," Peter suggests. "Just because they are guys at home with kids, it doesn't mean that we will hit it off. It is not a requirement that we have to become buddies." Linda concurs: "With the women there are so many more of them. I am sure they are not all friends with each other. But there are enough that you can develop a couple of friends."

Thus, with women heavily outnumbering men on the social landscape of parenting, many men express a sense of "dis-ease" as they move onto this female-dominated terrain, particularly in the years of parenting infants and toddlers. This issue of unease is further related to their status, not only as carers but also as non-earners or as secondary household earners.

Community Judgments of Fathers Who Relinquish Breadwinning: "I Felt I Wasn't Being a Good Man"

The social world of parenting is not the only arena to remain highly gendered: persistent gender ideologies relating to caring and earning play out in community sites as well. Every stay-at-home father interviewed referred in some way to the weight of social scrutiny exercised in communities and the pressure to be earning. Some fathers claimed that they were unaffected by this pressure but, nevertheless, the overwhelming majority admitted that they feel this social gaze upon them. Peter, a stay-at-home-father of two young sons for five years, described this quite well. His previous job in desktop publishing was gradually phased out, but he was able to maintain his connection with his former employer and take on contract work for about twelve hours a week from a home office. Despite very much identifying with the "stay-at-home father" label, he still felt compelled to tell people, especially other men, about his status as a working and earning father:

I've always – in social occasions, dinner parties, talking with other people, or whatever, with other men I guess especially – been able to talk about something I do in the "real world." And this has been kind of important socially. This doesn't make me sound limited, or stuck. I can show that I am able to work, although I have chosen to do this – to be a stay-at-home father.

Marc, who began staying at home fifteen years ago with his two young sons, also talked about the importance of being able to say that he was working: "It was hard at times and quite honestly ... I am not sure that I would have done it full-time for as long as I did if I had not been working part-time, if I didn't have some sense of worth." He further pointed to how different "moral" expectations weigh on women and men, and that both he and his wife felt pressure to fulfill their traditional gendered roles, with him "providing more money for the family" and his wife "filling her traditional role":

Back then, I think there were times when I felt I wasn't being a good man, by not providing more money for the family. And that I wasn't doing something more masculine. And there were times when my wife felt that she wasn't filling her traditional role as a wife and a mother.

Marc's words reflect those of Scott Coltrane a decade ago, when he observed that "the underlying equation of men with work and women with home has been surprisingly impervious to the labour market changes that have occurred over the past few decades" (Coltrane 1996, 26; see also Townsend 2002; Potuchek 1997). Further, whereas Marc mentioned how he felt judged for not "being a good man," Archie – in the quotation that opened this chapter – went further, suggesting that communities cast a suspicious gaze on men at home. At home for seven years, he reflects that men who stay home are judged as having something wrong with them because they do not have a "job" and they do not belong in that domestic role.

To be a primary caregiver without having achieved success as a breadwinner signals something out of sync with what many communities consider a socially acceptable role of male worker and parent. A male who is not formally engaged in paid work can spark community alarm bells if it seems that the father may have lost his job and was not in his caring situation because of a family choice. Theo, who left his job in the high-tech sector, points out: "Everybody assumed I was laid off." James, a gay and recently divorced father who took a four-month parental leave concurs:

I think there is still a stigma for men with staying-at-home, particularly around other men. I can't tell you how many times people ask as a first liner, "So, what do you do for a living?" When I answered, "I stay at home," most wondered – well, what happened?

Fathers with school-age children can juggle their children's school hours with their own part-time, flexible, or home-based paid work and have a comfort level with knowing that they are seen as earners while still doing their part to balance out family care. Nevertheless, as explored below, it is the fathers of infants and preschool children who feel particularly judged on their decision to be at home or to put their work on the back burner. Differences also play out between fathers of preschool children and those who care for school-aged children.

Community Judgments of Stay-at-Home Fathers with Infants: "The Incompetent Father Needing a Woman's Help to Get the Job Done"
Fathers of infants speak readily about the difficulties of moving through what several fathers called "estrogen-filled worlds." Most stay-at-home fathers narrated at least one uncomfortable or downright painful experience in infant playgroups or, more generally, on the community landscapes of preschool parenting. Some fathers glanced into the windows of this culture and quickly made the decision to avoid mother-dominated settings; they cited lack of time, fears that their child would catch a cold or flu, or the kids' schedules. Sometimes these reasons seemed justified. Other times it was clear that they were just avoiding one of the most female-dominated aspects of early parenting. For those who did venture out, many commented on feeling scrutinized for their competence level as carers. Craig, for example, who has one twin son with physical disabilities, reflects on how a recurring issue for him as a father is that "the incompetence thing comes into play" and social onlookers "very much want to make sure that the babies are okay." He points out that in situations where people know him, such as in his weekly visits to the physiotherapy clinic, his competence is not questioned. He relates: "I used to carry [my sons] in car seats with a diaper bag over my shoulder. I got known pretty quickly there, and there seemed to be a lot of other dads there as well." It was a different story, however, when he entered into other community settings where he was less well known. He remembers one particular setting where he was often "approached with offers of help. It was very much like the incompetent father needing a woman's help to get the job done."

Peter points to how these sentiments of assumed incompetence are particularly strong with young or preverbal children because onlookers may worry about the baby's care, while also assuming that the father is a secondary, and less competent, carer:

When I had a little tiny baby, there was always that sense that I was babysitting rather than taking care of my child like I do everyday – where I had to understand his wants and needs because he can't speak. That's where I felt it was very different from women. There was a bit of an assumption that I felt like I was just tiding things over until the *real mother* showed up, or the *person who really knew what they were doing* would show up. Maybe I just felt like I was under the microscope more. I don't continue to have that sensation. Because now that the kids are older, they can show it for themselves. The way we speak and interact, it shows that I know what I am doing. (Emphasis added)

At the end of his interview, Peter gives a frank assessment of the social acceptability of fathers as carers:

Even in a society where people believe that men and women are equal and can do just about everything, they don't really believe that men can do this with a baby, especially a really tiny baby.

To find a comfortable place in what are still female-dominated or "complex maternal" worlds (Bell and Ribbens 1994), stay-at-home fathers choose particular areas of community work and volunteering that fit traditional views of masculinity, such as assisting with children's sports; working in classrooms on tasks that require renovation, construction, or manual labour; and taking on leadership positions. Fathers' community involvement thus builds on traditional male interests while also providing for the possibility of constructing their own community networks on the basis of traditional areas of male connection such as sports (Messner 1987, 1990). A second related point is that fathers, particularly stay-at-home dads, view coaching and assisting in children's sports at school and in the community as both enjoyable for themselves and a way to ease community scrutiny of their decision to give up full-time paid work. What is implied here is the greater ease that fathers have as they navigate around both the social worlds of children in the years beyond the infant and toddler phases and the vestiges of resistance that exists in communities around fathers taking on primary care of very young children. This relates, more generally, to issues of time.

With Time, Involved Fathering Is Becoming More Acceptable: "It Has Gotten Easier"

One issue that emerges implicitly from the above discussion is the importance of time in understanding obstacles to involved fathering. First, as discussed in the preceding two sections, time matters because community acceptance of fathers as primary caregivers seems to grow as children mature. Time is also important in the sense of its chronological passing. In speaking to fathers whose experiences of being at home stretched from the mid-1990s to the early 2000s, it was striking how much changed over the course of that decade. With each passing year, it seems that the community acceptance of highly involved fathers improves significantly. Peter captured this increasing social acceptance of fathers when he noted that, although it had "gotten easier" over the six years he had been at home – between 1996 and 2002 – it still remained a "pretty alien environment," thus pointing to enduring gender differences in community parenting networks:

> It has gotten easier. I can walk into our community centre, and I can say hi to [the mothers there] and inquire after their kids and they after mine. But they're still around at the table at their regular coffee session that they have. And it wouldn't occur to them to invite a man. And I can kind of understand that ... They wouldn't invite a man to their reading group or whatever social experience they had a common bond with ... I have eventually made individual friendships with people. I haven't been included in any small group ... To me, as a man, that was a pretty alien environment, and it continues to be. It continues to be.

In a similar way, one couple, Aileen and Richard, parents of two young children and one infant, summed up the changes that had occurred in the two years that Richard had been at home with the children:

> *Aileen:* When he first started going to playgroups, nobody would talk to him.
> *Richard:* But now I go to three playgroups a week plus the library.

Conclusions

Drawing on my research on stay-at home fathers, I have argued for a wide conception of domestic responsibilities to include a dimension that is community-based, inter-institutional, and spatially located between households, as well as between households and other social institutions. This conceptualization of community responsibility opens up theoretical room for thinking of the community as a site and social institution that links up to research ideas about the underlying gender contract (see Introduction).

Focusing on community-level processes and the social networks that are part of caring work helps to illuminate the obstacles men continue to face when they attempt to share in the balancing of unpaid and paid work that typically falls on the shoulders of women. In spite of the enormous changes that have occurred in family, work, and state policies, practice, and ideologies, men still feel pressure to be good workers, and this can conflict with family commitments. Women, on the other hand, face pressures to be "good mothers" and this can, in turn, conflict with workplace commitments. What is striking is how these pressures, and the ensuing guilt about not meeting their responsibilities, seem to move in different directions for most mothers and fathers. Moreover, all of this is reinforced at the community level, where ideologies of who should be a primary parent and who should be a primary worker continue to unfold both ideologically and at the level of everyday practice. Within communities, several interrelated issues shape the ways in which heterosexual couples take on the community responsibility for children. As discussed in this chapter, these issues include deeply rooted gender differences in social networks; intersections between hegemonic masculinity and men's friendship patterns; community judgments of gender, breadwinning, and the care of infants; and tensions for fathers in moving on predominantly female terrain.

Since I completed my study of stay-at-home fathers in 2004, my two follow-up studies on fathers in their first year of parenting continue to confirm and strengthen some of the findings gleaned from that first study, while also pointing to positive state policies and community-level programs that work to facilitate fathering involvement.[4] A key point emerging from the two latter studies is how fathers continue to face challenges in taking on community responsibility in the early phases of parenting, and that this can matter profoundly in terms of the overall balance of how paid work and unpaid work get done by women and men. Nevertheless, as mentioned earlier in this chapter, Canadian men are forming child-related networks around traditional areas of male connection such as sports and other athletic activities. As these endeavours are increasingly seen as critical to children's physical, developmental, and social well-being, the place of fathers and men in community settings and their investment in the care of children is likely to increase (Marsiglio 2008).

A second positive change in Canada has been the dramatic increase by Canadian parenting resource centres of programs directed toward assisting fathers in making connections with other fathers. Such programs have become increasingly noticeable in communities in the past five years and include specialized attention to particular groups of fathers – including gay dads, teen dads, and fathers from ethnic minorities. One of our findings relates to the critical importance for community and health-based programs focused on the infant and preschool years to move from a mother-centric focus to one that also includes fathers, seeking to provide times and spaces for fathers only (Bader and Doucet 2005).

Finally, the extension of parental leave in Canada – from six months to one year – and the increased use of parental leave by fathers to care for infants (Marshall 2003; Pérusse 2003) could, I argue, lead to fathers' greater role in the creation of community networks. Many stay-at-home fathers in my study commented on the importance of having time at home, away from the intense demands of paid work, to establish a close connection with their children. Similar comments are consistently emerging in my new study on fathers and parental leave (McKay and Doucet 2010). As more fathers take up parental leave in Canada, this could lead to men taking on more of the community responsibility for parenting and, thus, potentially shifting the gendered weight of family care.

In a book focused mainly on the intersections between work, family, and state in considering how gender, paid work, and caring work are framed – discursively, ideologically, and in practice – this chapter adds the critical importance of considering the community as an institutional arena wherein a number of non-state and non-market institutions interact to solidify gendered assumptions and practices related to earning and caring. I build not only on a wide base of feminist scholarship on care, kin work, community, and international development studies but also from Jane Jenson's articulate description of the "welfare diamond" as one in which responsibilities for care are mapped across states, markets, families, and communities (Jenson 2007, 55).[5] As Jenson notes, most discussions of the responsibility for care draw on the notion of the "welfare triangle," which can overlook the ways in which communities are critical to how caring is configured in the lives of women and men (see Esping-Andersen et al. 2002). A focus on communities also illuminates the largely invisible labour that women have taken on as part of their caring responsibilities, as well as what facilitates and impedes men's participation in this important realm of care work.

Notes

1 According to Statistics Canada, stay-at-home fathers (about 111,000 of them in 2002) increased 25 percent from 1992 to 2002, whereas stay-at-home mothers have decreased by approximately the same figure (Statistics Canada 2002a). Moreover, there has been a sixfold increase in the proportion of single-earner families with a stay-at-home father between 1976 (two out of every hundred single-earner families or 2 percent) and 2005 (twelve out of every hundred or 12.5 percent) (Statistics Canada 2008a), and women are primary breadwinners in nearly one-third of Canadian two-earner families (Sussman and Bonnell 2006).

2 This study is part of a larger study of 118 fathers who self-identify as primary caregivers of their children (see Doucet 2006a, 2006b). Fathers were recruited through a wide sampling strategy that included ads in school newsletters, varied community centres, mainstream Canadian newspapers, and many small community papers. Several fathers were found through snowball sampling. The sample included participation from 15 fathers from visible ethnic minorities, 4 Aboriginal fathers, and 9 gay fathers. Most of the fathers were found in Ottawa (60 percent or 70 of 118), with the remaining 40 percent of fathers coming from cities, towns, and rural areas in eight provinces.

3 Data were analyzed with my research team through the use of the "Listening Guide" (Doucet and Mauthner 2008; Mauthner and Doucet 1998, 2003; Brown and Gilligan 1993), which is a multi-layered approach to transcript reading that incorporates reflexivity, narrative analysis, and theoretical analysis. A final stage of analysis entailed a lengthy process of coding using the data analysis computer program ATLAS.ti.

4 One of the studies was a SSHRC (Social Sciences and Humanities Research Council)-funded study of fathers and parental leave, carried out collaboratively with PhD student Lindsey McKay (2004-08); the second was a study of new fathers, which was part of a larger SSHRC-CURA (Community-University Research Alliances) project on fathering involvement – co-led by Kerry Daly and Ed Bader (2004-09).

5 I am grateful to Karen Foster, PhD student at Carleton University, for reminding me of Jenson's important concept. Thanks also to Karen Foster and Caitlin Oleson for editorial assistance.

8

Addressing the Interlocking Complexity of Paid Work and Care: Lessons from Changing Family Policy in Quebec

Patrizia Albanese

The Québécois family was among the first objects of sociological study in Canada (Nett 1996) but has since declined in popularity, at least in English Canada. It is not clear why, given recent policy shifts aimed at assisting families with integrating paid work and care. Quebec has gone from having the highest birth rates in the country to having among the lowest (Duchesne 2006). It has the highest rates of common-law unions (Statistics Canada 2002b), as well as shared and sole father custody following separations (Juby, Le Bourdais, and Marcil-Gratton 2005), with a seemingly more equitable way of calculating child support (Quebec 2004b). There is also reduced-fee childcare, which is believed to contribute to Quebec's high women's labour force participation rates (Roy 2006). But it was not always so.

Historically, Quebec stood out for its high fertility rates (Gauvreau and Gossage 2001; Miner 1938), the Roman Catholic Church's domination of private and public life, economic forwardness (rapidly industrializing from 1851 to 1896) and backwardness, and later its "quiet" reformation, sharp fertility declines, and pronatalist policies (Krull 2007; Baker 1994). Today, although Canada is classified as a liberal welfare state, relying on the free market rather than generous state support to families and social programs (Esping-Andersen 1990), Quebec is closer to a social democratic model in its policy intents and generosity (Krull 2007; Baker 2006). Quebec is governed by a different legal tradition in its civil law from the rest of Canada and has had a turbulent history in Canada, yet there are interesting trends suggesting that we should revisit its policies and practices.

Brief Historical Overview

In 2007, the population of Quebec exceeded 7,687,000 (Statistics Canada 2007a). Of these, about 6 million are believed to descend from French settlers (Laberge et al. 2005, 287) and can trace their origin to 1608 – the date of the founding of Quebec City, in New France, the first European settlement in the region. In 1759, the French were defeated in battle, and the colony passed into British hands.[1] For the next two centuries, while the English dominated their economy, the Québécois were guaranteed the right to use their language, be governed in civil law by the French Civil Code, and practise Catholicism. Crucially, the Roman Catholic Church played a central role in their lives, dominating education, health, and social welfare.

The Church also had a key role in maintaining a distinct Québécois identity – traditional, rural, and religious – seemingly averting assimilation by promoting high birth rates through what is commonly known as *la revanche des berceaux* – the revenge of the cradle. Being predominantly rural and religious, Québécoise women born in 1826 had an average of over eight children (Dumont et al. 1987). While birth rates declined – those born in 1845 had about six, and those born in 1867 had about five (ibid.) – Laberge and colleagues (2005) note that the fecundity rate of Québécoise women varied little from the time of New France until the end of the nineteenth century. At that point, fertility rates across Canada began to fall, but less so in Quebec. For example, in 1926, the total fertility rate for Canadian women was just under 3.5 births, whereas in Quebec it was almost 4.5 (Milligan 2002). It took another fifty years before rates in Quebec dipped sharply below others in Canada. The province's families were clearly affected by its unique cultural, legal, economic, and political history.

Confederation resulted in the creation of a decentralized governance structure, in which the federal government controlled the armed forces, communications, international relations, immigration, trade, and taxation. Education, employment, and health and welfare remained under provincial jurisdiction, resulting in a patchwork of policies and programs across the country – "tangled hierarchies" as Mahon (2006, 463) calls them. Because of Roman Catholic domination and the persistence of French legal tradition, relief and social welfare in Quebec were built on the humanitarian foundations of Catholicism and private charity. Unlike other jurisdictions after Confederation, municipalities in Quebec had no legal obligation to assist the poor (Greaves et al. 2002).

In rural Quebec, families engaged in subsistence farming during relatively short farming seasons. Winter months saw many men away at lumber camps or working in resource extraction (McRoberts 1988), so that women were responsible for basic survival (Dumont et al. 1987) and the reproduction of daily life. But life was harsh, and infant mortality rates continued to be high into the early twentieth century (Mercier and Boone 2002). With urbanization, traditional patriarchal views persisted, particularly regarding paid work, perceived typically as men's domain, and family responsibilities were cast as women's – except that a husband was still "head of the family" and many unmarried women worked in factories in Quebec and New England (Waldron

2005; Roussel 2003; Rocher 1962). Many women administered social assistance in hospitals, orphanages, shelters, and parish halls, under the domination, of course, of the male-only clergy (Dumont et al. 1987, 197).

Under Roman Catholic control, social programs remained paternalistic. For example, in 1937, Quebec was among the last provinces to enact legislation to assistant "needy" mothers, one of the first continuous programs of social assistance in the province (Morel 2002). Poor women were assisted only by virtue of being mothers, and eligibility depended on their worthy conduct as such. The 1933 Montpetit Commission, Quebec's social insurance commission, noted that "every needy mother who requests a grant should ... be of good character and able to bring up her children in good moral conditions" (Commission Montpetit 1933, cited in Morel 2002, 39).[2] As proof of her worthiness, she had to provide "reasonable guarantees of her competency to give her children the care of a good mother" (ibid) by presenting "at least two certificates, one provided by a member of a religious denomination and the other by a disinterested person unrelated to the claimant" (Laroche 1950, cited in ibid.). The needy mothers' allowance was used to control women's access to jobs (Morel 2002), but employed women were also disadvantaged. Dumont and colleagues (1987, 206) note that "whatever a city woman's civil and economic status, she was a second-class citizen. Deprived of a number of legal and political rights, she had little access to education and was a prisoner of the reproductive function." This was largely because of the clergy's grip on education and civil society, which lasted virtually unchallenged until the 1950s.

Quebec Family Demography and Policies, 1960s-1990

Under Maurice Duplessis' Union Nationale government, which ruled for most years between 1936 and 1960, economic matters remained in the hands of Anglo-Canadian and American private enterprise, and the Catholic Church controlled social matters.[3] Only after Duplessis' death in 1959 was change possible – his death marked the beginning of the Quiet Revolution. Under Liberal leader Jean Lesage, and with René Lévesque, the future separatist premier and founder of the Parti Québécois, as a minister, Quebec began to readjust its course, challenging the Church's domination of civic life and English-speaking domination of the economy. The Lesage government sought to reform public services and modernize, secularize, and nationalize Quebec society. Almost immediately, population growth slowed, while public spending and the number of civil servants grew dramatically (Couton and Cormier 2001). The Quiet Revolution and the Church's loss of ideological hegemony transformed Quebec families and family policies.

With declining religiosity and a mushrooming civil service, the level of education of Quebecers increased, family size shrunk, and an increasing number of people chose cohabitation over legal marriage (Gervais and Gauvreau 2003; Bashevkin 1983). By 2002, of all developed countries and regions studied, Roy and Bernier (2007) found that Quebec ranked lowest in the number of marriages, was among those where divorce was most prevalent, and ranked second only to Iceland in the number of births outside marriage. Quebec was unique compared with both the rest of Canada and other developed nations in the intensity and speed with which total fertility rates (TFR) dropped. It went from having "the highest fertility level among developed countries in 1960 to one of the lowest in 1987" (TFR was 1.4 – Roy and Bernier 2007, 11).

Although the Quiet Revolution introduced a range of programs (some universal) that sought the economic advancement of francophones through state intervention (Béland and Lecours 2006), the labour force participation rate of women (twenty-five to forty-four years) remained below the Canadian average at 30 versus 36 percent (Roy 2006).[4] Social policies shifted away from Catholic paternalism and were more progressive, yet they were not feminist-informed and, after the mid-1980s, became pronatalist (Krull 2007; Baker 1994).

Quebec's new family policies embodied a combination of progressivism and nationalism (Béland and Lecours 2006). Rapidly declining birth rates raised fears among Quebec nationalists that Québécois culture would decline, but there was also a commitment to fight poverty and provide support for children and families. This blend of nationalism and progressivism was evident in a 1987 provincial Liberal Party commitment to provide public support for the cost of child rearing to boost birth rates while encouraging parents to seek employment (Jenson 2001). The 1988 Parental Wage Assistance Program sought to draw parents into the labour force by providing a wage supplement to families with small earned incomes and offering extra support for childcare expenses (ibid.). But one of the most controversial parts of this plan involved the introduction of financial assistance to larger families. These included allowances for newborns that paid women $500 for a first birth, $1,000 for a second, and $8,000 for third and subsequent births; a family allowance for all children under eighteen years; and additional allowances for children under six (Krull 2007; Milligan 2002; Jenson 2001). These programs ushered in a controversial period – 1988 to 1997 – that saw anti-pronatalist feminists and other social interventionists battle non-interventionist and pronatalists (Krull 2007). Milligan (2002), for example, recently lamented the program's demise, presenting evidence from Quebec birth registry data that the policy had been successful in increasing fertility. It was less successful in assisting women, who were still responsible for social reproduction. Single mothers and poor families especially struggled. More had to be done, and differently. By 1996, a feminist-informed policy shift occurred, aimed at transforming social assistance, using a multifaceted approach, unmatched and often in sharp contrast to initiatives in the rest of the country.

The Changing Economy, Social Reproduction, and Conditions Leading to Policy Shifts

Fertility rates in Canada have, for the most part, been declining, yet the proportion of women in the labour force with young children has been increasing steadily. Between 1995 and 2004, women's labour force participation rates increased, particularly for women aged between twenty-five and fifty-four (Luffman 2006). By 2005, 81 percent of women in this group were in the labour force (Marshall 2006), as were 71.9 percent of mothers with young children (Roy 2006). For all workers, the average time spent on paid and unpaid work also increased, particularly for women (Marshall 2006). Although women have always been involved in the daily and inter-generational reproduction of people and their labour power (Bezanson 2006), and with the distribution of paid and care work remaining inequitable, working mothers struggled in a changing and increasingly insecure labour market (Stinson 2006; Perrons 2000). As Ehrenreich (1984) noted, men unexpectedly thrived on fast food and the purchase of domestic services, but children still need care (see McDowell et al. 2006) – and women were still doing most of it.

With cuts to public expenditures and the increasing privatization of the Canadian economy, "good" jobs for women, in the public sector in particular, were replaced with insecure, low-waged, part-time employment (Stinson 2006; Statistics Canada 1998). Family earnings instability and inequality grew throughout the 1990s (Morissette and Ostrovsky 2005), increasing a family's reliance on two or more incomes. Privatization and global restructuring resulted in widespread worker displacement and increased worker alienation (Silver, Shields, and Wilson 2005). The gendered outcomes of this restructuring at national and international levels are profound, with mothers bearing a disproportionate share of the cost of social reproduction (Bezanson 2006; McDaniel 2002b; Bakker 1996). Poignantly, Pearson (2007, 736) notes that "the increasing informalisation of employment ... has left the majority of the female workforce outside regimes of welfare and social protection at the very historical moment when they have taken a vanguard role."

Like the rest of Canada, Quebec felt the economic squeeze and its disproportionate weight on women with young children. Unlike the rest of Canada, it made serious efforts to do something about it. As a result of economic shifts, Quebec struggled with high unemployment and growing public concern with high school dropout rates (Tougas 2001b). As "a way out of a 12 percent unemployment rate," the Quebec government challenged the private sector and civil society to find strategies to help stimulate the economy (Neamtam 2005, 72). Representatives from government, the private sector, and the social economy – organizations and enterprises involved in the production of goods and services that are not private, for profit, or public (Neamtam 2005) – came together with proposals in a 1996 Summit on the Economy and Employment. Recognizing women's contribution to social reproduction, the summit and resultant white paper proposed redesigning family policy through new benefits and public institutions. Quebec also drew upon some of its existing strengths, which included strong feminist voices such as Fédération des femmes du Québec president Françoise David; feminists and social democrats holding high cabinet responsibilities, for example, Pauline Marois and Louise Harel; social activists and elected members of the National Assembly, for example, Camil Bouchard; and femocrats scattered throughout the Quebec bureaucracy. These progressive-feminist ministers and bureaucrats vocally recognized the difficulties mothers faced trying to balance paid work and family (Tougas 2001b).

At the same time, the province has a history of formal and informal community and non-profit organizations' involvement in the social economy (Neamtam 2005; Couton and Cormier 2001). According to Neamtam (2005, 73), in Quebec "the social economy accounts for over 10,000 collective enterprises and community organizations that employ over 100,000 workers and have sales of over $4.3 billion." Some new policies on childcare and *centres de la petite enfance,* discussed below, draw upon existing networks of voluntary associations and community-oriented tradition. With this in place, a major policy shift ensued.

Quebec's Family Policies, Mid-1990s to the Present
Since the mid-1990s, the Government of Quebec has been unfolding components of a family policy unparalleled in North America, aimed at addressing the multi-dimensional and complex interplay of work and family and promoting gender equity and reducing family poverty (Roy and Bernier 2007). At the 1996 Summit on the Economy and Employment, the province's premier announced a significant shift away from the 1987 reforms in family policies. The 1997 white paper argued for policy coherence and integration across domains – across social assistance, early childhood education, and employment. Its goals were to ensure fairness by offering universal support to families, providing more assistance to low-income families, facilitating a balance between work and parenting, and fostering child development and equal opportunity (Jenson 2001; Paquet n.d.).

To more adequately address the complexity and multi-dimensionality of this issue and eliminate some wrangling across ministries, a new ministry was formed by amalgamating and transforming existing ministries into the Ministère de la Famille et de l'Enfance (whose name has since changed to

Ministère de la Famille et des Aînés), with a budget of $500 million (Krull 2007). The ministry's agenda was threefold: (1) to establish a child allowance program for low-income families to supplement the Canada Child Tax Benefit (CCBT), (2) to implement a more comprehensive maternity-parental leave insurance plan, and (3) to provide a network of government-regulated and subsidized childcare facilities that offer quality educational programs for children under twelve (Krull 2007). To help fund the new system, the government abolished its allowances, paying up to $8,000 to families with young children and newborns. It also repatriated its part of the federal CCBT and recovered sums allotted for provincial childcare income tax deductions (Tougas 2001b).

A simplified family allowance – child assistance – was introduced to work with the federal National Child Benefit (Roy and Bernier 2007). Quebec's income tax laws were also reformed, removing parents' refundable tax credit for childcare expenses – the federal one remains. Parents could no longer write off childcare expenses on provincial income tax returns, because, in 1997, as a cornerstone of the new family policy, Quebec introduced $5-per-day childcare for four year olds using childcare at least three days a week, regardless of family income and employment status (Quebec 2003; Bégin et al. 2002; Tougas 2001a, 2001b, 2002). By 2000, all children regardless of age or financial need were eligible. The Act Respecting Child Day Care (Quebec 1997) transformed the childcare services office that was established in 1980. The government also introduced full-time, full-day kindergarten for five year olds in the public school system and special access to kindergarten for four year olds living in at-risk neighbourhoods. This was funded by school boards and controlled by the Ministère de l'Éducation. It was expected that full-day kindergarten would free up funds for reduced-rate childcare for children under four years (Tougas 2001b).

The government expanded school daycares – providing reduced-rate childcare ($5 per day per child) for school-aged children (five to twelve years) in need of before- and after-school care. Children between the ages of five and twelve could have access to childcare between 6:30 a.m. and 6:30 p.m. on regular school days from September to June for a maximum of twenty days per four-week period, with an annual maximum of two hundred days (Japel, Tremblay, and Côté 2005). Since their introduction, school daycare services increased by approximately 75 percent between 1997 and 2005. By 2004-05, there were 1,613 daycare services in Quebec schools, resulting in 81 percent of public elementary schools offering these services (Commission on Elementary Education 2006). In 2005, just over 230,000 children attended school daycares, representing 39.6 percent of children in public elementary schools in the province (ibid.; see also Tougas 2001b). Like full-day kindergarten, school boards under the Ministère de l'Éducation funded this program.

In 1998, to monitor changes in child development, a joint initiative of the Direction Santé Québec of the Institut de la statistique and a team of researchers from a number of universities established the Quebec Longitudinal Study of Child Development. The group conducted annual surveys on a representative sample of 2,223 children born in Quebec between October 1997 and July 1998. Its goals included following the children's social, emotional, and cognitive development across diverse socio-demographic contexts and monitoring their use of childcare services (Jetté 2000).

In 2006, Quebec offered its own more generous and flexible parental insurance plan. For the rest of Canada, Employment Insurance (EI) maternity and parental benefits have been unchanged since 2001. In the mean time, Quebec negotiated its withdrawal from the federal benefits program to offer its own system, which came into effect January 2006 (Phipps 2006). The Quebec plan offers two options: the "basic plan," with a longer duration but lower replacement rates in the second part of the leave, and the "special plan," with a shorter total duration but higher replacement rates (Quebec 2007; Phipps 2006). In both plans, the eligibility criteria are more equitable than the national EI plan; the EI eligibility is six hundred hours of employment, compared with $2,000 in earnings in the Quebec plans (Phipps 2006). The replacement rate is also more generous in Quebec. The EI basic rate is 55 percent for fifteen weeks maternity and thirty-five weeks of parental leave to a maximum of $39,000. Quebec's "basic plan" offers 70 percent for the first twenty-five weeks and 55 percent for the next twenty-five, to a maximum of $57,000. The "special plan" offers 75 percent for fifteen weeks maternity, twenty-five weeks parental, and three weeks fathers-only leave, to a maximum of $57,000.[5] With improved parental benefits, changes to family allowance, extended kindergarten, and reduced-rate childcare, Quebec is committed to helping families with young children in ways that the federal and other provincial governments are not. This is especially evident in the case of childcare services.

Ten Years of Childcare (Promises) in Canada and Quebec

In Canada, promises of a national childcare strategy have come on and off political tables with few concrete results. Changes appeared in the late 1990s, with the federal, provincial, and territorial governments' 1997 development of the National Children's Agenda (NCA), followed in 2000 by the Federal/Provincial/Territorial Early Childhood Development (ECD) Agreement, and in 2003 by the Multilateral Framework on Early Learning and Child Care. The Government of Quebec agreed with the objectives of the NCA but did not participate in its development because it wished to assume full responsibility over its own programs aimed at families and children (Canada 1997). The NCA confirmed that children's well-being was a national priority, and the ECD and the Multilateral Framework concretely outlined commitments to enriching provincial early learning and care programs. In the 2005 federal budget, the minority Liberal government indicated its intention to provide additional funding to the provinces for investment in early learning and childcare "in the amount of $700 million ... for 2004-2005 and 2005-2006, and a further $4.1 billion to be transferred over four years beginning in 2006-2007" (Canada and Quebec 2005, 3). After years of cuts, more federal funds seemed to be going to programs serving families with children.

A minority Conservative government took office in early 2006 and replaced past funding commitments with its own Universal Child Care Benefit, which gives families $100 monthly before tax for each child under six and professes to provide parents with more "choice" in childcare (Canada 2006). Despite cuts, provincial governments continue to subsidize childcare for low-income families, but for others, spaces are expensive and in short supply. Given the cost and availability of existing spaces, the promise of a national childcare plan remains unfulfilled. Only Quebec seemed committed to change this.[6]

Quebec introduced a reduced parental-contribution regulated system of educational childcare in 1997. Parents paid $5 per day per child, and those who qualified because of less income paid $2 per day.[7] In 2004, the general fee was increased to $7 per day. In 1997, Quebec had 78,864 regulated childcare spaces and, by 2003, it gained close to 90,000 more (Japel, Tremblay, and Côté 2005). Between 2001 and 2004, close to 60 percent of all spaces created in Canada were in Quebec, amounting to 43 percent of all children registered in daycare (Roy 2006). Quebec's Bill 145 set up a network of early childhood and childcare agencies and *centres de la petite enfance* (CPEs) out of non-profit childcare centres and family care agencies for children up to twelve years old (Tougas 2001a, 2001b).[8] CPEs are linked to coordinating offices in place to support and regulate childcare in a region. Each is a non-profit organization with a parent-dominated board. A CPE's board must include at least seven members, at least five of whom are parents who use services at that centre. One member must come from the business, institutional, social, education, or community sectors, and no more than two can be staff members of the centre (Quebec 2006). Individual caregivers in private homes can participate in the low-fee program but must be recognized by a childcare coordinating office – linked to a CPE – but they cannot care for more than six children, including no more than two under the age of eighteen months; this limit includes the provider's children under age nine. With an adult assistant, each caregiver can look after a maximum of nine children, with no more than four under the age of eighteen months (ibid.). In 2007, there were 165 accredited coordinating offices, with approximately a thousand CPEs, representing about forty thousand workers, the third-largest private employer in Quebec (Association Québécoise des Centres de la Petite Enfance 2007).

Japel, Tremblay, and Côté's analysis of the Quebec Longitudinal Study of Child Development (QLSCD) data found that the majority of childcare settings – including unregulated services, which were used by about 10 percent of respondents – attended by QLSCD children met the basic criteria of quality, but their educational component was minimal. One in eight failed to meet minimum standards, whereas one in four provided good to excellent care, echoing results from the Institut de la statistique du Québec study *Grandir en qualité*. Although more should be done to improve quality, non-profit centres were found to score higher than for-profit ones when it came to quality.

Using *Grandir en qualité* data, Cleveland and colleagues (2007) compared CPEs – non-profit centres – and *garderies* – for-profit/commercial centres – on several variables and found that on average 47 percent of wages in commercial centres went to trained educators, compared with 70 percent going to trained teachers in non-profit centres. They also found differences in average wages ($12.72 in commercial centres versus $15.81 in non-profit CPEs) and education and training of teachers – 27 percent of educators in commercial centres had only a high school diploma, compared with 7 percent of teachers in non-profit CPEs. Furthermore, different regulations were in place regarding staffing. Whereas CPEs were required to maintain a ratio of two qualified staff out of every three in 70 percent of the operating time, for-profit garderies required only one out of three qualified staff 50 percent of the time. Recent data also show that preschool spaces in CPEs receive $44 per day per child from the government, whereas for-profit centres receive between $32 and $49 per day per child, depending on age (ibid.).

With this level of funding, some argue that Quebec has focused too much on childcare and not enough on other options for parents, particularly stay-at-home mothers. Baril, Lefebvre, and Merrigan (2000), for example, suggest that there is no strong evidence that universal subsidized daycare generates greater benefits than other programs aimed at assisting families with young children and, in fact, 72 percent of families actually received less financial assistance from the provincial government in 1998 than they did before the introduction of $5-per-day childcare. They argue that it is too large a financial obligation, jeopardizing other programs. Is this indeed the case? Has Quebec fulfilled its aims of fighting poverty, increasing parental employment, and assisting children and families?

Is Quebec's New Family Policy Meeting Its Goals?
According to Cleveland and Krashinsky (2001b, 2), "the incremental social and economic benefits of a publicly financed system of early learning and childcare services for children aged two to five exceed the cost by a margin of at least two to one." In other words, there have been many social and economic benefits of the publicly funded system.

As noted above, in 1976, the labour force participation rate of women in Quebec was well below the Canadian average – 30 percent versus 36 percent. It caught up to the Canadian average by 1999, surprisingly quickly, and since 2000 has surpassed it by 4.2 percentage points – 76 percent versus 71.8 percent (Roy 2006). Many have noted that it was $5-per-day childcare that helped move Quebec from below average to consistently above average rates (Lefebvre and Merrigan 2008; Cleveland 2007; Roy and Bernier 2007; Roy 2006). Even critics of the program, for instance, Baker, Gruber, and Milligan (2005), note an increase in labour force participation rates of married and common-law mothers with children in low-fee childcare. They also calculate that, in a single year, increased government income tax revenues were sufficient to cover 40 percent of the cost of providing low-fee childcare services.

Overall, the proportion of two-parent families with children under age six whose parents are employed went from 56.2 percent in 1996 to 67.4 percent in 2004 and 68.3 percent in 2005 (Quebec 2007). Similarly, the proportion of lone-parent families with children under age six whose parent is employed went from 45.8 percent in 1996 to 64.4 percent in 2004 and to 63.5 percent in 2005 (ibid.). Roy and Bernier (2007, 41) conclude that "except for the Nordic countries, the women-men (paid work) activity rate ratio is higher in Quebec than in all the other developed countries, which indicates a more widespread adoption of the dual-income household and a move farther away from the traditional model."

Lefebvre and Merrigan (2008) found that low-fee childcare in Quebec had a substantial and significant effect in developing stronger labour force attachment and higher incomes among mothers. Analyzing Statistics Canada's Survey of Labour and Income Dynamics data, they found strong growth in weeks and hours worked among educated and less educated Quebec mothers with very young children relative to the rest of Canada after 1998.

In 2002, Quebec passed Bill 112, committing the government to an action plan aimed at cutting poverty in half by 2012 (Quebec 2004a). The province has been seeing positive results on this front. For example, between 1996 and 2006, the number of adults and children on monthly employment assistance – social security – declined, and their average benefits increased (Quebec 2007). In 1996, 558,361 adults and 254,888 children were receiving an average monthly benefit of $380.54. By 2006 the numbers had dropped to 383,857 adults and 123,683 children receiving an average monthly benefit of $461.78 (ibid.). According to Campaign 2000 (2006, 2), "Quebec is the only province where child poverty rates have been consistently declining since 1997." It attributes this to the "package of family support benefits implemented in 1997, including rapid expansion of affordable early learning and childcare services, an expanded child benefit and enhanced parental leave" (ibid.).

Family poverty rates have declined, but what has happened to fertility rates in the province? Although births outside marriage continue to rise in Quebec – in 1996, 52.8 percent of births were outside marriage, compared with 59.3 percent in 2005 – the overall total fertility rate remains low (Quebec 2007). In 1996, the total fertility rate in Quebec was 1.61. It dropped to 1.48 by 2004 and rose slightly to 1.51 in 2005 (Roy and Bernier 2007). However, a recent source notes: "Quebec's birth rate exceeded the national average for the third consecutive quarter, a feat not seen since the 1970s" (Statistics Canada 2007a). Overall, measures put in place since 1997 aimed at assisting families with managing the complexity of paid work and care work seem, for the most part, to have had positive outcomes. But what has all this meant for average families in the province? For women? Have their lives changed? Improved?

An Empirical Look at Reduced-Rate Childcare in Western Quebec

In 2004, I began doing research assessing the impact of $5-per-day (increased to $7-per-day) childcare using qualitative interviews with mothers and childcare providers, and a year later, fathers, living in a community located on the Quebec-Ontario border. The study involved a francophone community made up of two adjoining towns in western Quebec. I interviewed sixteen mothers and seventeen childcare providers. I conducted follow-up interviews a year later with ten mothers and new interviews with ten fathers of children in daycare.[9] The community is in a part of the province that until recently was a prosperous logging region. Many of the town's men still work in the economically hard-hit softwood lumber industry, in one of the remaining paper or lumber mills in the region. Two of these mills have recently closed.[10] Many women work in traditional service sector jobs, including sales, food services, health, and childcare; others commute to jobs up to one and a half hours away.

Many were struggling with cuts to the softwood lumber industry that disproportionately affected this region (Dufour 2002; Statistics Canada 2002c). Families increasingly depended on income from women's work, with many entering traditional low-paid pink-collar service jobs that often required long commutes. One of the fastest growing types of employer in the region is customer service call centres, which profit from a low-paid, bilingual, female labour force. Despite low wages, long commutes, and irregular hours, most saw their jobs as necessary for their family's economic well-being (Albanese 2006). Many said keeping their jobs depended on $7-per-day childcare. All mothers noted that $7-per-day childcare was not only a necessity – to work or study – but beneficial to their children as well. All stated that their children were acquiring skills they could not acquire with a sitter or relative. Some noted that their children were learning more in daycare than they themselves could teach them because of time constraints and irregular work schedules (ibid.). Some explained that, to a certain extent, $7-per-day childcare improved domestic relations, as they are experiencing less financial stress and less conflict at home. Mothers believed that with this program they were not only able to seek or return to paid work but could "afford" to work part-time or take minimum-wage jobs. If childcare was more costly, some explained, low-paid and part-time employment would hardly cover the cost of care (ibid.), as informal care in the grey or underground economy cost $20-a-day per child.

Having $7-per-day childcare proved to be advantageous for employability and the general well-being of mothers; it somewhat improved family stability and provided some economic stability for a community in economic flux. On the other hand, families had a difficult time juggling long commutes, irregular shift work, overtime hours, and childcare centre hours of operation. They reported that commutes and shift work made drop-off and pickup of children complicated, often requiring a network of support from friends, extended family, and sitters. Families superimposed this informal network of care on top of the province's childcare program to meet and manage the challenges of juggling shift work and commutes – a hallmark of Canada's new economy. Interviews with mothers and fathers revealed that women did much more managing of childcare and work schedules than their male partners. Even so, many mothers wondered aloud how women in the rest of Canada managed without low-fee childcare.

Conclusions and Lessons for Canada
In the current global economy, women's paid work is increasingly necessary for family subsistence. As this is happening, we have also been witness to retrenchment of the welfare state, with women inheriting the global offloading of unpaid or underpaid care (Pearson 2007; McDaniel 2002b). In parts of Europe, welfare state redesign, despite cuts, has involved improvements in formal childcare arrangements, as they have been deemed integral to social reproduction in post-industrial economies (Mahon 2006). In contrast, in Canada, the federal government has been withdrawing from previous commitments to childcare, and no governments but Quebec's seem to have recognized the importance of assisting families, and especially women, with the complexity of balancing paid work and family through a package of reforms and initiatives. Quebec's policy shifts seem to recognize and take into account the intricate, interdependent, and rich interplay of work and care in the lives of Québécois families, as demonstrated by its introduction of a multi-pronged approach to social policy and service provision.

Although Quebec was not always in the forefront of social reform, and in fact was a latecomer to state-funded services, it did much to transform an antiquated system of social support from Catholic paternalism to nationalist pronatalisms to feminist-informed policy and practice. Even with limitations, including long waiting lists, the need to improve quality, and the need for more flexible options, Quebec's model of childcare, coupled with its generous and diverse package of reforms, is unprecedented in North America. According to Morel (2002, 29), "Quebec's family policy is the most progressive in Canada, particularly with regard to public child-care services." It adds that "the parental leave policy currently proposed by the Quebec government is also well ahead of what exists in other Canadian provinces," noting that in this regard, "Quebec serves as a model" (ibid.). In sum, at a time when women's work – paid and unpaid – has been central to the international drive for cheap and productive labour (Pearson 2004), it is high time that the Canadian state contribute, following the Quebec model, to assisting mothers in bearing their disproportionate share of the cost of social reproduction.

Notes

The work in this chapter has been supported by grants from the Social Sciences and Humanities Research Council (Standard Research Grant); Ryerson University and the Social Sciences and Humanities Research Council (Standard Institutional Grant/SSHRC-SIG); and the Ryerson University New Faculty Research Fund.

1 Contrary to popular belief, from 1608 to the mid-1800s, women in the colony held more rights than other women in North America, including the right to vote (1791-1849) and own property; the Coutume de Paris did not eradicate a married woman's legal existence (Dumont et al. 1987).

2 This is not unlike some of the welfare reforms that reintroduced the policing of the social and sexual lives of single mothers under the Mike Harris Conservative government in Ontario in the 1990s (see Little and Morrison 1999).

3 In the 1950s, the number of priests, nuns, and monks exceeded the number of people employed by the government (Stevenson 2006).

4 After assuming power, Lévesque's government raised minimum wage to $3 per hour, the highest rate in North America (McRoberts 1988).

5 The figure on the Ministère de l'Emploi et de la Solidarité sociale website in 2007 was $59,000.

6 Between 1992 and 2004, allocations for childcare in Quebec increased $1.42 billion, whereas the increase for the rest of Canada was $221 million (Friendly and Beach 2005).

7 The Quebec government pays $31 per day or 82 percent of the cost (Krull 2007).

8 Despite resisting it – by having a moratorium on new licences since 1995 – Quebec also has for-profit *garderies* that are centre-based facilities operating outside the CPE but still provide services at $7 per day (Quebec 2006).

9 Interviews were one hour long, in the subject's home or workplace, and recorded. Non-probability, snowball sampling was used. I included mothers from different class and educational backgrounds, with children of diverse ages, and who used home and larger care centres. I contacted every daycare centre in the community and interviewed staff at the larger centre – a supervisor, an administrator, four educators, and two assistants – and six of eleven home daycares – six owners and three assistants.

10 Since these interviews and before the publication of this book, this last mill, too, has closed.

Part 3
Feminist-Informed Family Initiatives and Family Visions

9
Beyond the "Cultural" Landscape of Care: Queering Childcare, Caregiver, and Work
Justyna Sempruch

The "Cultural" Landscape of Care

The troublesome relation between care and economy has become paradigmatic for gender equality discussions across North American and European feminist research (see, for example, Heisz 2007; Morley 2006; Appelbaum et al. 2002; Timpson 2001; Folbre 1995). A standpoint shared by many is that the emotional value of care cannot be represented on account of its psychic and, therefore, impenetrable nature. In fact, a cultural consensus has already developed (Koehn 1998; Noddings 1984; Gilligan 1982) that takes maternal emotion – and the desire to care that derives from it – as economically unrepresentable, and thus part of the private, rather than the public, domain. This consensus is based on collectively imagined links between femininity, connection, and attachment, rather than on the position of the autonomous caring subject and speaks to the constitution and organization of female and male bodies, memories, and desires as fundamentally different (see Noddings 1984 and Gilligan 1982 for a discussion of "feminine care"). The emotional value of care also speaks to the individual (typically female) responsibility for care, raising questions about the ethics of care (Tronto 1993), as well as about the broader socio-cultural forces that underlie unpaid domestic labour. Indeed, although care work is frequently perceived as an individualized domestic responsibility, more wide-ranging definitions of care involving community and social commitment (Ruddick 1995; Tronto 1993; Fisher and Tronto 1990) suggest that care should be viewed as a complex activity of preserving bodies, selves, and environment. But even these definitions of care ground their discourse in the moral and ethical epistemology of gender (Walker 1998; Hekman 1995; Okin 1989), which marks care as a feminine domain of sociality.

It is not my intention to deny the ethical importance of any of these approaches to care, though in this chapter I focus on the social construction of care and its symbolic exclusion from definitions of economically measurable value. Specifically, I argue that socially constructed gender differences in relation to care secure the suspension of the feminine on the outside of economy-driven masculine scripts of value. Implying intimacy, connection, and trust, care links foremost with affection; all are typically not measurable in economic terms. In this sense, although femininity remains in relation to emotional engagement, care work is much talked about as providing reassurance and encouragement (Smart 1999), nurturing a psychological connection between individuals (see Mandell and Wilson, this volume). In other words, care work (that is, caregiving in contradistinction to self-care), is not marked as masculine and, hence, is not symbolically equated with economic activity.

Interestingly, and this argument will start my discussion, care work maintains a significant socio-cultural significance, often glorified in neo-conservative national practice across post-industrial cultures. Women in particular are encouraged to perform care work, as their moral and, in fact, natural duty to nation, tradition, or culture. This type of "moral" rather than economic activity takes place at home, with little recognition in economy-driven policy making, positioning women and care as the constitutive "other" to the masculine performance of work outside the home for a wage. As earlier chapters in this book suggest, the roots of such a welfare system are anchored in traditional norms of masculine value, which shape the broader meanings of rationality and progress. These norms, as any other norms of value, rest on the assumption that to be different means to be of lesser value. Because the cultural construction of domestic labour as feminine and wage labour as masculine is rooted in links between masculinity, rationality, and progress, to be defined as different or other than the masculine norm is also to be of lesser productive significance.

Defined by the logics of such differentiation, those who stay at home to care are plunged into strenuous negotiations between responsibility for another human being and their own dependence on a financial provider. In most Western societies, this can take place either directly through a breadwinner or indirectly through welfare provisions. The underlying logic splits care into economically devalued care for others (marked as a feminine subject position) on the one hand, and an ability to care for oneself and provide economically for others (marked as masculine) on the other. Following this dichotomy, the emotional value of care and its almost complete economic devaluation have over time created distinct forms of social subordination (on this see Fraser 2003). This subordination rests foremost on the underlying contract between genders, in which caregivers usually exchange their reproductive value for financial protection. Even if these genders are much more symbolical today than they were in the past, the cultural patterns of the gender contract continue to shape specific notions and fantasies of home and family.

To sum up these preliminary thoughts, although glorified and indispensable, the feminine values with respect to pregnancy, caregiving, and domestic work remain unjustified in terms of economic profitability and are often reduced to the unattractive marginalities of life (Sempruch 2005). This contradiction becomes all the more troubling across post-industrial cultures as newly emerging family forms struggle to develop their own relationships to work and care. In this vein, recent socio-economic studies on the decline of the male-breadwinner family across North America and western Europe, and the increasing diversity of family and employment patterns, have recognized the urgency in redefining the normative understandings of care, work, and balance (Halpern and Murphy 2005; Duxbury, Higgins, and Coghill 2003; Baker 2001; Jenson 2001; Lewis 2001; Mandell and Duffy 2000). Specifically in this chapter, I engage alternatives to the metaphors of care in relation to gender while following philosophical and political insights into the subjectivity of gender as well as the psychic fields of unrepresentability associated with care.[1]

I begin my discussion with the argument that despite popular rhetoric of difference, male and female bodies are ultimately much more alike than they are dissimilar (on this see also Hamington 2004). Against this rather obvious thought, gender distinctions persist in most research on care. Also, sexual orientation has become such a politically charged obstacle for caring that labels such as "gay" and "straight" appear as if two completely different species were addressed (ibid., 135). Even more sensitive ethical discourses tend to represent care for others as part of women's moral identity, whereas male care for others is imagined to result from some more immediate social requirements animated by duty (Bubeck 1995).[2] I see such polarized understanding of bodies as caught within the "heterosexual matrix" (Butler 1990, 42) and its "natural" morphology, which define the economic substance and materiality of bodies in terms of their reproductive capacity. This thinking follows Judith Butler's school of post-structuralist thought about the collapse of sex and gender into one and the same category of a social construction. In other words, we are not only labelled with a sex but also compelled to perform our corresponding gender and desires in accord with the socio-political requirements of a heterosexual norm. It is in this social and cultural context that the economic substance and materiality of bodies are defined in terms of their reproductive capacity.

Following this argument, gendered constructions of parenting and kinship are politically charged at the same time that they are perceived as natural. In fact, any parental sex/gender, as well as any legacy of kinship, has substantially less to do with nature and more to do with the socio-political discourse of nature established as a politically neutral domain. To give an example, heterosexual relations in the idealized marital form represent the norm by which parental rights are measured, preferably if they secure re-production in a biological way. In this sense, a heterosexual framework shapes institutional practices of parenting that make alternatives difficult and undesirable (Dunne 2000). Access to and eligibility for social benefits are linked to normative assumptions about sexuality. In length of time, maternal leave takes precedent to paternal leave, and welfare rights often exclude same-sex couples (Demczuk et al. 2002), while the self-perpetuating notion of a stay-at-home mother restricts single-parenting choices (see, for example, Hunsley 1997; Lightman 1997; Harris 1996).

As numerous feminist studies have suggested, women (as caregivers) have already begun to shift boundaries of domestic invisibility (see, for example, Aptheker 1989; Bakker 1996; Card 1996; Arendell 2000; Armstrong and Kits 2004) and to reshape their specifically gendered relation to care. These shifts are important, but meaningful socio-cultural transformations of care work must expand the focus to those who are usually excluded. In other words, if women as caregivers remain at the centre of feminist discussions, the subjectivity of care will continue to be seen as a feminine domain. Another growing body of research suggests that men/fathers are rather marginal to childcare policies and culturally unacknowledged for their increased partici-pation in the private sphere (see, for example, Seward et al. 2006; Allen and Hawkins 1999; Ross 1994; Bertoia and Drakich 1993). Stay-at-home fathers raising their children are still typically perceived as "losers" incapable of finding a "proper job," whereby the job itself is measured with traditional masculine norms of economic performance and has serious implications for the social and political economy of the household (see, for example, Ger-shuny, Godwin, and Jones 1994). Ultimately, it seems that equality will not be achieved if the normative masculine subject remains centralized as a breadwinner position and the involvement of men/fathers in childcare considered an addendum to family and work policies. I argue, then, that destabilizing and creatively repossessing gendered care lies at the core of the solution to the so far devalued subject of care work. I also believe that to overcome the split between the cultural and economic value of care, the caregiving subject necessitates a decisive shift toward an affirmingly flexible and much more subjective understanding of parental identity.

Expanding the meanings of fathering beyond the heterosexual discourse offers an illustration of such destabilization and reordering of gender binar-ies. Gay fathers, for example, provide the care requirements typically per-formed by both a mother and a father, while occupying neither of these subject positions in a conventional, hetero-normative way. Indeed, because gay fathering challenges traditionally accepted embodiments of care, it in-vites a radical rethinking of the masculine subject, as well as cultural repos-session of the imaginary and material institution of care as a feminine act.

The Fantasy of Home as a Private Space

Family, as my argument above suggests, intersects with a complex web of cultural ordering and disordering of gender.[3] The concept, as well as family practice, operates as a social container for the political economy of sexuality and its culturally reproduced meanings. Most importantly for my discussion, family is not a passive ideology of the historical contract between genders but a structure capable of subverting the symbolic laws that shape the cultural and economic order.

Although national constructions of home and family are always historically specific, they converge in the nineteenth-century maturation of capitalist states and the post-Second World War welfare-oriented ideology of responsibility for those who could not afford to support themselves. This paternalistic nature of the welfare state has become a common point of departure for many feminist analyses (see, for example, Sempruch, Willems, and Shook 2006a; Jenson 2003, 2004a; Bashevkin 2002; Silius 2002; Sainsbury 1999; Tyyskä 1995). The Western labour market presumed by postwar policy makers was based on the assumption of a male population in secure, full-time wage employment; women were considered either economically inactive or else supplementary workers performing mainly unpaid work at home.[4] It was further presumed by policy makers that men made a wage sufficient to support not only themselves but also their family (that is, their wife and children). This gender contract, defined in social research as the economic institution of a family wage, has structured the division between productive and reproductive labour and become a powerful incentive to enter into and remain in a marriage, regardless of subjective feelings (see Amato 2004b; Card 1996; Stacey 1996). A prerequisite for the functioning of such economic dependencies, traditional marriage constitutes the reason why informal care, conflated with empathy, is not considered work, as opposed to formal and less formal caregiving jobs (Fudge and Vosko 2001; Luxton and Corman 2001; Brodie 1995, 1996; Brody 1990). Thus, the specific cultural meanings and practices surrounding welfare, care, and employment policies have made caregivers take on cheap and temporary family-work solutions, often coming at the costs of gender equality (Foster and Broad 2002; Cleveland and Krashinsky 2001a, 2001b).

Consequently, the postwar gender contract has opened up questions of the citizenship right to economic independence via paid employment and social care service (Johnson 2002). Although many women, usually equally with men, engage today in full-time employment, they continue to perform unpaid domestic duties (Fudge 2001; Mirchandani 2000; O'Connor, Orloff, and Shaver 1999).[5] Moreover, within the policy domain, issues marked as feminine, such as care and emotional investments, are poorly represented or deemed too subjective as publicly valid positions. In national decision-making governmental structures, femininity continues to be infantilized and rendered non-essential, and caregivers' political inputs – which can offer an important perspective on community needs – are invisible. This dynamics of care and economy, a love-versus-money debate, is all the more fundamental, as it grounds the contemporary field of care as a psychic constitution. At this point, I would like to expand this line of thought and argue that care as a psychic constitution not only disenfranchises the feminine subject in terms of economy but also secures its exclusion from political representation.

Constructions and desires of home are strongly influenced by the privileges of the upper-middle classes, whereby the economic sphere of the public as masculine, competitive, and individualistic is contrasted to a home that offers feminine warmth and care as an antidote to a cruel outside world (see, for example, Marshall 1991). Consolidating motherhood as a legitimized source of pleasure, the safe domestic refuge combines fantasies of home not only as a feminine sphere but also a place of privacy, sterile sexuality, and moral purity. All these fantasies are relevant for the practice of social citizenship, as they maintain the heterosexist foundations of sexual difference and of private versus public space. Within this dominant social imaginary, the home continues to reproduce femininity as well as its distinct and incompatible relation to the public realm, despite the rising neo-liberal policy focus on the capacity of all citizens to support themselves via paid employment (Panitch and Swartz 2003; Bashevkin 2002; Giele 2002; Orloff and Shaver 1999; Kitchen 1997).[6]

The anecdotal question in this context is whether caregiving, especially in its gendered, hetero-normative version, can become a source of full-time inspiration while it is constructed as a package of devalued domestic activities for those who planned or were on their professional paths (Vincent, Ball, and Pietikainen 2004). The subjective ways through which we perceive and enact family and gender reveal that there is both an oversight and a danger in such polarization of work and life. Western societies consist of a diversity of family enactments. For some couples, parenting works; for many others, it doesn't. Some couples wish to have no children (see Gerson 2002; Gillespie 2000; Veevers 1980); others will never have any for various reasons. Some women value career over motherhood; still others may not pursue any specific career plans independently of whether they are mothers. Yet, amid such diversity of family enactments, the social construction of maternal absence, or absence of maternal desire as deviant and unnatural, makes women's subjectivity impossibly caught up within the collective image of mothering (see also Gustafson 2005; DiQuinzio 1999). On the other side of the spectrum, there are women who do not have as many children as perhaps desired and women who choose alternative kinship models. For example,

Ahmed (2004, 153) analyzes working-class lesbian parents who might not wish to be "like other families" and "might not be able to afford being placed outside the kinship networks" within their local communities. The persistence of these subjectivities, and the difficulties they create in the context of real-world diversity, points to precisely the question that lies at the heart of my chapter: How do we resolve gender typologies in relation to care?

Specifically, typologies based strictly on gender are often problematic, whereas the continuous, although increasingly absurd, dichotomy between the private and the public spheres contributes to a rather unproductive gender politics that as a rule is inherently static and does not capture newly emerging family patterns.[7] Thus, to expand our understanding of contemporary subjectivities, I now move on to discuss the political meanings of body in relation to care. If care continues to be understood as a psychic-emotional drive unreadable in terms of economy, we should perhaps ask how this unreadable domain of care is implicated in the construction of normative economic terms and conditions. Why does the very prospect of becoming economically useful depend on our acceptance of the current economic devaluation of care? It seems that to become economically significant, or to act in economically recognizable ways, requires that we subscribe to normative conditions of the economy. Following this inquiry, care as work becomes at once an ethical injunction and a political affair.

Situating care work, especially caregiving, within a broader socio-political context requires recognition of several important connections between the cultural value of care, preserved, for example, as motherhood ideology (Rothman 1989), and the economic value of care understood as work. Drawing on post-Foucauldian readings of body, what crosscuts these two understandings of the value of care might be referred to as "libidinal economy," a term that draws attention to the way in which the cultural production and consumption of gender, identity, and desire is linked to the economic practices and power relationships that underlie gendered family enactments. Precisely, "libidinal economy" refers to a specific organization of our sexuality, desires, and affects within or into sociality, whereby the social constitutes an essential part of the subject's psychic development and transformation. In other words, libidinal economy connects the cultural and economic value of care at the point where femininized care and the social production of the desire to perform a self-sacrificial version of motherhood reproduce the gendered economic relationships that devalue care work. Precisely, as a social field of force, libidinal economy promotes a heterosexual norm, as well as economic and cultural practices that replicate the norm (see Butler 1990). In this sense, not only our subjectivity but also our gendered bodies, desires, and affects are maintained by the combined impact of social and economic power relations, and they are always political.

Rendering subjectivity and embodiment political as such is in fact not an issue. The problem is with a politics that is founded on one dominant form of desire, which, as a primary and constitutive drive, affects not only our subjectivity but also our understanding of and acting upon our economic autonomy. This argument, with its complex gender implications, is crucial to my analysis and will now recur in the theme of embodied care (Hamington 2004) as the least readable domain of the libidinal economy.

Embodied Subjectivity and Care

So far I have referred to the historical contract between genders in order to situate the social consequences of feminine embodiedness. In the following discussion, I focus on the subjectivity of gender positions in relation to care work. I argue that culturally inherited patterns of sexual difference are of far more significance than the actual anatomical distinctions that designate bodies as female and male. Ultimately, my argument points to affectivity, desire, and pleasure as potential political and economic sites of subject autonomy. In this context, subject autonomy would imply sovereignty in terms of choices about reproduction, family, and work. Clearly, such choices are often shaped by interdependencies and the need for care faced by most individuals at some point in life. Acknowledging this, I propose to define subject autonomy as a form of "bodily complexity" – a term implying the importance of embodied subjectivity rather than the gender one identifies or is identified with.

In this respect, post-structuralist scholars have postulated the body as a "wilful choice" (see, for example, Griffin and Braidotti 2002, 232), that is, a material space of power that dictates and negotiates its own subjectivity. What this implies is that body can change as a subject, if desire activates such choice, and that sexuality and pleasure are central to this activation (ibid). Whereas subjectivity is shaped by forces of libidinal economy (sexuality, desire, pleasure), family, as an embodied multiple subject, reproduces such forces as internalized identity containers in their specific historical contexts of power. In this vein, our "embodiedness," or bodily materiality (Braidotti 2002), exists within biological limits but foremost within cultural boundaries that are also the first contours of the subject in the process of becoming.[8] Kinship within this framework of materiality has become an ultimate foundation of the subject, giving rise to cultures, traditions, and nations.

But desire can also generate various forms of resistance to the prevailing socio-cultural order. Considering that caregiving has been primarily constituted as feminine, the desire to provide care can be defined as a subjective passion, a "psychic space" of feminine affects. Following Julia Kristeva (1995, 29), it is within this psychic space that affects materialize between bodily organs and social customs (see also Irigaray 1985 and Butler 1997).[9] One's subjectivity depends on this space, as it generates linguistic meaning and collectively internalized relations between the body and culture. Subjectivity, so to say, is always embodied and therefore specific to one's particular psychic space of body. Yet such embodiment, or bodily specificity, is by no means limiting. On the contrary, it allows and even stimulates multiple preferences, which might be compatible or only partly compatible with the assigned gender. Thus, because our specific embodied subjectivity depends on our interpolation into a particular psychic space rather than on our biological composition, it is possible, for example, for an individual who has been sexed as male to internalize the desire to care.

Another reason why I focus on subjectivity is because the construction of masculine and feminine subject positions does not necessarily imply any exclusiveness of actual gendered desires or performances – either in relation to caregiving or self-care. In fact, the many uses of care discourse demonstrate the centrality of flexible subjectivity to everyday negotiations that also require the ability to "perform gender" within the family context (see, for example, Mandell 2002). Care work in this case refers both to the ability and desire to care for oneself and for the other family members. "Doing family," a term widely connoted in post-structural theories, might indeed best describe the current post-industrial family condition. Relying on the habits of empathy and subconscious processing of responsibility, family members negotiate their positions in many different ways, which both require and move beyond gender politics. Men may care for children while women work, economic circumstances may necessitate unconventional divisions of domestic chores, and children of both sexes may desire or be required to parent younger siblings at various times and in various ways. Importantly, these complex social interactions take place mostly without conscious perception or intentional formulation of care as work (see Hamington 2004).

Resistance and conceptual fluidity in the understanding of how the subject is constructed are therefore important to gender equality debates, as policies often display the tendency to universalize the categories of male and female bodies as always one or the other. Moving the discussion beyond the typical heterosexual household, the concept of nuclear family excludes not only same-sex/queer couples or single parenting as such but also various forms of heterosexual families that do not conform to hetero-normative assumptions about parenting (VanEvery 1995). Thus, while heterosexuality itself is clearly more of an injunction than a personal preference (Valverde 1987, 366), even heterosexual parents do not "choose" care-work solutions out of a number of equally valid, equally respected standards of choice. To quote Valverde, "Given the enormous social weight of heterosexism, one cannot accurately describe heterosexuality as merely a personal preference, as though there were not countless social forces pushing one to be heterosexual" (ibid.).

Clearly, choices that deviate from hetero-normative assumptions about gender are more difficult to enact, both economically and socially. This limitation in itself constitutes a form of repression forcing subjects to enact socially imposed or socially pleasing roles.

Although gender relations within the family have undergone conceptual shifts over the last decades, the continuously fixed division of categories constrains the emergence of intersectional subjectivities. In this sense, although family as a nuclear middle-class household consisting primarily of a mother, father, and children is no longer a pervasive reality, it is still a focus of policy attention (Brodie 1996; Phoenix, Woollett, and Lloyd 1991). Equally, the male breadwinner–dependent female caregiver ideology continues to serve as a signifying structure of the household norm, reducing grandparents and possibly other family members to redundant, invisible, or marginally attached bodies.

Summing up my argument so far, care intersects with the materiality of human reproduction, sexuality, and kinship and is therefore central to the conception of body as well as to differences that surround its social constitution. I also believe, in agreement with Fraser and Honneth (2003), that one cannot read off the economic subordination of care directly from the cultural order nor its cultural value from its economic devaluation. Since caring crosscuts public and private habits and imagination (see discussions by Martin-Matthews 2007; Hays 1996; Fisher and Tronto 1990), it blurs many of the established categories of knowledge about care (Hamington 2004). The ethically unyielding approach to care is neither primarily an economic nor a cultural one but one that recognizes subjectivity and care as always already specifically embodied. This approach accommodates differentiation, divergence, and subjective interaction between gender, desire, family, and work, all constituting the meanings of care. Drawing precisely on these intersections, I argue for the centrality of embodied care – a concept that offers the necessary ethical orientation and policy framework through which to resolve diverse inequalities in relation to wage labour and unpaid work in the household (see also Robinson 2006; Armstrong and Kits 2004; Appelbaum et al. 2002; Burggraf 1997).

Caregivers' Work across the Axis of Social Citizenship

The dichotomy between pro-market and non-marketable values has its own "complex and systematic logic," a logic that demarcates the economy of private and public distinctions (Gal 2000, 261). Inherently rooted in capitalist hierarchies of power, this logic also structures the ways in which the discursive schism between the public and the private shapes social constructions of specific genders across the axis of family and work (on social security regulations, see, for example, Marshall 2009; Marsiglio 1995; Sainsbury 1993). Working precisely against such constructions, feminist economists have long claimed that unpaid domestic work is critical for many employers whose profits hinge on paying workers less than the true value of their labour (Halpern and Murphy 2005). Increasingly relevant are studies examining post-industrial cultures of long working hours in which caregivers cannot compete and still provide care (Ehrenreich and Hochshild 2003; Appelbaum 2001; Beaujot 2000). This is most evident in the context of the best-paid and most privileged employment positions, where everyone must play according to the rules, regardless of gender or family situation.

Canada can serve as an example of such a post-industrial culture, in which having children is mainstreamed as a lifestyle choice, though this choice is simultaneously losing its popularity. Because of inadequate politics of public policies and the continued relevance of gendered care, raising children has become equivalent to giving up on more exclusive and otherwise more accessible lifestyle choices. Especially in large urban centres, there is both a growing popularity of middle-class childless couples pursuing fast-track professional careers and a growing number of single mothers living below the poverty level. An increasing number of stay-at-home fathers rely entirely on their partners' income. What these and many other family diversifications have in common (see Krull's and Baker's chapters, this volume) is the economic devaluation of care work at home (see also an excellent discussion by Macdonald 1998).

Like many types of paid work, especially knowledge-based work associated with leadership positions, care involves an ability to perform several tasks simultaneously and necessitates various forms of flexibility to prioritize tasks according to their urgency (Crittenden 2004; Silius 2002). Yet the time spent accomplishing domestic tasks is literally invisible, the form of work itself thought of as culturally inherited or even innate (DeVault 1991, 56-57), and understood to create its own psychic recompensations and pleasures.[10] Although the economic value of paid employment is never a question, the assessment of time invested in the private sphere remains a difficult and always only an approximate task. The much-discussed phenomenon of the double burden as affecting women in heterosexual relationships (Jacobs and Gerson 2004; Hochschild 1989, 1997) derives precisely from such devaluation. Clearly, too, such burden can triple in the context of immigrant or culturally different (usually non-Anglo-Saxon or non-Québécois) families in Canada. In this respect, Sara Ruddick (1995, 46) offers an analysis of care that removes it from the traditional cultural framework and defines it as an "emotional labour." Ruddick's analysis captures the effort and energy involved in care and avoids passive notions of instinctual or even morally driven care, providing a venue for expanding the concept of worker toward those who perform unwaged care work.

Today, as the heterosexual household continues to be the site for extensive cross-subsidization of economic activity between family members, most

Canadian households with children operate on the basis of the one-and-a-half breadwinner model. The contract between genders, as discussed earlier, increasingly implies dual earning, marginalized care, and repression of subjectivities. But even if we reject informal caregiving as a form of paid work, what remains open is the question of how primary caregivers who interrupt paid work in order to care for their family members should be defined in terms of social citizenship (Baker, Gruber, and Milligan 2005; Ackers 2004; Rubery and Grimshaw 2003; Zetlin and Whitehouse 2003).[11]

Social citizenship is of interest here not only in relation to the theme of embodied care but also in terms of how welfare states secure caregiver's personal autonomy or capacity to form autonomous households. For example, the Canada Child Tax Benefit, a program thought to embody social citizenship but in fact intrinsically supporting the reproduction of gendered care and work, provides caregivers with minimal state financial support: never enough to keep a single mother out of poverty but a sufficient bonus to those with access to a male breadwinner's income. Paradoxically, although citizenship includes the entitlement to social provision (Fraser and Honneth 2003), this right does not necessarily secure a decent life. As Fraser and Honneth (2003, 46) argue, receiving welfare is "usually considered grounds for disrespect, a threat to, rather than a realization of, citizenship," while in the area of social services, the word "public" is often pejorative. In Canada, social assistance plans are indeed stigmatized and undesirable (see, for example, Little 1998) and maintain continuously depreciatory meaning at a time when public services such as childcare and schooling are increasingly seen as imperative for the practice of social citizenship.

Social citizenship is therefore a useful category for the analysis of national welfare states and their social policy programs and also for interpreting the transformation of feminist cultures. Traditionally, feminist discussions of citizenship focused rhetorically on its exclusionary reinforcement of masculine power in terms of actual paid workforce participation. Such discussions revolved around women's right to participate equally with men in the economy. More recently, feminist social research has resulted in a redefinition of social citizenship to incorporate the right to provide care – through paid leave or equal treatment in part-time work – and the right to be cared for – through social care services. The issues at stake are not only the redistribution of income and social security rights but also the redistribution of social care services and unpaid caregiving. Public schools, childcare, and public health services are the key elements of this practice, of which the underlying premise is the economic recognition of care. This recognition implies access to caregiver-friendly jobs and public childcare services that are of good quality and tailored to the needs of working parents. Significantly, it explicitly implies caregivers' entitlement to equal respect, regardless of gender, age, or origin (Bleijenbergh, Bruijn, and Bussemaker 2004).

Queering Childcare and Caregivers' Work

As an immediate thought, a gender-neutral concept of parenting is politically problematic, and neutrality is not the point. Rather, it is a matter of a shifting subject position, that is, a form of gender flexibility that would engage in a dialogue with the socio-historically constructed exclusivity of "mother" as a caregiver. I therefore propose a perspective, which, in accord with the theoretical framework discussed earlier, defines caring as a politically charged position rather than as an anatomy-related essence. Femininity, motherhood, masculinity, and other such typologies are labels or performances both activated and/or abandoned for specific cultural and economic reasons. Changing political shifts in the war and postwar decades in the activation of mothers as primary workers when women workers were needed and as primary caregivers when birth rates were sinking are indisputable examples of such social acts. Significantly, caregiving requires both providing and nurturing, and it does so independently of gender, blood, or any other type of relation (see Rothman 1989). One simply cannot care without providing. Although women still overwhelmingly fill the maternal, nurturing role, men certainly can. The fact that relatively few are encouraged to do so connects with the continuing disadvantaging of caregivers in terms of their economic value.[12]

To follow on this theoretical thread, the symbolic repression of femininity is not "merely cultural" but cultural with significant political implications for culture as a paradigm of institutionalized authority (on this, see J. Butler 2002). As discussed earlier, this authority rewards the conforming and stigmatizes undesired forms of sexuality. The symbolic repression remains interwoven with cultural frameworks of kinship, while an insight into how parental roles have been socially constructed offers us a move toward their potential elasticity. By means of illustrating such elasticity, I introduce the notion of queering childcare, which underlies my conviction that employment of a positional simultaneity of gender is crucial to the feminist critiques of care practice. Such simultaneity is directly linked to the previously discussed subject becoming its resistance and capacity for flexibility and change. Queering thus offers a perception of care as a form of a flexible implementation and supplementation of values that no longer privileges women as those with exclusionary access to reproduction or men as those in control of the productive economy, allowing for an argument that fathers can also be constructed as marginal to the normative order (see Amato 2004a; Ross and Brott 1999; Brandth and Kvande 1998; Frey 1997; Cohen 1993; Bozett and Hanson 1991; Bronstein and Cowan 1988). Such a relational definition of care can shift as much as the various forms of family and work patterns that increasingly shape the post-industrial culture of Canada (see, for example, Lowe 2007). In the end, the question is not whether men or women are better caregivers, but who gets to become one, who is fit to endure in the role, and at what socio-economic costs? Following a queer (or positional) simultaneity of gender, the values, costs, and political relevance of care can be recognized and redistributed across gender identities. This queer simultaneity in relation to care speaks directly to parental rather than maternity leaves, affordable and good-quality childcare centres, and equal pay attainments. Today's debates on childcare are still primarily framed in the context of women's employment and the gendered division of domestic labour (CCAAC 2004; Statistics Canada 2003a, 2003b; CIDA 1999).

In demystifying modes of dialectical representation, a caution is required. The historical universalism of the masculine subject continues today as a form of fake gender sameness. This subject position coincides with self-consciousness of masculine agency and entitlement (for example, the postwar family wage–based employment, as previously discussed). On the contrary, the female subject, or subject embodied with female attributes, is deprived of such privileges within the symbolic system, through either lack or displacement of its material presence in culture. In this sense, the embodied subject competes for survival in the world of phallocentric regularities, in which the "female condition," independent of the gender that adopts it, constitutes a subject enveloped in a stigma of negative differentiation. A good example here is still typically a mother unable to keep up with the speed of her career and facing alternative solutions to paid work. Sexual difference is thus "both the subject around which feminists have gathered in their recognition of a general [female] condition, and the concept that needs to be analysed critically" (Braidotti 2002, 171). Difference, or the otherness of femininity, has its point of departure in a linguistic absence (Irigaray 1985) but needs to be strategically linked to the political project of providing representation for the female subject (Braidotti 2002, 171). To read Irigaray and Braidotti together, there is no sentimentality involved in the reappraisal of the maternal/material feminine. Both acknowledge the institution of motherhood as the site of women's capture within the "specular logic of the same" (11) and contrast this institution with maternity (O'Reilly 2004) as a powerful site of the social. The remaining question in my study is: How do we move from feminist maternity without losing its political insight and ultimately queer the notion of caregiving as duty and obligation but also as pleasure?

My answer to this question forms the concluding theoretical argument of this chapter. As I believe, the move from one politically significant position, such as feminist reappraisal of maternity, toward a broader pluralistic formulation of childcare amounts to a recognition and redistribution (Fraser and Honneth 2003) of cultural inscriptions of power across various forms of gender interaction within family, work, employment, and citizenship practice. Recognition in this framework refers to "a collective repossession of the images and representations of woman such as they have been encoded in language, culture, science, knowledge, and discourse and consequently internalized in the mind, body and lived experience of women" (Braidotti 2002, 171). Redistribution, on the other hand, is a strategy that parallels Judith Butler's call to dismantle the phallocentric framework through the implementation of subversive acts within this framework (see also discussions of mimetic strategy by Braidotti 2002 and Irigaray 1985). What should be recognized is the economic value of care, which then in the form of repetitive acts can be redistributed across spaces of collective normativity – that is, across family, work, employment, and citizenship structure. Both premises rest on the tasks of establishing autonomies outside constructed identities and affirming repeated interventions that validate these autonomies in culture. To follow on this thought with West and Zimmerman (1987), and also Coltrane's formulation (1989, 1996) of "doing gender," the domestic sphere provides the opportunity for expressing, confirming, and sometimes transforming the meanings of masculinity (Cooper and Baker 1996). Doing gender differently or performing family clearly impacts on newly emerging cultural values, as well as on conceptions of pleasure. To use Coltrane's example, the routine practice of sharing childcare and an ongoing personal involvement of a father can reconstruct him as a competent caregiver (Day and Lamb 2004; Dowd 2000; Daly 1993; Coltrane 1989).

Drawing on these examples, the political economy of desire and pleasure becomes a necessary intervention into debates on work and family reconciliation because it does not limit these debates to women's issues but, rather, grounds them in the political matrix of social gender relations. Such a standpoint involves the understanding that culture and economy act upon maternity, paternity, and commitment in culture-specific and economy-driven ways (see Coontz 2004; Collier 1999; May 1998; McKenna 1993). Thus, as long as certain choices are punished while others are presented as natural and normative, it is naive to describe the process of conformity and/or deviance from socially normalized lifestyles as a simplistic or homogenous affair. As Ahmed (2004, 153) argues, "Maintaining an active politics of 'transgression' not only takes time, but may not be psychically, socially or materially possible for some individuals and groups given their ongoing and unfinished commitments and histories." For example, it is difficult to discuss queer kinships without taking into account the contested concept of sexual citizenship within private-public discourses (Richardson 2000, 106). Sexual citizenship, not unlike the social, forms a model of rights and duties, again merging the domestic and public spheres of discourse. Sexual citizenship demarcates the "boundaries of tolerance or rejection, inclusion or exclusion" (108), rendering these boundaries simultaneously fixed and unstable.

Following this thought, the issue of same-sex marriage becomes a claim for socio-legal recognition that demystifies the private-public distinction, so that the private economy of desire is brought into a more public discourse of citizenship and is no longer a domestic matter. Ironically, as Judith Butler noticed, one might say that through marriage, "personal desire acquires a certain anonymity and interchangeability, becomes, as it were, publicly mediated and, in that sense, a kind of legitimated public sex" (2002, 23). The binaries are thus both reproduced and always of a transgressive nature (Gal 2000, 266) that allows alternative forms of kinship across social acts so that they might eventually enter the sphere of legitimacy and order.

In feminist rethinking of household economy, queering childcare seems essential to challenging the exclusivity of a female caregiver, as it suspends the most fundamental distinctions in terms of which gender does what. Consequently, it necessitates a redefinition of the boundaries, meanings, and contents of parental care (Nelson 1992, 2006b; Dunne 2000; Marsiglio 1995; Ambert 1994), though everyday encounters with mainstream ideals do not always make this task easy. As parents, a gay couple in Canada faces challenges both in terms of traditional notions of family and the non-procreative nature of homosexuality. Although their positioning outside conventionality may enable more creative approaches to parenting and care, their need for social recognition, and legal validation of the co-parent, results in sexuality being scrutinized under the public limelight: "There's a thing that if you want to be acknowledged as a parent, you just had to come out. It's the only way to explain that you're a parent" (Dunne 2000, 14). Following Dunne's argument, lesbian parents often navigate through the given, heterosexually coded, terminology to describe their understanding of kinship. Moreover, while challenging traditional notions of what constitutes family, they implicitly threaten the heterosexual monopoly on reproduction. Actually, to concur with Dunne, lesbian parenting represents "a radical and radicalizing challenge to heterosexual norms that govern parenting roles and identities," rather than a chance to incorporate lesbians "into the mainstream as honorary heterosexuals" (24).

Ultimately, what is most appealing about alternative kinship is the necessary subjective impetus for re-examining affiliations built upon social and sexual identities (see, for example, Rake 2001; Picchio 1998). In this sense, sexuality as a "private" bodily expression is always already a public expression as an assumed social consequence of a body that can be mapped as married, divorced, single, and more. Since there is no simple continuum of public to private, perhaps the discourse of sexual citizenship ought to be interpreted as a subjective reflection of contemporary reimaginings of family. In other words, the apparent ambiguity between the private and public spheres can actually open up new ways for anti-essentialist thinking about home and family through a discourse of libidinal economy. Such a positional perspective on parenting offers a way to avoid the limitations of the gendered body, as it is no longer a map of semiotic inscriptions or culturally enforced codifications but a surface for political embeddedness in the process of cultural mediation (Braidotti 2002, 21).

The Philosophy of Equal Treatment: Conclusions and Suggestions

Following intra-European policy developments over the last decade and a half, "women's concerns, needs and aspirations should be taken into account and assume the same importance as men's concerns in the design and implementation of policies" (European Commission 1996, 67). Paralleling this gender mainstreaming approach, the European Commission recognized persistent gender inequalities, which continue to require the implementation of "specific actions" in favour of women. In this sense, equal opportunities were already underscored by the logics of masculine sameness, shaping conditions of gender neutrality. This, in turn, enforced masculinization of the female life cycle without elevating femininity as an economically valued subject position. In fact, the Treaty of Amsterdam (1998) reinforced the use of positive action programs by underpinning them with a commitment to mainstreaming equal opportunities throughout all the European Union activities (for an excellent discussion on this, see Lombardo 2005). Such reinforcement inevitably led to new legislation on equal pay, equal treatment, parental leave, and maternity rights, as well as on sexual harassment at work. Protection of part-time, fixed-term, and contracted work was also part of the package. Still, the dialectical suspension between masculine sameness and femininized difference remained inherent to policy making. The more recently proposed dual-track approach – gender mainstreaming and specific actions (European Commission 2003) – clearly draws on the continued necessity to understand and remedy gender inequality by implementing policies in a combined dimension of redistribution and recognition practices.

There also seems to be a fundamental tension between the feminist pursuit of equal opportunities and the governmental policy-making pursuit of economic efficiency (see OECD 2005; Towns 2002; see also Albanese's reflections on some of the tensions in the context of Quebec, this volume). As numerous feminists have argued, the European Union's mainstreaming strategy "has been selective in its use of feminist theory," with consequences that often recognize "gendered processes on structural, interpersonal and symbolic levels" but do not "locate these in an analysis of patriarchy" and heteronormativity (Booth and Bennett 2002, 431). Gender mainstreaming can therefore "appear to be a diluted version of positive action strategies" and may appear irrelevant to actual choices available to caregivers. As Booth and Bennett (441) suggest, "What shapes specific tendencies in policy making is a desire to maintain rather than subvert the 'status' of current power structures." The best example here is the tendency of federal governments "to outwardly promote equal opportunities in the public sphere but without recognizing the needs for assistance and equality in the private sphere. Consequently, feminist scholars have been critical of a mainstreaming strategy and have been slow to make a contribution to the policy debate" (ibid.).

In the past, equal treatment emerged as a socio-political consequence of the gender contract and was focused on the assumption that women and men may equally be breadwinners. Today, however, asymmetrically rising levels of female labour market participation have diffused the underlying principles of equality. As Yuval-Davis (1997) has long argued, liberal understandings of social citizenship are based on notions of gender-neutral, racially neutral, and regionally homogenized individuals who are strangers to one another, rather than on differently empowered, positioned, and interrelated individuals and communities. On the contrary, embodied subjectivity and the potential changes it activates at various points of caregivers' lives are not valid for policy making. Whereas the ongoing challenge is largely defined as how to ensure that caregivers might be able to secure employment and upward mobility, the differences between working cultures and systems as well as more gender subjective and, in fact, multiple subject positions in relation to care must also be part of the picture.

The striking lack of definitive relationships between particular policies and changes in outcomes oftentimes shows that the family-work relation is not only a product of various social, economic, and political factors but is also culture-specific and subjectively defined.[13] The diversity of factors impacting families has been well captured by a 1993 intra-European survey, which identified the most influential determinants affecting the number of children across social strata. In descending order, most crucial were (1) housing, (2) the economic situation and unemployment, (3) the cost of raising children, (4) work-time flexibility, and (5) the availability of good-quality childcare and parental leave (Hantrais and Letablier 1996). Whereas flexibility and parental leave regulation appears toward the end of the list, neither family benefits nor tax relief were seen as important. On the contrary, economic stability seems to be more significant than the actual policy intervention, especially if the latter has not been culturally internalized. Following numerous comparative studies of family-work policies across Europe and North America (see, for example, Gornick, Heron, and Eisenbrey 2007; Misra, Budig, and Moller 2007; Evans, Lippoldt, and Marianna 2001), despite the centrality of care to the successful implementation of gender mainstreaming, there is no systematic assessment of caregiving impact on policy initiatives (see, for example, CEU 2005; United Nations, OSAGI 2001). It remains, therefore, imperative to investigate the actual philosophy behind policy discourse as affected by organizational innovations and also the culture-specific conditions in which these innovations operate.

Still, childcare policies are of importance for the family structure, as they directly reflect on cultural and economic norms as discursively constituted and therefore fixed. The most evident drawback is that there is no simple policy solution for achieving optimal arrangements of work and family. Rather, it seems necessary to separate cause and effect in policy making and to identify the different and more subjective variables in policy objectives. As previously argued, gender-fixed and culturally homogeneous initiatives may not result in expected outcomes because of more subjective as well as shifting positions in relation to childcare. This is particularly so in the case of parents belonging to specific ethnicities and cultures that dictate varied acceptable and desirable conditions for care.

The balance itself cannot be objectified for all, since that would ground such aspirations in a fixed and alleged family constellation (for example, the nuclear model is still typical for policy making). As complex and demanding as it sounds, a strategic diversification of interventions may be the only possible policy solution to result in actual equality improvement. However, the extent to which subjectivities have been integrated into family patterns and adopted by working culture needs attention on several fronts. The dilemma of task sharing, single parenting, and the question of who constitutes family goes hand in hand with the changing norms and cultures of work, as well as of welfare policies, which in Canada function often as "patchworks of purpose" (Boychuk 1998, 41; see also Roos, Trigg, and Hartman 2006; Bradbury 2005; Mahon 2005; Duxbury and Higgins 2001; Baker and Tippin 1999). In many areas of Canadian law and policy making, pervasively institutionalized androcentric values are codified across ethnicities, race, dis/abilities, and age. Despite growing mobility and employment opportunities for women in Canada, the socio-political topography of work, especially top governmental and managerial positions, privileges qualities associated with normative masculinity. On the other hand, codes of femininity, coupled with immigrant or minority positions, suffer from "status subordination," which takes the form of trivializing, objectifying, and stereotypical depictions in the media (Fraser and Honneth 2003, 21). Changing this status, like defining the balance, requires the systematic and ongoing replacement of particularly centralized value patterns with those expressing other types of logic. This task resonates with my theoretical argument to repeatedly dismantle hetero-normative assumptions through recognition and redistribution of other less privileged positions (see Fraser and Honneth 2003; Braidotti 2002; Butler 1990; Irigaray 1985). Taking into account the actual experience of different groups across gender, origin, or sexual orientation could certainly serve as a starting point for such a practice of restructuring. Although broader organizational change has yet to be realized, should it not follow, policy making adhering to one dominant normative regulation will continue as a socio-juridical system in which traditionally constructed roles are reinforced in the form of disseminated regulations. Also, if gender equality is to be seen as more than a "women's issue," its pursuit necessitates a substantial alteration of the male incentive structure (see Ranson 2001). At present, it appears unlikely that even the most progressive parental-leave policy will alone make a substantial difference. Workplace efforts for gender equality reflect this mixed legacy. At one extreme, mothers' exclusion continues – carried out informally, where formal restrictions are now illegal – and, hence, specific policy actions in favour of women might still be required. At the other extreme, equality will not be achieved without decentring the normative masculine subject. Thus, to subvert the institutionalized practice of motherhood as unpaid or economically devalued domestic activity (see, for example, Campbell and Carroll 2007; Baker 2004; Crittenden 2001), it would seem urgent to engage in a politically meaningful strategic alliance of caregivers across genders, origins, and cultures. What I specifically find imperative for policy making is to include fathers in taking on an equal share in domestic labour while focusing on the actual incentives for abandoning the masculine subject positions, still instilled with responsibility for financial providing.

Finally, an exclusive focus on household neglects an equally important aspect of family-work conflict: the actual conditions of work. How do workplace structures and culture shape parental experiences, and how does the workplace exacerbate work-life relations? Especially for those working deregulated hours, work aspects such as flexibility, autonomy, and control are likely to matter as much as working time (Conaghan and Rittich 2005; Fine-Davis 2004). In a similar fashion, the supply and demand for family-friendly options, such as flexible scheduling and educational (read "good-quality") childcare services, are of importance but far from widespread (Leira 2002; Milton 2001; Doherty, Friendly, and Oloman 1998). Intact with this recognition, it seems urgent to consider the hidden costs of family-supportive workplace policies. Even when options are formally available, in a high-opportunity work environment they entail subjective, unspoken, but very real penalties and dangers. Hence, caregivers often perceive that making use of policies related to family support jeopardizes long-term prospects for career advancement (Jacobs and Gerson 2004).

Following these fronts of policy focus, care work must be simultaneously addressed at levels of family, work organization, and broader conditions of social justice. The radical introduction of parental rights – like "daddy quotas" in Norway and Sweden – has already added to the visibility of men in care work (Kvande 2000), but such acts can be seen as emancipatory only if they do not create new marginalizations (LaRossa 1988). Similarly, policies aimed at the recognition of women's difference in caring responsibilities can be helpful only if they are used to enhance women's employment access or status. The fact that such improvements have not taken place is attested to by the fact that men still outnumber women in terms of seniority and higher wages (Webster 2001). The glass ceiling restricting women's career and development prospects, in particular their seniority and responsibility, remains firmly in place. On the other hand, gender-neutral strategies can increase the burden on caregivers without fundamentally shifting the gender division in domestic responsibilities.

Clearly, the recognition of subjectively defined experiences must be part of policy promotion. Subjectivity, in a broader socio-political sense, has implications for governments and their policy agenda and cannot be resolved exclusively from women's or a household perspective. In this light, political and social factors are closely interrelated in their shaping of production, distribution, and consumption (Jenson and Sineau 2001, 242). Such interrelatedness shapes a necessary understanding that political choices about childcare provisions are multi-faceted (Baker 2010; Doherty, Friendly, and Forer 2002) and never simply made on the premise that it is natural for families to take care of their own children and that childcare services are naturally excluded from social policy (Prentice 2001). It demands that our understanding of caregiving, especially as a form of unpaid emotional activity, undergoes transformation from the devalued toward a developed subject position (Sempruch 2006). What needs to be acknowledged as changing is not merely the terminology or metaphorical representation of the caregiving subject but the very structure of subjectivity (Braidotti 2002) and the social relations that maintain traditional discourses on care and family values (Boyd 2003; Boyd 2002; Stacey 1996).

Finally, if care, in its full complexity, is to be understood as a set of social relations that shape and are shaped by access to variously defined citizenship rights, such as sexual, socio-cultural, and political citizenship, then all three aspects must be targeted simultaneously. In other words, care is a combined issue of the continuous alterations in family arrangements, both in terms of sexuality and culture and the changing patterns of employment that create new challenges for the workplace (Statistics Canada 2006a, 2006c; Haney and Pollard 2003; Dickinson and Schaeffer 2001; Fudge and Vosko 2001; Carniol 2000; Deakin 2000; Standing 1997). As identities become more fluid and more contextual than ever, it is necessary not only to look at how mothers and fathers are discursively shaped under particular forms of inclusion and exclusion but also to effectively queer socio-economic citizenship through alternative kinship models. In all these intermingling "patterns of becoming" (Braidotti 2002, 169), both social challenges and cultural anxieties call for a new approach to the work-life balance: a gender-flexible approach that would serve as a necessary navigational tool to embrace the various enactments of the changing patterns, and in a much-needed feminist fashion.

Notes

1 "Subjectivity" in this context refers to the political aspects of human sexuality, desires, and affects, extending the traditional definitions of care and emotion beyond the fantasy of its private subsistence. On this, see Sara Ahmed (2004), Rosi Braidotti (2002), and Luce Irigaray (1985).

2 Elisabet Bubeck (1995) favours the view that care ethics is gendered as feminine because of social constructions of the female body as emotionally driven, in contrast to the male body, which is predominantly driven by socio-economic rules and role requirements. Duty, respectively, is understood here in terms of a masculine role as a breadwinner.

3 As much feminist work argues, home as a neo-liberal space of privacy shapes the experiences of parenting, whereby partners share the same nuclear structure but infinitely differentiate between carefully assigned roles in that structure: caregivers and providers, femininity and masculinity, desires and obligations, mothers and fathers – these designations being indices of the complex network of values (see, for example, Baxter, Hewitt, and Haynes 2008; Armstrong and Kits 2005; Baker and Phipps 1997; Luxton 1997).

4 Although the manifestations of this employment relationship vary by region and country (Korpi 2000), reflecting social, political, and legal traditions, the broad normative employment features are also a product of international labour regulation (ILO 2005).

5 Vast research suggests also that women have not gained much from the labour market restructuring that has accompanied the move to the liberal forms of the "knowledge society," whereas the levels of women's occupational segregation are constantly increasing (see OECD 2007a and UNDP 1995).

6 Particularly in the Canadian context, Bashevkin (2002) investigates welfare reform during the Mulroney era, notorious for disregarding single mothers and rendering welfare reform unaffordable.

7 For different reasons, however, both conservative and liberal policies rely on such passive approaches to gender, employment, and care (see, for example, Panitch and Swartz 2003). One approach simply prioritizes strong job protection based on the family wage model; the other focuses on unregulated labour markets and the politics of choice. Neither of these policies projects a much-needed gender-flexible and community-focused approach to care.

8 For the most compelling discussions on this, see Gilles Deleuze's "Mysticism and Masochism" (1967, trans. Michael Taormina) in *Desert Islands and Other Texts, 1953-1974*, ed. David Lapoujade, 131-34 (New York: Semiotext(e), 2004) and further work by Deleuze with Felix Guattari (for example, *A Thousand Plateaus: Capitalism and Schizophrenia*, trans. Brian Massumi [Minneapolis: University of Minnesota Press, 1987] and Judith Butler's *The Psychic Life of Power: Theories of Subjection* [1997]).

9 Care, as a central concern to the notion of embodied subjectivity, relates to Merleau-Ponty's formulation of knowledge and bodily acts as re-creating and maintaining knowledge through habits. Feminist philosophers, such as Luce Irigaray, Iris Young, and Judith Butler, advocate a reinterpretation of Merleau-Ponty (see Hamington 2004).

10 The daily "invisible" work performed by caregivers compares with the paid work of the largest industries of the "visible" economy. In the most industrialized countries, the total hours spent on unpaid household work amounts to at least half of the hours of paid work in the labour market. Up to 80 percent of this unpaid labour is performed by women (United Nations 1995, 97).

11 The risk in rejecting informal caregiving as a form of paid work is that legitimizing the home as a site of wage-earning could contribute to the maintenance of a caregiving norm that encourages women's confinement to the private sphere and reinforces long-standing patterns of occupational and industrial segregation (see, for example, Vosko 2006; Gershuny and Sullivan 2003).

12 Following feminist systematic rewritings of "natural care" into "economic force," the constructs of "mother" and "father" are always formed in relation to the socio-economic marginality of feminized care and women's vulnerability to poverty (Christopher 2002; Hobcraft and Kiernan 2001; Baker and Tippin 1999; Bryson 1998; Little 1998; Evans 1996; Folbre 1995).

13   Regarding the lack of definitive relationships between particular policies and changes in outcomes, the available indications from comparative country reviews do reveal, however, that women in Sweden, Denmark, and Finland tend to manage work and family responsibilities better than anywhere else in Europe and benefit more from policy interventions. For example, women in those countries do better materially over their life course, though there is evidence of an increasing polarity between well-educated, professional women in two-earner families and young single mothers or women in poorly paid work (for a thorough discussion, see Lewis 1993).

10
Working-Time Regimes, Flexibility, and Work-Life Balance: Gender Equality and Families
Judy Fudge

Time, like pay, provides a standard metric, and both are central elements in every employment relationship (Beaujot 2000, 24; Bosch 1999, 131). Time and pay are also key sources of conflict between employees and employers; but unlike conflicts over pay, conflicts over time cannot be resolved by expanding the pie (Jacobs and Gerson 2004, 2). There are only so many hours in a day, and the demands on people's time – to earn an income, to have affective relationships, to care for others, and to enjoy leisure – are often irreconcilable. How time is allocated between these different spheres of social activity not only affects the well-being of individuals and families (Higgins, Duxbury, and Johnson 2004; Duxbury and Higgins 2002, 2003), it also influences the level of equality between people, especially between men and women, in a society (Bosch 1999; Rubery, Smith, and Fagan 1998). Control over working time is about choice and power.

For these reasons, working time has long been "at the heart of political and social debate" (Anxo et al. 2004b, 1), as well as the subject of legal regulation. Since the mid-nineteenth century, laws imposing limits on the length of the workday have been a central and constant demand of the labour movement, with employers resisting these attempts to interfere with their prerogative to control working time. In the nineteenth century, the first legislation limiting hours of work was designed to protect women and child workers in specific industries (Conaghan 2006; Tucker 1990). Almost immediately after the First World War, the International Labour Organization adopted its first convention, which established the eight-hour day and the forty-eight-hour week as general standards for industry (ILO 2005, 2-6).[1] Despite these early demands, the form of legal regulation did not shift from protecting specific groups of workers to establishing general working-time standards until the end of the Second World War. Through a blend of legislation and collective bargaining, a standard working day of eight hours and working week of forty hours – with companion entitlements to overtime,

time-off work, and paid vacations – emerged across industrialized countries at the end of the Second World War and took root during the 1950s and 1960s (Bosch 1999; Campbell 1997, 201). These norms balanced protection for employees against flexibility for employers, and they were based on a division of labour for household and caring responsibilities in which women did this work on an unpaid basis (Mutari and Figart 2000, 39).

Over the past twenty years, there has been a profound change in the distribution of paid working time; the standard workday and workweek are in decline. According to Deborah Figart and Lonnie Golden (2000, 2), "A social organization of time that served to synchronize hours of work and leisure for much of the 20th century is gradually disintegrating. Working time is becoming more differentiated and variable, triggered by a combination of economic, technological, and cultural influences." The growing diversification, decentralization, and individualization of hours that people work has resulted in increasing conflict between employers' business interests and workers' needs and preferences and poses challenges for gender equality in the division of labour (ILO 2005, 9). Control over working time is prominent in public policy once again.

In this chapter I examine a central component of working-time regimes – the legal regulation of daily and weekly hours of paid employment – and how the federal working-time regime reinforces a gendered division of paid and unpaid labour and contributes to increased stress experienced by working mothers in particular.[2] I begin by introducing the concept of working-time regime and describing its central elements. The focus in this section is on the legal rules that regulate daily and weekly working time, and the goal is to demonstrate how these apparently gender-neutral legal rules are based on a profoundly gendered division of unpaid – and especially caring – labour. In the next section, I briefly describe the key elements of the hours-of-work rules of the federal working-time regime.[3] This sketch is followed by a discussion of the distribution of paid and unpaid work, emphasizing the gendered nature of this distribution in Canada. Having set out the conceptual, legal, and empirical aspects of the federal hours-of-work regime, I turn to public policy dimensions of the lack of fit between a working-time regime that was developed in the 1960s and contemporary working-time practices. This section focuses on how flexibility and work-life balance are defined, and how public policy trade-offs are identified, measured, and evaluated. Once again, the emphasis is on the gendered nature of these trade-offs, which is further explored in a summary of the findings of a major study of family-work conflict in Canada. One of the goals of this discussion is to re-examine the persistent ways in which the dichotomy of family and work is perpetuated by the assumption that paid work and life/family are independent. I conclude the chapter by offering proposals for reconciling work and family life in a manner that promotes gender equality, a caring society, and social solidarity, and in doing so seeks to contribute to the feminist-informed discussion of how a balance between paid work, family, and life can be achieved.

Working-Time Regimes: Components and Types

The legal regulation of working time has taken three general forms: (1) laws aimed at the protection of particular groups of workers, such as women and children; (2) standardized limits on working time combined with restrictions on the scheduling of work – for instance, limits on shift work and provision for rests, breaks, and more; and (3) the regulation of "new" working-time arrangements – for instance, part-time work, temporary work, or leave provisions.[4] The different forms coexist, but one form tends to dominate the others, though which form dominates changes over time.[5]

After the Second World War, the second form prevailed in most industrialized countries in the Organisation for Economic Co-operation and Development (OECD). The standard – or norm – of working time was "40 hours per week, distributed in equal daily segments over the daytime hours from Monday to Friday and joined with paid annual leave and public holiday entitlements equivalent to several weeks per year" (Campbell 1997, 201). The standard employment relationship, which consists of full-time, full-year continuous employment providing both a family wage and a range of social entitlements, stabilized this working-time regime. It was based on a male-breadwinner–dependent wife model for allocating time between paid work and leisure (Conaghan 2002; Fudge and Vosko 2001; Supiot 2001). This working-time norm was supported by a web of regulation at the national and international levels that imposed limits on normal hours of work and premiums for long or unsocial – evening, night, and weekend – work (Supiot 2001). As Deirdre McCann (2004, 10-11) notes, these regulations "stemmed partly from a concern for the needs of workers for both health and safety protection and for adequate time outside paid work, usually conceptualized as 'leisure' time in the gendered assumption that it would not involve other forms of labour."

Legally prescribed norms operate alongside voluntary and customary norms, including those derived from collective bargaining, to create a national system of regulation known as a working-time regime. There are three general types of regulation: (1) state-initiated, in which statutory regulation and state interventions are crucial; (2) negotiated regulation, in which collective agreements at the industrial and plant level dominate; and (3) market-based regulation, in which agreements on working time are reached at the enterprise or individual level (Lee 2004, 31). Although a specific form of regulation may dominate in a specific regime – for example, state-initiated in France as compared with market-based in the United States and United Kingdom – most, like the federal jurisdiction in Canada, are composed of all three. Moreover, the relationship between the legal regulation of working time and actual work hours is neither direct nor uncontroversial. Different legal approaches and divergent labour markets, as well as the prevailing institutional and regulatory framework in a country, have a profound impact on the actual hours worked by different groups of people (32).

Working-time regimes are a major influence on working-time practices. They "act to limit or extend variations in working hours for full-timers, promote or discourage part-time work and unsocial working hours, and influence the terms and conditions under which overtime, unsocial or atypical work contracts are taken" (Rubery, Smith, and Fagan 1998, 75).[6] Differences in working-time regimes lay in the specific characteristics of national institutions, the features of particular sectors, and the strategies adopted by firms and trade unions (Bosch 1995, 17). However, it is possible to classify working-time regimes by identifying the key components of a regime and looking at the relationship between them and working-time practices.

The key components of a working-time regime are (1) restrictions on the hours and scheduling of work, (2) paid time-off work, (3) leaves of absence from work, and (4) the treatment of working-time arrangements that deviate from the norm. The first component is the most complex, since it is as much involved with establishing procedures for authorizing exceptions and extensions to hours-of-work rules as it is with setting standards. Each working-time regime comprises a model or norm of standard working time and a series of carefully crafted provisions for formal variation from this norm. In addition, there is also "informal variation," which occurs when the employment relationship falls outside the scope of regulation.[7]

The working-time regime that was based on the standard employment is under increasing pressure.[8] On the demand side, the process of globalization, the intensification of competition, the spread of digital technologies, and the rise of just-in-time production and the twenty-four-hour service economy have led to the proliferation of flexible forms of working time that diverge from the standard. Standard reference points in working-time regulation, such as daily and weekly working time or the boundary between standard working time and overtime, are increasingly blurred (Bosch 1999). On the supply side, demographic changes such as the feminization of the labour force, the increasing labour force participation of women with young children, the shift to dual-earner households, and changes in the life course – for example, lifelong learning and longer life spans – have led to various working-time arrangements that do not conform to the norm (ILO 2005, 9; Anxo et al. 2004b, 2; Tergeist 1995, 10). The number of people working part-time has increased, and the range of family-related leaves to which workers are entitled has widened.

Working-time regimes have significant distributive consequences, one of the most profound of which is the relationship between working time and gender equality.[9] Using a taxonomy that focused on long working hours and high levels of unsocial hours in twelve countries in Europe in the mid-1990s, Jill Rubery, Mark Smith, and Collette Fagan (1998, 72) found a correlation between particular working-time norms and national regulatory regimes, with varying distributive effects for men and women. They discovered that although women performed the bulk of the domestic labour across Europe, the extent and degree of the inequality in women's paid work varied between countries and depended on the national working-time regime. Using a framework that emphasizes the degree of flexibility in work hours and relative gender equity in work schedules and economic roles, Deborah Figart and Ellen Mutari (2000, 851-52) identified four working-time regimes in the European Union with very different outcomes for gender equity. They found, in general, that the countries with shorter workweeks have a lower gap between men's and women's labour market behaviour (866).

Several researchers have found that divergent patterns of working time are associated with the institutional and regulatory environment in which they operate (Anxo et al. 2004a, 63-64; Jacobs and Gerson 2004, 146; Bosch 1999). Deregulation and wage inequality exacerbate the polarization (too few and too many) of hours of work (Bosch 1999). Countries with weak and ineffective statutory regulation, decentralized bargaining, and individual agreements exhibit the largest variation in working time across industries and individuals (Anxo et al. 2004a, 64). The increase in annual working time of full-time employees is particularly marked in countries where income inequalities have widened and labour markets have been deregulated. Canada is an example of such a country (Morissette and Johnson 2005; Bosch 1999, 135-37 and Table 3; Morissette, Myles, and Garnet 1994).

The Federal Working-Time Regime
Hours-of-work laws influence the supply and demand for labour in two ways: by imposing obligations on employers to pay an overtime premium once employees work beyond specified thresholds, and by establishing limits on maximum hours of work and requirements for minimum rest periods for employees. Standard workdays and workweeks function as triggers or thresholds for overtime pay. Limits on maximum hours of work and requirements for minimum rest periods prohibit employees from working hours in excess of the limits or during rest periods.

Hours of work in the federal jurisdiction are highly regulated in comparison with other jurisdictions in Canada. The Canada Labour Code, Part III, provides a standard and maximum workweek, as well as a standard workday.[10] Since the code imposes daily and weekly overtime thresholds and maximum hours of work in a week, it provides various mechanisms for injecting flexibility into these requirements and restrictions. These mechanisms are

(1) exemptions, (2) averaging or flexible scheduling, (3) permits from an official, (4) regulations that provide special rules for specific sectors, (5) emergencies, and (6) custom or practice.

There are many exemptions to hours-of-work rules in the code. Most employees of Crown corporations are covered, whereas federal public service employees are not. Managers and professionals are also exempt from overtime entitlements and limits on maximum hours of work on the grounds that they have both autonomy and bargaining power and, thus, do not need nor conform to restrictions on hours of work. There are specific regulations for many transportation industries, including railways, aviation, shipping, and trucking. Some of these regulations exempt the employees in the industry or undertaking from the hours-of-work provisions entirely. Other regulations provide specific rules for that industry or undertaking. In general, the code provides minimum standards that prevail over collective agreements. However, if employees are covered by a collective agreement, their union can authorize variations from the legislative standards in cases where the variation is permitted.

Under the federal code, the standard hours of work is eight in a day and forty in a week, and these standards function as daily and weekly thresholds for entitlement to overtime pay of one and one-half times the regular wage for every hour worked above the standard. The code provides flexibility to employers for overtime obligations by permitting overtime averaging, providing for modified work schedules, allowing work practices to prevail over legal rules in limited circumstances – switching shifts between employees – and designing special rules via regulations for specified industries. Each of these different mechanisms for varying standards is subject to different requirements and a different level or type of scrutiny, and all enable employers to reduce the cost of employing workers for long hours. Under the code, the maximum number of hours an employee is permitted to work in one week with a single employer is forty-eight. The code provides for flexibility regarding this limit through the following mechanisms or in the following circumstances: exemptions, averaging agreements, ministerial permits, emergencies, and regulations.

An individual right to refuse overtime and long hours of work in the federal jurisdiction does not match the flexibility for employers to vary the hours-of-work rules. Nor does the code provide employees much flexibility to determine their schedules or to vary their regular work hours to accommodate family obligations or education. The code does not limit the use of split shifts or unsocial hours.[11] Moreover, it does not provide for equal or comparable treatment with respect to pay or benefits of part-time work – work that is usually scheduled for fewer hours than the number usually scheduled for full-time employees.

Not only are the hours-of-work rules provided in the code very flexible but there is evidence that many employers simply ignore them. A series of evaluation studies of Part III of the code conducted in the late 1990s indicated that there was a widespread failure to comply with hours-of-work rules in the federal jurisdiction, that overtime hours were increasing, and that family-work conflict was on the rise.[12] Moreover, this finding was confirmed by the federal Labour Standards Review Commission headed by Harry Arthurs (HRSDC 2006, ch. 9). Survey data indicated that there was a high proportion of chronic overtime in the federally regulated sector. Both employers and employees reported a very high incidence of regular overtime; 45 percent of federally regulated employers and 42 percent of federally regulated employees reported workdays of longer than eight hours and workweeks that were longer than forty hours – compared with 31 percent of provincially regulated employers (HRDC 1998, 41). Moreover, a significant proportion – 24 percent – of federally regulated employers reported that the percentage of their employees working over forty hours a week had increased in the past two years (ibid.). In 2004, 21.5 percent of employees with federally regulated employers regularly worked overtime (Lowe 2005, Figures 5 and 6). Richard Chaykowski and George Slotsve (2008) found that employees in the federal jurisdiction worked on average 2.4 hours of unpaid overtime per week, compared to workers in the other Canadian jurisdictions who worked only 1.8 hours. This finding led them to conclude that enforcement of overtime pay is an area that should be addressed.

Hours of Paid and Unpaid Work in Canada

In Canada, there has been a growing diversification, decentralization, and individualization of working time. Between 1976 and 1998, the proportion of employees working thirty-five to forty hours a week declined from 65 percent of all workers to 54 percent, whereas the proportion of employees working more or fewer hours increased (Hall 1999). By the mid-1960s, the standard working week levelled off and stabilized at thirty-seven to forty hours of work over five days (Ontario, 1987, 13). During the period from 1976 to 1998, patterns of working time polarized, and the prevalence of the standard working week declined. However, recent research has revealed that long hours of work have been declining (Usalcas 2008), and this decline is "more likely to affect men's average hours since they have traditionally been more likely to work long hours" (Marshall 2009, 8).

The increasing labour force participation of women has accompanied the diversification in working-time arrangements. Men and women have very different work schedules (Sheridan, Sunter, and Divery 1996, C-6). Women are – and historically have been – far more likely than men to work short hours of employment. In 1998, 50 percent of women and just 28 percent of men worked less than thirty-five hours per week (Hall 1999, 30).[13] Men historically have, and continue to, outnumber women at the long hours end of the distribution. At least twice as many men than women worked between forty-one and forty-nine hours a week – 15 percent compared with 7 percent – and women were much less likely than men to work very long hours. In 1998, 6 percent of men and 1 percent of women worked more than sixty hours a week (ibid.). However, more recently there has been a convergence of paid work hours within dual-earner couples (Marshall 2009).

Hours worked also vary by industry and occupation. Long hours are more common in goods-producing industries – where men predominate – and short hours are more common in service-producing industries – where women are crowded (Hall 1999, 32). Trades and production workers put in the most paid overtime (36). Type of occupation also accounts for some of the variation in hours worked; long hours are common among managers. In 1998, 38 percent of managers worked more than forty hours a week, with 14 percent putting in between forty-nine and fifty-nine hours, and another 8 percent working sixty hours or more (33). Not surprisingly, men are much more likely to be managers than are women. Between 1998 and 2004, the percentage of male managers in the labour force ranged from 5.8 to 5.4, whereas the percentage of women managers in the labour force ranged from 3.2 to 3.1 (Statistics Canada 2004b). Professionals also work long hours; nearly 25 percent worked more than forty hours a week. However, professionals were less likely than managers to work very long hours – only 4 percent worked over sixty hours – and more likely than managers to work less than thirty-five hours a week – 38 percent.[14]

Despite the diversification in paid working hours, the average length of daily hours of paid work has increased considerably between 1986 and 2005, from 506 minutes to 536 minutes (Turcotte 2007, 5). Moreover, the average length of the working day has major implications for time spent each day with family members, which dropped an average of forty-three minutes between 1986 and 2005. The increase in the average number of hours spent in work during the typical workday is the factor that contributed most to the decline in time spent with family between 1986 and 2005, accounting for 39 percent of the decrease in family time.

However, behind the averages is a gendered division of household labour. Although men and women increasingly share this labour, including caring for children, women in heterosexual couples continue to devote appreciably more time to parenting than men. Women workers living with a male spouse and a child under five spent an average of forty-seven minutes more each day with family members than did men with a similar family structure. By contrast, there was no significant difference in the time spent with family members between lone-women and lone-men parents; however, women constitute three-quarters of lone parents. Overall, the increase in women's employment explains the decline in the amount of time spent with family (Turcotte 2007).

The gendered division of labour within the family is linked with women's paid employment. Despite the huge increase in women's labour force participation since the 1960s, women's share of unpaid work has remained the same, at about two-thirds of the total.[15] This domestic work includes caring for children and other family members, such as elders; housework; and emotional labour. In 2001, women were twice as likely as men to spend at least thirty hours a week on cooking and cleaning or on childcare, and twice as many men as women say they do no domestic work at all. Women also spend more time caring for elderly parents than do men, and they are more likely than men to reduce their hours of paid work to accommodate caring responsibilities (Jenson 2004b, 14). Unpaid labour is distributed unequally even when both men and women are working full-time. On average, women work two more weeks a year than men do when both paid and unpaid work are combined.[16]

Although there has been a trend toward equal sharing in household labour, the change in the division of labour does not match women's labour force participation (Marshall 2006). Moreover, the imbalance in the division of household labour is linked to marital conflict, reduced physical and mental well-being, and reduced wages for women. The average daily time spent on paid work, housework, and other unpaid household duties – including childcare – for those aged twenty-five to fifty-four has increased steadily over the past twenty years, rising from 8.2 hours in 1986 to 8.8 hours in 2005 (ibid.). This change is a result of the increase in paid labour, which rose from an average of 4.7 hours per day in 1986 to 5.4 hours in 2005. In all family types, daily participation rates for housework continued to be significantly higher for women than for men. However, a women's income in a heterosexual couple influences both the time she and her male partner spend on housework. When women in such couples have an income of $100,000 or higher, the division of paid labour and housework between heterosexual couples is likely to be split equally (ibid.).

Even though dual-earner heterosexual couples working full-time both contribute eight hours of total labour each day, the men in such households are more likely than the women to spend more time at a job (6.6 versus 5.9 hours) and less time on housework (1.4 versus 2.1 hours). Not only were the women in these households more likely to do more of the housework, they also felt the most responsibility for anticipating, planning, and organizing what needed to be done (Marshall 2006).

The proportion of women working part-time is twice as high as the proportion of men (Cooke-Reynolds and Zukewich 2004, 24; Comfort, Johnson, and Wallace 2003, 18-22). The growth in the part-time workforce outpaced the growth in the full-time workforce by a ratio of three to one between the late 1970s and the 1990s. Part-time employees represented 20 percent of the labour force in 1999 (Comfort, Johnson, and Wallace 2003, 10). Although one-third of part-time employees work short hours because they cannot find full-time jobs, the majority report working part-time by choice. One of the most frequently cited reasons by women for working part-time is family responsibilities. For over thirty years, women have consistently represented 70 percent of the part-time workforce (ibid.). And although the quality of part-time jobs differs – indeterminate and ongoing part-time jobs provide more benefits than do temporary ones – full-time work is much more likely to provide a greater array of benefits than any type of part-time work (Zeytinoglu and Cooke 2005, 56-57). The data suggest that the flexibility that women gain through part-time work may create costs in terms of job quality (Comfort, Johnson, and Wallace 2003, 10).

Public Policy and the Legal Regulation of Working Time
Much has changed in the Canadian labour market since the key features of federal law regulating hours of work were put in place in the mid-1960s (Jenson 2004b; Fudge and Vosko 2001). There is a growing misfit between the legal standard and working-time practices. The public policy question is how to respond. In a 2004 policy brief, the OECD (2004, 6) cautioned that

> a first lesson for policymaking is that working time is at the nexus of a number of policy concerns, including achieving strong economic growth, an inclusive labour market that supports high employment rates and conditions that allow employees to achieve a balance between work and the rest of their lives. This means that policymakers should avoid focusing narrowly on how work hours affect a single policy objective and be alert to potential trade-offs. For example, the flip-side of the growth advantage associated with an increase in per capita hours is the "time crunch" faced by working parents and the possibility that a "long hours culture" is undermining the work-life balance in certain professions. Similarly, flexibility in working hours may be detrimental to family life if it takes the form of non-standard work schedules dictated by the logic of just-in-time staffing for the "24/7" economy, rather than an increased chance for workers to select the work schedule that best reconciles their work with their family life.

To determine the policy trade-offs, it is important first to identify the policy interests at stake, and then it is necessary to assess the benefits and the costs of different policies. This is not a simple task. There are questions of the definition and the meaning of terms, as well as issues relating to the identification of relevant interests and principles involved regarding working time. For example, the meaning of "flexibility" is not at all clear. The term denotes a wide variety of practices, even when it comes to flexible working-time arrangements, and which arrangements are considered to be flexible depends on both perspective and interest (Fredman 2005; Messenger 2004b, 153; Picchio 1998; Bosch 1995, 38). Moreover, family-work reconciliation and work-life balance policies that are primarily directed at women will not change the opportunity costs associated with women's choice to care so long as men can choose not to care. Thus, policies that enhance individual choice need to attend to the broader structures of employment and social provisioning and the processes of socialization, as well as the power imbalance between men and women. Assessing the effects of different policies is also complex; costs and benefits can be direct and indirect, measured on a short-term or long-term basis, and they can be distributed in various ways.

Working-time flexibility and achieving a better balance between work and life are the issues that consistently dominate the contemporary working-time debate (OECD 2004). It is important to decode what these terms mean.

Flexibility

There has been an increased interest in the flexible scheduling of work by both employers and employees.[17] However, the use of the common term "flexibility" to express both employers' and employees' pressures for changes to the working-time standards does not mean that their interests are identical or that the range of policies used to make paid working time more flexible are compatible. Campbell (1997, 209) argues that

> a more scrupulous examination ... reveals that they involve two opposed conceptions of flexibility. For employers the common theme has been the desire to increase the flexibility of the supply of labour in order to meet the perceived constraints of the enterprise ... For employees, on the other hand, the common theme has been a desire to secure greater flexibility from the employing enterprise in order to respond to the constraints in the individual's extra-enterprise activities and responsibilities.[18]

The question of flexibility often comes down to the issue of control: who gets to choose how hours of work are scheduled. Laws and policies influence not only who gets to make the choices but also the range of choices that can be made. Different choices involve different trade-offs.

In the 1980s, pressures for flexibility from employers mounted – they wanted arrangements for the variable distribution of working hours. These are methods of organizing working time that allow for its adjustment in accordance with variations in the volume of an undertaking's activities over a certain period, and by extending hours over their normal length on certain days and shortening them on other days so that the total length of the working hours over the period does not exceed certain limits.[19] Transposed into legal form, according to International Labour Organization researcher Deidre McCann (2004, 12), "'flexibility' has involved the relaxation of restrictions on varying and individualizing working time schedules and on work during unsocial hours introduced with the goal of increasing capital utilization and extending opening hours."

Overtime hours, the cost of which was reduced through the introduction of reference periods over which overtime premiums and working-time limits can be averaged, have been very popular among certain employers. Other employers prefer to use part-time work to increase flexibility. Part-time work tends to be associated with lower wages, fewer benefits, and less opportunity for career advancement (Fagan 2004, 140). Manufacturing, which is predominantly male, and retail, which is predominantly female, appear to follow different paths in scheduling working time. In manufacturing, which is capital intensive, hours of work are extending, whereas in retail, where increased costs are incurred through longer operating hours, cheaper part-time work is substituted for more expensive working-time arrangements (Bosch and Tergeist 1995, 211-12). These industry-specific forms of flexibility have profound gender impacts.

In the 1990s, employees' preference for increased flexibility to balance work and personal and family life reached the public policy agenda. The increased labour force participation rate of women with young children, the growth in dual-earner and lone-parent households, the aging population, the declining birth rate, and the need for longer education and lifelong learning have led to a demand for increased diversity in working hours. In part, this demand for a variety of different working-time arrangements has led to the increase in non-standard work, especially part-time work (Fredman 2005; Fagan 2004). But the problem with non-standard work as a solution to the time crunch is that much non-standard work is poorly paid and lacks benefits, which makes it difficult for these workers, the majority of whom are women, to be economically self-sustaining (Fredman 2005; Fudge 2005). The difficulty in combining paid work with personal needs and family demands has led to increased stress, and research has begun to reveal the costs to individuals, employers, and society in general – lower fertility and higher health care costs – of the conflict between work and life (OECD 2005; Higgins, Duxbury, and Johnson 2004; Duxbury and Higgins 2002, 2003). Working-time flexibility for employees is about work-life balance.

"Flexibility" is also used to describe forms of regulation that allow for a menu of working-time arrangements and that involve a range of techniques – other than command and control – for establishing standards and enforcing the norms. Individual opt-out and collective derogations are legal techniques of providing flexibility to deviate from general standards and restrictions. The legal requirement to prepare risk-management plans that replace legal rules is an example of a more flexible form of regulation.[20] The Canadian government is on record at the International Labour Organization as wanting more flexible legal norms and more flexible forms of regulating working time. Although the government reaffirmed its commitment to protecting workers, it claims that the provisions of Conventions No. 1 and 30, which provide the standard eight-hour workday and forty-eight-hour workweek, are too restrictive to meet the needs of employees for flexible and varied work arrangements (ILO 2005, 87). However, the difficulty in balancing flexibility with protection is that as working time becomes more flexible, there is a risk that working hours will actually become longer, since they can no longer be so easily monitored (Bosch 1999, 148). Thus, there is a strong possibility that employer-driven flexibility and regulatory flexibility may exacerbate work-life conflict.

Work-Life Balance

Work-life policies build upon the family-work and family-friendly policies that began to be popular in the 1980s. In the late 1990s, the term "work-life" replaced "family-work" to signal that conflicts between work and life can potentially affect all workers, not just caregivers and family members (Brady 2008; Johnson, Lero, and Rooney 2001, 3). The increased attention to the social, medical, and work consequences of the stress resulting from work-life conflict helps to explain the broader focus (Higgins, Duxbury, and Johnson 2004; Duxbury and Higgins 2002, 2003). So too is the growing recognition of the need to develop working-time policies that are attentive both to life cycle and to the need for lifelong learning. The health and safety of workers was the initial rationale that was offered for limits on the hours of work (ILO 2005, 10), and it continues to feature as a component of work-life policies. However, the policy focus is increasingly upon assessing the extent and costs of work-life conflict. Linda Duxbury and Chris Higgins, who directed a major research project exploring work-life conflict and its costs in Canada, conceptualize work-life conflict

> to include role overload (RO) (having too much to do and too little time to do it in) as well as role interference (when incompatible demands make it difficult, if not impossible, for employees to perform all their roles well). Role interference, in turn, can be divided into two factors: family to work interference (FTW) and work to family interference (WTF). In the first case, interference occurs when family-role responsibilities hinder performance at work ... In the second case, interference arises when work demands make it harder for an employee to fulfill their family responsibilities. (Duxbury and Higgins 2001, 3)[21]

There is now a growing body of reliable data of different kinds – detailed surveys, shorter questionnaires, qualitative studies – that demonstrates the costs of the growing conflict between work and life. Research on the health implications of working long hours has revealed that increasing hours of work is associated with greater cigarette and alcohol consumption, weight gain, and depression (Sheilds 2000, 49). Work-life conflict, especially role overload and work-to-family interference, results in a decline in physical and mental health, lower job satisfaction and commitment, and an increase in absenteeism and employee turnover. The evidence is not only that this conflict has a detrimental impact on the quality of life for workers and their families but also that employers and society are bearing the costs of this conflict (Higgins, Duxbury, and Johnson 2004; Duxbury and Higgins 2002, 2003). There is also growing concern that work-life conflict is contributing to the declining fertility rate in Canada, which has long-term implications for the country's ability to sustain economic growth and prosperity (Fredman 2005; OECD 2005, 18).

The goal of work-life balance policies is to institutionalize a form of family-friendly flexibility that enables workers to allocate their time between paid and unpaid work to meet their individual needs and domestic responsibilities (ILO 2005, 10). Family-friendly flexibility makes it easier for individuals and households to combine family life and working life by providing employees with the right to change their working hours to accommodate changes in family composition and to adjust to sudden changes in the family timetable. Key components of work-life balance policies are leave for family responsibilities and flexible working-time arrangements that allow employees to control the hours that they work.

Policy Trade-Offs: The Place of Gender Equality

A range of policy goals – economic growth, worker health, inclusive employment, and family-work balance – informs working-time regulations. In addition, a gender-sensitive analysis, attentive to the need to provide equal employment opportunities to women and men and to value unpaid care work, is also a crucial element in public policy. In fact, the OECD (2005, 11) identifies the promotion of gender equality as a key component of family-friendly policies. How these goals are ranked in importance will shape how the policy trade-offs are evaluated. The period for assessing the impact of the policies (short or long term) as well as the level of analysis at which they are assessed (individual or societal enterprise) will also influence the evaluation.

It is useful to identify and to evaluate some of the trade-offs involved in a specific policy. Flexibility to use overtime and long hours is a good example. In the short term, increasing working hours moderately and making them more flexible is likely to enhance the productivity of an individual enterprise. However, using excessively long hours is apt to have the opposite effect. There is substantial empirical evidence demonstrating that reductions in excessively long hours of work – over forty-eight hours per week – have resulted in substantial productivity gains (Anxo et al. 2004a, 205-6).

Moreover, a policy of extending hours of work and reducing overtime payments is also likely either to reinforce or exacerbate inequality between women and men in the division of labour between paid and unpaid work and in control over economic resources. This is because increasing limits on maximum hours of work and reducing the overtime premium through averaging agreements is likely to drive up employer demand for average overtime hours per employee – because of the reduced short-run marginal cost of overtime – and make working weeks and schedules more unpredictable (Gonas 2002, 63). This policy "runs the risk of actually making workplaces more family unfriendly than friendly, thus harming worker 'utility' on the balance" (Rubery, Smith, and Fagan 1998, 72). Moreover, since women, who continue to shoulder the heaviest burden of caring responsibilities, have a stronger preference than men do for flexible working hours, they are "vulnerable in relation to employer-driven flexibility and changing work hours" (Gonas 2002, 63). Part-time employment continues to be less likely to provide employment-related benefits than full-time work, but it continues to be disproportionately performed by women (Zeytinoglu and Cooke 2005, 56-57; Comfort, Johnson, and Wallace 2003, 10). The data suggest that the flexibility women gain through part-time work may bear costs in terms of job quality. Those with lower-status jobs are less likely to have either family-friendly work environments or access to employee benefits plans that cover some of the cost of needed services (CAALL 2002, 27).

Combined with the unequal gender division of labour in the household and family, employer-driven working-time flexibility will likely reinforce gendered and unequal patterns of working time that, in turn, will probably reinforce occupational segregation and labour market segmentation (Gonas 2002, 63; Rubery, Smith, and Fagan 1998, 72).[22] These kinds of policies are also likely to reinforce a declining fertility rate and create barriers to women's full participation in the labour force, which undermines economic growth in the long term (Fredman 2005; OECD 2005). Furthermore, family-work reconciliation policies that simply focus on individual choices to work less place the onus on workers to use family-friendly policies, even when doing so can endanger one's job, career, and financial security (Brady 2008; Jacobs and Gerson 2004, 180).

Balancing Work, Family, and Lifestyle

A major empirical study of work-life balance by Linda Duxbury and Chris Higgins, which produced a series of four reports, probes the individual and social consequences of work-life conflict.[23] Comparing their 1991 samples to those of 2001, Duxbury and Higgins found that working time had increased. Only one in ten respondents in 1991 worked over fifty hours in a week but, by 2001, one in four did. Simultaneously, the proportion of employees working between thirty-five and thirty-nine hours declined from 48 to 27 percent (Duxbury and Higgins 2002, 47). In 2001, 30 percent of the sample worked paid overtime, and men were more likely than women to work overtime (51). Forty-seven percent of the respondents perceived that they could refuse overtime if they wanted to. Since perceived control over one's time has been a key predictor of stress and work-life conflict, the fact that just under one-half of those working for large employers are able to control the amount of time they devote to paid overtime is very troubling (51). The proportion of employees who performed unpaid overtime almost doubled, from one in four of the respondents to one in two. The responses indicated that managers and professionals have a particularly difficult time meeting work demands within a regular workweek.

Duxbury and Higgins's study confirms that the time men spend on child-care has increased since 1991 to the extent that the time spent by women and men was almost equal in 2001. However, in 2001, the majority of both men and women indicated that women had the primary household responsibility for childcare (Duxbury and Higgins 2002, 64). This is an important finding, since "responsibility for a role has been found to have a higher positive association with stress than has time spent in role-related activities" (ibid.). Duxbury and Higgins also found that employees who have the greatest need for flexible work arrangements – that is, parents and employees with eldercare responsibilities – do not have access to them (ibid.). Managers, professionals, and private sector employees are more likely to have access to and to use flexi-time arrangements than non-professional employees.

The percentage of the workforce with high role overload has increased over the past decade; 58 percent of the respondents in the 2001 survey reported high levels of role overload – an increase of 11 percent over what was observed in the 1991 sample (Duxbury and Higgins 2003, 63). The data indicate that work-to-family interference was a real problem for one in four Canadians working for large employers; 38 percent of Canadians reported moderate levels of interference in 2001 (ibid.). High levels of caregiver strain – the stress involved in providing care to assist a disabled or elderly dependant – was reported by one in four of the respondents (69). Moreover, the evidence is clear that employed Canadians with dependant care responsibilities have the greatest difficulty in balancing work and family responsibility. Not surprisingly, women are more likely than men to report high levels of role overload and high caregiver strain; they devote more hours per week than men to activities such as child and eldercare, and they are more likely to have responsibility for those tasks (71-73).

Job type is associated with work-life conflict, although different types of jobs encounter different types of conflict. Managers and professionals who have higher demands at work are more likely than those in other jobs to experience high levels of role overload, whereas those in other jobs were likely to report higher levels of caregiver strain due to the financial stresses associated with eldercare (Duxbury and Higgins 2003, 75). When job type is taken into account, and work-life conflict is broken into its component parts, many of the gender differences in work-life conflict disappear, suggesting that "many of the gender differences in work-life conflict may be attributed to the fact that women are typically compressed into a different set of jobs than men" (xiv). However, managers and professionals were in better mental and physical health than were workers in other jobs, and Duxbury and Higgins suggest that the sense of control that managers and professional enjoy accounts for this difference. Women report higher levels of perceived stress, burnout, and depression than men, which indicates that such differences may have more to do with gender differences in socialization than in either work or non-work demands.

The study also sought to identify the major predictors of role overload, work-to-family interference, family-to-work interference, and caregiver strain, as well as the key factors that place employees at risk of the various forms of work-life conflict.[24] Duxbury and Higgins explored the demographic conditions and life circumstances of employees and examined the link between workplace culture and work-life conflict. In particular, they focused on both work or family cultural expectations in which employees are expected to put work ahead of family to advance and the culture of hours that refers to expectations that associate security and promotion with long hours of work. They found that work culture is the most powerful predictor of role overload for both men and women – work or family and long-hours cultures were strongly associated with role overload (Duxbury and Higgins 2005, 30-32). The amount of time spent in unpaid overtime a month plus the total number of hours spent in work per week key predictors of role overload for both men and women (35). However, the most important predictors of caregiver strain and family-to-work interference are associated with the family domain – family type and adult role responsibilities (33).

Organizational culture is a key predictor of role overload, work-to-family interference, and family-to-work interference for both men and women (Duxbury and Higgins 2005, 40-42). However, family type and adult roles are predictive of role overload and work-to-family interference for women but not for men. Women with a stay-at-home spouse reported lower levels of role overload and family-to-work interference but higher levels of work-to-family interference than other women. Women in this family type manifest work-life conflict patterns that are more typically reported of men (54).

There is a common conclusion in each of the four reports: the link between hours of work and role overload, burnout, and physical and mental health problems suggests that these workloads are not sustainable over the long term (Duxbury and Higgins 2002, 63;, 2005, 59; Higgins, Duxbury, and

Johnson 2004, 52). A clear contributing factor to role overload is the increased use of overtime. Non-professional employees fear that their refusal to work overtime will lead to job loss, while professionals worry that their careers will not progress (Higgins, Duxbury, and Johnson 2004, 52). Duxbury and Higgins (2003, 79) recommend that employers adopt measures to provide employees with flexibility in working-time arrangements and to increase employees control over their working time. Specifically, they suggest that employees be given the right to refuse overtime work; to take time off in lieu of overtime pay; to have paid childcare leave; and to acquire the opportunity to transfer from full-time to part-time work, which would provide pro-rated benefits, full seniority, and the right to return to full-time status.

Working-Time Regimes and Gender Equality

There is a gap between the working-time schedules that individuals need and prefer and those that they are required to work (Anxo et al. 2004a, 195). Employees want greater control over their working time. They also want a variety of work schedules: research indicates that employees' preferences are shaped by income, household composition, and gender. High-income employees would prefer to work fewer hours, whereas lower-income employees want to work more. Households in which there are two working adults desire fewer hours of work, whereas men who have an unemployed spouse prefer more. Married women with care responsibilities for younger children would prefer shorter work hours, whereas lone-parent mothers are willing to work more hours because they need the income (OECD 2005, 184; Drolet and Morissette 1997).

Employers also want greater control over scheduling working hours – they want to be able to arrange longer hours of work and to reduce their overtime costs. They have not voluntarily embraced work-life balance or family-friendly policies. The costs and benefits for employers of such policies "is a function of i) the difficulty with which (skilled) workers can be replaced and ii) how important it is to these that these workers have family-friendly support" (OECD 2005, 206). Moreover, policy makers in Canada "are hesitant to pass additional costs to Canadian employers in [the] face of competition with the United States" (ibid.).

At the federal level, the United States had adopted a market model for the regulation of its working time.[25] The Fair Labor Standards Act, the primary federal legislation setting nationwide employment standards, does not impose daily or weekly limits on numbers of hours worked. Instead, it imposes a standard workweek of forty hours, requiring that hours in excess of that standard be paid at a premium of time and a half the employee's regular wage. Although employers are not allowed to reduce the cost of overtime through averaging provisions or compressed workweeks, there are extremely broad exemptions to the overtime provisions.[26] Given such light regulation and very low union density, it is not surprising that a growing portion of employees in the United States work very long hours (Jacobs and Gerson 2004, 39). There is also a high degree of polarization in working time (163-65). Women continue to bear the brunt of family responsibilities, and this translates into the type of jobs they have and the income they earn (167-68).

One problem with this market model for regulating working time is that it shifts the costs of flexibility that enhances employer control over the scheduling of work to employees. Although employers bear some of the costs of excessive and unsocial hours through lost productivity, reduced morale and commitment, and increased absenteeism and benefits costs, they are able to shift a great deal of the costs onto workers, their families, and public services. As a group of experts on the regulation of working time has recently noted, "Estimates of costs vary, depending on whether the policy measures are considered as a short-term consumption or a long-term form of investment, and also whether the costs are calculated from a macro-economic societal level or from a enterprise perspective" (Anxo et al. 2004a, 207). They also note that, since the benefits of these policies are not reaped by enterprises alone, their cost should not be borne exclusively by enterprises but shared among government, employers, and workers (ibid.).

Another problem is that the market model has a very thin notion of choice. Choice is regarded as an endogenous property of free will, not shaped by the opportunities available and prevailing cultural norms. Women who choose to take on family responsibilities bear the burden of accommodating their home and work roles. Yet policy discourse has barely begun to register ideas about men's greater involvement in family life. As long as men can choose not to do domestic labour, women will have no choice but to do it, and occupations and employment will continue to be structured in ways that limit women's choices (Olson 2002; Probert 1997). Unless work-life balance policies address the structural sources of the time divide, they will continue to distribute the negative consequences of the choice to care disproportionately on women (Brady 2008; Jacobs and Gerson 2004, 180). The real freedom to choose paid work requires that a comparable value be attached to care independent of preference gains (Lewis and Giullari 2005, 90). As Rosemary Crompton (2006, 209) explains, "The gendered allocation of domestic work is the outcome of both material and normative factors."

Europe has taken a different approach to regulating working time, one that continues to impose limits on hours of work and provides greater flexibility for employees. The basic directive on the organization of working time stipulates minimum daily (eleven hours) and weekly (twenty-four hours) rest periods, and a maximum workweek (forty-eight hours). Flexibility for employers is provided through averaging agreements as well as individual and collective derogations, which are subject to time limits.[27]Annual paid leave must amount to at least four weeks. Moreover, the part-time work directive provides for parity in treatment of full-time and part-time work, as well as greater flexibility for employees to schedule working time.[28] Part-time employees are not to be treated in a less favourable manner than full-time employees unless the different treatment can be justified on objective grounds. Moreover, employers are obliged to give consideration to requests to transfer from full-time to part-time work and vice versa.

In theory, in Canada, the federal working-time regime falls midway between the market model of the United States and the European "social" model. Although the Canada Labour Code, Part III, regulates standard working time, it does little either to provide employees with access to flexible working time or to ensure that part-time work is treated comparably to full-time work. Moreover, in practice, the federal regime is moving closer to a market model, since many employers simply do not comply with the legislation (HRSDC 2006, ch. 9).

The hours-of-work rules for Canada's national infrastructure were established in the late 1960s. A standard forty-hour week and eight-hour day were combined with a limit of forty-eight hours per week, and employers were provided with flexibility through a range of averaging and excess-hour mechanisms. However, much has changed in the labour market over the past forty years. The legal regime has adapted to the changing demographics of the workforce by providing workers with job-protected leaves to accommodate family responsibilities. But these provisions were simply grafted on to the old working-time norms, and they have tended to reinforce the traditional division of labour between men and women for caring responsibilities (Fudge 2005). The drift toward a market model has exacerbated work-life conflict and has contributed to a gendered polarization in the distribution of paid working time.

One of the key elements in any policy to develop a more equitable distribution of paid and unpaid labour is to shift paid working-time norms in a direction that better accommodates and values socially important care work. Thus, it is important to revise hours-of-work laws that were devised for a gender contract based on a male breadwinner–dependent female caregiver model. Focusing on the federal jurisdiction, the standard workweek that functions as the overtime threshold should remain at forty hours. Overtime hours should be severely restricted – employees should be permitted to work only up to one hundred hours of overtime per year, and these overtime hours should not be transferred between employees. Employees should be entitled to choose between overtime pay at time and one-half the regular wage rate or time off at a rate of an hour and one-half for every hour of overtime worked. To give employers additional flexibility, workers could be entitled to another hundred hours of overtime per employee; however, the employer would be required to provide time off – at a rate of an hour and one-half for every hour of overtime worked – instead of overtime pay. These proposals would simplify the hours-of-work rules, since there would be no need for excess-hours permits or agreements to average excess hours.

It is important that the occupational exclusions should be repealed; not only do they lead to time-consuming demarcation disputes – the question of managerial status is a perennial problem – but they also promote a culture of long hours. Other than corporate officers, all managers should be covered by hours-of-work rules and overtime, and the onus should be on the employer to justify the exclusion of any particular manager. Professional employees should also be covered by hours-of-work rules and overtime provisions, subject only to professional responsibilities.

It is also important to provide employees with greater control over their working schedules. The right to refuse overtime goes some way toward achieving this goal. However, there is also a pressing need to improve the terms and conditions of part-time work. The timehas come to require employers to provide part-time workers with treatment comparable to full-time workers.[29] Part-time workers should be entitled to pro-rated benefits or payment in lieu of benefits at the employee's choice, and there should be no minimum weekly or annual hours threshold for this entitlement.[30] After thirty hours in a week, part-time employees should be entitled to the same benefits as full-time employees. Provisions facilitating part-time work and transitions between part-time and full-time employment are another important consideration (Fredman 2005). Instead of beginning with a full-fledged right to have the request accommodated by the employer, as is the case in the Netherlands (Burri 2006), it might be useful to follow Britain's example and begin with a right to have the employer consider the request (Collins 2005; Croucher and Kellier 2005).

Individual opt-outs from hours-of-work standards and limits should not be permitted because the evidence suggests that they dilute the regulation of working time and do not counteract the culture of long hours (Barnard, Deakin, and Hobbs 2003). Not only is it difficult to ensure that the agreement is based on the voluntary choice of the employee, but individual derogations from limits on excess hours make a mockery of any attempt to combat the culture of long hours (ibid.; Conaghan 2002). Variation either by the bargaining agent of the affected employees or a majority of the affected employees should be permitted, subject to an individual employee's right to refuse excess hours.

These proposals only begin to touch the surface of designing working-time policies and laws that are more sensitive to, and compatible with, the changing life cycle of Canadians. A life-cycle approach would also consider how to make paid working time more compatible with education, training, caring for elders, and phased-in retirement. Likewise, these proposals are based on four assumptions. First, caring is necessary and valuable labour for individuals, families, and society in general (Fudge 2005; Fudge and Cossman 2002). Second, caring will continue to be conducted primarily within a broad range of differently composed families and households because caring is essential to identity formation and a relational activity that is impossible fully to commodify (Lewis and Giulliari 2005). Third, caring is "coded rather than gendered in any essential sense," since men who have to – or choose to – assume a major caring role also face problems in developing their careers (Crompton 2002, 549). Fourth, changing men's roles is "necessary but not sufficient for achieving a true balance between work and family life in dual earner societies" (Crompton 2006, 217). Thus, greater control over working time through legislative mandates would make a major contribution to the recognition of the interdependence of employment, family, and life.

Notes

This chapter is based on a report titled "Control over Working Time and Work-Life Balance: A Detailed Analysis of the Canada Labour Code, Part III," prepared for the Federal Labour Standards Review Commission and submitted in February 2006.

1 The Hours of Work (Industry) Convention, 1919 (No. 1).
2 This chapter does not consider self-employment, though there is evidence that increasing numbers of women take up own-account self-employment to better balance the need to earn an income and fulfill domestic responsibilities (Fudge 2006).
3 Regulation of working time is divided between the federal and provincial governments in Canada, with federal jurisdiction confined to federally regulated undertakings such as banks, telecommunications, and transportation. This jurisdiction was selected because the Canada Labour Code, Part III, provides extensive regulation of daily and weekly working time, and it has recently been subject to review by an independent commission.
4 This typology is based on Bosch's classification (1999, 131-33) of International Labour Organization working-time conventions into four groups; I have collapsed two of his groups to make the second of my categories.
5 The first form of regulation of hours of work was introduced in the United Kingdom in 1833 to restrict the working hours of women in factories (Lee 2004). In Canada, the 1880s factory legislation restricted the hours of work of women in manufacturing and, in the 1930s, legislation restricting working time for women and children was extended to men. After the Second World War, across the country, legislation restricting the number of hours of work in a week and providing for annual vacations as well as general holidays was gradually enacted. Although British Columbia had legislation providing for maternity leave as early as 1921, most jurisdictions in Canada did not follow suit until the 1960s; it was not until 1971, after the unemployment insurance scheme began to provide maternity benefits, that such leave became universal. In the 1980s, attention shifted to parental leave and part-time work (Brennan 2000).
6 This claim is based on empirical research undertaken by the European Commission's network of experts on women's employment and covers working-time practices in the twelve countries that were members of the European Union in 1994.
7 Iain Campbell (1997, 201) explains that

> the generalization of a norm of standard working time does not mean that everyone, or even a majority of the economically active population, must work according to the norm. Variation can arise in two main ways – either formally or informally. Formal variation arises on the platform provided by the model of standard working time, and it represents the second fundamental component in the standardization of

working-time arrangements. It occurs as a result of provisions for deviation from the standard through leave, flextime arrangements, overtime, short-time working, work in unsocial hours, shift systems and non-standard employment contracts. Informal variation, by contrast, arises in the gaps in the regulatory system.

8   Rubery, Smith, and Fagan (1998, 91) identify "three types of pressures for the restructuring of working time ... to increase competitiveness, to reduce unemployment and to reconstruct the employment contract to make it more compatible with the trend towards dual-earner families."

9   Mutari and Figart (2001, 39) define gender equity as "a similar distribution of men and women across possible work schedules, along with higher levels of women's labour force participation and a relatively narrow wage gap. In addition, long hours jobs should be kept to a minimum so that breadwinners can be caregivers." Rubery, Smith, and Fagan (1998, 72) define equity in terms of the time allocation between the sexes and the time allocation between wage and non-wage work for both sexes.

10 Canada Labour Code, R.S. 1985, c. L-2, Part III.

11 The code prohibits night work only for those employees under the age of seventeen.

12 One report concluded that the survey supported "the view that non-compliance with the Code is widespread in a number of areas, particularly for normal hours of work and severance pay provisions. Lack of awareness may be a major driving force behind non-compliance with the Code, but there are also indications that deliberate non-compliance occurs for a small number of firms" (HRDC 1997, 44).

13 In part, this difference is because women's absence rate is almost twice that of men's.

14 Managers and professionals were the least likely to work paid overtime but the most likely to work unpaid overtime (Hall 1999, 36). Managers and professionals in most jurisdictions in Canada are excluded from the legal provisions pertaining to overtime pay.

15 Statistics Canada (2000, 111). Women with children are still less likely to be employed than women without children, and women who are lone parents are less likely than mothers in two-parent families to be employed.

16 Freeze (2001), reporting on *Statistics Canada General Social Survey: Time Use* (November 1999), http://www.statscan.gc.ca/.

17 For example, "an overriding finding" that emerged from a recent study of federal labour standards was that "employers and workers expressed a general desire for more flexibility in federally regulated workplaces to address workplace change" (HRDC 2000, 41).

18 Employers tend to want flexibility to reduce labour costs or to schedule labour to fit the needs of the operation in changing, competitive, and increasingly global markets. Employees tend to want more flexibility to design their own work schedules, and the labour force is increasingly heterogeneous in terms of preferences for scheduling working time.

19 This technique is known as "averaging" in most jurisdictions across Canada, although in Quebec it is known as "staggering."

20 A Canadian example of this type of flexibility is in the railway sector.

21 Duxbury and Higgins use a child's illness preventing attendance at work as an example of family-to-work interference and long hours preventing attendance at a family function as work-to-family interference.

22 Leave policies can also be designed either to reinforce or challenge the traditional gendered division of unpaid care labour provided by members of a household (Fredman 2005).

23 The empirical research spanned two decades. In 1989-1990, 25,000 Canadians were surveyed on issues relating to work-life conflict. In 2001, the survey was replicated and received responses from more than 31,500 employees in one hundred public, private, and not-for-profit organizations – each of which had at least five hundred employees. These large firms are more likely to be unionized and have policies to deal with work-life conflict.

24 For discussion of the research methodology, see Duxbury and Higgins (2005, ch. 2).

25 The Fair Labor Standards Act, 29 U.S.C. 201-219 (2000), passed in 1938, is the primary federal legislation governing national wage rates. State legislation also regulates working time.

26 These exemptions range from farm workers to transportation workers. In 2004, the "white-collar" exemption of executive, administrative, and professional employees was expanded. Code of Federal Regulations Pertaining to ESA, Title 29, Chapter V, Part 451, August 23, 2004.

27 Organization of Working Time (Basic Directive) 2003/88/EC.

28 Part-time Work Directive, 97/81/EC, amended by Council Directive 98/23/EC of 7 April 1998. For a discussion of this directive, see Fredman (2005).

29 As Zeytinoglu and Cooke (2005) discuss, the 1983 Commission of Inquiry into Part-Time Work, led by Joan Wallace, advocated comparable treatment for part-time workers.

30 Hours-of-work thresholds simply create an incentive for employers to schedule hours under the threshold to reduce costs.

11
The Increasing Invisibility of Mothering
Margaret Hillyard Little

I sit here at my desk watching the clock on my computer count away the hours, and now minutes, before I will go to get my daughter from daycare and mark the end of another shortened day of paid work, a day of fewer paid work hours because I have chosen this balance between family and employment. I have interviewed low-income single moms for more than twenty years about their experiences of mothering and welfare. And now I am a single mom, albeit in quite different circumstances from the women I continue to interview. For I am one of the relatively new breed of single moms: a single mom by choice.[1] When I recently interviewed low-income women, one of them startled me by asking: "You mean you are single by choice?" Her economic circumstances had never allowed her the privilege of choosing to be single, of choosing to raise her children on her own rather than relying on a partner who often caused considerable grief but did keep her from starvation and homelessness (Little 2005). This reminds me that the state's treatment of single mothers says much about the degree of choice available to all mothers. If the welfare cheque is woefully inadequate, then some single moms are forced to give up their children or their freedom to be single. If Employment Insurance does not cover all working mothers, then it denies parental leave to some and, subsequently, forces many mothers to work at least part-time during the first year of their baby's life. And if there is no national, subsidized, quality childcare program, then many mothers are forced to resort to inadequate childcare arrangements or remain home caring for their children when they want or need to do paid work. All of this speaks to the complex relationship between family, paid work, and unpaid work. This chapter attempts to understand the current neo-liberal version of this relationship by exploring the treatment of welfare single moms. Through the experiences of welfare single mothers, we will see that the Canadian neo-liberal state has helped to make mothering, in all its endless hours of care, more invisible.

By exploring the history of welfare policy's treatment of single mothers, we can better appreciate the tectonic shift in emphasis on women's paid versus unpaid work heralded by the neo-liberal era. For some time, feminist scholars have argued that Western liberal democracies established social programs on a two-tiered system. Couched in the discourse of individual citizenship and entitlement, one tier provided comparatively more generous, less stigmatized state payments predominantly to white males attached to the labour market. The other, characterized by intrusive moralistic regulation, provided means-tested, stigmatized meagre benefits predominantly to white women who made claims based on their dependent family status.[2] As the two-tier model suggests, women were and continue to be underrepresented in the social insurance, or first tier, and overrepresented in the social assistance, or second tier. When we observe the history of single mothers on welfare, we shall see the limitations of women's attachment to the second tier based on their maternal responsibilities. But through time, we shall also see the disappearance of these two distinct tiers as mothering becomes less and less a claim for state support.

Mothers First: Tracing Maternalism through the History of Mothers' Allowance

The introduction and development of welfare for single mothers in Canada during the early 1900s occurred during what is often termed the "maternal" era of state reform. In political and popular discourse, it was generally agreed that women's maternal duties made the genders quite distinct. During this period, the state and influential societal organizations defined women's role as deeply influenced by their imagined or real maternal responsibilities. Claims for women to obtain the vote or state financial support – through workers' compensation, mothers' allowances, or government supplements to the Canadian Patriotic Fund – were generally couched in maternal language (Little 1998, 7-17).[3] All of these policies supported a family wage model that assumed a male worker with dependent wife and children, or granted government support to the dependants if the male worker was absent or injured. This family wage model promoted a maternal ideology that assumed that a mother's first role was to care for her children, and this arrangement should be state supported under certain circumstances.

The campaign across the country for mothers' allowances clearly illustrated the maternal underpinnings of the call for state payments to low-income single mothers. Both male and female lobbyists promoted the notion of gender difference, advocating that women's "natural" role in life was that of caregiver, whereas men were "naturally" economic providers. Women's experiences as caregivers made them uniquely able to nurture both their families and society at large. It was argued that, if possible, every child needed his or her mother's constant attention and influence, and the state should provide financial support for this. Thereby, it was determined that low-income single mothers of the correct race and moral character should be encouraged to stay home and raise their children through regular state payments, as opposed to working full-time and having their children raised by others or placed in an orphanage. Of course, there was some disagreement about just which single mothers should be financially supported by the state and which ones were considered unworthy; race, ethnicity, religion, number of children, and moral character all played a role in this deliberation.

This maternalist ideology was gendered, but it was also elitist and racist. There has been some debate among American feminist scholars about whether this maternalist ideology crossed class and race divisions in the United States. But research of Canadian campaigns for mothers' allowances suggests that the debate in Canada was predominantly elitist, with labour and working-class advocates promoting a male worker with dependent wife and children familial model very similar to that of the emerging middle-class and bourgeois social reformers. And on the question of race, virtually all those who campaigned for mothers' allowance in Canada advocated a racist policy that shored up the Euro-Canadian single-mother-led family at the expense of most ethnic minority and Aboriginal single mothers. Yet the fact remains that most of those who campaigned for mothers' allowances and mothers' pensions in Canada espoused a maternalist philosophy that assumed that a mother's primary responsibility was to provide care for her children. Both social reformers and labour advocates promoted familial models characterized by a male breadwinner and dependent wife and children. For instance, these lobbyists clearly opposed collective childcare, which would have freed poor women to engage in full-time employment, while they promoted mothers' allowance.[4]

The welfare policy for low-income single mothers established in most provinces and eventually the territories was entrenched in this maternalist philosophy. In the 1920s, five of Canada's provinces had established a mothers' allowance policy, and all of these open policies encouraged the female recipients to see mothering as their primary responsibility.[5] The majority of mothers' allowance lobbyists, steeped in maternalist values, favoured policies that would not require mothers to work outside the home. In contrast, mothers' allowance payments were insufficient on their own and would require mothers to conduct some part-time paid work. Mothers' allowance administrators vehemently discouraged full-time work, advising part-time work that was carefully monitored. As a result, mothers' allowance recipients tended to be involved in low-paid, female-ghetto jobs. It was clear that their first job was to be in the home and that financial security would come only with remarriage. As a result, this policy encouraged a maternal ideal that met Anglo-Saxon middle-class standards rather than the long-term interests of its recipients. Women were persuaded to undertake part-time paid work and unpaid domestic work – neither of which would lead to economic security. Administrators advised mothers on just what type of work they could do to earn money and still receive their allowance. Part-time work in the home that utilized the "natural" domestic skills of the mother was the preferred option. In fact, policy administrators insisted that single mothers refuse factory work in favour of domestic work such as selling pies, sewing, and laundry, even though factory work paid substantially more.

The rise of male unemployment in the 1930s did little to dramatically challenge the maternalist underpinnings of mothers' allowance policy in Canada. Feminist historians argue that this was a period of gender crisis, as both masculine and feminine prescribed roles were challenged by the economic difficulties of the era. Gender boundaries were under enormous stress as men's jobs disappeared and the female labour force expanded. Margaret Hobbs argues that these gender identities underwent perhaps their biggest challenge of the modern industrial period during the Depression era (Hobbs 1993a, 1993b).[6] Mothers' allowance rates across the country remained woefully inadequate during this difficult time. As in the past, single moms were forced to find some paid work to supplement their allowance. There is evidence from case files to demonstrate that mothers' allowance administrators reinforced traditional gender roles over the economic needs of the family. There were complaints from the public that mothers' allowance recipients were taking jobs away from others who could not receive public assistance. So although there was considerable gender slippage in "women's" and "men's" work in the larger community, the traditional definitions of women's work were carefully maintained by the mothers' allowance administrators. In the case of mothers' allowance recipients, their paid work was never to interfere with their primary responsibility: the care of their children. As in the 1920s, it remained clear in the 1930s that mother work was their first and most important job.[7]

The Second World War and the immediate postwar period raised new challenges about the role of women in society. Social programs such as Family Allowances (1944) and Unemployment Insurance (1940) demonstrated that the Canadian wartime and immediate postwar welfare state would be premised on a family wage model where men were assumed to be the primary breadwinners and women remained in the home providing unpaid domestic care. Unprecedented employment opportunities characterized the war years and had a dramatic impact on welfare programs. Those considered employable who were unable to find work during the Depression were quickly absorbed into the expanding war economy. Even marginal workers, namely, the partially disabled, single mothers, and even seniors, were attractive to employers during this economic boom. Increased employment opportunities also led to increased surveillance. In Ontario, the mothers' allowance administrators became suspicious of the possibility of mothers and children secretly doing paid work while collecting their mothers' allowance cheques. Consequently, the Ontario government almost doubled its number of mothers' allowance investigators in the early 1940s to ferret out single mothers or their children who were secretly doing paid work.

Through financial regulation of women and children in the postwar era, the nuclear family unit was remodelled. During this period of rapid social and economic change, the family model was used to quiet anxieties and achieve both political and personal goals. On the political front, this model was to exemplify the success of capitalism and Western democracy. And, personally, a home filled with children was to create a feeling of warmth and security – a haven from threatening social, economic, and political forces outside the door (May 1988, 16-36).[8]

Mothers' allowance regulation reflected this desire to preserve and bolster the nuclear family model. Although the policy extended eligibility to new groups of single mothers, regulations continued to favour the nuclear family. Administrators did send mothers outside the home in search of paid work, but this action did not threaten the male-breadwinner family model as the ideal familial unit. Mothers were not encouraged to take jobs that would lead to long-term financial security. Rather, they were urged to reinforce their domestic skills through paid work. The mothers' allowance policy assumed that these single mothers were only temporarily in the labour force and would return to their domestic subservient role if and when the right male breadwinner came along. Simultaneously, mothers' allowance amendments concerning children encouraged the young to extend their time as familial dependants and, consequently, prolong a mother's duties within the home. Also in support of this familial ideal, the mothers' allowance administration offered rehabilitation services for incapacitated husbands by the mid-1950s so that they could once again become the breadwinners.[9]

The 1960s and 1970s saw the consolidation of the Canadian welfare state – some existing programs were expanded, including Unemployment Insurance, as was subsidizing of post-secondary education, while certain new universal policies were introduced, such as medicare and seniors' benefits. And the Canada Assistance Plan committed the federal government to fifty-fifty unlimited cost-sharing for health care, education, and welfare, as well as the creation of federal guidelines for these programs that perceived welfare as a right to all those in economic need. These programs helped to solidify a popular belief that the Canadian state could and should help to improve the socio-economic lives of its citizens. Although this is considered the golden age of the Canadian welfare state, large groups of ethnic minorities and women did not benefit equally from the arrangement. Those without full-time employment did not receive the full benefit of these more generous welfare state entitlements. Thus, the maternal ideology of a previous era was not significantly challenged by the war and postwar welfare state. An ideology that promoted the female-caretaker norm fit well with the more generous state benefits for the (male) full-time worker.[10] Although single mothers were not granted state support to the same degree as full-time male workers, and in fact the family wage model worked to perpetuate gender inequalities, there was still a recognition that these women should be acknowledged, however inadequately, for their maternal responsibilities.

The history of mothers' allowance in Canada from its introduction in the early 1900s to the early 1980s demonstrates that the state saw low-income single mothers' first responsibility as their unpaid domestic work. Despite dramatic changes in the labour market during this period, a maternalist philosophy continued to influence much of Canadian welfare for single mothers through the 1920s, the unemployment crisis of the 1930s, and the demand for female workers during the Second World War and the immediate postwar period. During this entire period, welfare payments to single mothers were inadequate. Because the payments did not begin to meet the real needs of single mothers, it was assumed that these women would supplement their government cheques with paid employment. But welfare administrators were adamant that this employment not interfere with mothering responsibilities. In addition, administrators permitted only the most gendered employment. It was only in the mid-1990s and the early twenty-first century, when a neo-liberal regime was entrenched, that this belief that single mothers are first and foremost mothers was dramatically challenged.

Neo-Liberalism: Mothers Are Workers

The neo-liberal era has heralded seismic changes in the way the Canadian state views mothering, particularly for low-income single moms. Neo-liberalism is an ideology that dramatically changes how we perceive the role of the state, the economy, and the individual. It advocates decreased state regulation of capital and often increased state regulation of the marginalized – that is, the poor, criminals, and so on. It promotes lower direct taxation and increased individual and market responsibility for various services. And through more punitive and restrictive social policies, the neo-liberal state blames the individual, rather than the market, for poverty and unemployment.[11] Such dramatic changes in state policy have affected all women, but especially those most dependent on the state, such as low-income single mothers.

Under a neo-liberal regime, women are predominantly viewed as gender-neutral workers. The male breadwinner–dependent female caregiver model assumed by the Canadian state in the immediate postwar Keynesian welfare state era is no longer. Instead, the majority of women, both with and without young children, are involved in paid work. For example, in 2001, almost 70 percent of mothers with children under six were in the labour force, and the majority were working full-time.[12] Yet the Canadian state virtually ignores the mothering responsibilities of women in the workforce. Year after year, the federal government has refused to establish a national affordable, quality childcare program. Federal-provincial agreements such as the Canada Assistance Plan and the Established Programs Financing Act were replaced with the Canada Health and Social Transfer, which reduced funding to the provinces and encouraged them to place restrictions on eligibility. This policy change has had a tidal effect on provincial social policies and services. First, numerous efforts to support workers and families from health care and education to community services and welfare have all been scaled back in the neo-liberal era. The result is that caring work is increasingly privatized, with middle- and upper-income workers employing low-paid precarious women workers, often women of colour, to fulfill caring responsibilities.[13] And at the same time, policies that receive the least popular support, namely, benefits and services for the most marginalized, are the ones most vulnerable to cuts and eligibility restrictions.

These changes in the economy-family-state nexus have implications for all women but particularly for the most marginalized. Welfare policy across this country, from the early 1900s to the 1980s, implicitly recognized mothering as the first duty of poor single mothers. This is no longer the case for most contemporary welfare policy in Canada. In the late 1980s, there were attempts in various provinces to place more emphasis on paid work for these single mothers. For instance, in 1989, the Ontario Liberal government established the Supports to Employment Program (STEP) to help ease the transition from welfare to paid work. STEP increased earning exemptions, provided special exemptions for training allowances, provided for the first months' costs of childcare, and offered start-up benefits for people starting new jobs. And the New Democratic Party government that followed produced a report that recommended that each single mother on welfare have an employment counsellor who would establish an "opportunity plan," an agreement about how a single mother planned to transition to full-time work.[14] Other provinces went even further to move low-income single mothers toward employment. Among the most ambitious projects were New Brunswick Works (NB Works) and the Self-Sufficiency Project in New Brunswick and British Columbia. NB Works, which ran in the 1990s, provided long-term training compared with most programs for welfare recipients, thereby allowing low-income women to gain academic upgrading and skills training that would make them able to compete for stable jobs at living wages. Participants, 84 percent female, were provided with allowances at least equal to their previous welfare cheques and a childcare allowance. They participated in a community work placement following academic upgrading and training of their choice.[15] The Self-Sufficiency Project, which ran from 1992 to 1995, supplemented the wages of single mothers who were welfare recipients for up to three years, provided they were employed a minimum of thirty hours a week and remained off welfare. The purpose of these self-sufficiency projects was to financially supplement the earnings of the participants for a certain period, thereby lifting these people out of working poverty. This supplement helped single mothers pay for childcare, transportation, and other employment-related expenses. It was assumed that the participants were being trained in employment-related skills while on the job. It was also assumed that these women would be able to find better-paying jobs once the program ended.

But most of these retraining and wage-supplement programs specifically designed for poor single mothers did not lead to employment. The 1980s and early 1990s was a period of high unemployment; despite some retraining or supplements to their wages, poor single mothers generally could not find permanent employment. NB Works participants found that they were not able to complete their educational goals before the program disbanded. And some participants of the Self-Sufficiency Project had difficulty finding employment and were concerned that they would not be able to meet their childcare and other employment-related expenses once the supplement to the poorly paid job ended (Ford et al. 2003, ch. 2 and 4; McFarland 2003, 201). Consequently these programs did very little to remove single mothers from poverty. Instead of investing in job opportunities so that single mothers would have a light at the end of the retraining tunnel, government abandoned the entire project of retraining poor single mothers. Today, there is virtually no training program across the country specifically designed for poor single mothers.

Although the Self-Sufficiency Project and NB Works provided low-income single mothers with a choice of whether to enter training or employment, the writing was on the wall. Through these programs, a single mother could choose to spend the majority of her time in unpaid caring work, or she could choose to juggle unpaid and paid work. But even these choices were limited given that these welfare policies did not adequately appreciate the realities of women's paid and unpaid work responsibilities. It is hardly a choice to participate in an employment program if the alternative is to try to survive on welfare payments that do not meet basic needs. However, today, most neo-liberal welfare policies no longer present even these limited choices. Instead, single mothers are forced to be in the workforce and, in many cases, they can be denied welfare if they are not conducting some type of paid or volunteer work outside the home. In Quebec, the welfare benefit is reduced when a mothers' youngest child enters school. The Ontario Conservative government in 1997 established workfare that ties most welfare to employment or employment-related activity. Single mothers with children four years or older are expected to be involved in workfare activities or paid work and can be cut off all welfare payments if they do not comply. Some provincial welfare programs are more severe. Both Saskatchewan and Alberta welfare programs consider a mother to be employable when her youngest child is six months old. And British Columbia's welfare program states that an applicant must prove two years prior work experience before she or he can be eligible for welfare.[16] Welfare programs that emphasize a current or previous attachment to the workforce clearly erode a single mother's choice to stay at home full-time and raise her children. For the first time in the history of welfare in Canada, poor single mothers are now considered paid workers, in some instances completely interchangeable with single childless adults. This development is what some feminist scholars call the gender-blind nature of neo-liberal policy. For now, welfare does not appreciate single mothers as having considerable unpaid caring responsibilities. Instead, these responsibilities are increasingly ignored as these women are treated as employable, requiring few if any supports to enter the paid-work world.

The main feature of welfare-tied-to-employment programs is their focus on individual characteristics such as educational level, job-seeking skills, work habits, the ability to write resumés, interviewing skills, and interpersonal presentation skills.[17] Increasingly, there is little recognition of mothering responsibilities that might interfere with a mother's time and commitment to paid work. Where previous welfare programs attempted to pay some lip service to childcare needs for mothers, and the better ones helped financially compensate low-income working mothers for their childcare costs, the situation has changed. Low-income mothers transitioning from welfare to paid work receive less financial compensation for childcare expenses than before. Interviews with such women demonstrate time and again that these mothers are forced to place their children in substandard childcare arrangements because of the prohibitive costs and limited availability of state-regulated daycare. Mothers transitioning from welfare to paid work are most often part of the precarious part-time employment sector, with work shifts that vary from day to day and week to week and do not fit the nine-to-five timeframe of most licensed childcare. These mothers constantly worry about their childcare arrangements as they shuffle their children from one unregulated space to another, juggling the irregularity of multiple part-time jobs and inconsistent work shifts. Neither their unpaid caring responsibilities nor the responsibilities of those who replace them in these duties are addressed by welfare policies that focus on transitioning people from welfare to paid employment regardless of the monetary or intangible costs to the mother or the next generation. As workfare and welfare tied to employment have become the norm in this neo-liberal age, so has the increasing invisibility of caring work conducted by mothers and their replacements.

The Canadian state is not without contradictions in its treatment of mothering. Even though there is a general trend toward the invisibility of mothering, there are small pockets of policy in which the state recognizes and reaffirms mothering. The federal government does recognize some caring responsibilities through tax-based incentives and certain social policies, but these have been dramatically scaled back in the neo-liberal era. For more than three decades, Ottawa provided monthly Family Allowances to all families with children.[18] This has been replaced with the National Child Benefit (NCB), a benefit for low- and moderate-income families.[19] However, many provinces clawback the NCB from parents on welfare. This has the effect of the state recognizing this unpaid caring work for working poor families but not acknowledging this role among welfare poor families. Clearly, such policies demonstrate that the state is choosing which types of parenting to support and which to ignore. As well, Employment Insurance (EI) eligibility has been severely restricted. The proportion of the unemployed receiving EI has dropped from 83 percent in 1989 to 42 percent in 1997. Among those who have become ineligible are the more marginal workers who are employed less than full-time, with little job security.[20] This describes many working-class and working-poor women. The federal government's childcare contribution of $100 per month per child under six years old recognizes unpaid childcare at the same time as it makes it impossible for low-income parents to rely solely on this income to care for a child. Thus, the Canadian state recognizes some mothering but, at the same time, policies have restricted just which mothers should be financially supported and under what conditions.

Challenging Neo-Liberal Understandings of Mothering

The increasing invisibility of mothering creates new challenges for feminist scholars and activists. We need to be cautious about how to frame our demands on the neo-liberal state. We need to revisit and refine our old claims upon the state. But first, we need to re-examine the feminist demand for employment. The problem is not jobs but the types of jobs and the fact that these jobs provide virtually no flexibility to a mother's caring responsibilities. Therefore, we must insist on a qualified position about low-income single moms' involvement in the workforce. These women must be able to choose when they wish to join the workforce and under what conditions. The social safety net must support their entry into the workforce, but it must also support their decision to fulfill their unpaid caring responsibilities. Second, we need to be cautious of feminist demands that focus on children at the expense of adults. As the neo-liberal state blames adults for poverty and unemployment, it has embraced a discourse calling for the alleviation of child poverty and promoting social policy that separates children's needs from that of their parents. As feminists, we need to refocus the magnifying glass back on mothers. Poor mothers are raising poor children, and it is the mothers' poverty that must first be addressed. The neo-liberal state is quick to establish educational and surveillance mechanisms for poor mothers. Programs that instruct mothers in proper nutrition and child-rearing techniques are helpful only when the mothers have adequate financial support. The increased surveillance and capture of low-income children through Children's Aid Societies does not address the underlying cause of much child abuse and neglect: poverty.

Finally, as feminists, we need to demand increased state support of mothering. We have been quick to see the limitations of the maternalist discourse of the nineteenth century; however, we need to make room for a political argument that embraces motherhood and all its demands and duties. American scholar Gwendolyn Mink (1998) has urged us to reconsider the maternalist argument and has encouraged us to see the class and race differences among our experiences of mothering. As feminist scholars and activists, we need to ensure that we are asking nothing more of our low-income sisters than we do of ourselves. All mothers should be able to choose the family-employment balance that works best for them. All single mothers must know that there is a social safety net that will adequately provide for them and make it possible to carry out their mothering responsibilities. This means a welfare rate that is livable and not tied to employment. This means retraining programs that lead to better-paid jobs and are flexible to the demands of single motherhood.[21] This includes EI that ensures coverage for all who are recently unemployed and parental leave for all new parents. And this means a comprehensive, quality national childcare program that accommodates single mothers who do paid work at nights or on weekends, or who have work schedules that vary week to week. This is but a beginning list of demands we need to make on the neo-liberal state, but I believe it is critical that every demand we make must recognize and value mothering. We must make it possible for low-income single mothers to choose how to balance family and employment. And in this choice, we must make it possible for them to choose to be and to remain proud single mothers.

Notes

1 Since the 1980s, there has been a rise of professional women choosing to raise children on their own. For further discussion of this phenomenon, see Mikki Morrissette (2008), especially the Introduction.

2 I am providing only the basic outline of an argument that has seen much discussion and refinement over the last twenty years. Key figures in this debate include Ann Shola Orloff (1993), Carole Pateman (1992), Barbara Nelson (1990), Nancy Fraser (1989), and Diane Pearce (1978, 1985). My own attempt to apply this theory to the Canadian case is presented in an unpublished paper, "Workers and Mothers: A Comparison of Ontario Mothers' Allowance and Ontario Workers' Compensation, 1920-40," June 1993, Canadian Social Welfare Conference, St. John's, Newfoundland.

3 A nationalist charity organization administered and financed the Canadian Patriotic Fund, which provided monthly allowances to soldiers' dependent wives and children; the organization received federal, provincial, and municipal government grants to supplement these allowances.

4 For a more detailed analysis of the campaign for mothers' allowance and mothers' pensions in Canada, see Little (1998, 1-28), Jane Ursel (1992, 125-74), and Veronica Strong-Boag (1979).

5 Mothers' allowance was established in Manitoba in 1916, Saskatchewan in 1917, Alberta in 1919, and Ontario and British Columbia in 1920. Nova Scotia and New Brunswick established commissions to investigate and recommend mothers' allowances in the early 1920s, but no policy was enacted at the time. In 1930, Nova Scotia passed and implemented mothers' allowances, and in New Brunswick a similar act was passed in 1930 but not administered until 1943. Prince Edward Island enacted mothers' allowance in 1949; Newfoundland passed legislation when it joined Canada in 1949.

6 For further discussion of the gender crisis of the 1930s, see Gordon (1994, ch. 7) and Pierson (1990, 78).

7 For detailed analysis of Ontario Mothers' Allowance 1930s case files and the careful scrutiny of recipients' paid work options, see Little (1998, 89-96).

8 Elaine May's work on postwar American families has made an enormous contribution to our understanding of this period. She demonstrates a strong relationship between political and familial values, arguing that the political ideology of the period provoked a desire for domestic security within the family home.

9 For further details of the Second World War and immediate postwar period and the administration of Ontario Mothers' Allowance, see Little (1998, 107-38).

10 For elaboration on this argument, see Fudge and Vosko (2003, 183-209).

11 For more detailed discussion of the neo-liberal features of the Canadian state and its impact on women, see Bezanson and Luxton (2006, 3-10), Bakker (1996), and Brodie (1996).

12 Organisation for Economic Co-operation and Development, *Babies and Bosses: Reconciling Work and Family Life* (2005, 70), cited in Bezanson and Luxton (2006, ch. 5).

13 For discussion of precarious women workers who do caring work, see Sedef Arat-Koc (2006) and Bakan and Stasiulis (2005).

14 For more details about changes in emphasis toward the employment of welfare recipients, see Little (1998, 139-63).

15 For a detailed discussion of NB Works, see McFarland and Mullaly (1996).

16 For further discussion of neo-liberal welfare reforms in British Columbia, see Little and Marks (2010).

17 For further discussion of employability programs, see Baker and Tippin (1999, 37-70).

18 One exception to this universal policy was the federal government's treatment of Inuit people. Instead of a monthly allowance cheque, Inuit families received food and staples that were insensitive to Inuit culture; see Kulchyski and Tester (1994).

19 For a more detailed discussion of the National Child Benefit, see McKeen and Porter (2003, 119-22).

20 For a more detailed description of the impact of Unemployment Insurance changes on workers, and women in particular, see McKeen and Porter (2003, 117-19) and Porter (2003).

21 For further discussion of the type of retraining programs that we need to offer low-income single mothers, see Little (1998).

A Feminist Vision for Caring-Employment Integration in Canada
Susan A. McDaniel

In recent years, the concept of reflexive postmodernity has guided much sociological consideration of work and family changes, including perhaps particularly feminist approaches. Women are thought to be freed of both tradition and structures, including social roles, as we navigate our lives as pilots of our own destinies. Choice and individualization are deemed natural accompanying constructs to reflexive postmodernity. Work and family, thus, are seen as choices we, as women, make from an array of possible options with few and diminishing social constraints. Both a theoretical and political discourse focusing on balancing work and family and on individual strategizing to manage work and family simultaneously underscore the choice motif. Indeed, a Policy Research Initiative *Horizons* issue (Canada, Policy Research Initiative 2006) on this topic is significantly titled "Work and Life Balance: Better Choice, Flexibility and Policy Opportunities."

Each of the chapters in this volume works, in different ways, to demystify the family-work relationship or prevailing gender contract that holds that women are, or should be, the predominant balancers of work and family: that work, for women, is separate from their lives as women. This latter image is evoked by the image of "work-life balance," as if work is not part of life. In this chapter, a feminist vision of caring and employment integration is offered, based on social science research and new theorizations of work and family. Two pivotal concepts to this new vision are social citizenship and social provisioning, which open the door to seeing the social structural nests in which choices do and do not occur. Caring and paid employment will be unlocked from the vice-grip, on the one hand, of the discourse on caring as women's forte and the source of their "difference" and, on the other hand, of the neo-liberal agenda that values women's participation in the labour market but deems caring responsibilities private or familial. The ethos of neo-liberalism embodies the values and norms of market rationality, of primacy of the individual as economic actor, of choice, of control over one's fate, and of personal responsibility. The concepts of social citizenship and particularly of social provisioning call these neo-liberal precepts into sharp question.

In interrogating the underlying premises of conceptualizing women's contemporary lives in terms of a family-work – or sometimes a work-life – balancing act, the contributors to this volume echo Catherine Krull's opening chapter in questioning, on several planes, the assumptions behind changes in women's labour market participation and in secular changes in family. My chapter moves on to a frontal discussion of the rhetoric of family-work balance, suggesting new theorizations of societal participation. Its major importance, I believe, lies in the proposal for unlocking the vice-grip of gendered caring scripts and of the neo-liberal promotion of "choice" as well as its consequences for women who "do it all." To draw on Michèle Fitoussi's title of her best-selling book (1987), *La ras-le-bol des superwomen* (Superwomen Are Fed Up), so are their families! In this volume, the point is theoretically expanded by Justyna Sempruch, who shows how newer policies in Europe seem to view mothering as worthy of either a second track in terms of labour market participation or something that necessitates special concessions to women, and only to women. With this opening in mind, I now elaborate on the intermingling notions of choice, necessity, diversity, and balance and their possible usage for feminist ends in care work.

Changes in Market Participation: Choice versus Necessity?

As discussed by Maureen Baker and Margaret Hillyard Little in this volume, women's participation in the paid labour market in Canada has been increasing, regardless of whether they are mothers. As Little mentions in her chapter, in 2001 in Canada, almost 70 percent of mothers with children under age six were in the labour force, and the majority were working full-time. In Quebec, as discussed in Patrizia Albanese's chapter, the proportion is even higher, though it started at a much lower level than in Canada thirty years ago. The maternalist views and policies of a previous era, when mothering was given some priority, have been disregarded by the neo-liberal agendas of recent decades. Women have become neutral sources of paid labour, regardless of their caring responsibilities on the home front. A heavy economic curtain has occluded their mothering – an important point Albanese and Baker explore in the policies of Quebec and Canada. Donna Baines and Bonnie Freeman make a similar observation in their chapter on indigenous people's perspectives and experiences.

With women's remuneration for paid work remaining considerably less than men's, women's work seldom results in economic security. For lone mothers, to follow empirical evidence cited by Baker, economic security is more likely to be enhanced by marriage than by their own labours. This has led to the initiation of social policies in the United States to encourage marriage as the solution to poverty among low-income lone mothers, which some have called "wedfare" (Jenson and St. Martin 2006). It could be, and has been argued, that women remain where they are as dependants, but instead of dependence on the state, they depend on a man. Their social citizenship, or full societal participation, in both situations is compromised, as is their vital contribution to social provisioning for their families and for society. Men on whom women are asked by policy to rely economically may be as financially insecure and undependable as the neo-liberal state has become for low-income lone mothers. But women are forced by these policies to use traditional feminine wiles to catch and keep a man as the means of keeping a roof over their and their children's heads. It is a Faustian bargain for all, but particularly for women in a feminist age. The postwar gender contract, which is anchored in women's caring and feminine subjectivity, as outlined by Sempruch, is therefore reinforced by policy.

Intertwining work and family and its ever-present gender subtext becomes even more complex when it is recognized that women with the highest earning power are less likely to marry, less likely to have children, and, if married or in a union, less likely to remain coupled than women with less earning power. This tendency is noted in Baker's chapter. An intricate calculus of choice, non-choice, gender politics, and persistent structures of social inequalities are thus operative here. That the same cannot be said of high-earning men who differentially have spouses and children is telling.

One popular narrative of women's rapidly increasing labour market participation is women's choice to work, cast at times as a rights issue emanating from feminist politics. Just as Fudge in her chapter makes it clear that a gap exists between what people want in terms of working hours and what they get, a similar gap exists between working and the choice to work. There seems little doubt that for some women, particularly the high-earning women mentioned above, work may appear to surface observers to be a choice. But is it a choice if these women are more likely to be single or post-union, or does it, rather, serve as the only source of support for themselves and whatever dependants they might have? For the vast majority of women and men who are not high earners, work is necessary because they must support their families.

The choice rubric is still curiously gendered when it comes to working. For most of human history, just as today, most people worked because they had to: to eat, to be sheltered, and to live. Work and life are not separate now and never have been. A unified object is not balanced; it is more like holding. Hence, the focus on choice to work for women is a highly gendered and distinctly inaccurate image. Is it asked whether men make a choice to work? Generally not, and this has its own set of perils for men who care full-time or even part-time, as Andrea Doucet's chapter compellingly reveals. Choice to work for women does not exist in reality, as all women, except perhaps the extremely rich who remain luxuriously leisured and lovely, work either for pay or as unpaid workers in their families – most doing both – without choice. Provisioning is what working women are doing in both paid work and caring work. "'Social provisioning' is a [term] that draws attention away from images of pecuniary pursuits and individual competition, and toward notions of sustenance, cooperation, and support" (Power 2004, 6). Care work and paid work are both provisioning for families.

Monumental challenges are posed for working women who are mothers with dependent children, particularly preschool children, in what arrangements to make for childcare. Since familial caring has become more and more of a back-burner issue on the political agenda in Canada – with the exception of Quebec, as evident in Albanese's chapter – children are almost seen as being "stored" quietly, whereas the "real action" is the paid work. This has long been apparent in the popular but completely incorrect phrase "taking time off to have children." Margrit Eichler's chapter shows how competencies acquired in caring and in housework writ large are not acknowledged as such. She quotes Linda Butler (1993, 80) to show how this wheedles its way into women's ways of thinking about what they do: "Women cannot attempt to claim credit or reward for competence which they do not even know they possess." If these skills acquired in caring and housework are invisible and unacknowledged by the women who possess them, it is easy to see how difficult it becomes to transfer the skills into the paid economy as useful and usable. If childcare is not deemed a valued skill at home even by mothers, then it is not seen as such in the paid labour market either. Both Krull and Sempruch repeatedly argue that such diminishing of roles reinforces essentialist thinking about care work. Expectedly, childcare workers are generally poorly paid and not much valued and, of course, they are foremost differentially women. So, children can be "stored" while women engage in the real thing – paid work.

As discussed by Judith Fudge and by Ann Duffy and Norene Pupo in their chapters, the issues involved in childcare connect with issues of working hours, and with work in the new economy, more often in low-pay service jobs with limited security, lower benefits, and so on. Childcare, in this sense, has direct implications for labour market policy, as considered by Sempruch. Less pay alone, even without the conflating issues of unpredictable and nonstandard hours of work, means decidedly fewer options for childcare. Except in Quebec, as suggested by Albanese, quality care tends to be expensive and often not available for times other than the standard white-collar workday. Talk about a human capital investment in the children model of social policy is not borne out in practice when working women or parents often have little choice but to leave their children with untrained sitters while they work. Children learn little, parents worry about them, and no one really benefits. The hard-won architecture, decades on the federal political lobbying drawing boards, for a national childcare program was in place just as the new Conservative government of Stephen Harper came to power in 2006. The Harper government quickly replaced it with a universal program whereby all parents of young children receive a direct payment to use, as they wish, for childcare. If sufficient childcare does not exist, having that money in one's pocket cannot make it suddenly appear. Only Quebec, as Albanese discusses, has chosen to do something serious about these challenges.

Also, to follow Baker's suggestion, many other countries do a better job than Canada in providing policies that enable work and caring for women while keeping poverty levels low. Canada seems to rely, sometimes implicitly, on an outdated male breadwinner–female caregiver model. Quebec, by contrast, rose to the occasion with a coalition of feminist groups, including some key feminists in government, the civil service, and non-profit voluntary organizations, and shifted its policy focus in the 1990s. Albanese reveals in her chapter how Quebec developed a network of policies that recognize the value of family caring while acknowledging the need for more women in the paid labour market. A key pillar of these policies was affordable childcare for preschool and school-age children. The growth in school daycares skyrocketed. This growth was accompanied by a monitoring of child development outcomes and expanded parental insurance schemes with more equitable eligibility criteria than the federal Employment Insurance plan. Quebec now has a sex ratio of paid work higher than any country in the world, with the exception of the Nordic countries. The Quebec childcare program is not without problems, but it is unprecedented in North America and has worked to the benefit of both children and their working parents.

Is Family Diversity a Choice Array?

Families are discussed often in the literature of many disciplines as being diverse and implicitly choice-driven. It is as if a smorgasbord of choices is laid out, and we choose the one suited to us. This is consistent with the social science stance of reflexive postmodernity. Of course, questions arise immediately about the degree of choice involved in being a lone mother with limited income in the wake of divorce from an abusive spouse, or the choice involved in living as a lesbian couple or in an immigrant multigenerational family. Krull's and Sempruch's chapters point not only toward restrained familial choices but also to the culturally scripted pushes toward normative heterosexuality and conformance with unrealistic cultural gender ideals. The "choice" rubric fades quickly with only the addition of a little extra thought. Yet the economist's image of choice for women seems to lurk behind many contemporary approaches to family diversity, child-bearing, labour force participation, and other dimensions of current family change.

The choice rubric may not be appropriate for most in the families in which or with whom they live, but it is applicable to a small subset of women, and a few men, who choose to be parents without being in a nuclear family. Little informs us in her chapter that she is a lone mother by choice. Albanese tells us about the reality of choice in Quebec to have births outside traditional legal marriage, which in 2005 included the majority – 59.3 percent – of children born. These examples, although important in revealing choices in family, and increasingly so in the case of common-law unions with children, still do not diminish emphasis on the point that we, on average, do not choose from an array of possible family styles. For most of us, choices are limited, if not constrained.

Work and Family: A Balancing Act for Women

For most of human existence, and in the overwhelming majority of places in the world today, both men and women simultaneously work and have families. Without work and family, we probably would not be here today, as our ancestors had to work to care for their families. And without family, there would be no "us," descendents. Similarly, people in most of the world work and have families for the same reason: need and survival. Family and work are not separable in Aboriginal cultures, as Baines and Freeman eloquently reveal in their chapter. If this is so, how did we get to the balancing metaphor so prevalent today? Two possible explanations are offered. First, both work and family have been dramatically recalibrated of late. Early on, work was moved out of family and family enterprises into a separate location, thereby making it much more difficult to integrate and coordinate. Many of the dimensions of recent changes are revealed in the chapters that make up this volume. Most important of late may be the shift brought about by neo-liberalism and globalization to a new kind of economy, as Krull and Sempruch outline in their introduction to this volume. There is also the time squeeze of longer and more diverse work hours in a 24/7 service economy (see the chapter by Fudge); the advent of technologies keep us on short tethers to work even when we are not at work per se; the expense of housing near where we work makes for longer and longer commutes; and the list goes on. In the realm of family, there are equally seismic changes, most notably the instability of relationships demanding from us great amounts of time, emotional energy as well as worry, and the vastly increased demands of child rearing with a strong focus on child-centred development and outcomes.

The second reason has received a little less attention. Until recently, family and work were considered separate spheres by policy makers and by researchers often located in different places in universities (Edwards and Wajcman 2005, 44). It is now increasingly apparent to researchers, if not as much perhaps to policy makers, that work organizations are not separate from the societal contexts in which they exist, including changing family contexts, and that family and caring are not separate from the economy (Power 2004).

The earlier perception of work as separate from family may come down to the perception – held until recently in many work organizations – that men were the breadwinners and real workers; conversely, women were seen as only secondary workers who would leave the workforce or work part-time to accommodate family work. At any rate, women in segmented labour markets were not central to the functioning of the workplace and could be easily replaced with other, lower-paid women.

But as ideas about family began to change, numerous bits of evidence began tumbling out in the popular media about long hours logged at work; about work being a retreat – for women in particular – from the huge demands of family (Hochschild 1997); about the length of commutes to and from work leaving less time for family; about children struggling in inadequate childcare; and about parents – again, particularly women – frazzled by the mounting time pressures. As well, the traditional division of labour on the home front, while not dissolving by any means, was slipping as the foundation for separate gendered spheres diminished. Then there are the concepts of the work-rich, those who work too many hours, and the work-poor, those who cannot get enough hours at any one job to survive and help support their families. The latter often take on multiple jobs, whereas the former spend more time at work, meaning that family gets put behind in both instances. Parental relationships with children and spousal relationships are seen as the casualties of these work challenges.

The relationship of women's paid work to their unpaid family work has been sharply recalibrated – see the chapters by Fudge and by Duffy and Pupo. In some ways, it can be argued that increases in women's paid employment have drawn more attention – both by working women themselves and by social scientists – to the amount of unpaid family work women have traditionally done. Serious attempts have been proffered to capture and measure in monetary terms how much that work is worth. As well, many efforts have been made to inquire about what men do at home and what women do. The answers are not pretty, as Eichler reveals in the opening section of her chapter. Some have summed it up as a 2000s division of labour in the workplace with a 1950s division of labour by gender at home. Others call it a second shift for women.

That said, it is clear, as Eichler points out, that unpaid work is typically seen as taking away from the focus on paid work. This is so much the case that women leave the labour market more often than men to do the requisite family work that they feel they must do. This has the effect of confirming the belief that women are not as committed to paid work as men, that they are really secondary workers, constituted as women by their caring. The development of provisions for childcare is being increasingly framed in the context of policies addressing work-life balance for women, to preserve their paid workforce participation. Despite this motivation, social care and the need for it has been brought more into focus (Charles and Harris 2007). This is apparent in the majority of chapters in this volume.

The family-work balance is further parsed by whether the women in question are poor or well-off and whether they have a spouse. As Little shows, class was and remains fundamentally important in policies on assistance to women in need. Like Little, Baker discusses the double standard of family-work for poor lone mothers, who, in accordance with neo-liberal precepts, are deemed to be paid workers primarily with little cognizance of their mothering roles (Gazso 2007). Women on social assistance in Alberta, for example, are expected to be in paid work when their children are only three months old (ibid.). Choice is certainly not a rubric applicable to women who depend on state sustenance.

Baines and Freeman paint a very different and refreshing picture of family-work balance by looking at Aboriginal peoples. The separate spheres approach is simply inapplicable, they argue, because socially important activities such as resistance to injustice and social activism do not fall into work or family but are sustaining activities. Rather, mothering, family life, work, and social activism are intertwined with women's identities, lives, and everyday practices. Indigenous models of women's roles have always perplexed colonial rulers, as the colonial wage-labour system perplexes Aboriginal people. Nuclear families matter much less than families over time, in generations, and circles. For women in Haudenosaunee society, caring is united with governance, leadership, and political activism. It is a decidedly public activity. Work, then, is defending the land and the culture and sustaining the generations. It is social provisioning. Not only is balancing not an apt metaphor here, but it simply misses the central notion that work and family are both infused with greater caring about perpetuation, justice, community, culture, and sustaining ways of life. It is, in essence, social provisioning.

New Research and Theorizations of Work-Family and Gender
Analyses of work that treat family as separate and gender as an analytical variable must be seen as flawed or, at the very best, outdated. Work is more than wage labour; it includes caring work, unpaid work, and work done as resistance to a dominant discourse or way of life. Family is work, hard and very demanding work at times. Places where money is earned can no longer take the view that male employees have wives or partners to look after them and their families on the home front. And they can no longer see women as secondary workers, whatever segmented roles women may still play in the workplace.

Nor does a choice rubric work in considering work or family lives: "The idea either that family life is governed by individuals making rational choices or that it consists of individuals choosing 'biographies and lifestyles, rather than following predetermined roles' is questioned by evidence which shows that 'individual goals are seen through the lens of family responsibilities and negotiated within wider social normatives'" (Duncan and Irwin 2004, 391-92, cited in Charles and Harris 2007, 279). People work and have families. The two are inextricably linked and dependent one on the other. Within the structures of inequality, choices are made, but the choices are constrained and for the most part not free. Structures and human agency are mutually reinforcing. Structures such as social institutions of work and family do not *do* anything per se, but they create environments where choices are constrained and where sometimes few or no real choices exist. People behave in accordance with the structural conditions in which they are placed or find themselves and, in so doing, perpetuate the relevant cultural or social expectations. Put another way, relations of domination and subordination are embedded in social institutions, and people detect those relations and respond accordingly. This book speaks volumes about relations of dominance, particularly patriarchal and state dominance. Relations of ruling are ferreted out explicitly in Baines and Freeman's chapter as the schism around which women's identities and behaviours are structured.

A relatively new conceptualization that is useful here is that of social citizenship, or the granting of rights and privileges on the basis of full citizenship (Brodie 1997, 2007; McDaniel 2004). What seems to have happened of late is that citizenship rights have been eclipsed by market citizenship. Access to paid employment has increasingly become the central dimension of social integration and a main, or only, route to accessing welfare and social rights in the post-industrial world (Leon 2005, 204). We see this happening very clearly with neo-liberal welfare-to-work policies that push women with caring responsibilities out the door into waged employment with little or no concern for their social citizenship rights to care for their children. The concept of social citizenship and what it entails opens a deeper understanding of the social structural nests in which choices occur, or do not, about work and family.

Neo-liberalism and the shift toward the neo-liberal state represent a shift in citizenship regimes. Women displaced by the shifting regimes have no space to advocate for change or equality. It has fallen to corporations to invoke "solutions" such as flex-time – family-friendly policies that are seen as accommodation, not workplace change, to women's inherent familial caring responsibilities. This resonates with Krull's argument in the opening chapter of this book that underlying much of the family-work conceptualization is an essentialist view of gender-appropriate domains. Women get little say in how they would like to see change, except in the instances of Quebec and some Aboriginal communities. In the rest of Canada, women's political voices have been drowned out either as special interests (and men's aren't?) or as speaking about women's issues, considered passé. Yet so-called women's interests have been increasingly politicized as our voices have been silenced. Women's interests are typically the interests of people generally.

Changing theorizations of gender also matters to our understanding of family-work challenges. Katherine Marshall (2000), for example, interrogates difference as opposed to diversity, and post-structuralist approaches and critiques, such as that presented by Sempruch in this volume, have contributed greatly to understandings and interpretive frameworks on this question. In their focus on discourse and culture, postmodernists in particular may be critiqued in that they are risking a focus on materially grounded factors that still persist, such as structural inequalities and discrimination. And yet, although gender does not simply signify difference but is productive of difference (Marshall 2000), moving beyond the binaries and essentialism of gender is imperative. Echoing Krull in the opening chapter of this volume, family is less what we *are* than what we *do*. Even such a leading postmodernist voice as Pierre Bourdieu (2005, 17) takes a structuralist lens when he says: "We cannot understand individual choices unless we take into account their objective structures and their transformation."

Unlocking the Vise-Grip

Unlocking the Vise-Grip, on the one hand, of the discourse on caring as gendered and private and, on the other hand, of the neo-liberal agenda of valuing labour market participation by women is far from an easy task. Caring is at once constructed as an inherent womanly art, valued greatly, and yet socially undervalued and undermined. The concept that caring is too valuable to monetize is still prevalent. This tends to make it appear as an essential trait – an assumption in need of deep interrogation, as Krull and Sempruch suggest in the Introduction. It further renders care as something men should avoid to a large extent for fear of being seen as less masculine. Doucet's chapter explores these issues in depth.

The degree and depth of presumption about caring moves to the fore when, confronting aging populations and increasing numbers of women in the paid workforce, worries about a "caring crunch" are expressed (Hunsley 2006). It is expected, without much questioning, that women will care for elders, just as they always have, in both families and in the workforce, for low pay. Nancy Mandell and Sue Wilson question this assumption. A full employment model for women, espoused by European Union policies (Hantrais 2004; Gauthier 2001), is inconsistent with a model of women as pre-eminently responsible for organizing, if not doing, care for the young, old, and infirm. Unknotting the time bind is a key to unlocking the vice-grip * (Lapierre-Adamcyk, Marcil-Gratton, and Le Bourdais 2007; Hochschild 1997).

What is needed is collective mobilization to change the work culture that supports being constantly in a time bind. The cultural zeitgeist is firmly in place so that one must be running constantly with an imperatively coordinated schedule – not only for work but also the family – to be seen as a valuable, contributing member of post-industrial society. Families are prisoners and architects of this bind as much as are workplaces.

A Feminist Vision of Work-Family

An ideal world would be one in which men and women both have access to the good jobs, without gender contracts on the family front being presumed. But that is not sufficient by itself. Men and women, in an ideal world, would also participate fully and equally in the care work at home, including caring for children, aging relatives, sick friends and family, each other, and members of society outside their families. And even that is insufficient without the addition of supportive communities and public institutions.

These ideals are dreamy and more difficult – much more difficult – to implement than to envision. The reasons are revelatory, and some are well articulated in the chapters in this volume. First is the relatively new notion in the social sciences, but not at all new in human experience and life, that work and family are simply inseparable. Balancing, then, is not an appropriate conceptualization when we see paid work and family care as two sides of the sustainability and survival coin, of social provisioning. Families need money to live in a developed society in which housing, food, transportation, and clothes must be bought on the market, not made at home or bartered. Selling one's labour on the market is the means by which money needed to support families is gained. So, work is far from antithetical to families, whether the work is done by women or by men.

Second are the gendered webs of contradictory myths surrounding both paid work and family care. This is well summed up in a series of axioms:

- Men expect to work, and most prepare for it all their lives.
- Women more often hedge their bets on preparing for lifetime work until they find a life's partner.
- Both men and women want children, on average, but only women generally expect and plan to pull back on job or career to have children.
- We say we value children, but we privatize their raising and devalue mothering.
- The children of poor mothers are seen as needing less mothering than those in better-off families, as evidenced by neo-liberal social assistance policies.

The conundrum of caring is a tough, tough nut, as demonstrated by the plethora of recent research and theorization on the topic. Even tougher, however, is the concept that work includes caring for families and communities, and that caring is a competence learned by doing what is undervalued even, or particularly, by those who do it.

A new feminist paradigm of work and family is one in which gender does not matter to either work or care. A shared work-valued care model recognizes the value of care as work and redistributes more equitably the costs and benefits of caring for both young and old, both of which, after all, are public "goods." Provisioning is an emerging feminist concept that characterizes all we do for our families and ourselves, whether in paid work or in family, in private or in public.

"Provisioning" is used in multiple and diverse ways. It is an internet term to describe coordinating or connecting computer systems. It is used commonly in ecological studies of birds and animals to describe how groups work together to sustain their young and their communities. The term is also used in macro-economics and in reference to public provision of basic social goods such as health care or unemployment insurance. A basic tenet of social provisioning is that "caring labor and domestic labor are vital parts of any economic system and should be incorporated into the analysis from the beginning, not shoehorned in as an afterthought" (Power 2004, 4). There is, in other words, no possibility of separating paid work from other kinds of economically important contributions such as caring and unpaid work in families. But social provisioning is more than unity of paid work with family work. The term emphasizes process as well as outcomes. The ways in which we provide for ourselves, both paid and unpaid, are included, as are the processes of community caring as valued economic contributions. The inclusion of community and wider society makes social provisioning an inherently political concept. It can illuminate the ways a society organizes itself to produce and reproduce material life. Once spotlighted, change is often a next step. Schild (2002) shows how reliance on a social provisioning model in Chile, with a focus on social inclusion and political movements, can be empowering toward fundamental political change.

Social provisioning takes both family and work out of their gendered, essential garments. The organization of social provisioning is not the "natural" outcome of market or gender. Rather, its organization reflects relations of power – social power. Its organization therefore is subject to change, human will, and negotiation. In broadening the conceptualization of what constitutes economic activity, social provisioning enables deeper understanding of the interdependency of paid work with unpaid work and caring (Neysmith and Reitsma-Street 2005). Individuals are seen as a part of systems that connect and interconnect, rather than as atomized actors making choices based on either self-interest or societal expectation.

It is not difficult then to see how the concept of social provisioning could be the guiding concept for a better future for work and family for women as we move beyond the trapeze image of a balancing act between paid work and all the rest of our lives. The concept of provisioning can be used in multiple ways to explore how innovative social movements of women provide for themselves, their families, their communities, and their societies in increasingly challenging times.

References

Abrahams, Naomi. 1996. Negotiating Power, Identity, Family, and Community: Women's Community Participation. *Gender and Society* 10(6): 768-96.

Ackers, Louise. 2004. Citizenship, Migration and the Valuation of Care in the European Union. *Journal of Ethnic and Migration Studies* 30(2): 373-96.

Ahmed, Sara. 2004. *The Cultural Politics of Emotion*. Edinburgh: Edinburgh University Press.

Akyeampong, Ernest B. 2006. Unionization. *Perspectives on Labour and Income* 7(8): 18-32.

Albanese, Patrizia. 2006. Small Town, Big Benefits: The Ripple Effect of $7/Day Child Care. *Canadian Review of Sociology and Anthropology* 43(2): 125-40.

Allen, Karen R., and Alexis J. Walker. 1992. Attentive Love: A Feminist Perspective on the Caregiving of Adult Daughters. *Family Relations* 41(3): 284-89.

Allen, Sarah M., and Alan J. Hawkins. 1999. Maternal Gatekeeping: Mothers' Beliefs and Behaviors that Inhibit Greater Father Involvement in Family Work. *Journal of Marriage and Family* 61: 199-212.

Amato, Paul R. 2004a. Parenting through Family Transitions. *Social Policy Journal of New Zealand* 23(12): 31-44.

–. 2004b. Tension between Institutional and Individual Views of Marriage. *Journal of Marriage and Family* 66: 959-65.

Ambert, Anne-Marie. 1994. An International Perspective on Parenting: Social Change and Social Constructs. *Journal of Marriage and Family* 56: 529-43.

–. 2006a. *Changing Families: Relationships in Context*. Toronto: Pearson.

–. 2006b. *One-Parent Families: Characteristics, Causes, Consequences, and Issues*. Toronto: Vanier Institute of the Family.

Anderson, Kim. 2000. *Recognition of Being: Reconstructing Native Womenhood*. Toronto: Second Story Press.

Anxo, Dominique, Colette Fagan, Sangheon Lee, Deirdre McCann, and Jon C. Messenger. 2004a. Implications for Working Time Policies. In Messenger 2004a, 195-211.

Anxo, Dominique, Colette Fagan, Deirdre McCann, Sangheon Lee, and Jon C. Messenger. 2004b. Introduction: Working Time in Industrialized Countries. In Messenger 2004a, 1-9.

Appelbaum, Eileen. 2001. Transformation of Work and Employment and New Insecurities. In *The Future of Work, Employment and Social Protection,* ed. P. Auer and C. Daniel, 15-37. Geneva: International Labour Organization.

Appelbaum, Eileen, Thomas Bailey, Peter Berg, and Arne L. Kalleberg. 2002. Shared Work – Valued Care: New Norms for Organizing Market Work and Unpaid Care Work. *Economic and Industrial Democracy* 23(1): 125-31.

Aptheker, Bettina. 1989. *Tapestries of Life: Women's Work, Women's Consciousness, and the Meaning of Daily Experience*. Amherst: University of Massachusetts Press.

Arat-Koc, Sedef. 2006. Whose Social Reproduction? Transnational Motherhood and Challenges to Feminist Political Economy. In Bezanson and Luxton 2006, 75-92.

Arber, Sara, and Jay Ginn. 1991. *Gender and Later Life: A Sociological Analysis of Resources and Constraints.* London: Sage.

Arendell, Terry. 2000. Conceiving and Investigating Motherhood: The Decade's Scholarship. *Journal of Marriage and Family* 62(4): 1192-209.

Armstrong, Pat, and Hugh Armstrong. 1990. *Theorizing Women's Work.* Toronto: Garamond Press.

Armstrong, Pat, and Olga Kits. 2004. One Hundred Years of Caregiving. In *Caring from/ Caring About,* ed. Karen R. Grant, Carol Amaratunga, Pat Armstrong, Madeline Boscoe, Ann Pederson, and Kay Willson, 45-73. Aurora, ON: Garamond Press.

–. 2005. Public and Private: Implications for Care Work. *Sociological Review* 53(2): 167-87.

Association Québécoise des Centres de la Petite Enfance. 2007. *Les CPE en Chiffres.* http:// www.aqcpe.com/.

Atkinson, Robert D. 2006. Building a More-Humane Economy. *The Futurist,* May-June: 44-49.

Attias-Donfut, Claudine. 1995. *Les solidarities entre generations.* Paris: Nathan.

Babbage, Maria. 2010. Ontario to Offer Full-Day Kindergarten in 600 Schools. *Globe and Mail,* 11 January.

Bader, Ed, and Andrea Doucet. 2005. *Canadian Community Organizations and New Fathers: A Report of the New Fathers Cluster of the Father Involvement Research Alliance (FIRA).* Guelph, ON: FIRA-CURA Project, University of Guelph.

Bailey, Sue. 2007. No Tory Child-Care Plan as Parents Face Long Waits, Rising Fees. *Canadian Press,* 22 January.

Baines, Carol, Patricia M. Evans, and Sheila Neysmith. 1998. Caring: Its Impact on the Lives of Women. In *Women's Caring: Feminist Perspectives on Social Welfare,* ed. C. Baines, P.M. Evans, and S. Neysmith, 11-35. Toronto: Oxford University Press.

Baines, Donna. 2004a. Caring for Nothing: Work Organization and Unwaged Labour in Social Services. *Work, Employment and Society* 18(2): 267-95.

–. 2004b. Pro-Market, Non-Market: The Dual Nature of Organizational Change in Social Services Delivery. *Journal of Critical Social Policy* 24(1): 5-29.

–. 2004c. Seven Kinds of Work – Only One Paid: Raced, Gendered and Restructured Care Work in the Social Services Sector. *Atlantis: A Women's Studies Journal* 28(2): 19-28.

Bakan, Abigail, and Daiva Stasiulis. 2005. *Negotiating Citizenship: Migrant Women in Canada and the Global Context.* Toronto: University of Toronto Press.

Baker, Maureen. 1994. Family and Population Policy in Quebec: Implications for Women. *Canadian Journal of Women and the Law* 7(1): 116-32.

–. 1995. *Canadian Family Policies: Cross-National Comparisons.* Toronto: University of Toronto Press.

–. 2001. *Families, Labour and Love: Family Diversity in a Changing World.* Sydney: Allen and Unwin.

–. 2004. Devaluing Mothering at Home: Welfare Restructuring and Perceptions of "Mother-work." *Atlantis: A Women's Studies Journal* 28(2): 51-60.

–. 2005. Medically Assisted Conception: Revolutionizing Family or Perpetuating a Nuclear and Gendered Model? *Journal of Comparative Family Studies* 36(4): 521-43.

–. 2006. *Restructuring Family Policies: Convergences and Divergences.* Toronto: University of Toronto Press.

–. 2008. Low-Income Mothers, Employment and Welfare Restructuring. In *New Zealand, New Welfare,* ed. N. Lunt, M. O'Brien, and R. Stephens, 69-77. Melbourne: Cengage Learning.

–. 2009. Working Their Way Out of Poverty? Gendered Employment in Three Welfare States. Special issue, *Journal of Comparative Family Studies* 40(4): 617-34.

–. 2010. *Choices and Constraints in Family Life.* Toronto: Oxford University Press.

Baker, Maureen, and Shelley Phipps. 1997. Family Change and Family Policy: Canada. In *Family Change and Family Policies in Britain, Canada, New Zealand and the U.S.,* ed. S. Kamerman and A. Kahn, 137-273. Oxford: Oxford University Press.

Baker, Maureen, and David Tippin. 1999. *Poverty, Social Assistance and the Employability of Mothers: Restructuring Welfare States.* Toronto: University of Toronto Press.

Baker, Michael, Jonathan Gruber, and Kevin Milligan. 2005. Universal Child Care, Maternal Labor Supply and Family Well-Being. NBRE Working Paper 11832, National Bureau of Economic Research, Cambridge, MA.

Bakker, Isabella. 1996. Introduction: The Gendered Foundations of Restructuring in Canada. In *Rethinking Restructuring: Gender and Change in Canada*, ed. I. Bakker, 3-28. Toronto: University of Toronto Press.

Balbo, Laura. 1987. Crazy Quilts: Rethinking the Welfare State Debate from a Woman's Point of View. In *Women and the State*, ed. A. Showstack Sasson, 45-71. London: Hutchinson.

Baril, Robert, Pierre Lefebvre, and Philip Merrigan. 2000. Quebec Family Policy: Impact and Options. IRPP *Choices* 6(1): 1-52.

Barnard, Catherine, Simon Deakin, and Richard Hobbs. 2003. Opting Out of the 48-Hour Week: Employer Necessity or Individual Choice? An Empirical Study of the Operation of Article 18(1)(b) of the Working Time Directive in the UK. *Industrial Law Journal* 32(4): 223-52.

Barreiro, Jose, ed. 1992. *Indian Roots of American Democracy*. Ithaca, NY: Akwe:kon Press.

Bartholet, Elizabeth. 2005. Abuse and Neglect, Foster Drift, and the Adoption Alternative. In Haslanger and Witt 2005, 223-33.

Bashevkin, Sylvia. 1983. Social Change and Political Partisanship: The Development of Women's Attitudes in Quebec, 1965-1979. *Comparative Political Studies* 16(2): 147-72.

–. 2002. *Welfare Hot Buttons: Women, Work, and Social Policy Reform*. Toronto: University of Toronto Press.

Baxter, Janine, Belinda Hewitt, and Michele Haynes. 2008. Life Course Transitions and Housework: Marriage, Parenthood and Time Spent on Housework. *Journal of Marriage and Family* 70(2): 259-72.

Beaujot, Roderic. 2000. *Earning and Caring in Canadian Families*. Peterborough, ON: Broadview Press.

–. 2004. *Delayed Life Transitions: Trends and Implications; Contemporary Family Trends*. Ottawa: Vanier Institute of the Family.

Beaujot, Roderic, and Don Kerr. 2004. *Population Change in Canada*. 2nd ed. Don Mills, ON: Oxford University Press.

Beaupré, Pascale, Pierre Turcotte, and Anne Milan. 2006. Junior Comes Back Home: Trends and Predictors of Returning to the Parental Home. *Canadian Social Trends* 82 (Winter): 28-34.

Beavon, Daniel, and Martin Cooke. 2003. An Application to the UN Human Development Index and Registered Indians in Canada, 1996. In *Aboriginal Conditions: Research as a Foundation for Public Policy*, ed. J.P. White, P.S. Maxim, and D. Beavon, 201-21. Vancouver: UBC Press.

Bégin, Louise, Louise Ferland, Gaétane Girard, Chantal Gougeonet. 2002. *School Daycare Services*. Quebec: Government of Quebec.

Béland, Daniel, and André Lecours. 2006. Sub-State Nationalism and the Welfare State: Québec and Canadian Federalism. *Nations and Nationalism* 12(1): 77-96.

Bell, Linda, and Jane Ribbens. 1994. Isolated Housewives and Complex Maternal Worlds – the Significance of Social Contacts between Women with Young Children in Industrial Societies. *Sociological Review* 42(2): 227-62.

Bengtson, Vern L. 2001. The Burgess Award Lecture – Beyond the Nuclear Family: The Increasing Importance of Multigenerational Bonds. *Journal of Marriage and Family* 63(1): 1-16.

Bertoia, Carl, and Janice Drakich. 1993. The Fathers' Rights Movement: Contradictions in Rhetoric and Practice. *Journal of Family Issues* 14(4): 592-615.

Bezanson, Kate. 2006. Gender and the Limits of Social Capital. *Canadian Review of Sociology and Anthropology* 43(4): 427-43.

Bezanson, Kate, and Meg Luxton, eds. 2006. *Social Reproduction: Feminist Political Economy Challenges Neo-Liberalism*. Montreal and Kingston: McGill-Queen's University Press.

Bibby, Reginald W. 2004. *The Future Families Project: A Survey of Canadian Hopes and Dreams*. Toronto, Vanier Institute of the Family. http://www.vifamily.ca/.

Bird, Delys, Wendy Were, and Terri-Ann White, eds. 2003. Future Imaginings: Sexualities and Genders in the New Millennium. In *From Shared Expectations to Profound Ambivalence: Australia's Gender Culture in the 1950s and the 1990s*, ed. Belinda Probert, 25-42. Claremont, WA: University of Western Australian Press.

Blaisure, Karen R., and J. Koivunen. 2000. Incorporating a Discussion of Equality in Couple Education Programs. *Family Science Review* 13(1-2): 74-95.

Bleijenbergh, Inge, Jeanne de Bruijn, and Jet Bussemaker. 2004. European Social Citizenship and Gender: The Part-Time Work Directive. *European Journal of Industrial Relations* 10(3): 309-28.

Blume, Libbi B., and Thomas W. Blume. 2003. Toward a Dialectical Model of Family Gender Discourse: Body, Identity, and Sexuality. *Journal of Marriage and Family* 65: 785-94.

Bolderson, Helen, and Deborah Mabbett. 1991. *Social Policy and Social Security in Australia, Britain and the USA*. Aldershot: Avebury.

Bookman, Ann. 2003. *Starting in Our Own Backyards: How Working Families Can Build Community and Survive in the New Economy*. New York: Routledge.

Booth, Christine, and Bennett Cinnamon. 2002. Gender Mainstreaming in the European Union: Towards a New Conception and Practice of Equal Opportunities? *European Journal of Women's Studies* 9(4): 430-47.

Borrell, Carme, C. Muntaner, J. Benach, and L. Artazcoz. 2004. Social Class and Self-Reported Health Status among Men and Women: What Is the Role of Work Organisation, Household Materials Standards and Household Labour? *Social Science and Medicine* 58: 1869-87.

Bosch, Gerhard. 1995. Synthesis Report. In OECD 1995.

–. 1999. Working Time: Tendencies and Emerging Issues. *International Labour Review* 138(2): 131-49.

Bosch, Gerhard, and Peter Tergeist. 1995. Proceedings of the OECD Experts' Meeting on Flexible Working Time Arrangements: The Role of Bargaining and Government Intervention. In OECD 1995.

Bourdieu, Pierre. 2005. *The Social Structures of the Economy*. Cambridge: Polity Press.

Bourgeault, Ron. 1988. The Struggle of Class and Nation: The Canadian Fur Trade, 1670s to 1870. *Alternate Routes* 8: 74-122.

Boychuk, Gerald William. 1998. *Patchworks of Purpose: The Development of Provincial Social Assistance Regimes in Canada*. Montreal and Kingston: McGill-Queen's University Press.

Boyd, Elisabeth. 2002. Being There: Mothers Who Stay at Home, Gender and Time. *Women's Studies International Forum* 25(4): 463-70.

Boyd, Susan B. 2003. *Child Custody, Law, and Women's Work*. Toronto: Oxford University Press.

Bozett, Frederick W., and Shirley M.H. Hanson, eds. 1991. *Fatherhood and Families in Cultural Context*. New York: Springer.

Bradbury, Bettina. 2000. Single Parenthood in the Past: Canadian Census Categories, 1891-1951, and the "Normal" Family. *Historical Methods* 33(4): 211-17.

–. 2005. The Social, Economic and Cultural Origins of Contemporary Families. In *Families: Changing Trends in Canada*, 5th ed., ed. M. Baker, 71-98. Toronto: McGraw-Hill Ryerson.

Bradshaw, Jonathan, and Naomi Finch. 2002. A Comparison of Child Benefit Packages in 22 Countries. UK Department for Work and Pensions Research Report 174. Leeds: Corporate Document Services.

Brady, Michelle. 2008. Absences and Silences in the Production of Work-Life Balance Policies in Canada. *Studies in Political Economy* 81: 99-128.

Braidotti, Rosi. 2002. *Metamorphoses: Towards a Materialist Theory of Becoming*. Cambridge: Polity Press.

Brandth, Berit, and Elin Kvande. 1998. Masculinity and Child Care: The Reconstruction of Fathering. *Sociological Review* 46(2): 293-313.

Brave Heart, Maria Yellow Horse. 2000. *Wakiksuyapi*: Carrying the Historical Trauma of the Lakota. *Tulane Studies in Social Welfare* 21-22: 245-66.

Braverman, Lois. 1989. Beyond the Myth of Motherhood. In *Women in Families: A Framework for Family Therapy*, ed. M. McGoldrick, C.M. Anderson, and F. Walsh, 227-43. New York: W.W. Norton.

Brennan, Deborah. 2007. The ABC of Child Care Politics. *Australian Journal of Social Issues* 42(2): 213-25.

Brodie, Janine. 1995. The De-Re-Gendering of Social Policy. *Canadian Watch* (3)1.

–. 1996. Canadian Women, Changing State Forms, and Public Policy. In *Women and Canadian Public Policy,* ed. J. Brodie, 1-24. Toronto: Harcourt Brace.

–. 1997. Meso-Discourses, State Forms and the Gendering of Liberal-Democratic Citizenship. *Citizenship Studies* 1: 223-42.

–. 2007. Reforming Social Justice in Neo-Liberal Times. *Studies in Social Justice* 1(2): 93-107.

Brody, Elaine. 1990. *Women in the Middle: Their Parent-Care Years.* New York: Springer.

Bronstein, Phyllis, and Carolyn Cowan, eds. 1988. *Fatherhood Today: Men's Changing Role in the Family.* New York: Wiley and Sons.

Brown, Lyn Mikel, and Carol Gilligan. 1993. Meeting at the Crossroads: Women's Psychology and Girls' Development. *Feminism and Psychology* 3(1): 11-35.

Bryceson, Deborah F., and Ulla Vuorela. 2002. Introd. to *The Transnational Family: New European Frontiers and Global Networks,* ed. D.F. Bryceson and U. Vuorela, 3-30. New York: Oxford University Press.

Bryson, Valerie. 1998. *Feminist Debates: Issues of Theory and Political Practice.* Houndmills: Macmillan.

Bubeck, Elisabet. 1995. *Care, Gender, and Justice.* Oxford: Clarendon Press.

Buchanan, Ruth. 2006. 1-800-New Brunswick: Economic Development Strategies, Firm Restructuring, and the Local Production of "Global" Services. In Shalla 2006, 177-202.

Buchignani, Norman, and Christopher Armstrong-Esther. 1999. Informal Care and Older Native Canadians. *Aging and Society* 19: 3-32.

Budgeon, Shelley, and Sasha Roseneil. 2004. Beyond the Conventional Family. *Current Sociology* 52(2): 127-34.

Burggraf, Shirley P. 1997. *The Feminine Economy and Economic Man.* Reading: Addison-Wesley.

Burri, Susanne. 2006. Flexibility and Security, Working-Time and Work-Family Policies. In Fudge and Owens 2006, 305-28.

Butler, Judith. 1990. *Gender Trouble: Feminism and the Subversion of Identity.* New York: Routledge.

–. 1993. *Bodies That Matter: On the Discursive Limits of Sex.* New York: Routledge.

–. 1997. *The Psychic Life of Power: Theories of Subjection.* Stanford, CA: Stanford University Press.

–. 2002. Is Kinship Always Already Heterosexual? *Differences* 13(1): 14-44.

–. 2003. The Question of Social Transformation. In *Women and Social Transformation,* ed. Elizabeth Beck-Gernsheim, Judith Butler, and Lidia Pulgvert, 5-21. New York: Peter Lang.

–. 2004. *Undoing Gender.* New York: Routledge.

Butler, Linda. 1993. Unpaid Work in the Home and Accreditation. In *Culture and Processes of Adult Learning: A Reader,* ed. M. Thorpe, R. Edwards, and A. Hanson, 66-86. London: Routledge.

CAALL (Canadian Association of Administrators of Labour Legislation). 2002. *Work-Life Balance: A Report to Ministers Responsible for Labour in Canada.* Ottawa: Canadian Association of Administrators of Labour Legislation Ad Hoc Committee.

Calasanti, Toni. 2006. Gender and Old Age: Lessons from Spousal Care Work. In Calasanti and Slevin 2006, 269-94.

Calasanti, Toni, and Kathleen F. Slevin. 2001. *Gender, Social Inequalities and Aging.* Walnut Creek, CA: AltaMira Press.

–, eds. 2006. *Age Matters: Realigning Feminist Thinking.* London: Routledge.

Calliste, Agnes. 2003. Black Families in Canada: Exploring the Interconnections of Race, Class, and Gender. In *Voices: Essays on Canadian Families,* 2nd ed., ed. M. Lynn, 243-70. Scarborough, ON: Thomson Nelson.

Campaign 2000. 2006. *Oh Canada! Too Many Children in Poverty for Too Long; 2006 Report Card on Child and Family Poverty in Canada.* http://www.campaign2000.ca/.

Campbell, Iain. 1997. Working-Time: Comparing Australia and Germany. In *Work of the Future: Global Perspectives,* ed. P. James, W.F. Veit, and S. Wright, 198-222. St. Leonards, NSW: Allen and Unwin.

Campbell, Lori D., and Michael Carroll. 2007. The Incomplete Revolution: Theorizing Gender When Studying Men Who Provide Care to Aging Parents. *Men and Masculinities* 9(4): 491-508.

Canada. 1997. *Public Dialogue on the National Children's Agenda – Developing a Shared Vision.* http://www.socialunion.ca/.

–. 2006. *Welfare Incomes.* Ottawa: Minister of Public Works and Government Services.

–. Policy Research Initiative. 2006. Work and Life Balance: Better Choice, Flexibility and Policy Opportunities. *Horizons* 8(3): 1-2.

Canada and Quebec. 2005. *Canada-Quebec Agreement on Early Learning and Child Care.* http://action.web.ca/home/crru/.

Canadian Press. 2007. Nuclear Family Still Thrives in Some Parts of Canada. 12 September. http://www.ctv.ca/.

–. 2008. Auditor: Foster Care Failing Native Children. 6 May. http://www.thestar.com/.

Cancian, Francesca M. 2004. From Role to Self: The Emergence of Androgynous Love in the 20th Century. In *Public and Private Families: A Reader,* 4th ed., ed. A. Cherlin, 75-91. New York: McGraw-Hill.

Caplan, Leslie J., and Carmi Schooler. 2006. Household Work Complexity, Intellectual Functioning, and Self-Esteem in Men and Women. *Journal of Marriage and Family* 68: 883-900.

Card, Claudia. 1996. Against Marriage and Motherhood. *Hypatia* 11(3): 1-23.

Carniol, Ben. 2000. *Case Critical: Challenging Social Services in Canada.* 4th ed. Toronto: Between the Lines.

Carroll, Michael, and Lori Campbell. 2008. Who Now Reads Parsons and Bales? Casting a Critical Eye on the Gendered Styles of Caregiving Literature. *Journal of Aging Studies* 22: 24-31.

Carroll, William K. 2004. *Corporate Power in a Globalizing World.* Toronto: Oxford University Press.

Castellano, Marlene Brant. 2002. *Aboriginal Family Trends: Extended Families, Nuclear Families, Families of the Heart.* Nepean, ON: Vanier Institute of the Family.

CCAAC (Child Care Advocacy Association of Canada). 2004. *From Patchwork to Framework: A Child Care Strategy for Canada.* Toronto: CCAAC.

CEU (Council of the European Union). 2005. A Central Role for Gender Mainstreaming. In *Beijing +10: Progress Made within the European Union; Report from the Luxembourg Presidency of the Council of the European Union.* http://www.emancipatieweb.nl/uploads/2096/UB006798.pdf.

Chalmers, Jenny, and Trish Hill. 2005. Part-Time Work and Women's Careers: Advancing or Retreating? Paper presented at the Australian Social Policy Conference, Sydney.

Chappell, Neena L., and Margaret J. Penning. 2005. Family Caregivers: Increasing Demands in the Context of 21st-Century Globalization? In *The Cambridge Handbook of Age and Aging,* ed. M.L. Johnson, 455-62. New York: Cambridge University Press.

Charles, Nickie, and Chris Harris. 2007. Continuity and Change in Work-Life Balance Choices. *British Journal of Sociology* 58(2): 277-95.

Chaykowski, Richard, and George Slotsve. 2008. The Extent of Economic Vulnerability in the Canadian Labour Market and Federal Jurisdiction: Is There a Role for Labour Standards? *Social Indicators Research* 88(1): 75-96.

Che-Alford, Janet, and Brian Hamm. 1999. Under One Roof: Three Generations Living Together. *Canadian Social Trends* 53 (Summer): 6-9.

Cherlin, Andrew J. 1999. *Public and Private Families.* Boston: McGraw-Hill.

–. 2004. The Deinstitutionalization of American Marriage. *Journal of Marriage and Family* 66: 848-61.

–. 2006. On Single Mothers "Doing" Family. *Journal of Marriage and Family* 68: 800-3.

Childs, John Brown. 2003. *Transcommunality: From the Politics of Conversion to the Ethics of Respect.* Philadelphia: Temple University Press.

Chisholm, June F. 1999. The Sandwich Generation. *Journal of Social Distress and the Homeless* 8(3): 177-80.

Chrisjohn, Roland, and Sherri Young. 1997. *The Circle Game: Shadows and Substance in the Indian Residential School Experience in Canada.* Penticton, BC: Theytus Books.

Christopher, Karen. 2002. Welfare State Regimes and Mothers' Poverty. *Social Politics* 9(1): 60-86.

Chung, Lucy. 2006. Education and Earnings. *Perspectives on Labour and Income* 7(6): 9-12.

CIDA (Canadian International Development Agency). 1999. *Policy on Gender Equality.* Ottawa: Minister of Public Works and Government Services.

Clark, Warren. 2007. Delayed Transitions of Young Adults. *Canadian Social Trends* 84 (Winter): 14-22.

Clement, Wallace, and Leah F. Vosko, eds. 2003. *Changing Canada: Political Economy as Transformation.* Montreal and Kingston: McGill-Queen's University Press.

Cleveland, Gordon. 2007. *The Benefits and Costs of Quebec's Centres de la Petite Enfance.* http://action.web.ca/home/crru/.

Cleveland, Gordon, Barry Forer, Douglas Hyatt, Christa Japel, and Michael Krashinsky. 2007. *An Economic Perspective on the Current and Future Role of Nonprofit Provisions of Early Learning and Child Care Services in Canada: Final Project Report.* http://childcarepolicy.net/.

Cleveland, Gordon, and Michael Krashinsky. 2001a. Financing Early Learning and Child Care in Canada. Discussion paper prepared for the Canadian Council on Social Development's National Conference on Child Care in Canada – Child Care for a Change! Shaping the 21st Century, Winnipeg.

–, eds. 2001b. *Our Children's Future: Child Care Policy in Canada.* Toronto: University of Toronto Press.

Clio Collective. 1987. *Quebec Women: A History.* Toronto: Women's Press.

Cohen, Aaron, and Catherine Kirchmeyer. 1995. A Multidimensional Approach to the Relations between Organizational Commitment and Nonwork Participation. *Journal of Vocational Behavior* 46: 189-202.

Cohen, Theodore F. 1993. What Do Fathers Provide? Reconsidering the Economic and Nutriment Dimensions of Men as Parents. In *Men, Work and Family,* ed. J.C. Hood, 1-22. London: Sage.

Collier, Richard. 1999. Men, Heterosexuality and the Changing Family: (Re)Constructing Fatherhood in Law and Social Policy. In *Changing Family Values,* ed. G. Jagger and C. Wright, 38-58. London: Routledge.

Collins, Hugh. 2005. The Right to Flexibility. In Conaghan and Rittich 2005, 99-124.

Collins, Patricia Hill. 1990. *Black Feminist Thought: Knowledge, Consciousness, and the Politics of Empowerment.* New York: Routledge.

–. 1994. Shifting the Center: Race, Class and Feminist Theorizing about Motherhood. In *Representations of Motherhood,* ed. D. Bassin, M. Honey, and M.M. Kaplan, 56-74. New Haven, CT: Yale University Press.

–. 2000. *Black Feminist Thought: Knowledge, Consciousness, and the Politics of Empowerment.* Rev. 10th anniversary ed. New York: Routledge.

–. 2004. *Black Sexual Politics: African Americans, Gender, and the New Racism.* London: Routledge.

Coltrane, Scott. 1989. Household Labor and the Routine Production of Gender. *Social Problems* 36(5): 473-90.

–. 1996. *Family Man: Fatherhood, Housework, and Gender Equity.* New York: Oxford University Press.

–. 2004. Elite Careers and Family Commitment: It's (Still) about Gender. *ANNALS of the American Academy of Political and Social Science* 596: 214-20.

Comfort, Derrick, Karen Johnson, and David Wallace. 2003. *Part-Time Work and Family-Friendly Practices in Canadian Workplaces.* Ottawa: Statistics Canada.

Commission on Elementary Education. 2006. *School Daycare Services: Placing Quality at the Heart of Priorities.* Quebec: Government of Quebec.

Conaghan, Joanne. 2002. Women, Work and Family: A British Revolution? In *Labour Law in an Era of Globalization: Transformative Practices and Possibilities,* ed. J. Conaghan, R.M. Fischl, and K. Klare, 54-73. London: Oxford University Press.

–. 2006. Time to Dream? Flexibility, Families, and Working Time. In Fudge and Owens 2006, 101-30.

Conaghan, Joanne, and Kerry Rittich. 2005. *Labour Law, Work, and Family: Critical and Comparative Perspectives*. Oxford: Oxford University Press.

Conference Board of Canada. 2006. *Canada's Demographic Revolution: Adjusting to an Aging Population*. Ottawa: Conference Board of Canada.

–. 2007. *Too Few People, Too Little Time: The Employer Challenge of an Aging Workforce*. http://www.conferenceboard.ca/.

Connell, Robert W. 1987. *Gender and Power: Society, the Person and Sexual Politics*. Cambridge: Polity Press.

–. 2000. *The Men and the Boys*. Cambridge: Polity Press.

Connelly, Mary Patricia. 1978. *Last Hired, First Fired*. Toronto: Women's Press.

Connidis, Ingrid Arnet. 2002. The Impact of Demographic and Social Trends on Informal Support for Older Persons. In *Aging and Demographic Change in Canadian Context*, ed. D. Cheal, 105-32. Toronto: University of Toronto Press.

Connidis, Ingrid Arnet, and Julie Ann McMullin. 2002. Sociological Ambivalence and Family Ties: A Critical Perspective. *Journal of Marriage and Family* 64(3): 558-67.

Conway-Turner, Kate. 1999. Older Women of Color: A Feminist Exploration of the Intersections of Personal, Familial and Community life. *Journal of Women and Aging* 1(2/3): 115-30.

Cooke-Reynolds, Melissa, and Nancy Zukewich. 2004. The Feminization of Work. *Canadian Social Trends* 72 (Spring): 24-29.

Cooney, Teresa, and Peter Uhlenberg. 1992. Support from Parents over the Life Course. *Social Forces* 71(1): 63-84.

Coontz, Stephanie. 1992. *The Way We Never Were: American Families and the Nostalgia Trip*. New York: Basic Books.

–. 1997. *The Way We Really Are: Coming to Terms with America's Changing Families*. New York: Basic Books.

–. 2004. The World Historical Transformation of Marriage. *Journal of Marriage and Family* 66(4): 974-79.

Cooper, Mick, and Peter Baker. 1996. Fathering: The Nurturing Man. In *The MANual: The Complete Man's Guide to Life*, ed. M. Cooper and P. Baker. New York: Thorsons.

Cornell, Drucilla. 2005. Adoption and Its Progeny. In Haslanger and Witt 2005, 19-46.

Correll, Shelley, Stephen Benard, and In Paik. 2007. Getting a Job: Is There a Motherhood Penalty? *American Journal of Sociology* 112(5): 1297-338.

Cournoyer, Dave. 2006. http://daveberta.ca/. (Accessed May 2007.)

Couton, Phillippe, and Jeffrey Cormier. 2001. Voluntary Associations and State Expansion in Quebec, 1955-1970. *Journal of Political and Military Sociology* 29: 19-45.

Coward, Ros. 1997. The Heaven and Hell of Mothering: Mothering and Ambivalence in the Mass Media. In *Mothering and Ambivalence,* ed. Wendy Hollway and Brid Featherstone, 111-18. London: Routledge.

Cowdery, Randi S., and Carmen Knudson-Martin. 2005. The Construction of Motherhood: Tasks, Relational Connection, and Gender Equality. *Family Relations* 54: 335-45.

Cranford, Cynthia J., Leah F. Vosko, and Nancy Zukewich. 2006. The Gender of Precarious Employment. *Relations Industrielles/Industrial Relations* 58(3): 454-82.

Cranswick, Kelly. 1997. Canada's Caregivers. *Canadian Social Trends* 47 (Winter): 2-6.

Cranswick, Kelly, and Thomas Derrick. 2005. Elder Care and the Complexities of Social Networks. *Canadian Social Trends* 77 (Summer): 10-15.

Creese, Gillian. 2007. Racializing Work/Reproducing White Privilege. In Shalla and Clement 2007, 192-226.

Crittenden, Ann. 2001. *The Price of Motherhood: Why the Most Important Job in the World Is Still the Least Valued*. New York: Metropolitan Books.

–. 2004. *If You've Raised Kids, You Can Manage Anything: Leadership Begins at Home*. New York: Gotham.

Crompton, Rosemary. 2002. Employment, Flexible Working and the Family. *British Journal of Sociology* 53(4): 537-58.

–. 2006. *Employment and the Family: The Reconfiguration of Work and Family Life in Contemporary Societies.* Cambridge: Cambridge University Press.

Croucher, Richard, and Clare Kellier. 2005. The Right to Request Flexible Working in Britain: The Law and Organizational Realities. *International Journal of Comparative Labour Law and Industrial Relations* 21(3): 503-20.

Cruikshank, Jane. 2007. Lifelong Learning and the New Economy: Rhetoric or Reality? *Education Canada* 47(2): 32-36.

Curry, Bill, and Gloria Galloway. 2008. We Are Sorry. *Globe and Mail,* 12 June.

Daly, Kerry. 1993. Through the Eyes of Others: Reconstructing the Meaning of Fatherhood. In *Men and Masculinities: A Critical Anthology,* ed. T. Haddad, 203-12. Toronto: Canadian Scholars' Press.

–. 2000. *Changing Patterns of Time in Families.* Ottawa: Vanier Institute of the Family.

–. 2004a. *The Changing Culture of Parenting.* Ottawa: Vanier Institute of the Family.

–. 2004b. VIF 40th Anniversary Lecture: Reframed Family Portraits. Ottawa: Vanier Institute of the Family.

Daly, Mary, and Katherine Rake. 2003. *Gender and the Welfare State.* Cambridge: Polity Press.

Das Gupta, T. 1999. The Politics of Multiculturalism: "Immigrant Women" and the Canadian State. In *Scratching the Surface: Canadian Anti-Racist Thought,* ed. E. Dua and A. Robertson, 187-206. Toronto: Women's Press.

–. 2000. Families of Native People, Immigrants, and People of Colour. In Mandell and Duffy 2000, 146-87.

Davis, Angela. 2001. Racism, Birth Control and Reproductive Rights. In *Women, Race and Class,* ed. A. Davis, 202-21. London: Women's Press.

Day, Randal, and Michael Lamb, eds. 2004. *Conceptualizing and Measuring Fathers' Involvement.* Mahwah, NJ: Lawrence Erlbaum.

Deakin, Simon. 2000. *The Many Futures of the Contract of Employment.* Cambridge: ESRC Centre for Business Research/University of Cambridge Press.

Delphy, Christine. 1984. *Close to Home: A Materialist Analysis of Women's Oppression.* Amherst: University of Massachusetts Press.

Demczuk, Irène, Michèle Caron, Ruth Rose, and Lyne Bouchard. 2002. *Recognition of Lesbian Couples: An Inalienable Right.* Ottawa: Status of Women Canada.

Dennerstein, Lorraine, Emma Dudley, and Janet Guthrie. 2002. Empty Nest or Revolving Door? A Prospective Study of Women's Quality of Life in Midlife during the Phase of Children Leaving and Re-Entering the Home. *Psychological Medicine* 32(3): 545-50.

Deutsch, Francine M. 1999. *Halving It All: How Equally Shared Parenting Works.* Cambridge, MA: Harvard University Press.

DeVault, Marjorie. 1991. *Feeding the Family: The Social Organization of Caring as Gendered Work.* Chicago: University of Chicago Press.

Dickinson, Torry D., and Robert K. Schaeffer. 2001. Fast Forward: Work, Gender, and Protest in a Changing World. Lanham, MD: Rowman and Littlefield.

Diebel, Linda. 2007. The Kidd Clan Is Fielding Eight Candidates in the Upcoming Election: Here, It's All in the (Coalition) Family. *Toronto Star,* 24 September.

Dienhart, Anna. 1998. *Reshaping Fatherhood: The Social Construction of Shared Parenting.* London: Sage.

Di Leonardo, Micaela. 1987. *The Female World of Cards and Holidays: Women, Families, and the Work of Kinship.* Chicago: University of Chicago Press.

Dillaway, Heather. 2006. Good Mothers Never Wane: Mothering at Menopause. *Journal of Women and Aging* 18(2): 41-53.

DiQuinzio, Patrice. 1999. *The Impossibility of Motherhood: Feminism, Individualism and the Problem of Mothering.* London: Routledge.

Doherty, Gillian, Martha Friendly, and Barry Forer. 2002. *Child Care by Default or Design? An Exploration of Differences between Non-Profit Canadian Child Care Centres Using the You Bet I Care! Data Sets.* Occasional Paper 18, Child Care Resource and Research Unit, Toronto.

Doherty, Gillian, Martha Friendly, and Mab Oloman. 1998. *Women's Support, Women's Work: Child Care in an Era of Deficit Reduction, Devolution, Downsizing and Deregulation.* Ottawa: Status of Women Canada.

Doucet, Andrea. 2000. There's a Huge Difference between Me as a Male Carer and Women: Gender, Domestic Responsibility, and the Community as an Institutional Arena. *Community Work and Family* 3(2): 163-84.

–. 2001a. Can Boys Grow into Mothers? Maternal Thinking and Fathers' Reflections. In *Mothers and Sons: Feminism Masculinity, and the Struggle to Raise Our Sons,* ed. A. O'Reilly, 163-83. London: Routledge.

–. 2001b. You See the Need Perhaps More Clearly than I Have: Exploring Gendered Processes of Domestic Responsibility. *Journal of Family Issues* 22(3): 328-57.

–. 2004. Fathers and the Responsibility for Children: A Puzzle and a Tension. Special issue, *Atlantis: A Women's Studies Journal* 28(2): 103-14.

–. 2006a. *Do Men Mother?* Toronto: University of Toronto Press.

–. 2006b. Estrogen-Filled Worlds: Fathers as Primary Caregivers and Embodiment. *Sociological Review* 23(4): 695-715.

Doucet, Andrea, and Natasha S. Mauthner. 2008. What Can Be Known and How? Narrated Subjects and the Listening Guide. Special issue, *Qualitative Research* 8(3): 399-409.

Dowd, Nancy E. 2000. *Redefining Fatherhood.* New York: New York University Press.

Dreby, Joanna. 2006. Honor and Virtue: Mexican Parenting in the Transnational Context. *Gender and Society* 20(1): 32-59.

Drolet, Marie, and Rene Morissette. 1997. *Working More? Working Less? What Do Canadian Workers Prefer?* Ottawa: Statistics Canada.

Dua, Enakshi. 1999. Beyond Diversity: Exploring the Ways in Which the Discourse of Race Has Shaped the Institution of the Nuclear Family. In *Scratching the Surface: Canadian Anti-Racist Thought,* ed. E. Dua and A. Robertson, 237-60. Toronto: Women's Press.

Duchesne, Louis. 2006. *La situation démographique au Québec – Bilan 2006.* Quebec: Institut de la statistique du Québec.

Dufour, Daniel. 2002. *The Lumber Industry: Crucial Contribution to Canada's Prosperity.* Manufacturing Overview Research Papers. Ottawa: Statistics Canada.

Dumont, Micheline, Michèle Jean, Marie Lavigne, and Jennifer Stoddart. 1987. *Quebec Women: A History.* Toronto: Women's Press.

Duncan, Simon, and Sarah Irwin. 2004. The Social Patterning of Values and Rationalities: Mothers' Choices in Combining Caring and Employment. *Social Policy and Society* 3(4): 391-99.

Dunne, Gillian. 2000. Opting into Motherhood: Lesbians Blurring the Boundaries and Transforming the Meaning of Parenthood and Kinship. *Gender and Society* 14(1): 11-35.

Duran, Eduardo, Bonnie Duran, Marie Yellow Horse Brave Heart, and Susan Yellow Horse. 1998. Healing the American Indian Soul Wound. In *International Handbook of Multigenerational Legacies of Trauma,* ed. Y. Danieli, 341-54. New York: Plenum Press.

Duxbury, Linda, and Christopher Higgins. 2001. *Work-Life Balance in the New Millennium: Where Are We? Where Do We Need to Go?* Ottawa: Canadian Policy Research Networks.

–. 2002. *The 2001 National Work-Life Conflict Study: Report One.* Ottawa: Health Canada.

–. 2003. *Work Life Conflict in Canada in the New Millennium: A Status Report.* Ottawa: Health Canada.

–. 2005. *Who Is at Risk? Predictors of Work Life Conflict; Report Four.* Ottawa: Health Canada.

Duxbury, Linda, Christopher Higgins, and Donna Coghill. 2003. *Voices of Canadians: Seeking Work-Life Balance.* Hull: Human Resources Development Canada.

Edwards, Paul, and Judy Wajcman. 2005. *The Politics of Working Life.* Oxford: Oxford University Press.

Eggbeen, David J., and Dennis P. Hogan. 1990. Giving between the Generations in American Families. *Human Nature* 1: 211-32.

Ehrenreich, Barbara. 1984. Life without Father: Reconsidering Socialist-Feminist Theory. *Socialist Review* 73: 48-57.

Ehrenreich, Barbara, and Arlie Hochschild. 2003. *Global Woman: Nannies, Maids, and Sex Workers in the New Economy.* New York: Metropolitan Books.

Eichler, Margrit. 1981. The Inadequacy of the Monolithic Model of the Family. *Canadian Journal of Sociology* 6(3): 367-88.

–. 1988. Nonsexist Research Methods: A Practical Guide. New York: Allen and Unwin.

–. 1997a. *Family Shifts: Families, Policies and Gender Equality.* Oxford: Oxford University Press.

–. 1997b. Feminist Methodology. *Current Sociology* 45: 9-36.

–. 2001. Biases in Family Literature. In *Families: Changing Trends in Canada,* 4th ed., ed. M. Baker, 51-66. Toronto: McGraw-Hill Ryerson.

–. 2005. The Other Half (or More) of the Story: Unpaid Household and Care Work and Lifelong Learning. In *International Handbook of Educational Policy,* ed. Nina Bascia, Alister Cumming, Amanda Datnow, Keith Leithwood, and David Livingstone, 1023-42. Dordrecht: Springer.

–. 2008. Just Women's Stuff: Lifelong Learning through Unpaid Household Work. In *The Future of Lifelong Learning and Work: Critical Perspectives,* ed. D. Livingstone, K. Merchandani, and P. Sawchuk. Rotterdam: Sense Publishers.

Eichler, Margrit, and Patrizia Albanese. 2007. What Is Household Work? A Critique of Assumptions Underlying Empirical Studies of Housework and an Alternative Approach. *Canadian Journal of Sociology* 32(2): 227-58.

Eichler, Margrit, and Ann Matthews. 2005. Was ist Arbeit? Eine Betrachtung aus der Perspektive Hausarbeit unbezahlter [What is work: A view from the perspective of unpaid housework]. In *Leben und Wirtschaften: Geschlechterkonstruktionen durch Arbeit* [Life and business: Gender construction through work], ed. W. Ernst, 17-34. Munster: LIT-Verlag.

–. 2007. What Is Work? Looking at All Work through the Lens of Unpaid Housework. In *Sociology in Canada: A Reader,* ed. L. Tepperman and H. Dickinson, 133-36. Oxford: Oxford University Press.

Elvin-Nowak, Ylva, and Helene Thomsson. 2001. Motherhood as Idea and Practice: A Discursive Understanding of Employed Mothers in Sweden. *Gender and Society* 15(3): 407-28.

Emberley, Julia V. 2001. The Bourgeois Family, Aboriginal Women, and Colonial Governance in Canada: A Study in Feminist Historical and Cultural Materialism. *Signs* 27: 59-85.

Esping-Andersen, Gøsta. 1990. *The Three Worlds of Welfare Capitalism.* Cambridge: Polity Press.

–, ed., with Duncan Gallie, Anton Hemerijck, and John Myles. 2002. *Why We Need a New Welfare State.* Oxford: Oxford University Press.

European Commission. 1996. *Communication on Incorporating Equal Opportunities for Women and Men in All Community Policies and Activities.* COM (96) 67 final. Brussels: European Commission.

–. 2003. *Integrating the Gender Dimension in the Sixth Framework Program of the European Commission.* Annex 4, Centre for Strategies and Evaluation Service. Brussels: European Commission.

Evans, John, Douglas C. Lippoldt, and Pascal Marianna. 2001. *Labour Market and Social Policy: Trends in Working Hours in OECD Countries.* Occasional Paper Number 45, 17-59. Organisation for Economic Co-operation and Development, Paris.

Evans, Patricia. 1996. Single Mothers and Ontario's Welfare Policy: Restructuring the Debate. In *Women in Canadian Public Policy,* ed. J. Brodie, 151-71. Toronto: Harcourt Brace.

Fagan, Colette. 2004. Gender and Working Time in Industrialized Countries. In Messenger 2004a, 108-46.

Farrar, Angela, and Laverne Gyant. 1998. African-American Women, Family and Hospitality Work. *Marriage and Family Review* 28: 125-41.

Fast, Janet. 2005. Caregiving: A Fact of Life. *Transition* (Summer): 4-9.

Fausto-Sterling, Anne. 1999. Is Gender Essential? In *Sissies and Tomboys: Gender Nonconformity and Homosexual Childhood,* ed. M. Rottnek, 52-57. New York: New York University Press.

–. 2000. *Sexing the Body: Gender Politics and the Construction of Sexuality.* New York: Basic Books.

–. 2003. The Problem with Sex/Gender and Nature/Nurture. In *Debating Biology: Reflections on Medicine, Health and Society,* ed. S.J. Williams, L. Birke, and G.A. Bendelow, 123-32. London: Routledge.

FCPO (Family Coalition Party of Ontario). 2010. Homepage and Policies. http://www.familycoalitionparty.com.

Fenstermaker Berk, Sarah. 1985. *The Gender Factory: The Apportionment of Work in American Households.* New York: Plenum.

Figart, Deborah M., and Lonnie Golden. 2000. Introduction and Overview: Understanding Working Time around the World. In *Working Time: International Trends, Theory and Policy Perspectives,* ed. L. Golden and D.M. Figart, 1-17. New York: Routledge.

Figart, Deborah M., and Ellen Mutari. 2000. Work Time Regimes in Europe: Can Flexibility and Gender Equity Coexist? *Journal of Economic Issues* 34(4): 847-71.

Fine, Michael, and Caroline Glendinning. 2005. Dependence, Independence or Interdependence? Revisiting the Concepts of "Care" and "Dependency." *Ageing and Society* 25(4): 601-21.

Fine-Davis, Margaret. 2004. *Fathers and Mothers: Dilemmas of the Work-Life Balance: A Comparative Study in Four European Countries.* Dordrecht: Kluwer Academic Publishers.

Fisher, Bernice, and Joan Tronto. 1990. Towards a Feminist Theory of Caring. In *Circles of Care: Work and Identity in Women's Lives,* ed. E. Abel and M.K. Nelson, 35-62. Albany: State University of New York Press.

Fiske, J., and Rose Johnny. 2003. The Lake Babini First Nation Family: Yesterday and Today. In *Voices: Essays on Canadian Families,* 2nd ed., ed. M. Lynn, 181-98. Toronto: Thomson Nelson.

Fitoussi, Michèle. 1987. *La ras-le-bol des superwomen* [Superwomen Are Fed Up]. Paris: Calmann-Lévy.

Fletcher, Alice. 1888. The Legal Conditions of Indian Women. In *Report of the International Council of Women, Assembly of the National Woman Suffrage Association,* ed. Rufus H. Darby. Washington, DC: International Council of Women.

Fogg-Davis, Hawley. 2005. Racial Randomization: Imagining Nondiscrimination in Adoption. In Haslanger and Witt 2005, 247-64.

Folbre, Nancy. 1995. Holding Hands at Midnight: The Paradox of Caring Labor. *Feminist Economics* 1(1): 73-92.

Ford, Reuben, David Gyartmati, Kelly Foley, and Doug Tattrie, with Liza Jimenez. 2003. *Can Work Incentives Pay for Themselves?* Ottawa: Social Research and Demonstration Corporation.

Foster, Lori, and Dave Broad. 2002. *The Child Care Policy That Wasn't.* Regina: Social Policy Research Unit, University of Regina Press.

Fournier, Suzanne, and Ernie Crey. 1997. *Stolen from Our Embrace: The Abduction of First Nations Children and the Restoration of Aboriginal Communities.* Vancouver: Douglas and McIntyre.

Fox, Bonnie. 2009. *When Couples Become Parents: The Creation of Gender in the Transition to Parenthood.* Toronto: University of Toronto Press.

Fox, Bonnie, and Meg Luxton. 2001. Conceptualizing Family. In *Family Patterns and Gender Relations,* ed. B. Fox, 22-33. Toronto: Oxford University Press.

Fraser, Nancy. 1989. *Unruly Practices: Power, Discourse, and Gender in Contemporary Theory.* Minneapolis: University of Minnesota Press.

–. 1997. *Justice Interruptus: Critical Reflections on the Postsocialist Condition.* New York: Routledge.

–. 2003. Social Justice in the Age of Identity Politics: Redistribution, Recognition and Participation. In *Redistribution or Recognition? A Political-Philosophical Exchange,* by Nancy Fraser and Axel Honneth, 7-109. London: Verso.

Fredman, Sandra. 2005. *Control over Time and Work-Life Balance: Comparative/Theoretical Perspective.* Ottawa: Human Resources and Skills Development Canada.

Freeman, Bonnie. 2007. Indigenous Pathways to Anti-Oppressive Practice. In *Doing Anti-Oppressive Practice: Building Transformative, Politicized Social Work,* ed. D. Baines, 95-111. Toronto: Fernwood.

Freeze, Colin. 2001. Women Outwork Men by Two Weeks Every Year. *Globe and Mail,* 13 March.

Frenette, Marc. 2007. Life after High Tech. *Perspectives on Labour and Income* 8(7): 5-13.

Frey, Michael. 2004. Ist der "Arbeitskraftunternehmer" weiblich? "Subjektivierte" Erwerbsorientierungen von Frauen in Prozessen betrieblicher Diskontinuitaet [Is There a Female

Entreprenuerial Workforce? "Subjective" Income Orientation of Women in the Process of Work Discontinuity]. *Arbeit* 13(1): 61-77.

Frey, Ron. 1997. How We Prevent Men from Parenting by Insisting They Remain Fathers. *Social Alternatives* 16(3): 23-25.

Friendly, Martha, and Jane Beach. 2005. Trends and Analysis: Early Childhood Education and Care in Canada, 2004. Toronto: Childcare Resource and Research Unit, University of Toronto.

Fruhauf, Christine A., Shannon E. Jarrott, and Katherine R. Allen. 2006. Grandchildren's Perceptions of Caring for Grandparents. *Journal of Family Issues* 17(7): 887-911.

Fudge, Judy. 2001. Flexibility and Feminization: The New Ontario Employment Standards Act. *Journal of Law and Social Policy* 16: 1-22.

–. 2005. The New Gender Contract: Work-Life Balance or Working-Time Flexibility? In Conaghan and Rittich 2005, 261-88.

–. 2006. Self-Employment, Women, and Precarious Work: The Scope of Labour Protection. In Fudge and Owens 2006, 3-27.

Fudge, Judy, and Brenda Cossman. 2002. Introd. to *Privatization, Law, and the Challenge to Feminism,* ed. B. Cossman and J. Fudge, 3-40. Toronto: University of Toronto Press.

Fudge, Judy, and Rosemary Owens, eds. 2006. *Precarious Work, Women and the New Economy: Challenging Legal Norms.* Oxford: Hart.

Fudge, Judy, and Leah Vosko. 2001. Gender, Segmentation and the Standard Employment Relationship in Canadian Labour Law and Policy. *Economic and Industrial Democracy* 22: 271-310.

–. 2003. Gender Paradoxes and the Rise of Contingent Work: Towards a Transformative Political Economy of the Labour Market. In Clement and Vosko 2003, 183-209.

Gal, Susan. 2002. A Semiotics of the Public/Private Distinction. *Differences* 13(1): 77-95.

Galabuzi, Grace-Edward. 2006. *Canada's Economic Apartheid: The Social Exclusion of Racialized Groups in the New Century.* Toronto: Canadian Scholars' Press.

Galarneau, Diane, Jean-Pierre Maynard, and Jin Lee. 2005. Whither the Workweek? *Perspectives on Labour and Income* 6(6): 5-17.

Gauthier, Anne Hélène. 1996. *The State and the Family: A Comparative Analysis of Family Policies in Industrialized Countries.* Oxford: Clarendon Press.

–. 2001. Family Policies and Families' Well-Being: An International Comparison. In Cleveland and Krashinsky 2001b, 251-74.

Gauvreau, Danielle, and Peter Gossage. 2001. Canadian Fertility Transitions: Quebec and Ontario at the Turn of the Twentieth Century. *Journal of Family History* 26(2): 162-88.

Gazso, Amber. 2007. Balancing Expectations for Employability and Family Responsibilities While on Social Assistance: Low-Income Mothers' Experiences in Three Canadian Provinces. *Family Relations* 56(5): 454-66.

–. 2009. Reinvigorating the Debate: Questioning the Assumptions about the Models of "the Family" in Canadian Social Assistance Policy. *Women's Studies International Forum* 32(2): 150-62.

Gelles, Richard. 1987. *The Violent Home.* Newbury Park, CA: Sage.

–. 1994. Introd. to special issue on Family Violence. *Journal of Comparative Family Studies* 25(1): 1-6.

Gershuny, Jonathan, Michael Godwin, and Sally Jones. 1994. The Domestic Labor Revolution: A Process of Lagged Adaptation? In *The Social and Political Economy of the Household,* ed. M. Anderson, F. Bechhofer, and J. Gershuny, 151-97. Oxford: Oxford University Press.

Gershuny, Jonathan, and Oriel Sullivan. 2003. Time Use, Gender, and Public Policy Regimes. *Social Politics* 10(2): 205-28.

Gerson, Kathleen. 2002. Moral Dilemmas, Moral Strategies, and the Transformation of Gender: Lessons from Two Generations of Work and Family Change. *Gender and Society* 16(1): 8-28.

Gervais, Diane, and Danielle Gauvreau. 2003. Women, Priests and Physicians: Family Limitation in Quebec, 1940-1970. *Journal of Interdisciplinary History* 34(2): 293-314.

Gerzer-Sass, Annemarie. 2004. Familienkompetenzen als Potential einer innovativen Personalpolitik. In *Kompetenzentwicklung im Wandle: Auf dem Weg zu einer informellen*

Lernkultur? [Family as Potential for an Innovative Workforce Policy: Competence in Change – The Path towards an Informal Learning Culture?], ed. B. Hungerland and B. Overwien, 89-112. Wiesbaden: Verlag für Sozialwissenschaften.

Ghalam, Nancy Zukewich. 1997. Attitudes toward Women, Work and Family. *Canadian Social Trends* 46 (Fall): 13-17.

Giele, Janet Z. 2002. Decline of the Family: Conservative, Liberal, and Feminist Views. In *Public and Private Families,* ed. A. Cherlin, 378-93. New York: McGraw-Hill.

Gillespie, Rosemary. 2000. When No Means No: Disbelief, Disregard, and Deviance as Discourses of Voluntary Childlessness. *Women's Studies International Forum* 23(2): 223-34.

Gilligan, Carol. 1982. *In a Different Voice: Psychological Theory and Women's Development.* Cambridge, MA: Harvard University Press.

Gindin, Sam, and Jim Stanford. 2006. Canadian Labour and the Political Economy of Transformation. In Shalla 2006, 379-94.

Ginn, Jay. 2001. Risk of Social Exclusion in Later Life: How Well Do the Pension Systems of Britain and the US Accommodate Women's Paid and Unpaid Work? *International Journal of Sociology and Social Policy* 21(4/5/6): 212-44.

Glenn, Eveleyn Nakano. 1994. Social Constructions of Mothering: A Thematic Overview. In *Mothering: Ideology, Experience and Agency,* ed. E.N. Glenn, G. Chang, and L.R. Forcey, 1-29. New York: Routledge.

Goetz, Anne Marie. 1997. Introduction: Getting Institutions Right for Women in Development. In *Getting Institutions Right for Women in Development,* ed. A.M. Goetz, 1-28. London: Zed Books.

Gonas, Lena. 2002. Balancing Family and Work – To Create a New Social Order. *Economic and Industrial Democracy* 23(1): 59-66.

Goodman, Catherine Chase. 2007. Family Dynamics in Three-Generation Grandfamilies. *Journal of Social Issues* 28(3): 355-79.

Gordon, Linda. 1994. *Pitied but Not Entitled: Single Mothers and the History of Welfare.* New York: Free Press.

Gornick, Janet C., Alexandra Heron, and Ross Eisenbrey. 2007. *The Work-Family Balance: An Analysis of European, Japanese, and U.S. Work-Time Policies.* EPI Briefing Paper 189. http://www.sharedprosperity.org.

Gouthro, Patricia A. 2000. Globalization, Civil Society and the Homeplace. *Convergence* 33(1/2): 57-76.

–. 2002. Education for Sale at What Cost? Lifelong Learning and the Marketplace. *International Journal of Lifelong Education* 21(4): 334-46.

–. 2005. A Critical Feminist Analysis of the Homeplace as Learning Site: Expanding the Discourse of Lifelong Learning to Consider Adult Women Learners. *International Journal of Lifelong Education* 24(1): 5-19.

Grana, Sheryl J., Helen A. Moore, Janet K. Wilson, and Michelle Miller. 1993. The Contexts of Housework and Paid Labor Force: Women's Perceptions of the Demand Levels of Their Work. *Sex Roles* 28(5-6): 295-306.

Grant, Agnes. 1996. *No End of Grief: Indian Residential Schools in Canada.* Winnipeg: Pemmican.

Grant, Tavia, and Wallace Immen. 2008. Bummed Out at Work? Join the Club. *Globe and Mail,* 2 May.

Greaves, Lorraine, Colleen Varcoe, Nancy Poole, Nancy M. Morrow, Joy Johnson, Ann Pederson, and Lori Irwin. 2002. *A Motherhood Issue: Discourses on Mothering under Duress.* Ottawa: Status of Women Canada. http://dsp-psd.pwgsc.gc.ca/Collection/SW21-99-2002E.pdf.

Greenaway, Norma. 2007. Pro-Family Group Quits Gay Marriage Fight. *Ottawa Citizen,* 27 September. http://www.canada.com/ottawacitizen/.

Greenhaus, Jeffrey, and Gary N. Powell. 2006. When Work and Family Are Allies: A Theory of Work-Family Enrichment. *Academy of Management Review* 31(1): 72-92.

Griffin, Gabriele, and Rosi Braidotti. 2002. Introduction: Configuring European Women's Studies. In *Thinking Differently: A Reader in European Women's Studies,* ed. G. Griffin and R. Braidotti, 1-28. London: Zed Books.

Grosz, Elizabeth. 1995. *Space, Time and Perversion*. New York: Routledge.

–. 2005. *Time Travels: Feminism, Nature, Power*. Durham: Duke University Press.

Grundy, Emily. 2005. Reciprocity in Relationships: Socio-Economic and Health Influences on Intergenerational Exchanges between Third Age Parents and Children in Great Britain. *British Journal of Sociology* 56(3): 291-312.

Grundy, Emily, and John C. Henretta. 2006. Between Elderly Parents and Adult Children: A New Look at the Intergenerational Care Provided by the "Sandwich Generation." *Aging and Society* 26: 707-22.

Grzywacz, Joseph G., David M. Almeida, and Daniel McDonald. 2002. Work-Family Spillover and Daily Reports of Work and Family Stress in the Adult Labor Force. *Family Relations* 51: 28-36.

Grzywacz, Joseph G., and Adam B. Butler. 2005. The Impact of Job Characteristics on Work-to-Family Facilitation: Testing a Theory and Distinguishing a Construct. *Journal of Occupational Health Psychology* 10(2): 97-109.

Guiffrida, Douglas. 2005. Othermothering as a Framework for Understanding African American Students' Definitions of Student-Centered Faculty. *Journal of Higher Education* 76(6): 701-23.

Gustafson, Diana L. 2005. The Social Construction of Maternal Absence. In *Unbecoming Mothers: The Social Production of Maternal Absence*, ed. D.L. Gustafson, 23-48. New York: Haworth Press.

Habtu, Roman, and Andrija Popovic. 2006. Informal Caregivers: Balancing Work and Life Responsibilities. *Horizons* 6(3): 27-34.

Hall, Karen. 1999. Hours Polarization at the End of the 1990s. *Perspectives on Labour and Income* 11(2): 28-37.

Hallamore, Christopher. 2007. *Aging Workforce and Looming Labour Shortages Begin to Shape Bargaining in 2007*. Ottawa: Conference Board of Canada.

Halpern, Diane, and Susan Murphy. 2005. From Balance to Interaction: Why the Metaphor Is Important and How We Study Work-Family Interactions. In *From Work-Family Balance to Work-Family Interaction*, ed. D.F. Halpern and S.E. Murphy, 3-9. Mahwah, NJ: Lawrence Erlbaum.

Hamington, Maurice. 2004. *Embodied Care: Jane Addams, Maurice Merleau-Ponty, and Feminist Ethics*. Bloomington: University of Illinois Press.

Han, Wen-Jui. 2008. Shift Work and Child Behavioural Outcomes. *Work, Employment and Society* 22(1): 67-87.

Haney, Lynne, and Lisa Pollard, eds. 2003. *Families of a New World: Gender, Politics and State Development in a Global Context*. New York: Routledge.

Hann, Arwen, and Kim Thomas. 2007. Threat to Free Care of Young. *The Press*, 23 January.

Hansen, Karen V. 2005. *Not-So-Nuclear Families: Class, Gender and Networks of Care*. New Brunswick, NJ: Rutgers University Press.

Hantrais, Linda. 2000. *Social Policy in the European Union*. 2nd ed. Basingstoke: Macmillan.

–. 2004. *Family Policy Matters: Responding to Family Change in Europe*. Bristol: Policy Press.

Hantrais, Linda, and Marie-Therese Letablier. 1996. *Families and Family Policy in Europe*. London: Longman.

Hareven, Tamara K. 1996. *Aging and Generational Relations over the Life Course: A Historical and Cross-Cultural Perspective*. Berlin: W. de Gruyter.

Harjo, Joy, and Gloria Bird. 1997. *Reinventing the Enemy's Language: Contemporary Native Women's Writings of North America*. New York: W.W. Norton.

Harris, Kathleen Mullen. 1996. Life after Welfare: Women, Work and Repeat Dependency. *American Sociological Review* 61: 407-26.

Harrison, Trevor W., and John W. Friesen. 2004. *Canadian Society in the Twenty-First Century: A Historical Sociological Approach*. Toronto: Pearson Prentice Hall.

Haslanger, Sally. 2005. You Mixed? Racial Identity without Racial Biology. In *Adoption Matters: Philosophical and Feminist Essays*, ed. S. Haslanger and C. Witt, 265-89. Ithaca, NY: Cornell University Press.

Haslanger, Sally, and Charlotte Witt, eds. 2005. *Adoption Matters: Philosophical and Feminist Essays*. Ithaca, NY: Cornell University Press.

Hasselkus, B.R., and R.O. Ray. 1988. Informal Learning in the Family: A Worm's Eye View. *Adult Education Quarterly* 39(1): 31-40.

Hays, Sharon. 1996. *The Cultural Contradictions of Motherhood.* New Haven, CT: Yale University Press.

Head, Simon. 2003. *The New Ruthless Economy: Work and Power in the Digital Age.* Oxford: Oxford University Press.

Heisz, Andrew. 2007. *Income Inequality and Redistribution in Canada: 1976 to 2004.* Analytical Studies Branch Research Paper Series, Minister of Labour. Ottawa: Statistics Canada.

Heisz, Andrew, and Sebastien LaRochelle-Côté. 2006. *Summary of Work Hours Instability in Canada.* Analytical Studies Branch Research Series, Minister of Industry. Ottawa: Statistics Canada.

Hekman, Susan J. 1995. *Moral Voices, Moral Selves: Carol Gilligan and Feminist Moral Theory.* College Park: Pennsylvania State University Press.

Hertz, Rosanna. 2006. Talking about "Doing" Family. *Journal of Marriage and Family* 68: 796-99.

Hertz, Rosanna, and Faith I. Ferguson. 1998. Only One Pair of Hands: Ways That Single Mothers Stretch Work and Family Resources. *Community, Work, and Family* 1: 13-37.

Hessing, Melody. 1993a. Environmental Protection and Pulp Pollution in British Columbia: The Challenge of the Emerald State. *Journal of Human Justice* 1: 29-45.

–. 1993b. Making the Connections: Ecofeminist Perspectives on Women and the Environment. *Alternatives* 19: 14-21.

Higgins, Chris, Linda Duxbury, and Karen Johnson. 2004. *Report Three: Exploring the Link between Work-Life Conflict and Demands on Canada's Health Care System.* Ottawa: Health Canada.

Hill, Barbara-Helen. 2002. *Shaking the Rattle: Healing the Trauma of Colonization.* Penticton, BC: Theytus Books.

Hill, E. Jeffrey. 2005. Work-Family Facilitation and Conflict, Working Fathers and Mothers, Work-Family Stressors and Support. *Journal of Family Issues* 26(6): 793-819.

Hill, Richard. 1992. Oral Memory of the Haudenosaunee Views of the Two Row Wampum. In Barreiro 1992, 149-59.

Hobbs, Margaret. 1993a. Equality and Difference: Feminism and the Defence of Women Workers during the Great Depression. *Labour/Le Travail* 32: 201-23.

–. 1993b. Rethinking Antifeminism in the 1930s: A Response to Alice Kessler-Harris. *Gender and History* 5(1): 4-15.

Hobcraft, John, and Kathleen Kiernan. 2001. Childhood Poverty, Early Motherhood and Adult Social Exclusion. *British Journal of Sociology* 52(3): 495-517.

Hochschild, Arlie. 1989. *The Second Shift: Working Parents and the Revolution at Home.* New York: Viking.

–. 1997. *The Time Bind: When Work Becomes Home and Home Becomes Work.* New York: Henry Holt.

Holdsworth, Clare. 2007. Intergenerational Inter-Dependencies: Mothers and Daughters in Comparative Perspective. *Women's Studies International Forum* 30: 59-69.

Hondagneu-Sotelo, Pierette. 2007. Domestica: Immigrant Workers Cleaning and Caring in the Shadows of Affluence. Berkeley: University of California Press.

Hondagneu-Sotelo, Pierrette, and Ernestine Avila. 1997. "I'm Here, but I'm There": The Meaning of Latina Transnational Motherhood. *Gender and Society* 11(5): 548-71.

hooks, bell. 2000. *Feminist Theory: From Margin to Center,* 2nd Ed. Boston: South End Press.

–. 2009. *Belonging: A Culture of Place.* New York: Routledge.

Hooyman, Nancy R., and Judith G. Gonyea. 1999. A Feminist Model of Family Care: Practice and Policy Directions. *Journal of Women and Aging* 11(2/3): 149-69.

HRDC (Human Resources Development Canada). 1997. Evaluation and Data Development Strategic Policy. In *Evaluation of Federal Labour Standards (Phase I): Final Report.* Ottawa: Human Resources Development Canada.

–. 1998. Evaluation and Data Development Strategic Policy. In *Evaluation of Federal Labour Standards (Phase II): Final Report.* Ottawa: Human Resources Development Canada.

–. 2000. *A Study Concerning Federal Labour Standards: Balancing Work, Family and Learning in Canada's Federally Regulated Workplaces.* http://www.hrsdc.gc.ca/.

–. 2006. Fairness at Work: Federal Labour Standards for the 21st Century. Ottawa: Supply and Services Canada.

Huber, Evelyne, and John Stephens. 2001. *Development and Crisis of the Welfare State: Parties and Policies in Global Markets.* Chicago: University of Chicago Press.

Hunsley, Terrance. 1997. *Lone Parent Incomes and Social Policy Outcomes: Canada in International Perspective.* Montreal and Kingston: McGill-Queen's University Press.

–. 2006. Work-Life Balance in an Aging Population. *Horizons* 8(3): 3-13.

Iacovetta, Franca. 2006. Recipes for Democracy? Gender, Family, and Making Female Citizens in Cold War Canada. In *Moral Regulation and Governance in Canada,* ed. A. Glasbeek, 169-87. Toronto: Canadian Scholars' Press.

ILO (International Labour Organization). 2005. *Report III (Part 1B): General Survey of the Reports Concerning the Hours of Work (Industry) Convention, 1919 (No. 1), and the Hours of Work (Commerce and Offices) Convention, 1930 (No. 30).* Geneva: ILO.

Ipsos Reid. 2006a. Most Mothers in Ontario (77%) Feel "Starved for Energy." 8 May poll. http://www.ipsos-na.com/.

–. 2006b. Parents in Western Canada Feeling Squeezed for Time. 15 June poll. http://www.ipsos-na.com/.

Irigaray, Luce. 1985. *This Sex Which Is Not One.* Ithaca, NY: Cornell University Press.

Jacobs, Jerry A., and Kathleen Gerson. 2004. *The Time Divide: Work, Family and Gender Inequality.* Cambridge, MA: Harvard University Press.

Japel, Christa, Richard E. Tremblay, and Sylvana Côté. 2005. Quality Counts: Assessing the Quality of Day Services Based on Quebec Longitudinal Study of Child Development. IRPP *Choices* 11(5): 1-42.

Jenson, Jane. 2001. Family Policy, Child Care and Social Solidarity: The Case of Quebec. In *Changing Child Care: Five Decades of Child Care Advocacy and Policy in Canada,* ed. S. Prentice, 39-62. Halifax: Fernwood.

–. 2003. *Redesigning the "Welfare Mix" for Families: Policy Challenges.* Discussion Paper F/30. Ottawa: Canadian Policy Research Networks.

–. 2004a. Canadian Policy Research Network – Family Network: A Decade of Challenges. Keynote address at "A Decade of Choices: Consequences for Canadian Women" conference, Women's Economic Summit, Ottawa.

–. 2004b. *Catching Up to Reality: Building the Case for a New Social Model.* CPRN Social Architecture Papers, Research Report F/35. Ottawa: Canadian Policy Research Networks.

–. 2004c. Changing the Paradigm: Family Responsibility or Investing in Children. *Canadian Journal of Sociology* 29(2): 169-92.

–. 2007. The European Union's Citizenship Regime: Creating Norms and Building Practices. *Comparative European Politics* 5: 53-69.

Jenson, Jane, and Mariette Sineau. 2001. Citizenship in the Era of Welfare State Redesign. In *Who Cares? Women's Work, Childcare, and Welfare State Redesign,* ed. J. Jenson and M. Sineau, 240-65. Toronto: University of Toronto Press.

Jenson, Jane, and Denis St. Martin. 2006. Building Blocks for a New Social Architecture: The LEGO Paradigm of an Active Society. *Policy and Politics* 34(3): 429-52.

Jetté, Mireille. 2000. The ELDEQ, 1998-2002, A First Annual Longitudinal Study of Quebec Newborns. *Isuma* 1(2): 118-22.

Johnson, Jennifer A., and Megan S. Johnson. 2008. New City Domesticity and the Tenacious Second Shift. *Journal of Family Issues* 29(4): 487-515.

Johnson, Karen L., Donna S. Lero, and Jennifer A. Rooney. 2001. *Work-Life Compendium 2001: 150 Statistics on Work, Family and Well-Being.* Guelph, ON: University of Guelph Centre for Families, Work and Well-Being.

Johnson, Rebecca. 2002. *Taxing Choices: The Intersection of Class, Gender, Parenthood, and the Law.* Vancouver: UBC Press.

Juby, Heather, Celine Le Bourdais, and Nicole Marcil-Gratton. 2005. Sharing Roles, Sharing Custody? Couples' Characteristics and Children's Living Arrangements at Separation. *Journal of Marriage and Family* 67: 157-72.

Kalinowski, Tess. 2007. Commute's True Cost – Family Time. *Toronto Star,* 13 December.

Kamerman, Sheila B., and Alfred J. Kahn. 2001. Child and Family Policies in an Era of Social Policy Retrenchment and Restructuring. In *Child Well-Being, Child Poverty and Child Policy in Modern Nations: What Do We Know?* ed. K. Vleminck and T. Smeeding, 501-24. Bristol: Policy Press.

Kaplan, E. Ann. 1992. *Motherhood and Representation: The Mother in Popular Culture and Melodrama.* London: Routledge.

Kaufman, Michael. 1999. Men, Feminism, and Men's Contradictory Experiences of Power. In *Men and Power,* ed. J.A. Kuypers, 59-83. Halifax: Fernwood.

Keefe, Janice, and Pamela J. Fancey. 2002. Work and Eldercare: Reciprocity between Older Mothers and Their Employed Daughters. *Canadian Journal on Aging* 21(2): 229-41.

Keefe, Janice, Carolyn Rosenthal, and François Béland. 2000. The Impact of Ethnicity on Helping Older Relatives: Findings from a Sample of Employed Canadians. *Canadian Journal on Aging* 19(3): 317-42.

Kirchmeyer, Catherine. 1992a. Nonwork Participation and Work Attitudes: A Test of Scarcity vs. Expansion Models of Personal Resources. *Human Relations* 45(8): 775-95.

–. 1992b. Perceptions of Nonwork-to-Work Spillover: Challenging the Common View of Conflict-Ridden Domain Relationships. *Basic and Applied Social Psychology* 13(2): 231-49.

–. 1993. Nonwork-to-Work Spillover: A More Balanced View of the Experiences and Coping of Professional Women and Men. *Sex Roles* 9(10): 531-52.

–. 1995. Managing the Work-Nonwork Boundary: An Assessment of Organizational Responses. *Human Relations* 48(5): 515-36.

Kitchen, Brigitte. 1997. The New Child Benefit: Much Ado about Nothing. *Canadian Review of Social Policy* 39 (Spring): 65-74.

Klein, Ralph. 2006. Time Runs Out in Alberta for Anti-Gay Marriage Bill. CTV News, 10 May.

Koehn, Daryl. 1998. *Rethinking Feminist Ethics: Care, Trust and Empathy.* London: Routledge.

Kopun, Francine. 2006. Commuters Say They Enjoy the Ride. *Toronto Star,* 8 November.

Korpi, Walter. 2000. Faces of Inequality: Gender, Class, and Patterns of Inequalities in Different Types of Welfare States. *Social Politics* 7(2): 127-91.

Kristeva, Julia. 1995. *New Maladies of the Soul.* New York: Columbia University Press.

Krull, Catherine. 2006a. Cultural Diversity and Adaptation: Canada's Ethnic and Immigrant Families. In Ambert 2006a, 86-116.

–. 2006b. Historical and Cross-Cultural Perspectives on Family Life. In Ambert 2006a, 31-57.

–. 2007. Families and the State: Family Policy in Canada. In *Canadian Families Today: New Perspectives,* ed. D. Cheal, 254-72. Don Mills, ON: Oxford University Press.

–. 2010. Investing in Families and Children: Family Policies in Canada. In *Canadian Families Today: New Perspectives,* 2nd ed., ed. D. Cheal, 254-73. Don Mills, ON: Oxford University Press.

Kulchyski, Peter, Don McCaskill, and David Newhouse, eds. 1999. *In the Words of the Elders: Aboriginal Cultures in Transition.* Toronto: University of Toronto Press.

Kulchyski, Peter, and Frank Tester. 1994. *Tammarniit (Mistakes): Inuit Relocation in the Eastern Arctic, 1939-1963.* Vancouver: UBC Press.

Kvande, Elin. 2000. The Introduction of the "Fathers' Quota" and "Time Account Scheme" in Norway. Paper presented at the Oxford Seminar on Re-Definitions of Women's Relationship to Employment.

Laberge, A.M., J. Michaud, A. Richter, E. Lemyre, M. Lambert, B. Brais, and G.A. Mitchell. 2005. Population History and Its Impact on Medical Genetics in Quebec. *Clinical Genetics* 68(4): 287-301.

Lan, Pei-Chia. 2003. Maid or Madam? Filipina Migrant Workers and the Continuity of Domestic Labor. *Gender and Society* 17(2): 187-208.

Lapierre-Adamcyk, Éveline, Nicole Marcil-Gratton, and Céline Le Bourdais. 2007. Working Schedules: In Search of a Balance between Family Time and Economic Well-Being. In *Ages, Generations and the Social Contract,* ed. J. Véron, S. Pennec, and J. Legaré, 343-56. Dortrecht: Springer.

LaRossa, Ralph. 1988. Fatherhood and Social Change. *Family Relations* 37(4): 451-57.

Le Bourdais, Céline, and Évelyne Lapierre-Adamcyk. 2004. Changes in Conjugal Life in Canada: Is Cohabitation Progressively Replacing Marriage? *Journal of Marriage and Family* 66(4): 929-42.

Lederman, John. 1999. Trauma and Healing in Aboriginal Families and Communities. *Native Social Work Journal* 2(1): 59-90.

Lee, Christina, and Jenny Porteous. 2002. Experiences of Family Caregiving among Middle-Aged Australian Women. *Feminism and Psychology* 12(1): 79-96.

Lee, Sangheon. 2004. Working-Hour Gaps: Trends and Issues. In Messenger 2004a, 29-59.

Lefebvre, Pierre, and Philip Merrigan. 2008. Child-Care Policy and the Labor Supply of Mothers with Young Children: A Natural Experiment. *Journal of Labor Economics* 26(3): 519-48.

Legall, Paul. 2006. [Title not available]. *Hamilton Spectator,* 23 March.

Leira, Arnlaug. 2002. *Working Parents and the Welfare State: Family Change and Policy Reform in Scandinavia.* Cambridge: Cambridge University Press.

Leon, Margarita. 2005. Welfare State Regimes and the Social Organization of Labour: Childcare and the Work/Family Balance Dilemma. *Sociological Review* 53(2): 204-18.

Levin, Irene. 2004. Living Apart Together: A New Family Form. *Current Sociology* 52: 223-40.

Lewis, Jane, ed. 1993. *Women and Social Policies in Europe: Work, Family and the State.* Aldershot: Edward Elgar.

–. 2001. The Decline of the Male Breadwinner Model: Implications for Work and Care. *Social Politics* 8(2): 152-69.

–. 2003. *Should We Worry about Family Change?* Toronto: University of Toronto Press.

Lewis, Jane, and Susanna Giullari. 2005. The Adult Worker Model Family, Gender Equality and Care: The Search for New Policy Principles and Problems of a Capabilities Approach. *Economy and Society* 34(1): 76-104.

Lewis, Jane, Philip Noden, and Sophie Saree. 2008. Parents' Working Hours: Adolescent Children's Views and Experiences. *Children and Society* 22(6): 429-39.

Li, Chris, Ginette Gervais, and Aurelie Duval. 2006. *The Dynamics of Overqualification: Canada's Underemployed University Graduates.* Ottawa: Minister of Industry.

Lightman, Ernie S. 1997. "It's Not a Walk in the Park": Workfare in Ontario. In *Workfare: Ideology for a New Under-Class,* ed. E. Shragge, 85-107. Toronto: Garamond.

Lindsay, Colin. 2008. *Are Women Spending More Time on Unpaid Domestic Work than Men in Canada?* Catalogue no. 89-630 X. Ottawa: Statistics Canada.

Litt, Jacquelyn, and Mary Zimmerman. 2003. Global Perspectives on Gender and Carework: An Introduction. *Gender and Society* 17(2): 156-65.

Little, Don. 1999. *Employment and Remuneration in the Services Industries since 1984.* Analytical Paper Series, Minister of Industry. Ottawa: Statistics Canada.

Little, Margaret Hillyard. 1998. *No Car, No Radio, No Liquor Permit: The Moral Regulation of Single Mothers in Ontario, 1920-1997.* Oxford: Oxford University Press.

–. 2005. *If I Had a Hammer: Retraining That Really Works.* Vancouver: UBC Press.

Little, Margaret Hillyard, and Lynne Marks. 2010. A Closer Look at the Neo-Liberal Petri Dish: Welfare Reform in British Columbia and Ontario. *Canadian Review of Social Policy.*

Little, Margaret Hillyard, and Ian Morrison. 1999. "The Pecker Detectors Are Back": Regulation of the Family Form in Ontario Welfare Policy. *Journal of Canadian Studies* 34(2): 110-36.

Liu, Lichun Willa. 2007. New Home, New Learning: Chinese Immigrants, Unpaid Housework and Care Work. In *The Future of Lifelong Learning and Work: Critical Perspectives,* ed. D. Livingstone, K. Merchandani, and P. Sawchuk. Rotterdam: Sense Publishers.

Livingstone, David. 2000. *Exploring the Icebergs of Adult Learning: Findings of the First Canadian Survey of Informal Learning Practices.* Toronto: OISE-University of Toronto.

–. 2005. Expanding Conception of Work and Learning: Recent Research and Policy Implications. In *International Handbook of Educational Policy,* ed. Nina Bascia, Alister Cumming, Amanda Datnow, Kenneth Leithwood, and David Livingstone, 977-95. New York: Springer.

Loder, Tondra. 2005. African American Women Principals' Reflections on Social Change, Community Othermothering, and Chicago Public School Reform. *Urban Education* 40(3): 298-320.

Lombardo, Emanuela. 2005. Integrating or Setting the Agenda? Gender Mainstreaming in the European Constitution – Making Process. *Social Politics* 12(3): 412-32.

Lorinc, John. 2008. 9 to 5? We Just Need You from Noon to 2. *Globe and Mail,* 5 April.

Lowe, Elaine. 2006. What a Difference 50 Years Makes: Coming of Age, Then and Now. *Transition Magazine* 36(1).

Lowe, Graham. 2005. *Control over Time and Work-Life Balance: An Empirical Analysis.* Report prepared for the Federal Labour Standards Review Committee. Ottawa: Human Resources and Skills Development Canada.

–. 2007. *21st-Century Job Quality: Achieving What Canadians Want.* Ottawa: Canadian Policy Research Networks.

Luffman, Jacqueline. 2006. Core-Age Labour Force. *Perspectives on Labour and Income* 7(9): 5-11.

Lupton, Deborah, and Lesley Barclay. 1997. *Constructing Fatherhood: Discourses and Experiences.* London: Sage.

Luxton, Meg. 1980. *More than a Labour of Love.* Toronto: Women's Press.

–. 1997. Feminism and Families: The Challenge of Neo-Conservatism. In *Feminism and Families: Critical Policies and Changing Practices,* ed. Meg Luxton, 10-26. Halifax: Fernwood.

Luxton, Meg, and June Corman. 2001. *Getting by in Hard Times: Gendered Labour at Home and on the Job.* Toronto: University of Toronto Press.

Lyon, Dawn. 2006. The Organization of Care Work in Italy: Gender and Migrant Labor in the New Economy. *Indiana Journal of Global Legal Studies* 13(1): 207-24.

Lyons, Oren. 1984. Spirituality, Equality and Natural Law. In *Pathways to Self-Determination: Canadian Indians and the Canadian State,* ed. L. Little Bear, M. Boldt, and J.A. Long, 5-13. Toronto: University of Toronto Press.

Macdonald, Carmen L. 1998. Manufacturing Motherhood: The Shadow Work of Nannies and Au Pairs. *Qualitative Sociology* 21(1): 25-48.

MacDonald, Martha, Shelley Phipps, and Lynn Lethbridge. 2005. Taking Its Toll: The Influence of Paid and Unpaid Work on Women's Well-Being. *Feminist Economics* 11(1): 63-94.

Macdonald, Ryan. 2007. *Not Dutch Disease, It's China Syndrome: Insights on the Canadian Economy.* Analytical Paper Series, Minister of Industry. Ottawa: Statistics Canada.

Mackinnon, Catherine. 1982. Feminism, Marxism, Method and the State: An Agenda for Theory. *Signs* 7: 515-44.

Maher, Jane Maree, Jo Lindsay, and Suzanne Franzway. 2008. Time, Caring Labour and Social Policy: Understanding the Family Time Economy in Contemporary Families. *Work, Employment and Society* 22(3): 547-58.

Mahon, Rianne. 2005. *The OECD and the Reconciliation Agenda: Competing Blueprints.* Toronto: Childcare Resource and Research Unit, University of Toronto Press.

–. 2006. Of Scalar Hierarchies and Welfare Redesign: Childcare in Three Canadian Cities. *Transactions of the Institute of British Geographers* 31(4): 452-66.

Mahoney, Jill. 2006. Empty Nests More Rare. *Globe and Mail,* 4 October.

Mandell, Deena. 2002. *Deadbeat Dads: Subjectivity and Social Construction.* Toronto: University of Toronto Press.

Mandell, Nancy, and Ann Duffy. 2000. *Canadian Families: Diversity, Conflict and Change.* 2nd ed. Toronto: Harcourt Brace.

Mandell, Nancy, Susan Wilson, and Ann Duffy. 2008. *Connection, Compromise and Control: Canadian Women Discuss Midlife.* Toronto: Oxford University Press.

Marks, Nadine F. 1998. Does It Hurt to Care? Caregiving, Work-Family Conflict, and Midlife Well-Being. *Journal of Marriage and Family* 60: 951-66.

Marshall, Hariette. 1991. The Social Construction of Motherhood: An Analysis of Childcare and Parenting Manuals. In Phoenix, Woollett, and Lloyd 1991, 66-85.

Marshall, Katherine. 2000. *Configuring Gender: Explorations in Theory and Politics.* Peterborough, ON: Broadview Press.

–. 2003. Benefiting from Extended Parental Leave. *Perspectives on Labour and Income* 4(3): 5-11.

–. 2006. Converging Gender Roles. *Perspectives on Labour and Income* 18(3): 7-19.

–. 2007. The Busy Lives of Teens. *Perspectives on Labour and Income* 8(5): 5-15.

–. 2009. The Family Work Week. *Perspectives on Labour and Income* 10(4): 5-12.

Marsiglio, William, ed. 1995. *Fatherhood: Contemporary Theory, Research, and Social Policy.* London: Sage.

–. 2008. *Men on a Mission: Valuing Youth Work in Our Communities.* Baltimore, MD: Johns Hopkins University Press.

Marsiglio, William, Paul Amato, Randal D. Day, and Michael E. Lamb. 2000. Scholarship on Fatherhood in the 1990s and Beyond. *Journal of Marriage and Family* 62: 1173-91.

Martin-Matthews, Anne. 2007. Situating "Home" at the Nexus of the Public and Private Spheres. *Current Sociology* 55(2): 229-49.

Mauthner, Natasha, and Andrea Doucet. 1998. Reflections on a Voice-Centred Relational Method of Data Analysis: Analysing Maternal and Domestic Voices. In *Feminist Dilemmas in Qualitative Research: Private Lives and Public Texts,* ed. J. Ribbens and R. Edwards, 119-44. London: Sage.

–. 2003. Reflexive Accounts and Accounts of Reflexivity in Qualitative Data Analysis. *Sociology* 37(3): 413-31.

May, Elaine Tyler. 1988. *Homeward Bound: American Families in the Cold War Era.* New York: Basic Books.

May, Larry. 1998. Paternity and Commitment. In *Masculinity and Morality,* ed. L. May, 24-40. Ithaca, NY: Cornell University Press.

McCann, Deirdre. 2004. Regulating Working Time Needs and Preferences. In Messenger 2004a, 10-28.

McClure, Margaret. 1998. *A Civilised Community: A History of Social Security in New Zealand, 1898-1998.* Auckland: Auckland University Press.

McDaniel, Susan A. 2001. "Born at the Right Time?" Gendered Generation and Webs of Entitlement and Responsibility. *Canadian Journal of Sociology* 26(2): 193-14.

–. 2002a. Generational Consciousness of and for Women. In *Narrative, Generational Consciousness and Politics,* ed. B. Turner and J. Edmunds, 89-110. Boulder, CO: Rowman Littlefield.

–. 2002b. Women's Changing Relations to the State and Citizenship. *Canadian Review of Sociology and Anthropology* 9(2): 125-49.

–. 2004. Generationing Gender: Justice and the Division of Welfare. *Journal of Aging Studies* 18(1): 27-44.

–. 2008. The "Growing Legs" of Generation as a Policy Construct: Reviving Its Family Meaning. *Journal of Comparative Family Studies* 40(2): 243-53.

McDowell, Linda, Kevin Ward, Colette Fagan, Diane Perrons, and Kath Ray. 2006. Connecting Time and Space: The Significance of Transformations in Women's Work in the City. *International Journal of Urban and Regional Research* 30(1): 141-58.

McFarland, Joan. 2003. Public Policy and Women's Access to Training in New Brunswick. In *Training the Excluded for Work,* ed. M. Cohen, 193-213. Vancouver: UBC Press.

McFarland, Joan, and Bob Mullaly. 1996. NB Works: Image vs. Reality. In *Remaking Social Policy: Social Security in the Late 1990s,* ed. J. Pulkingham and G. Ternowetsky, 202-19. Halifax: Fernwood.

McGraw, Lori A., and Alexis J. Walker. 2004. Negotiating Care: Ties between Aging Mothers and Their Caregiving Daughters. *Journals of Gerontology* 59B (6 November): S324-S32.

McKay, Lindsey, and Andrea Doucet. 2010. "Without Taking Away Her Leave": A Canadian Case Study of Couples' Decisions on Fathers' Use of Paid Leave. *Fathering* 8(3): 300-320.

McKeen, Wendy, and Ann Porter. 2003. Politics and Transformation: Welfare State Restructuring in Canada. In Clement and Vosko 2003, 109-34.

McKenna, Kate. 1993. (Dis)Honouring Father(s). In *Men and Masculinities: A Critical Anthology,* ed. T. Haddad, 59-75. Toronto: Canadian Scholars' Press.

McMahon, Martha. 1995. *Engendering Motherhood: Identity and Self-Transformation in Women's Lives.* New York: Guilford Press.

McRoberts, Kenneth. 1988. *Quebec: Social Change and Political Crisis.* Toronto: McClelland and Stewart.

Mederer, Helen J. 1993. Division of Labour in Two-Earner Homes: Task Accomplishment versus Household Management as Critical Variables in Perceptions about Family Work. *Journal of Marriage and Family* 55: 133-45.

Mercier, Michael, and Christopher Boone. 2002. Infant Mortality in Ottawa, Canada, 1901: Assessing Cultural, Economic and Environmental Factors. *Journal of Historical Geography* 28(4): 486-507.

Messenger, Jon C., ed. 2004a. *Working Time and Workers' Preferences in Industrialized Countries: Finding the Balance.* New York: Routledge.

–. 2004b. Working Time at the Enterprise Level: Business Objectives, Firms' Practices and Workers' Preferences. In Messenger 2004a, 147-94.

Messner, Michael A. 1987. The Meaning of Success: The Athletic Experience and the Development of Male Identity. In *The Making of Masculinities: The New Men's Studies,* ed. H. Brod, 193-209. Boston: Allen and Unwin.

–. 1990. Boyhood, Organized Sports, and the Construction of Masculinities. *Journal of Contemporary Ethnography* 18: 416-44.

Milan, Anne. 2000. One Hundred Years of Families. *Canadian Social Trends,* Catalogue no. 11-008 (Spring): 2-13.

Milan, Anne, and Brian Hamm. 2003. Across the Generations: Grandparents and Grandchildren. *Canadian Social Trends* 71 (Winter): 2-7.

Milan, Anne, Mireille Vezina, and Carrie Wells. 2007. *Family Portrait: Continuity and Change in Canadian Families and Households in 2006, 2006 Census.* Ottawa: Minister of Industry.

Milligan, Kevin. 2002. Quebec's Baby Bonus: Can Public Policy Raise Fertility? *Backgrounder* 57. Quebec: C.D. Howe Institute.

Milloy, John. 1999. *A National Crime: The Canadian Government and the Residential School System.* Winnipeg: University of Manitoba Press.

Milton, Penny. 2001. Education and Child Care: Confronting New Realities. In Cleveland and Krashinsky.2001b, 184-200.

Miner, Horace. 1938. The French-Canadian Family Cycle. *American Sociological Review* 3(5): 700-8.

Mink, Gwendolyn. 1998. *Welfare's End.* Ithaca, NY: Cornell University Press.

Mirchandani, Kiran. 2000. "The Best of Both Worlds" and "Cutting My Own Throat": Contradictory Images of Home-Based Work. *Qualitative Sociology* 23(2): 159-82.

Misra, Joya, Michelle J. Budig, and Stephanie Moller. 2007. Reconciliation Policies and the Effects of Motherhood on Employment, Earnings and Poverty. *Journal of Comparative Policy Analysis* 9(2): 135-55.

Mitchell, Barbara A. 2003. Would I Share a Home with an Elderly Parent? Exploring Ethnocultural Diversity and Intergenerational Support Relations during Young Adulthood. *Canadian Journal on Aging* 22(1): 69-82.

Mitchell, Mike. 1984. *Traditional Teachings.* Cornwall Island, ON: North American Indian Traveling College.

Moen, Phyllis, Julie Robison, and Donna Dempster-McClain. 1995. Caregiving and Women's Well-Being: A Life Course Approach. *Journal of Health and Social Behavior* 36(3): 259-73.

Monsebraaten, Laurie. 2007. Economist's Team Finds Casual Work "Toxic" to Society and to Employees. *Toronto Star,* 21 March.

Monture-Okanee, Patricia A. 1992. The Roles and Responsibilities of Aboriginal Women: Reclaiming Justice. *Saskatchewan Law Review* 56(1): 237-66.

Morel, Sylvie. 2002. *The Insertion Model or the Workfare Model? The Transformation of Social Assistance within Quebec and Canada.* Ottawa: Status of Women Canada. http://www.rwmc.uoguelph.ca/cms/documents/84/Morel_1-177.pdf.

Morgan, George. 2006. Work in Progress: Narratives of Aspiration from the New Economy. *Journal of Work and Education* 19(2): 141-51.

Morrissette, Mikki. 2008. *Choosing Single Motherhood.* Boston: Houghton Mifflin.

Morrissette, Rene, and Anick Johnson. 2005. *Are Good Jobs Disappearing in Canada?* Ottawa: Statistics Canada.

Morrissette, Rene, John Myles, and Picot Garnet. 1994. Earnings Inequality and the Distribution of Working Time in Canada. *Canadian Business Economics* 2(3): 3-16.

Morrissette, Rene, and Yuri Ostrovsky. 2005. *The Instability of Family Earnings and Family Income in Canada, 1986 to 1991 and 1996 to 2001.* Analytical Studies Branch Research Paper Series. Ottawa: Statistics Canada.

–. 2006. Earnings Instability. *Perspectives on Labour and Income* 18(4): 14-25.

Morissette, Rene, and Garnett Picot. 2005. *Low-Paid Work and Economically Vulnerable Families over the Last Two Decades*. Analytical Studies Branch Research Paper Series. Ottawa: Statistics Canada.

Morissette, Rene, Xuelin Zhang, and Marc Frenette. 2007. *Earnings Losses of Displaced Workers: Canadian Evidence from a Large Administrative Database on Firm Closures and Mass Layoffs*. Analytical Studies Branch Research Paper Series. Ottawa: Statistics Canada.

Morley, Louise. 2006. Theorising Gender Equity in Commonwealth Higher Education. In Sempruch, Willems, and Shook 2006b, 43-65.

Morton, Ted. 1998. Why Family Matters. *Calgary Sun,* 1 November. http://fathersforlife.org/.

Murphy, Brian, Paul Roberts, and Michael Wolfson. 2007. High-Income Canadians. *Perspectives on Labour and Income* 8(9): 5-17.

Mutari, Ellen, and Deborah M. Figart. 2001. Europe at a Crossroads: Harmonization, Liberalization, and the Gender of Work Time. *Social Politics* 8(1): 36-64.

Naples, Nancy. 1992. Activist Mothering: Cross-Generational Continuity in the Community Work of Women from Low-Income Urban Neighborhoods. *Gender and Society* 6(3): 441-63.

–. 2001. A Member of the Funeral: An Introspective Ethnography. In *Queer Families, Queer Politics: Challenging Culture and the State,* ed. Mary Bernstein and Renate Reimann, 21-43. New York: Columbia University Press.

National Council of Welfare, 2006. *Welfare Incomes*. Summer edition. Ottawa: Minister of Public Works and Government Services Canada.

Neamtam, Nancy. 2005. The Social Economy: Finding a Way between the Market and the State. *Policy Options* 26(6): 71-76.

Nelson, Barbara. 1990. The Origins of the Two-Channel Welfare State: Workmen's Compensation and Mothers' Aid. In *Women, the State, and Welfare,* ed. L. Gordon, 123-51. Madison: University of Wisconsin Press.

Nelson, Margaret K. 1992. Negotiated Care: The Experience of Family Day Care Providers. *Journal of Marriage and Family* 54(5): 474-72.

–. 2005. *The Social Economy of Single Motherhood: Raising Children in Rural America*. New York: Routledge.

–. 2006a. Families in Not-So-Free Fall: A Response to Comments. *Journal of Marriage and Family* 68(4): 817-23.

–. 2006b. Single Mothers "Do" Family. *Journal of Marriage and Family* 68(4): 781-95.

Nett, Emily M. 1996. Family Study in Canada during Sociology's Shifts from RC to PC to DC. *Canadian Review of Sociology and Anthropology* 33(1): 23-46.

New Zealand. 2006. Working for Families. http://www.workingforfamilies.govt.nz.

Neysmith, Sheila M., and Marge Reitsma-Street. 2005. Provisioning: Conceptualizing the Work of Women for 21st-Century Social Policy. *Women's Studies International Forum* 28: 381-91.

Noddings, Nel. 1984. *Caring: A Feminine Approach to Ethics and Moral Education*. Berkeley: University of California Press.

Noel, Jan. 2006. Power Mothering: The Haudenosaunee Model. In *Until Our Hearts Are on the Ground: Aboriginal Mothering, Oppression, Resistance and Rebirth,* ed. D.M. Lavell-Harvard and J. Corbiere Lavell. Toronto: Demeter Press.

O'Brien, Mary. 1981. *The Politics of Reproduction*. Boston: Routledge.

O'Conner, Deborah. 2007. Self-Identifying as a Caregiver: Exploring the Positioning Process. *Journal of Aging Studies* 21(2): 165-74.

O'Connor, Julia, Ann Shola Orloff, and Sheila Shaver. 1999. *States, Markets, Families: Gender Liberalism and Social Policy in Australia, Canada, Great Britain and the United States*. Cambridge: Cambridge University Press.

OECD (Organisation for Economic Co-Operation and Development). 1995. *Flexible Working Time: Collective Bargaining and Government Intervention*. Paris: OECD.

–. 2002. *OECD Employment Outlook*. Paris: OECD.

–. 2004. Clocking In and Clocking Out: Recent Trends in Working Hours. *OECD Observer: Policy Brief*. Paris: OECD.

–. 2005. *Babies and Bosses: Reconciling Work and Family Life.* Vol. 4, *Canada, Finland, Sweden and the United Kingdom.* Paris: OECD.

–. 2007a. OECD Family Database. www.oecd.org/els/social/family/database.

–. 2007b. *Society at a Glance: OECD Social Indicators.* Paris: OECD.

–. 2008a. *Employment Outlook.* Paris: OECD.

–. 2008b. *Growing Unequal? Income Distribution and Poverty in OECD Countries.* Paris: OECD.

Okin, Susan Moller. 1989. *Justice, Gender and the Family.* New York: Basic Books.

Oliker, Stacey J. 1989. *Best Friends and Marriage: Exchange among Women.* Berkeley: University of California Press.

Olson, Kevin. 2002. Recognizing Gender, Redistributing Labor. *Social Politics* 9(3): 380-410.

Ontario. Provincial Task Force on Hours of Work and Overtime. 1987. *Working Times: The Report of the Ontario Task Force on Hours of Work and Overtime (Phase 1).*

O'Reilly, Andrea. 2004. *From Motherhood to Mothering: The Legacy of Adrianne Rich's Of Woman Born.* Albany, NY: SUNY Press.

Orloff, Ann Shola. 1993. Gender and the Social Rights of Citizenship: The Comparative Analysis of Gender Relations and Welfare States. *American Sociological Review* 58: 303-28.

Orloff, Ann Shola, and Sheila Shaver. 1999. Gendering Theories and Comparisons of Welfare States. In O'Connor, Orloff, and Shaver 1999.

Osberg, Lars, Fred Wien, and Jan Grude. 1995. *Vanishing Jobs: Canada's Changing Workplaces.* Toronto: James Lorimer.

Owram, Douglas. 1999. The Family at Mid-Century. *Transition Magazine* 29(4). http://www.vifamily.ca/.

Pahl, Ray, and Liz Spencer. 2004. Personal Communities: Not Simply Families of "Fate" or "Choice." *Current Sociology* 52: 199-221.

Panitch, Leo, and Donald Swartz. 2003. Neo-Liberalism, Labour, and the Canadian State. In *From Consent to Coercion: The Assault on Trade Union Freedoms,* 3rd ed., ed. L. Panitch and D. Swartz, 183-222. Toronto: Garamond.

Paquet, Nicole. n.d. Toward a Policy on Work-Family Balance. Discussion paper, abr. ed. Quebec: Ministère de l'Emploi et de la Solidarité sociale.

Parke, Ross D. 1996. *Fatherhood.* Cambridge, MA: Harvard University Press.

Parsons, Talcott, and Robert Bales. 1955. *Family, Socialization and Interaction Process.* Glencoe, IL: Free Press.

Pateman, Carole. 1992. The Patriarchal Welfare State. In *Defining Women: Social Institutions and Gender Divisions,* ed. L. McDowell and R. Pringle, 223-45. Cambridge: Polity Press.

Pearce, Diane. 1978. The Feminization of Poverty: Women, Work and Welfare. *Urban and Social Change Review* 11: 28-36.

–. 1985. Toil and Trouble: Women Workers and Unemployment Compensation. In *Women and Poverty,* ed. Barbara C. Gelpi and Nancy Harstock, 141-61. Chicago: University of Chicago Press.

Pearson, Ruth. 2004. The Social Is Political. *International Feminist Journal of Politics* 6(4): 603-22.

–. 2007. Beyond Women Workers: Gendering CSR. *Third Work Quarterly* 28(4): 731-49.

Pence, Ellen, and Michael Paymar. 1993. *Education Groups for Men Who Batter.* New York: Springer.

Perrig-Chiello, Pasqualina, and François Hopflinger. 2005. Aging Parents and Their Middle-Aged Children: Demographic and Psychological Challenges. *European Journal of Aging* 2: 183-91.

Perrons, Diane. 2000. Care, Paid Work, and Leisure: Rounding the Triangle. *Feminist Economics* 6(1): 105-14.

Pérusse, Dominique. 2003. New Maternity and Parental Benefits. *Perspectives on Labour and Income* 4: 12-15.

Peskowitz, Miriam. 2005. *The Truth behind the Mommy Wars: Who Decides What Makes a Good Mother?* Emeryville: Seal Press.

Phipps, Shelley. 2006. Working for Working Parents: The Evolution of Maternity and Parental Benefits in Canada. IRPP *Choices* 12(2): 1-40.

Phoenix, Ann, Anne Woollett, and Eva Lloyd. 1991. *Motherhood: Meanings, Practices and Ideologies*. London: Sage.

Picchio, Antonella. 1998. Wages as a Reflection of Socially Embedded Production and Reproduction Processes. In *The Dynamics of Wage Relations in the New Europe*, ed. L. Clarke, P. de Gijsel, and J. Janssen, 195-214. London: Kluwer.

Pierson, Ruth Roach. 1990. Gender and the Unemployment Insurance Debates in Canada, 1934-1940. *Labour/Le Travail* 25: 77-103.

Pleck, Joseph H. 1985. *Working Wives, Working Husbands*. London: Sage.

Porter, Ann. 2003. *Gendered States: Women, Unemployment Insurance, and the Political Economy of the Welfare State in Canada, 1945-1997*. Toronto: University of Toronto Press.

Potuchek, Jean L. 1997. *Who Supports the Family? Gender and Breadwinning in Dual-Earner Marriages*. Stanford, CA: Stanford University Press.

Power, Marilyn. 2004. Social Provisioning as a Starting Point for Feminist Economics. *Feminist Economics* 10(3): 3-19.

Prentice, Susan. 2001. *Five Decades of Child Care Advocacy and Policy in Canada*. Halifax: Fernwood.

Presser, Harriet B. 2000. Nonstandard Work Schedules and Marital Instability. *Journal of Marriage and Family* 62(1): 93-111.

–. 2007. Toward a 24-Hour Economy: Implications for the Temporal Structure and Functioning of Family Life. In *Ages, Generations and the Social Contract*, ed. J. Véron, S. Pennec, and J. Legaré, 325-42. Dortrecht: Springer.

Preston, Valerie, Damaris Rose, Glen Norcliffe, and John Holmes. 2000. Shift Work, Childcare and Domestic Work: Divisions of Labour in Canadian Paper Mill Communities. *Gender, Place and Culture* 7(1): 5-29.

Probert, Belinda. 1997. Gender and Choice: The Structure of Opportunity. In *Work of the Future: Global Perspectives*, ed. P. James, W.F. Veit, and S. Wright. St. Leonards, NSW: Allen and Unwin.

Proffitt, Norma Jean. 2000. *Women Survivors, Psychological Trauma and the Politics of Resistance*. New York: Haworth Press.

Pupo, Norene, and Ann Duffy. 2007. Blurring the Distinction between Public and Private Spheres: The Commodification of Household Work – Gender, Class, Community and Global Dimensions. In Shalla and Clement 2007, 289-325.

Putnam, Robert D. 2000. *Bowling Alone: The Collapse and Revival of American Community*. New York: Simon and Schuster.

Pyper, Wendy. 2006. Balancing Career and Care. *Perspectives on Labour and Income* (22 November): 5-15.

–. 2007. Payday Loans. *Perspectives on Labour and Income* (22 February).

Quebec. 1997. *An Act Respecting the Ministère de la Famille et de l'Enfance and Amending the Act Respecting Child Day Care Centres. Bill 145*. Quebec: Ministère de la Famille et de l'Enfance.

–. 2003. *Development and Funding Scenarios to Ensure the Permanence, Accessibility and Quality of Childcare Services: Consultations 2003*. Quebec: Ministère de L'Emploi et de la Solidarité sociale.

–. 2004a. *Reconciling Freedom and Social Justice: A Challenge for the Future – Government Action Plan to Combat Poverty and Social Exclusion*. Quebec: Ministère de l'Emploi et de la Solidarité sociale. http://www.mess.gouv.qc.ca/.

–. 2004b. *Report of the Follow-Up Committee on the Quebec Model for the Determination of Child Support Payments*. Quebec: Ministère de la Justice.

–. 2006. *Family and Childcare Services – Childcare Services*. http://www.mfa.gouv.qc.ca/.

–. 2007. *Quebec Handy Numbers*. Institut de la statestique du Quebec. http://www.stat.gouv.qc.ca/.

Rake, Katherine. 2001. Gender and New Labour's Social Policies. *Journal of Social Policy* 30(2): 209-31.

Ranson, Gillian. 2001. Men at Work: Change or No Change in the Era of the New Father. *Men and Masculinities* 4(1): 3-26.

–. 2009. Paid and Unpaid Work: How Do Families Divide Their Labour? In *Families: Changing Trends in Canada,* 6th ed., ed. M. Baker, 108-29. Toronto: McGraw-Hill Ryerson.

–. 2010. *Against the Grain: Couples, Gender and the Reframing of Parenting.* Toronto: University of Toronto Press.

Ratansi, Yasmin. 2007. *Improving the Economic Security of Women: Time to Act.* Report on the Standing Committee on the Status of Women. Ottawa: House of Commons.

Red Horse, John. 1980. American Indian Elders: Unifiers of Indian Families. *Social Casework* (October): 490-93.

Reitsma-Street, Marge, and Sheila M. Neysmith. 2000. Restructuring and Community Work: The Case of Community Resource Centres for Families in Poor Neighborhoods. In *Restructuring Caring Labour: Discourse, State Practice, and Everyday Life,* ed. S. Neysmith, 142-63. Don Mills, ON: Oxford University Press.

Reyes, Angela. 2002. I'm Not Mad, I'm Postcolonial, a Woman, and a Mother: Introduction. In *Mothering across Cultures: Postcolonial Representations,* ed. A. Reyes, 1-31. Minneapolis: University of Minnesota Press.

Richardson, Diane. 2000. Constructing Sexual Citizenship: Theorizing Sexual Rights. *Critical Social Policy* 20(1): 105-35.

Risman, Barbara J. 1998. *Gender Vertigo: American Families in Transition.* New Haven, CT: Yale University Press.

Roberts, Dorothy. 2005. Feminism, Race and Adoption Policy. In Haslanger and Witt 2005, 234-56.

Robinson, Fiona. 2006. Beyond Labour Rights: The Ethics of Care and Women's Work in the Global Economy. *International Feminist Journal of Politics* 8(3): 321-42.

Rocher, Guy. 1962. Patterns and Status of French Canadian Women. *International Social Science Journal* 14(1): 131-37.

Ronning, Rolf. 2002. In Defence of Care: The Importance of Care as a Positive Concept. *Quality in Ageing: Policy, Practice and Research* 3(4): 34-43.

Roos, Patricia A., Mary K. Trigg, and Mary S. Hartman. 2006. Changing Families/Changing Communities: Work, Family and Community in Transition. *Community, Work and Family* 9(2): 197-224.

Roseneil, Sasha, and Shelley Budgeon. 2004. Cultures of Intimacy and Care beyond "the Family": Personal Life and Social Change in the Early 21st Century. *Current Sociology* 52(2): 135-59.

Ross, D. Parke, and Armin A. Brott. 1999. *Throwaway Dads: The Myths and Barriers That Keep Men from Being the Fathers They Want to Be.* Boston: Houghton Mifflin.

Ross, John Munden. 1994. *What Men Want: Mothers, Fathers, and Manhood.* Cambridge, MA: Harvard University Press.

Rothbard, Nancy P. 2001. Enriching or Depleting? The Dynamics of Engagement in Work and Family Roles. *Administrative Science Quarterly* 46: 655-84.

Rothman, Barbara Katz. 1989. *Recreating Motherhood: Ideology and Technology in Patriarchal Society.* New York: W.W. Norton.

Roussel, Jean-François. 2003. Roman Catholic Religious Discourse about Manhood in Quebec: From 1900 to the Quiet Revolution. *Journal of Men's Studies* 11(2): 145-55.

Roy, Francine. 2006. From She to She: Changing Patterns of Women in the Canadian Labour Force. *Canadian Economic Observer* 19(6): 3.1-3.10.

Roy, Laurent, and Jean Bernier. 2007. *Family Policy, Social Trends and Fertility in Quebec: Experimenting with the Nordic Model?* Quebec: Ministère de la Famille des Aînés et de la Condition féminine.

Rubery, Jill, and Damian Grimshaw. 2003. The State, the Family and Gender: From Domestic Work to Wage Employment. In *The Organization of Employment: An International Perspective,* ed. J. Rubery and D. Grimshaw. Basingstoke: Palgrave Macmillan.

Rubery, Jill, Mark Smith, and Colette Fagan. 1998. National Working-Time Regimes and Equal Opportunities. *Feminist Economics* 4(1): 71-101.

Rubin, Beth A., and Charles J. Brody. 2005. Contradictions of Commitment in the New Economy: Insecurity, Time, and Technology. *Social Science Research* 34: 843-61.

Rubin, Lillian B. 1985. *Just Friends: The Role of Friendship in Our Lives*. New York: Harper and Row.

Ruddick, Sara. 1995. *Maternal Thinking: Toward a Politics of Peace*. Boston: Beacon.

Ruderman, Marian N., Patricia J. Ohlott, Kate Panzer, and Sara N. King. 2002. Benefits of Multiple Roles for Managerial Women. *Academy of Management Journal* 45(2): 369-86.

Saccoccio, Sabrina. 2007. Revenge of the Only Children. CBC News in Depth, 3 July. http://www.cbc.ca/.

Sainsbury, Diane. 1993. Dual Welfare and Sex Segregation of Access to Social Benefits: Income Maintenance Policies in the U.K., the U.S., the Netherlands and Sweden. *Journal of Social Policy* 22(1): 69-98.

–. 1999. *Gender and Welfare State Regimes*. Oxford: Oxford University Press.

Salazar Parreñas, Rhacel. 2000. Migrant Filipina Domestic Workers and the International Division of Reproductive Labour. *Gender and Society* 14(4): 560-81.

–. 2001. Mothering from a Distance: Emotions, Gender, and Intergenerational Relations in Filipino Transnational Families. *Feminist Studies* 27: 361-89.

–. 2005. *Children of Global Migration: Transnational Families and Gendered Woes*. Palo Alto, CA: Stanford University Press.

–. 2008. *The Force of Domesticity: Filipino Migrants and Globalization*. New York: New York University Press.

Sarkisian, Natalia. 2006. "Doing Family Ambivalence": Nuclear and Extended Families in Single Mothers' Lives. *Journal of Marriage and Family* 68: 800-3.

Satz, Debra. 2007. Remaking Families: A Review Essay. *Signs* 32(2): 523-38.

Sauvé, Roger. 2002. *Connections: Tracking the Links between Jobs and Families; Job, Family and Stress among Husbands, Wives and Lone-Parents 15-64 from 1990 to 2000*. Ottawa: Vanier Institute of the Family.

–. 2009. *The Current State of Canadian Family Finances*. 2008 report prepared for the Vanier Institute of the Family. http://www.vifamily.ca.

Sayer, Liana C. 2005. Gender, Time and Inequality: Trends in Women's and Men's Paid Work, Unpaid Work and Free Time. *Social Forces* 84(1): 285-303.

Schild, Veronica. 2002. Engendering the New Social Citizenship in Chile: NGOs and Social Provisioning under Neoliberalism. In *Gender Justice, Development and Rights*, ed. M. Molyneux and R. Shahrashoub, 170-92. Oxford: Oxford University Press.

Schwartz, Pepper. 2004. Peer Marriage. *Social Problems* 26.

Seidler, Vic. 1992. Rejection, Vulnerability and Friendships. In *Men's Friendships: Research on Men and Masculinities*, ed. P.M. Nardi, 15-34. London: Sage.

–. 1997. *Man Enough: Embodying Masculinities*. London: Sage.

Sempruch, Justyna. 2005. Connecting Loose Ends: Domestic Labour, Illusion of the "Natural" and Global Economies. In *Culture and Power: Culture and Society in the Age of Globalization*, ed. E. Oliete, O. Seco, and A. Matamala, 117-32. Zaragoza: University of Zaragoza Press.

–. 2006. Women, Education and Employment: From the Devalued towards Developed Subject Positions. In Sempruch, Willems, and Shook 2006b, 116-32.

Sempruch, Justyna, Katharina Willems, and Laura Shook. 2006a. Intercultural Dialogues on Gender and Education. In Sempruch, Willems, and Shook 2006b, 9-40.

–, eds. 2006b. *Multiple Marginalities: An Intercultural Perspective on Gender in Education across Europe and Africa*. Konigstein: Helmer Verlag.

Sennett, Richard. 2006. *The Culture of the New Capitalism*. New York: Yale University Press.

Sevenhuijsen, Selma. 1998. *Citizenship and the Ethics of Care: Feminist Considerations on Justice, Morality, and Politics*. London: Routledge.

Sev'er, Aysan. 2010. All in the Family: Violence against Women, Children and the Aged. In *Canadian Families Today: New Perspectives*, 2nd ed., ed. D. Cheal, 237-53. Don Mills, ON: Oxford University Press.

Seward, Rudy Ray, Dale E. Yeatts, Lisa K. Zottarelli, and Ryan G. Fletcher. 2006. Fathers Taking Parental Leave and Their Involvement with Children: An Exploratory Study. *Community, Work and Family* 9(1): 1-9.

Shalla, Vivian. 2006. *Working in a Global Era: Canadian Perspectives*. Toronto: Canadian Scholars' Press.

Shalla, Vivian, and Wallace Clement, eds. 2007. *Work in Tumultuous Times: Critical Perspectives*. Montreal and Kingston: McGill-Queen's University Press.

Sharma, Ursula. 1986. *Women's Work, Class and the Urban Household: A Study of Shimla, North India*. London: Tavistock.

Shaw, Murray. 2004. Consolidating a Neoliberal Policy Bloc. In Carroll 2004, 154-79.

Shenandoah, Audrey. 1992. Everything Has to Be in Balance. In Barreiro 1992, 36-42.

Sheridan, Mike, Deborah Sunter, and Brent Diverty. 1996. The Changing Workweek: Trends in Weekly Hours of Work in Canada, 1976-1995. *Labour Force* 52(6): C-2–C-31.

Shewell, Hugh. 2004. *Enough to Keep Them Alive: Indian Welfare in Canada, 1873-1965*. Toronto: University of Toronto Press.

Shields, Margot. 2000. Long Working Hours and Health. *Perspectives on Labour and Income* 12(1): 49-56.

–. 2004. Stress, Health and the Benefit of Social Support. *Health Reports* 15(1): 9-38.

–. 2006. Unhappy on the Job. *Health Reports* 17(4): 33-37.

Shields, Margot, and Kathryn Wilkins. 2006. *National Survey of the Work and Health of Nurses in 2005: Provincial Profiles*. Catalogue no. 11-621-MIE2006052. Ottawa: Ministry of Industry.

Shragge, Eric. 1997. Workfare: An Overview. In *Workfare: Ideology for a New Under-Class*, ed. E. Shragge, 17-34. Toronto: Garamond Press.

Silius, Harriet. 2002. Feminist Perspectives on the European Welfare State. In *Thinking Differently: A Reader in European Women's Studies*, ed. G. Griffin and R. Braidotti, 31-48. London: Zed Books.

Silman, Janet. 1988. *Enough Is Enough: Aboriginal Woman Speak Out*. Toronto: Women's Press.

Siltanen, Janet, and Andrea Doucet. 2008. *Gender Relations in Canada: Intersectionality and Beyond*. Toronto: Oxford University Press.

Silver, Susan, John Shields, and Sue Wilson. 2005. Restructuring of Full-Time Workers: A Case of Transitional Dislocation or Social Exclusion in Canada? Lessons from the 1990s. *Social Policy and Administration* 39(7): 786-801.

Smart, Carol. 1999. *Family Fragments?* Malden, MA: Polity Press.

–. 2007. *Personal Life*. Cambridge: Polity Press.

Smart, Carol, and Bren Neale. 1999. *Family Fragments*. Cambridge: Polity Press.

Smith, Dorothy E. 1987. *The Everyday World as Problematic*. Toronto: University of Toronto Press.

Spar, Debora. 2006. *The Baby Business: How Money, Science, and Politics Drive the Commerce of Conception*. Boston: Harvard Business School Press.

Spencer, Emily. 2006. Lipstick and High Heels: War the Feminization of Women in Chatelaine Magazine, 1928-1956. PhD diss., Royal Military College of Canada.

Spitze, Glenna, and Mary P. Gallant. 2004. "The Bitter with the Sweet": Older Adults' Strategies for Handling Ambivalence in Relations with Their Adult Children. *Research on Aging* 26(4): 387-412.

Spitze, Glenna, and John R. Logan. 1992. Helping as a Component of Parent-Adult Child Relations. *Research on Aging* 14(3): 291-312.

Stack, Carol B. 1974. *All Our Kin: Strategies for Survival in a Black Community*. New York: Harper and Row.

St. John, Susan. 2008. Working for Families: Work, Families and Poverty. In *New Zealand, New Welfare: New Developments in Welfare and Work*, ed. N. Lunt, M. O'Brien, and R. Stephens, 78-91. Melbourne: Cengage Learning.

Stacey, Judith. 1996. *In the Name of the Family: Rethinking Family Values in the Postmodern Age*. Boston: Beacon Press.

–. 2004. Cruising to Familyland: Gay Hypergamy and Rainbow Kinship. *Current Sociology* 52: 181-97.

Stafford, Janine. 2002. *A Profile of the Childcare Services Industry*. Ottawa: Statistics Canada.

Standing, Guy. 1997. Globalization, Labour Flexibility and Insecurity: The Era of Market Regulation. *European Journal of Industrial Relations* 3: 7-37.

Stanford, Jim. 2008. Good Jobs Won't Appear without a Helping Hand. *Toronto Star,* 14 November.

Statistics Canada. 1998. 1996 Census: Labour Force Activity, Occupation and Industry, Place of Work, Mode of Transportation to Work, Unpaid Work. *The Daily,* 17 March.

–. 2000. *Women in Canada 2000: A Gender-Based Statistical Report.* Ottawa: Statistics Canada.

–. 2002a. *Annual Average 2002 Family Characteristics of Single Husband-Wife Families.* Labour Force Survey. Ottawa: Statistics Canada.

–. 2002b. *General Social Survey – Cycle 15 – Changing Conjugal Life in Canada.* Ottawa: Minister of Industry.

–. 2002c. Sawmills and Planing Mills. *The Daily,* 5 March.

–. 2003a. *Canada e-Book: The People – Working Hours.*

–. 2003b. *Women in Canada: Work Chapter Updates.* Ottawa: Statistics Canada.

–. 2004a. Grandparents Raising Their Children's Children. *Spotlight: Grandparents.* http://www.statcan.gc.ca/pub/.

–. 2004b. *Labour Force Estimates by Detailed Occupation, Sex, Canada, Province, Annual Average, 1987-2004.* Communications Canada, Depository Services Program STC catalogue no. 71F0004XCB. Ottawa: Statistics Canada.

–. 2005a. Divorces. *The Daily,* 9 March. http://www.statcan.gc.ca/.

–. 2005b. Fact Sheet: Education Indicators. *Perspectives on Labour and Income* 6(12): 29-43.

–. 2006a. Study: Changing Patterns of Women in the Canadian Labour Force. *The Daily,* 15 June.

–. 2006b. *The Wealth of Canadians: An Overview of the Results of the Survey of Financial Security 2005, Pensions and Wealth Surveys Section.* Ottawa: Minister of Industry.

–. 2006c. *Wives as Primary Breadwinners.* www.statcan.gc.ca/.

–. 2007a. *Quarterly Demographic Estimates: January to March 2007, Preliminary.* Ottawa: Statistics Canada.

–. 2007b. Study: Work Stress among Health Care Providers. *The Daily,* 13 November.

–. 2008a. *Canadian Demographics at a Glance.* Catalogue no. 91-003-X. Ottawa: Minister of Industry. http://www.statcan.gc.ca/.

–. 2008b. Census Snapshot – Immigration in Canada: A Portrait of the Foreign-Born Population, 2006 Census. *Canadian Social Trends* (April).

–. 2010. Definitions, Data Sources and Methods. http://www.statcan.gc.ca

Steiner, Leslie Morgan. 2007. *Mommy Wars: Stay-at-Home and Career Moms Face Off on Their Choices, Their Lives, Their Families.* New York: Random House.

Stephens, Mary Ann Parris, Melissa M. Franks, and Audie A. Atienza. 1997. Where Two Roles Intersect: Spillover between Parent Care and Employment. *Psychology and Aging* 12(1): 30-37.

Stevenson, Garth. 2006. *Parallel Paths: The Development of Nationalism in Ireland and Quebec.* Montreal and Kingston: McGill-Queen's University Press.

Stinson, Jane. 2006. Impact of Privatization on Women. *Canadian Dimension* 40(3): 27-32.

Stobert, Susan, and Kelly Cranswick. 2004. Looking after Seniors: Who Does What for Whom? *Canadian Social Trends* 74 (Autumn): 2-6.

Strain, Laurel A., and Neena L. Chappell. 1989. Social Networks of Urban Native Elders: A Comparison with Non-Natives. *Canadian Journal of Ethnic Studies* 21(2): 104-17.

Strauss, Murray, and Richard Gelles. 1990. *Physical Violence in American Families: Risk Factors and Adaptations to Violence in 8145 Families.* New Brunswick: Transaction.

Strauss, Murray, Richard Gelles, and Suzanne Steinmetz. 1986. The Marriage License as a Hitting License. In *Family in Transition,* 5th ed., ed. A. Skolnick and J. Skolnick, 290-303. Boston: Little, Brown.

Strohschein, Lisa. 2007. Challenging the Presumption of Diminished Capacity to Parent: Does Divorce Really Change Parenting Practices? *Family Relations* 56: 358-68.

Strong-Boag, Veronica. 1979. Wages for Housework: Mothers' Allowances and the Beginning of Social Security in Canada. *Journal of Canadian Studies* 4(2): 24-34.

Sumer, H. Canan, and Patrick A. Knight. 2001. How Do People with Different Attachment Styles Balance Work and Family? A Personality Perspective of Work-Family Linkage. *Journal of Applied Psychology* 86(4): 653-63.

Supiot, Alain. 2001. *Beyond Employment: Changes in Work and the Future of Labour Law in Europe.* New York: Oxford University Press.

Sussman, Deborah. 2006. Minimum Wage. *Perspectives on Labour and Income* 7(10): 12-17.

Sussman, Deborah, and Stephanie Bonnell. 2006. Wives as Primary Breadwinners. *Perspectives on Labour and Income* 7(8): 10-17.

Sydney Morning Herald. 2009. Budget Winners and Losers. 13 May. http://www.business.smh.com.au (accessed 2007).

Szinovacz, Maximiliane E. 2006. Families and Retirement. In *New Frontiers on Research on Retirement,* ed. Leroy O. Stone, 165-98. Ottawa: Statistics Canada.

Tergeist, Peter. 1995. Introd. to *Flexible Working Time: Collective Bargaining and Government Intervention.* Paris: OECD.

Thomas, Jacob. 1994. *Teachings from the Longhouse.* Toronto: Stoddart.

Throsby, Karen, and Rosalind Gill. 2004. "It's Different for Men": Masculinity and In Vitro Fertilization (IVF). *Men and Masculinities* 6(4): 330-48.

Thurer, Shari L. 1994. *The Myths of Motherhood: How Culture Reinvents the Good Mother.* New York: Houghton Mifflin.

Timpson, Annis-May. 2001. *Driven Apart: Women's Employment Equality and Child Care in Canadian Public Policy.* Vancouver: UBC Press.

Toronto Star. 2007. EI Cash Rich, Service Poor. 25 February. http://www.thestar.com/.

Tougas, Jocelyne. 2001a. *Child Care in Quebéc: Where There's Will, There's a Way.* Child Care Advocacy Association of Canada. http://action.web.ca/home/crru/.

–. 2001b. What We Can Learn from the Quebec Experience. In Cleveland and Krashinsky 2001, 92-105.

–. 2002. Quebec's Family Policy and Strategy on Early Childhood Development and Childcare. *Education Canada* 39(4): 20-22.

Towns, Ann. 2002. Paradoxes of (In)Equality: Something Is Rotten in the Gender Equal State of Sweden. *Cooperation and Conflict* 37(2): 157-79.

Townsend, Nicholas. 2002. *Package Deal: Marriage, Work and Fatherhood in Men's Lives.* Philadelphia: Temple University Press.

Tronto, Joan. 1993. *Moral Boundaries: A Political Argument for an Ethic of Care.* New York: Routledge.

Tucker, Eric. 1990. *Administering Danger in the Workplace: The Law and Politics of Occupational Health and Safety Regulation in Ontario, 1850-1914.* Toronto: University of Toronto Press.

Tucker, Robert C. 1972. *Philosophy and Myth in Karl Marx.* Cambridge: Cambridge University Press.

Turcotte, Martin. 2006. Parents with Adult Children Living at Home. *Canadian Social Trends* 80 (Spring): 2-10.

–. 2007. Time Spent with Family during a Typical Workday, 1986 to 2005. *Canadian Social Trends* 83 (13 February).

Twigg, Julia. 2004. The Body, Gender and Age: Feminist Insights in Social Gerontology. *Journal of Aging Studies* 18(1): 59-73.

Tyyskä, Vappu. 1995. *The Politics of Caring and the Welfare State: The Impact of the Women's Movement on Child Care Policy in Canada and Finland, 1960-1990.* Helsinki: Suomalainen Tiedeakatemia.

UNICEF (United Nations Children's Fund). 2005. *Child Poverty in Rich Nations.* Florence: Innocenti Research Centre.

–. 2008. *The Child Care Transition.* Report Card 8. Florence: Innocenti Research Centre.

UNDP (United Nations Development Programme). 1995. *Human Development Report.* Oxford: Oxford University Press.

–, OSAGI (Office of the Special Advisor on Gender Issues and the Advancement of Women). 2001. *Supporting Gender Mainstreaming.* New York: United Nations Publications.

Ursel, Jane. 1992. *Private Lives, Public Policy: 100 Years of State Intervention in the Family.* Toronto: Women's Press.

Usalcas, Jeannine. 2005. Youth and the Labour Market. *Perspectives on Labour and Income.* 6(11): 5-10.

–. 2008. Hours Polarization Revisited. *Perspectives on Labour and Income* 9(3): 5-15.

Valverde, Mariana. 1987. Lesbianism: A Country That Has No Language. In *Sex, Power, and Pleasure,* 75-108. Toronto: Women's Press.

Van Echtelt, Patricia E., Arie C. Glebbeek, and Siegwart M. Lindenberg. 2006. The New Lumpiness of Work: Explaining the Mismatch between Actual and Preferred Working Hours. *Work, Employment and Society* 20(3): 493-512.

VanEvery, Jo. 1995. *Heterosexual Women Changing the Family: Refusing to Be a Wife.* London: Taylor and Francis.

Veevers, Jean E. 1980. *Childless by Choice.* London: Butterworths.

Verberg, Norine. 2006. Family-Based Social Activism: Rethinking the Social Role of Families. *Studies in Political Economy* 2(1): 23-46.

Vincent, Carol, Stephen Ball, and Soile Pietikainen. 2004. Metropolitan Mothers: Mothers, Mothering and Paid Work. *Women's Studies International Forum* 27: 571-87.

Vincent, Clark E. 1966. Familia Spongia: The Adaptive Function. *Journal of Marriage and Family* 28(1): 29-36.

Vosko, Leah. 2002. Mandatory "Marriage" or Obligatory Waged Work: Social Assistance and Single Mothers in Wisconsin and Ontario. In *Women's Work Is Never Done: Comparative·Studies in Care-Giving, Employment, and Social Policy Reform,* ed. S. Bashevkin, 165-200. New York: Routledge.

–, ed. 2006. *Precarious Employment: Understanding Labour Market Insecurity in Canada.* Montreal and Kingston: McGill-Queen's University Press.

–. 2007. Gendered Labour Market Insecurities: Manifestations of Precarious Employment in Different Locations. In Shalla and Clement 2007, 52-97.

Wagner, Sally Roesch. 1992. *Akwe:kon Journal* 9(1): 4-15.

–. 2001. *Sisters in Spirit: Haudenosaunee (Iroquois) Influence on Early American Feminists.* Summertown, TN: Native Voices.

Waldron, Florencemae. 2005. Battle over Female (In)Dependence Women in New England Quebecois Migrant Communities. *Frontiers: A Journal of Women Studies* 26(2): 158-205.

Walker, Alexis, Clara Pratt, and Linda Eddy. 1995. Informal Caregiving to Aging Family Members. *Family Relations* 44: 402-11.

Walker, Gilian. 1990. *Family Violence and the Women's Movement: The Conceptual Practices of Power.* Toronto: University of Toronto Press.

Walker, Janet. 2003. Radiating Messages: An International Perspective. *Family Relations* 52: 406-17.

Walker, Karen. 1994. "I'm Not Friends the Way She's Friends": Ideological and Behavioral Constructions of Masculinity in Men's Friendships. *Masculinities* 2: 38-55.

Walker, Margaret Urban. 1998. *Moral Understandings: A Feminist Study in Ethics.* New York: Routledge.

Walmsley, Christopher. 2006. *Protecting Aboriginal Children.* Vancouver: UBC Press.

Walsh, Froma. 2003. *Normal Family Processes: Growing Diversity and Complexity.* New York: Guildford Press.

Walters, Vivienne, and Margaret Denton. 1997. Stress, Depression and Tiredness among Women: The Social Production and Social Construction of Health. *Canadian Review of Sociology and Anthropology* 34(1): 53-69.

Walzer, Susan. 1998. *Thinking about the Baby: Gender and Transitions into Parenthood.* Philadelphia: Temple University Press.

Waring, Marilyn. 1999. *Counting for Nothing: What Men Value and What Women Are Worth.* 2nd ed. Toronto: University of Toronto Press.

Warry, Wayne. 2000. *Unfinished Dreams: Community Healing and the Reality of Aboriginal Self-Government.* Toronto: University of Toronto Press.

Waters, Johanna L. 2002. Flexible Families? Astronaut Households and the Experiences of Mothers in Vancouver, British Columbia. *Social and Cultural Geography* 3: 117-34.

Wayne, Jane Holliday, Nicholas Musisca, and William Fleeson. 2004. Considering the Role of Personality in the Work-Family Experience: Relationships of the Big Five to Work-Family Conflict and Facilitation. *Journal of Vocational Behavior* 64: 108-30.

Weaver, Hilary, and Berry White. 1997. The Native American Family Circle: Roots of Resiliency. *Journal of Family Social Work* 2(1): 67-79.

Webb, Steve, Martin Kemp, and Jane Millar. 1996. The Changing Face of Low Pay in Britain. *Policy Studies* 17(4): 255-71.

Webster, Juliet. 2001. Reconciling Adaptability and Equal Opportunities in European Workplace. *Report for DG-Employment of the European Commission.* Brussels: European Commission.

Weeks, Carly. 2008. Interracial Relationships Rise 30 Per Cent in Five Years. *Globe and Mail,* 3 April. http://www.theglobeandmail.com/.

Weeks, Wendy. 1994. *Women Working Together.* Melbourne: Longman.

Weis, Lois. 2006. Masculinity, Whiteness, and the New Economy. *Men and Masculinities* 8(3): 262-72.

West, Candace, and Don Zimmerman. 1987. Doing Gender. *Gender and Society* 1(2): 125-51.

Williams, Cara. 2003a. Sources of Workplace Stress. *Perspectives on Labour and Income* 4(6): 5-12.

–. 2003b. Stress at Work. *Canadian Social Trends* 70 (Autumn): 7-13.

–. 2005. The Sandwich Generation. *Canadian Social Trends* 72 (Summer): 16-21.

Williams, Joan. 2000. *Unbending Gender: Why Family and Work Conflict and What to Do about It.* Oxford: Oxford University Press.

Williams, Philippa, Barbara Pocock, and Natalie Skinner. 2008. "Clawing Back Time": Expansive Working Time and Implications for Work-Life Outcomes in Australian Workers. *Work, Employment and Society* 33(4): 737-48.

Wittig, Monique. 1992. *The Straight Mind and Other Essays.* Boston: Beacon Press.

Wood, Stephen. 1989. The Transformation of Work? In *The Transformation of Work?* ed. S. Wood, 1-43. London: Unwin Hyman.

Young, Brigitte. 2001. The "Mistress" and the "Maid" in the Globalized Economy. *Socialist Register* 37: 287-327.

Yuval-Davis, Nira. 1997. *Gender and Nation.* London: Sage.

Zajicek, Anna, Toni Calasanti, Cristie Ginther, and Julie Summers. 2006. Intersectionality and Age Relations: Unpaid Care Work and Chicanas. In *Age Matters: Realigning Feminist Thought,* ed. T.M. Calasanti and K.F. Slevin, 175-97. New York: Routledge.

Zetlin, Di, and Gillian Whitehouse. 2003. Gendering Industrial Citizenship. *British Journal of Industrial Relations* 41(4): 773-88.

Zeytinoglu, Isik Urla, and Gordon B. Cooke. 2005. Non-Standard Work and Benefits: Has Anything Changed since the Wallace Report? *Relations Industrielles/Industrial Relations* 60(1): 29-66.

Zhang, Xuelin. 2009. Earnings of Women with and without Children. *Perspectives on Labour and Income* (March): 5-13.

Contributors

Patrizia Albanese is an associate professor in the Department of Sociology at Ryerson University. Her research interests include family policies, ethnic relations, gender and nationalism, and social inequality. She is the author of *Mothers of the Nation: Women, Family and Nationalism in Twentieth Century Europe* (2006); *Children in Canada Today* (2009); and *Child Poverty in Canada* (2010); co-editor (with Lorne Tepperman and James Curtis) of *Sociology: A Canadian Perspective*, 2nd ed.; and co-author of *More Than It Seems: Household Work and Lifelong Learning* (2010). She is also completing a book on youth in Canada (expected 2011). She is currently doing SSHRC-funded research on childcare in rural Ontario and Quebec and is working on projects on youth in Canadian Forces families (with Deborah Harrison, University of New Brunswick) and on the intergenerational transmission of problem gambling (with Lorne Tepperman, University of Toronto).

Donna Baines is an associate professor and teaches labour studies and social work at McMaster University. Her research focuses on restructuring in women's paid and unpaid care work; race, class, and gender in everyday work; and anti-oppressive social work practice. She has published extensively and in a wide variety of areas, including restructuring, health and safety, bullying, the organization of work for social workers, and social service public policy. Her articles have appeared in *Social Work, Journal of Health and Safety, Women and Work, Australian Social Work, Social Justice,* and *Studies in Political Economy,* among several other journals. Her recent work includes the second edition of the edited volume *Doing Anti-Oppressive Practice: Building Transformative, Politicized Social Work* (forthcoming 2011).

Maureen Baker is professor of sociology at the University of Auckland. Her research interests include family policies and trends, gendered work, restructuring welfare states, comparative social policy, reproduction, and gender identity. In 2008, she was made a fellow of the New Zealand Academy of the Humanities and in 2009 a fellow of the Royal Society of New Zealand. She has taught at several Canadian universities, including the University of Toronto and McGill University, as well as in Australia. She has also worked as a senior researcher for Canada's Parliament, specializing in social policy issues relating to families and women. She is the author of numerous books and articles on family and social issues, including *Choices and Constraints in Family Life,* 2nd ed. (2010), and *Families: Changing Trends in Canada,* 6th ed. (2009).

Andrea Doucet is a professor of sociology at Carleton University. She is co-author of a recent book titled *Gender Relations: Intersectionality and Beyond* (with Janet Siltanen, 2008) and of *Do Men Mother?* (2006), which was awarded the John Porter Tradition of Excellence Book Award from the Canadian Sociological Association. She was the 2007 (and eleventh) recipient of the SSHRC Thérèse F. Casgrain Fellowship for research on women and social justice, from which she is completing a book titled *Bread and Roses and the Kitchen Sink: American and Canadian Breadwinning Mothers in the 21st Century.* She has also published widely on reflexive and creative approaches to qualitative research and is co-author of a forthcoming book, *A Guide through Qualitative Analysis: Listening, Seeing and Reading Narrative Data* (with Natasha Mauthner, 2012).

Ann Duffy is a professor in the Department of Sociology and is cross-appointed to the Labour Studies Program at Brock University. She is also an active contributor to the MA program in Critical Sociology and the MA program in Social Justice and Equity Studies. Her published work reflects a long-term interest in employment, particularly part-time work, and its impact on women and older Canadians. Her most recent book is a co-authored examination of mid-life women's lives – *Connection, Compromise, and Control: Canadian Women Discuss Midlife* (2008). At present, she and Julianne Momirov are completing a second edition of *Family Violence: A Canadian Introduction.* She is also engaged in a SSHRC-funded research project that examines the impact of economic restructuring and job displacement on workers and their communities in Welland, Ontario.

Margrit Eichler is a professor of sociology and equity studies in education at the Ontario Institute for Studies in Education at the University of Toronto. A Fellow of the Royal Society of Canada, her research interests include family policy, reproductive and genetic technologies, feminist methodology, and an integrative approach to social in/equity that understands the issue of sustainability to be part of social stratification. She has over two hundred publications, including *Nonsexist Research Methods: A Practical Guide* (1991); *Change of Plans: Towards a Non-Sexist Sustainable City* (1995); *Family Shifts: Families, Policies and Gender Equality* (1997); *Feminist Utopias: Re-Visioning Our Futures* (2002); and *The Bias Free Framework: A Practical Tool for Identifying and Eliminating Social Biases in Health Research* (2006). Her latest book (co-edited) is titled *Minds of Our Own: The Invention of Feminist Scholarship 1967-1976* (2008).

Bonnie Freeman is an Algonquin/Mohawk PhD candidate from Six Nations of the Grand River in the Faculty of Social Work at Wilfrid Laurier University. She is also on faculty at McMaster University School of Social Work under an Aboriginal Pre-Doctoral Fellowship. Her doctoral work focuses on Aboriginal youth reclaiming their identity and well-being through cultural-based activism. She is also interested in areas of research that include self-determination in Aboriginal communities and public policy development; traditional Aboriginal cultural interventions in clinical social work practice; Aboriginal collective and community-healing cultural approaches; Aboriginal perspectives on anti-oppressive practices; and Indigenous health and wellness research. Her publications include *Indigenous Pathways to Anti-Oppressive Practice* (2007) and "An Aboriginal Community Model" (2007, *Native Social Work Journal*).

Judy Fudge is professor and Lansdowne Chair in Law at the University of Victoria. She has written extensively on employment and labour law, labour law history, pay equity, human rights at work, and the legal regulation of women's work. In 2009, she was awarded the Bora Laskin National Fellowship in Human Rights for her project Labour Rights as Human Rights: Unions, Women, and Migrants. Her publications include the co-edited *Work on Trial: Canadian Labour Law Struggles* (2010); the co-authored *Self-Employed Workers Organize: Law, Policy, and Unions* (2005); the co-edited *Precarious Work, Women and the New Economy: The Challenge to Legal Norms* (2006); and the co-edited *Privatization, Law and the Challenge to Feminism* (2002).

Catherine Krull is an associate dean, Faculty of Arts and Science, and an associate professor in the Department of Sociology (also a member of the Cultural Studies Graduate Program and cross-appointed to Women's Studies) at Queen's University. She is currently a research fellow at the Institute for the Study of the Americas, School of Advanced Study, University of London and has held other research fellowships at the Rockefeller Center, Harvard University (2007); Department of Sociology, Boston University (2007); and the Centre for International Studies, London School of Economics (2003). While she continues to write on the efficacy of Canadian family policies, her current research focuses on 1) a generational analysis of women's participation and resistance in Cuba's revolution, and 2) an analysis of the Cuban diaspora in Canada, Mexico, the United Kingdom, Spain, and the Dominican Republic.

Margaret Hillyard Little is an anti-poverty activist and professor in women's studies and political studies at Queen's University, Kingston, Ontario. She is the author of *If I Had a Hammer: Retraining That Really Works* (2005) and *No Car, No Radio, No Liquor Permit: The Moral Regulation of Single Mothers in Ontario* (1998), which won the Floyd S. Chambers Book Award in Ontario History. She is currently working on a SSHRC-funded research project titled "Who's Hurting Now? A Race, Class and Gender Analysis of Neo-Liberal Welfare Reforms in Canada." Her first job, though, is being a mom.

Nancy Mandell is a professor of sociology and women's studies at York University and a former Director of the Centre for Feminist Research and chair of the Sociology Department. Her research and teaching interests include gender, aging, schooling, and family. She has published articles and book chapters on parental involvement in monitoring children's homework, feminist aging studies, aging and embodiment, gendered and racialized forms of care work, and patterns of economic security among aging immigrant families. Her community-academic research protocol (Mandell and Whittington-Walsh 2004) based on community-based research is widely used across Canada. Her book *Conflict, Compromise and Choice: Canadian Women at Midlife 2008,* co-authored with Ann Duffy and Sue Wilson, examines the work, community, family, and intimate relationships of mid-life women and their involvement with the women's movement. She is currently leading a project funded by the Social Sciences and Humanities Research Council of Canada titled Worked to Death: Gendered and Racialized Patterns of Economic Security among Senior Immigrants.

Susan A. McDaniel is the Prentice Research Chair in Global Population and Economy, director of the Prentice Institute, and professor of sociology at the University of Lethbridge. Her research is on life course, demographic aging, generational relations, family change, and the social impacts of technology. She is the author of seven books and research monographs and over 170 research articles and book chapters and is a frequent keynote speaker at national and international conferences. She is a fellow of the Royal Society of Canada, the recipient of many research and teaching awards, and an advisor to governments in Canada, the United Kingdom, and the European Union on social statistics, social policies, science and technology, and innovation policies. Her current research projects include Inequalities in Canada and the United States in relation to later-life health risks; social engagement in mid-life; and intergenerational poverty.

Norene Pupo is past director of the Centre for Research on Work and Society (CRWS) and an associate professor in the Department of Sociology at York University. She has researched and published in the areas of women, work, and social policy; part-time employment, call centres, and shifting employment practices in the public sector; and unions and economic restructuring. She is co-author of *The Part-Time Paradox* and *Few Choices: Women, Work and Family* and is co-editor of *Good Jobs, Bad Jobs, No Jobs: The Transformation of Work in the 21st Century*. Her recent work is a SSHRC-funded project that focuses on restructuring work and labour in the new economy. She has recently edited a book on changes in the structure of work and labour processes, *Interrogating the New Economy,* with Mark Thomas. She is also editing a collection on changing conditions of work, *The Shifting Landscape of Work,* with Ann Duffy and Daniel Glenday. Through her role as director of the CRWS, Professor Pupo is editor of the centre's journal, *Just Labour.*

Justyna Sempruch is a researcher at the Centre for Gender Studies, University of Basel, Switzerland. She completed her PhD in comparative literature at the University of British Columbia (2003) and has published on philosophical and socio-political intersections of gender, nationality, and psychoanalysis, as well as on literature of cultural diaspora. She published her monograph, *Fantasies of Gender: The Witch in Western Feminist Theory and Literature* (2008), with Purdue

University Press Monograph Series in Comparative Cultural Studies and co-edited an anthology, *Multiple Marginalities: An Intercultural Dialogue on Gender in Education* (2006). More recently, she has taught and conducted research at Queen's University (Kingston, Ontario) while completing major transnational research funded by the Swiss National Foundation (2004-7) on the politics of parenting. Within this research scope, addressing the changing concepts of family as well as feminist understandings of women's participation in economy, she is preparing her second book for publication with Lambert Academic Publishing House in Germany.

Sue Wilson was a professor of sociology in the School of Nutrition at Ryerson University, where she taught research methods, professional practice, family studies, and nutrition communication. For several years before her untimely death, she was the associate dean of the Faculty of Community Services. Sue wrote several sociology textbooks, including *Women, Families and Work,* 4th ed. (1996), and several chapters in texts in the areas of family and women's work, midlife women's health, and caregiving. Her most recent publications include the co-authored book *Connection, Compromise, and Control: Canadian Women Discuss Midlife* (2008). She was also involved in research in the area of breast cancer and spirituality. She is sadly missed by colleagues, family, and friends.

Index

ABC Learning Centres (Australia), 56
Aboriginal families: Family Allowance program, 205n18; government policy, 29n3, 73-75; healing ceremonies, 75; languages, 18, 67; mothering traditions, 67-69; mothers' allowances, 196; multi-generational structure, 18-19, 38; role of women, 78-80, 213, 214; WALL Lifelong Learning Study, 87; work-life balance, 211, 213, 214-15. *See also* First Nations; Indigenous families
activism–social care paradigm, 71-72, 77-78
adoption, 14, 17, 18, 29n3
adult children, 13, 35-37, 46, 109, 110, 114nn11,14,16
adult grandchildren, 40
African Americans, 18-19, 37, 78
agricultural jobs, 105, 193n26
Ahmed, Sara, 161
Akhwa:tsire (family), 67, 68
Albanese, Patrizia, 96n5, 114n14, 130-43, 207, 209, 210, 211
Alberta: childcare, 57; mothers' allowance, 198, 205n5; parent-child relationship survey, 111; social spending, 54, 58; traditional family agendas, 17; welfare policy, 60, 202, 213
alcoholism, 23
Allen, Katherine R., 40
Alliance Party (New Zealand), 63n6
Aptheker, Bettina, 72, 76
Arthurs, Harry, 176
assimilation, 76, 77
au pair workers, 34
Australia: child payments and allowances, 59, 59t; childcare, 56, 56t, 58; eldercare, 42-43; employment and poverty rates, 53t; family wage, 48; income tax, 51;

maternal employment, 50-61; parental benefits, 54-55, 55t; part-time work, 51t; social spending, 59-60, 59t, 63n5
auto jobs, 101
Avila, Ernestine, 16
axioms on work and family, 216

baby boomers, 21, 44
"bad jobs," 49, 99, 100-103, 113n2
Baines, Donna, 67-80, 207, 211, 213, 214
Baker, Maureen, 17, 23, 47-63, 207-8, 210, 213
Baker, Michael, 139
Bales, Robert, 22
Baril, Robert, 139
Bashevkin, Sylvia, 168n6
Beaujot, Roderic, 23
Belgium, 60
benefits: assessing, 180, 181; child support allowances, 59, 59t, 133-34, 136, 140, 158, 203, 210; childcare subsidies, 55-57, 56t, 138, 143nn6-7; cross-national comparisons, 53-55, 55t, 137; income support payments, 60, 61; maternity leave, 54, 55, 63n6, 136-37, 150, 191n5; mothers' allowances, 195-99, 205n5; parental leave, 33, 112, 116, 128-29, 129n4, 189, 191n5, 204; for part-time work, 179, 184, 190, 193n29; paternal leave, 137, 143n5, 150; policy formation, 53-55, 55t, 63n7, 112, 160, 166, 192n22; reforms to family benefits, 58-60, 59t; seniors' benefits, 198; social benefits, 150, 195; universal family allowance, 58-59, 61, 63n2, 138, 210; vacation entitlements, 104. *See also* social spending; tax policy; welfare system
Bengston, Vern L., 19
Bennett, Cinnamon, 163

Bernier, Jean, 133, 140
Bibby, Reginald W., 11, 24-25
birth rates, 130, 131, 133, 141, 181, 211
births outside marriage, 133, 141, 211
black families. *See* African Americans
Blackfoot Confederacy, 72
blended families, 11
blood mothers, 19
body as social construction, 168n2. *See also* embodied subjectivity
boomerang kids, 35-37, 110
Booth, Christine, 163
Bosch, Gerhard, 191n4
Bouchard, Camil, 135
Bourdieu, Pierre, 215
Bowling Alone (Putman), 98
Bradbury, Bettina, 22
Braidotti, Rosi, 160
breadwinners. *See* male breadwinner system
Britain. *See* United Kingdom
British Columbia: maternity leave, 191n5; mothers' allowance, 198, 205n5; parent-child relationship survey, 111; regulation of working time, 191n5; Self-Sufficiency Project, 200-201; welfare policy, 202
Brody, Charles, 112-13
broken families, 11
Bryceson, Deborah F., 29n4
Bubek, Elisabeth, 168n2
Budgeon, Shelley, 26
Butler, Judith, 19-20, 27-28, 149, 161, 162, 168n9
Butler, Linda, 83-84, 87, 95, 209

Caledonia, Ont., 67, 72, 76, 77, 80n3
call centre work, 102, 141
Campbell, Iain, 180, 191n7
Campbell, Lori, 40
Canada: employment and poverty rates, 53t; health care system, 42, 105-6, 181, 198, 200; investing in children discourse, 58, 61, 137-38; regulation of working time, 172-76, 179-83, 188-91, 191n3, 191n5; unemployment rates, 113n2; WALL Lifelong Learning Study, 82, 86-94; wartime economy, 197-98. *See also* public policy; social spending; *and specific provinces*
Canada Assistance Plan, 198, 200
Canada Child Tax Benefit (CCTB), 136, 158
Canada Health and Social Transfer, 200
Canada Labour Code, 174-76, 189, 191n3, 192nn11-12

Canadian Charter of Human Rights, 76
Canadian General Social Survey, 42
Canadian Parliament, 76-77
Canadian Patriotic Fund, 195, 205n3
capitalist production system, 70-72, 156
Caplan, Leslie J., 81
care work/caregiving: benefits and burdens of, 41-43, 46; care provider networks, 43; care work–paid work relationships, 2, 3, 7, 25-28, 130-43, 168nn10-11, 206-18; concept of, 2-4, 6, 30-32, 46, 147-50, 153, 209; devaluation of, 43-44, 152, 157-58, 166, 215; domestic service workers, 16, 20, 33-35, 107, 113n8, 119, 147, 200; emotional nature, 3, 31-32, 41-43, 46, 147, 157, 178; fathers' participation, 32, 115-29; genderization/racialization of, 34-35, 45-46, 54; Hasselkus and Ray study, 83; Indigenous perspectives, 4, 67-80; informal care, 31-32, 46n1; intergenerational, 19, 30-46; mid-life care work, 35-39, 41, 46; neo-conservative philosophy, 148; policy implications, 43-45, 47-63, 130-43, 167-68; postcolonial discourse, 46; primary responsibility for, 33-34, 119, 147, 150, 154-55, 184, 188-89, 197; as psychic constitution, 152-54; socio-political context, 6, 31, 32, 34-35, 134, 148, 153-54, 166-67; spousal care, 40-41, 43; state support for earning and caring, 53-55; value of, 161, 215, 217. *See also* cultural landscape of care; elders/eldercare; fathers/fathering; grandparents/grandmothering; mothers/mothering
caring crunch, 215
Carnegie Council on Adolescent Research, 111
Carroll, Michael, 40
Catholic Church, 130, 131, 132, 143n3
CAW (Canadian Auto Workers), 113n5
cellphones, 105
centres de la petite enfance (CPEs), 138-39, 143n8
Changing Nature of Work and Lifelong Learning (WALL) Study, 82, 86-94, 90t, 96n5, 96nn8-9
Chappell, Neena L., 42
Châteauguay, Ont., 77
Chatelaine magazine, 22
Chaykowski, Richard, 176
Chief Cornplanter, 73
childcare, 47-63; availability, 58, 62, 194, 200, 202, 204, 209, 212; costs of, 55-58, 56t; cross-national comparisons, 55-58, 56t, 142; and divorce, 22; formulations

of, 160-61, 209; government subsidies, 47-48, 49, 58, 136-39, 143n7; by grandmothers, 38-39; in-home care networks, 43; by men, 112, 185; National Childcare Program, 204, 209-10; privatization, 106, 109, 137-39; public policy, 57, 164-65, 196, 204, 210, 212-13; Quebec programs, 130, 136, 137-39, 141-43, 143nn6-7, 209-10; queering childcare, 159-63; reduced-fee childcare, 130, 141-42; school daycare services, 136, 210; universal childcare, 26, 139; WALL Lifelong Learning Study, 89; women as primary caregivers, 185, 212. *See also* benefits; social spending
Child Care Advocacy Association of Canada, 58
Childcare Subsidy program (New Zealand), 58
children: Aboriginal children, 18; adult children, 13, 35-37, 46, 109, 110, 114n11, 114n14, 114n16; basis for social networks, 120-21; child abuse, 23, 204; child development programs, 137; child payments and allowances, 59, 59t, 133-34, 136, 158, 210; child poverty, 6, 53t, 58, 140-41; family time survey, 111; family values agendas, 16, 17; illness of, 192n21; impact of divorce on, 20, 22; Indigenous perspectives, 73, 75, 77; investment in children discourse, 58, 61, 203, 209; regulation of working time, 170-71, 191n5, 192n11. *See also* childcare; parenting; social spending
Children's Aid Societies, 204
Chile, 217
choice rubric, 208-10, 213
Chrisjohn, Roland, 75
citizenship, 158, 167, 214-15. *See also* social citizenship
Civil Marriage Act (Bill C-38), 14, 29n2
Clark, Helen, 63n6
Cleveland, Gordon, 139
cohabitation, 13, 25, 133
collective derogations, 181-82
Collins, Patricia Hill, 78
colonization, 4, 67-69, 72-76, 143n1, 213
Coltrane, Scott, 124, 161
common-law unions, 14, 15, 16, 25, 108, 130, 140, 211
community/community responsibility, 115-29; community-care services, 42, 217-18; defined, 116, 117-18, 127; judgments of stay-at-home dads (SAHDs), 115, 123-27, 150; methodology, 117; mothering, 19. *See also* fathers/fathering;

social networks
commuting, 104, 113n6, 142, 211, 212
competence/competency levels, 83-85, 89, 125, 132, 209, 217
computers/computer networks, 103, 104-5, 113n7
Conference Board of Canada, 45
Conservative Party (Canada), 57, 210
consumer price index, 59
consumerism, 1, 23, 79, 103, 109
contract work, 5, 101, 103, 123
Cooke, Gordon B., 193n29
Cornell, Drucilla, 12
corporations, 99-100, 106, 113n5, 180, 216
Côté, Sylvana, 139
Cournoyer, Dave, 17
Cowdery, Randi S., 34
CPEs (centres de la petite enfance), 138-39, 143n8
Cranswick, Kelly, 39-40, 41-42
Crompton, Rosemary, 188
cultural healing, 4
cultural landscape of care, 147-69; background, 147-50; embodied subjectivity, 6, 149, 154-58, 160, 168nn1-2, 168nn9-10, 208; home as private space, 151-54, 168n3; philosophy of equal treatment, 163-67; queering childcare, 159-63. *See also* social citizenship
Curry, Bill, 18

Daly, Mary, 52
David, Françoise, 135
daycare. *See* childcare
Denmark, 50-60, 51t, 53t, 55t, 56t, 59t, 169n13
Denton, Margaret, 41
"dependency" concept, 21, 48-50, 148, 156, 195, 208, 213. *See also* male breadwinner system
Depression era, 197
Dillaway, Heather, 35
diversification: employment, 103-5; family structures, 14-15, 23-24, 37, 210-11
Divorce Act, 14
divorce/divorce rates, 13, 14, 16, 19, 20, 21-22, 24, 133
"doing family," 28, 152, 155, 161, 215
"doing gender," 27-28, 49, 116, 152, 155, 161
domestic service, 16, 20, 33-35, 107, 113n8, 119, 147, 200
domestic violence, 20, 23
Doucet, Andrea, 15, 115-29, 208, 215

Douglas Creek Estates protest, 67, 72, 80n3
downsizing, 101, 104-5, 111
dual-earner households, 108, 140, 173, 177, 181, 187, 191, 192n8
Duffy, Ann, 39, 98-114, 209, 212
Dumont, Micheline, 132
Dunne, Gillian, 162
Duplessis, Maurice, 132
Duxbury, Linda, 184-87, 192n21

economy: economic apartheid, 44; libidinal economy, 153-56, 162; low-wage economy, 6, 15, 16, 61-62, 114n12; political economy, 161-62. *See also* new economy
education/education levels: early childhood education, 57, 58, 138, 139, 140; G/L/B/T information prohibited in schools, 17; high school dropout rate, 134-35; informal learning, 81-97; kindergarten programs, 57; post-secondary education, 108-9, 110, 198; of primary wage earners, 33; in Quebec, 132, 134-35; WALL Lifelong Learning Study, 82, 86-94, 90t, 96n5, 96n8
Eggbeen, David J., 36
Ehrenreich, Barbara, 31, 134
Eichler, Margrit, 26, 81-97, 114n14, 209, 212
elders/eldercare: employment opportunities for older workers, 45; immigrants, 113n8; Indigenous families, 69, 73, 75; men as caregivers, 39-41; sandwich generation, 39-41; seniors' benefits, 198; women as primary caregivers, 42, 82, 178, 185-86, 215
Eli Lilly, family time survey, 111
embodied subjectivity, 6, 149, 154-58, 160, 168nn1-2, 168nn9-10, 208
employment: care work–employment relationships, 2, 3, 7, 25-28, 130-43, 168nn10-11, 206-18; changing nature of, 5, 6, 15-16, 48-50, 61-62, 99-106, 192n8; cross-national comparisons, 50-60; deregulation of, 5, 61, 174; downsizing, 101, 104-5, 111; family support policies, 15, 187, 189, 214; feminist perspectives, 203-4, 207-10, 213-14; full-time employment, 101, 215; gender equality, 5, 155, 174, 183-84, 187-91; glass ceiling, 167; good jobs/bad jobs, 49, 99, 100-103, 113n3; hours-of-work rules, 174-77, 184-85, 189-90, 191n7, 193n30, 211; housework skill set transferral, 5, 83-86, 87, 89-96, 90t, 157, 209;

impact of new economy, 98-114; intensification and diversification, 45, 96n8, 103-5, 113n6, 134, 142, 181-82; just-in-time workforce, 103; multiple job-holding, 5, 212; non-standard work, 5, 15-16, 100-102, 104, 113n4, 181-82; over-employment, 103; overqualified workers, 102; and poverty rates, 49, 53t; self-employment, 15, 101, 191n2; single-parent families, 61, 192n15, 203-4; women as secondary workers, 212. *See also* labour/labour markets; maternal employment; part-time work; working-time regimes
Employment Insurance (EI): eligibility, 63n7, 203, 210; feminist perspectives on, 204; parental leave programs, 55, 63n7, 112, 137, 194, 204. *See also* Unemployment Insurance
equal treatment philosophy, 160, 163-67
essentialism/essentialist thinking, 11-29, 32, 209, 214-15
Established Programs Financing Act, 200
"estrogen-filled" worlds, 122, 125
Euro-centrism, 77
Europe: childcare programs, 142, 210; part-time work regulations, 190; work-time regulation, 188-89, 191n6; working-hours study, 174. *See also specific countries*
European Commission, 163, 191n6
European Union (EU): competency levels for house work, 84-85; equal treatment policies, 163; social spending, 60; women full employment policies, 60, 215; working-time regimes, 174
extended families: demographics, 37-39; Indigenous families, 18-19, 69, 73-74, 75; marginalization, 156; mothering duties, 35; unpaid care roles, 70; value of, 18-19

factory work, 197
Fagan, Colette, 174, 192n8, 192n9
Fair Labor Standards Act, 187, 192n25
family: changing trends, 2-4, 11, 12-24, 28n1, 98-99, 151-56, 162, 210-13; class divisions, 107-8; cross-national comparisons, 51t, 52-53, 53t; essentialist theory, 11-12, 32, 214-15; families of choice, 19, 26-27, 210-11; family activism, 71-72, 79; family diversity, 14-15, 23-24, 37, 210-11; family-in-decline discourse, 16-17, 19, 24; family time, 111, 177; family values agendas, 16-17, 24; feminist perspectives, 2, 112, 210-14; gender

equality, 11-12, 19-20, 32, 125-28, 214-15; gender relations, 2, 112, 115-17, 131-32, 156; generalist approaches to, 68-72, 76; impact of new economy, 98-114, 142; importance of, 24-26; Indigenous perspectives, 67-80; members with disabilities, 38, 39; Mohawk term for, 67; neo-conservative views, 16-17, 24, 148; neo-liberal views, 2, 11, 152, 168n3, 199-204; non-standard families, 11, 18-20, 23, 28, 157; patriarchal basis for, 131; performativity/"doing family," 26-28, 152; policy implications, 43, 44, 58-60, 59t, 130-43, 214, 216; post-modernist views, 210-11; power relationships, 20, 21, 153-54; transnational, 15-16, 29n4. *See also* benefits; extended families; nuclear family; work and family discourse

Family Allowance program, 197, 203, 205n18, 210

Family Coalition Party, 16-17

family violence, 20

family wage model: dependency concept/gender contract, 48-50, 151, 195, 197; employment relationship, 15, 106, 160, 168n7, 172; gender inequality, 199; welfare state policy, 197

farm workers, 105, 193n26

fathers/fathering, 115-29; absentee fathers, 16; care work responsibilities, 33, 127-29, 161; community acceptance of, 126-27; cross-national employment comparisons, 50-60; daddy quotas, 166; gay fathers, 150; gendered family roles, 2, 112; and infants, 125-26; mid-life care work, 35; nuclear family ideal, 11-12; obstacles to caregiving, 119-28; parenting resource centers, 128-29; paternal leave, 137, 143n5, 150; single fathers, 117; social constructs, 168n12; social networking, 117-27; stress levels, 110. *See also* masculinity; men; stay-at-home dads (SAHDs)

Federal/Provincial/Territorial Early Childhood Development (ECD) Agreement, 137-38

Fédération des femmes du Québec, 135

femininity: cultural labels, 121, 147-48, 154-55, 159, 165; devaluation of, 152, 163, 166; gender flexibility, 6; otherness of, 160; socio-political discourse, 152. *See also* masculinity

feminism/feminist perspectives: care work–employment integration, 2, 3, 7, 25-28, 71, 206-187; choice rubric, 208-10, 213; citizenship/social citizenship, 158; community responsibilities, 119; cultural landscape of care, 147-69; decline of family, 16; embodied subjectivity, 6, 149, 154-58, 160, 168nn1-2, 168nn9-10, 208; equal treatment philosophy, 160, 163-67; home as private space, 71, 151-54, 168n3; nuclear family, 70-71; politicization of women's interests, 214-15; social provisioning, 206-7, 208, 209, 213, 216, 217-18; women's roles in labour force, 71, 80n2; work-family balance, 2, 6-7, 28, 213-18. *See also* gender/gender equality; maternalism; mothers/mothering; nuclear family

fertility rates, 14, 24, 130-31, 133-34, 141, 181, 184

Figart, Deborah, 171, 174, 192n9

financial services, 105, 114n10

Fine, Michael, 31-32

Finland, 54, 60, 169n13

First Nations: band councils, 68; care work and colonialism, 4-5; Douglas Creek Estates protest, 67, 76, 77, 80n3; Indian Act (Bill C-31), 76-77; Kanesatake-Oka protest, 76, 77, 80n3; kinship relations, 18, 70; resistance and self-determination, 69, 72, 76-80, 213; Six Nations Reclamation protests, 77; Sixties Scoop, 18, 29n3, 69, 75. *See also* Aboriginal families; Haudenosaunee Confederacy; Indigenous families

Fitoussi, Michèle, 207

Fletcher, Alice, 73

flexible work schedules: access to, 5, 46, 185, 188-90; averaging, 192nn19-20; Canada Labour Code, 174-75; and childcare, 204; flex-time, 214; gendered aspects, 176-79, 184; hours-of-work rules, 174-77, 184-85, 189-90, 191n7, 193n30, 211; labour market participation by women, 173, 176, 181, 192n9; non-standard work, 104, 113n4; revising, 6; work-life balance, 179, 180-82, 183, 187; worker control over, 190-91; working-time regimes, 46, 179, 180-82, 183; workplace change, 192n17. *See also* part-time work

foster care, 18

France, 53t, 54-55, 55t, 60

Fraser, Nancy, 156, 158

Freeman, Bonnie, 67-80, 207, 211, 213, 214

French Civil Code, 131

Frey, M., 95-96

friendships: cross-gender, 122-23; male friendships, 120-23
fringe banking, 114n10
frozen embryos, 14
Fruhauf, Christine A., 40
Fudge, Judy, 170-93, 208, 209, 211, 212

Gage, Matilda, 73
Galabuzi, Grace-Edward, 44
Gallant, Mary P., 43
Galloway, Gloria, 18
gays, 17, 23, 28, 150, 162
gender contract, 4, 127, 148, 151, 158, 164, 189, 206
gender/gender equality: axioms on work and family, 216; cross-gender friendships, 122-23; doing gender, 27-28, 49, 116, 152; employment, 5, 155, 174, 183-84, 187-91; family roles, 11-12, 19-20, 125-28, 214-15; feminist perspectives, 215; gender convergence, 111-12; gender politics, 208; gender relations, 2, 112, 115-17, 131-32, 156; glass ceiling, 167; housework divide, 24, 33-34, 112, 177-78, 184-86, 192n22, 212; mainstreaming, 163-65; neo-liberal philosophy, 199-200, 202; new economy, 111-13; public policy, 155, 160, 163-67, 183-84; social constructions, 6, 7, 161-62; social networks, 119-20, 122, 123-27; theorizations, 192n9, 215; wage gap, 44-45, 50, 52, 60, 63n4, 178, 192n9; work patterns, 15-16, 22, 27-28, 44-45, 49, 50-53, 102-3, 134. *See also* embodied subjectivity; femininity; male breadwinner system; masculinity
Gender Trouble (Butler), 27
General Motors, 101, 113n5
generational change, 98
genocide, 75, 76
Gerzer-Sass, Annemarie, 84-85, 87, 95
Getting Institutions Right for Women in Development (Goetz), 118
Ghalam, Nancy Zukewich, 34
Glendinning, Caroline, 31-32
globalization: global care chain, 31; impact on women's employment, 142-43; international corporations, 99, 180; labour/labour markets, 15-16, 61, 98, 101, 134, 142, 173, 192n17; multigenerational families, 37-38; work-family balance, 211
Goetz, Anne Marie, 118
Golden, Lonnie, 171
"good jobs," 100-103, 107, 108, 134, 203, 204, 216

Goodman, Catherine Chase, 37
goods-producing sector, 105, 177
grandchildren, 40, 43, 46
Grandir en qualité study (Quebec), 139
grandparents/grandmothering, 19, 28n1, 37-39, 43, 46, 156
Grant, Agnes, 74
Greenaway, Norma, 16
Grosz, Elizabeth, 12
Gruber, Jonathan, 139

Habtu, Roman, 39-40
Hansen, Karen V., 20
Harel, Louise, 135
Harper, Stephen, 16, 18, 210
Harris, Mike, 143n2
Hasselkus, B.R., 83
Haudenosaunee Confederacy: creation story, 76; Douglas Creek Estates (Ont.) protest, 67; role of family, 76-78; role of women, 67-69, 72-74, 76-78, 213. *See also* First Nations
healing ceremonies, 75
health care system, 42, 105-6, 181, 198, 200
Hertz, Rosanna, 28
heterosexuality/heterosexual couples: double burden for women, 157-58; dual-earner households, 108, 140, 173, 177, 181, 187, 191, 192n8; gendered ideals, 210-11; heterosexual matrix, 147-50; libidinal economy, 153-56, 162; sociopolitical discourse, 147-50, 152. *See also* femininity; masculinity; nuclear family; sexuality
Higgins, Christopher, 184-87, 192n21
high-tech bubble, 100
historical trauma, 75
Hobbs, Margaret, 197
Hochschild, Arlie, 31
Hogan, Dennis P., 36
home: feminist perspectives, 71; in-home care network, 43; as private space, 151-54, 168n3
homophobia, 121, 122
homosexuality, 17, 23, 28, 150, 162. *See also* gays; lesbians/lesbian parents
Hondagneu-Sotelo, Pierrette, 16
Honneth, Axel, 156, 158
hooks, bell, 19, 98
Horizons (Policy Research Initiative), 206
household cleaners. *See* domestic service
household income: child payments and allowances, 59t, 136, 210; childcare costs, 56t; cost of living, 60, 62; debt load, 108; dual-earner households, 108,

140, 173, 177, 181, 187, 191, 192n8;
employment and poverty rates, 53t;
gendered wage gap, 44-45, 50, 52, 60,
63n4, 178, 192n9; housing costs, 113n6;
single-earner families, 129n1; socio-
economic factors, 44, 107; stability/
instability, 134, 142. *See also* male breadwinner system; tax policy
household service work. *See* domestic
service
households/housework: commodified
household labour, 109; and competency
levels, 83-85, 89, 125, 209, 217; daily
participation rates, 168n10, 178; definition, 82-83, 88, 96n2; domestic responsibilities, 28, 31, 115-19, 124, 151-52,
169n13, 197-99; family time, 111, 177;
gendered housework divide, 24, 33-34,
112, 177-78, 184-86, 192n22, 212; home
as private space, 151-54, 168n3; informal
learning from, 81-97; multi-generational,
37; and self-esteem, 81; skill set transfer,
5, 83-86, 87, 89-96, 90t, 157, 209; skip-
generation households, 19; stereotypes,
83; stress levels, 81-82; WALL Lifelong
Learning Study, 82, 86-94, 90t, 96n5,
96n8. *See also* care work/caregiving;
family; household income
human rights, 17, 23

immigrants/immigrant families: burden
on women, 157; demographics, 14-15;
immigration policy, 19, 29n3; impact of
new economy, 106, 108, 109-11, 113n8;
income/income gap, 44-45, 102; 96n8;
multi-generational family structure,
18-19, 38; WALL Lifelong Learning
Study, 87-88
in vitro fertilization, 14
Inco, 101
income tax, 136, 140, 158
Indian Act (Bill C-31), 76-77
Indian agents, 68
Indigenous families: activist mothering,
71-72, 78; colonization and Indigenous
women's roles, 4, 67-69, 72-76, 143n1,
213; forced adoption, 18, 29n3; Indian
status, 77; productive labour system, 71;
resistance and self determination, 69,
72, 76-80, 213; revitalizing, 75-76; Six
Nations Reclamation protests, 77; Sixties
Scoop, 18, 29n3, 69, 75. *See also* First
Nations
individualism, 16, 112
individuation theory, 98-99
industrial sector, 105, 112

infants, 125-26, 131
informal care, 31-32, 46n1
information technology, 5
Institut de la statistique du Québec, 139
institutional arenas, communities as,
115-29
intergenerational family. *See* extended
families
International Labour Organization (ILO),
170-71, 181-82, 191n4
interracial marriage, 15
intimacy, 122
Inuit families, 205n18. *See also* Aboriginal
families
Ipsos Reid surveys, 110-11, 114n15
Ireland, 56, 56t
Irigaray, Luce, 160, 168n9
Iroquois Confederacy. *See* Haudenosaunee
Confederacy

Japel, Christa, 139
Jarrott, Shannon E., 40
Jenson, Jane, 129
job sharing, 107
job strain, 105-6
just-in-time workforce, 103, 173, 179

Kanesatake-Oka protest, 76, 77, 80n3
kindergarten, 57, 136
kinship relations: cultural frameworks,
149, 152-53, 159, 161, 162, 167; kin
work, 119, 129; significance, 18, 70, 154,
156
Kirchmeyer, Catherine, 86
Klein, Ralph, 17
Knudson-Martin, Carmen, 34
Krashinsky, Michael, 139
Kristeva, Julia, 154
Krull, Catherine, 1-7, 11-29, 206, 209,
210, 211, 214, 215

Laberge, A.M., 131
labour/labour markets: background, 4, 71;
changing nature of, 15-16, 48-50, 61-62,
99-106, 168nn4-5, 176-79; collective
bargaining and agreements, 170, 172,
175; dependence on unpaid labour, 81-
82; domestic/wage dichotomy, 147-48;
federal labour standards, 192n17; feminist perspectives, 24-25, 203-4, 207-10,
213-14; full employment for women, 71,
80n2, 81-82, 108, 184, 192n15; gendered patterns of work, 15-16, 22, 44-45,
49, 50-53, 111-12, 151; general work
flexibility, 5, 16, 46, 103; housework
skill set transfer, 5, 83-86, 87, 89-96, 90t,

209; immigrants, 102; impact of World War II, 197, 199; increasing participation by women, 15-16, 33-34, 42, 117, 133, 134, 140, 164; international regulations, 168n4; labour force shortages, 44; market segmentation, 184; neo-liberal perspectives, 199-200, 206-7, 215-16; Nordic countries, 210; occupational segregation, 168n5; overqualified workers, 102; productive labour system, 71, 80n1, 183; teenagers, 106, 110, 114n16; women as secondary workers, 212; women managers, 177. *See also* employment; flexible work schedules; maternal employment; part-time work
Labour Standards Review Commission, 176
labour unions/organized labour, 48-49, 100, 101, 113n5, 170, 172, 175
language, role of, 69
Lapierre-Adamcyk, Éveline, 19
layoffs. *See* downsizing
Le Bourdais, Céline, 19
learning through unpaid household work, 81-97; background, 82-86; WALL Lifelong Learning Study, 86-94, 90t, 96n5, 96n8
Leave It to Beaver, 22-23
Lee, Christina, 42
Lefebvre, Pierre, 139
Legall, Paul, 67
leisure time concept, 172
Lesage, Jean, 132
lesbians/lesbian parents, 17, 28, 153, 162, 210-11
Lévesque, René, 132, 143n4
Liberal Party (Canada), 57
Liberal Party (Quebec), 133
libidinal economy, 153-56, 162
life course theoretical models, 45
lifelong learning, 81-97, 173, 181
Lifelong Learning (WALL) Study, 82, 86-94, 90t, 96n5, 96nn8-9
Litt, Jacquelyn, 25, 26
Little, Margaret Hillyard, 194-205, 207, 211, 213
Livingston, David, 83, 96n5
Lockhead, Clarence, 12-13
Logan, John R., 35
lone-parent families. *See* single-parent families
low-wage economy, 6, 15, 16, 61-62, 114n12
Lowe, E., 23
lumber industry, 131, 141, 143n10
Luxton, Meg, 23-24

Magna International, 113n5
Mahon, Rianne, 131
male breadwinner system: breadwinner ideology, 127-28; evolving family structures, 123-28, 149, 150, 157-58; gender equality, 61, 62, 70, 164, 168n2; globalization, 16; judgments of fathers who relinquish breadwinning, 115, 123-27, 150; male breadwinner/dependent wife caregiver concept, 11-12, 19-21, 48-50, 148, 156, 195, 208, 213; in new economy, 112; and public policy, 15, 195-200, 210, 212, 213; traditional family wage models, 15, 195-98; women as breadwinners, 5, 32, 33, 117, 119, 129n1; working-time standards, 189. *See also* gender contract; nuclear family
managers, 176-77, 185-86, 190, 192n14
Mandell, Nancy, 30-46, 39, 215
Manitoba, 111, 198, 205n5
manufacturing sector, 101, 105, 181
marginalized groups: care work options, 31; elders, 69; globalization-created, 16; minorities, 14-15, 19, 23, 34-35, 37-38; working-class families, 23
market citizenship, 214
marketplace. *See* labour/labour markets
Marois, Pauline, 135
marriage: common-law, 14, 15, 16; companionate, 21; definition of "spouse," 14; demographics, 13-15, 21, 50, 132; and economic security, 207; ideal of, 29n6, 149-52, 162; interracial, 15; marital conflict, 23, 178; popularity of, 13, 20, 24-25, 29n6, 61, 151; same-sex, 14, 16, 17, 161-62; as solution to poverty, 207-8; spousal caregiving, 40-41
Marshall, Katherine, 33, 215
Marxism/Marxist theory, 70, 71, 80n2
masculinity: cultural labels, 159, 215; and gender equality, 163, 165; hegemonic masculinity, 120-23; judgments of stay-at-home dads (SAHDs), 115, 123-27, 150; male-incentive structure, 166; masculine value, 148; social constructions, 6, 27-28, 112, 155, 161; universalism, 160. *See also* fathers/fathering; femininity; men
maternal employment, 47-63; class differences, 49-50, 213; conflicting policy, 6, 47-48; cross-national comparisons, 50-60; "dependency" concept, 21, 48-50, 195; history, 61; low-wage economy, 6, 61-62; single-parent families, 61, 192n15; supplemental income, 48; and

trade unions, 48-49; welfare state, 48-49, 202, 213
maternalism, 195-99, 204, 205n5, 207
maternity, feminist perspectives, 160-61
maternity leave, 54, 55, 63n6, 136, 150, 191n5
matrilineal diasporas, 35
matrilineal societies, 72-77
MAW. *See* Mothers Are Women
May, Elaine, 205n8
McCann, Deidre, 180-81
McDaniel, Susan A., 24, 206-18
McGraw, Lori A., 42
McJobs, 105, 113n5
men: axioms on work and family, 216; care work participation, 32, 39-41, 42, 43, 46, 112, 115-29; male friendships, 120-22; in matrilineal societies, 74; nurturing role, 159; permanent full-time employment statistics, 100-103; self-reliance, 121-22; social networking, 120-23, 127-28; spousal care, 40, 43; working-time intensification, 103. *See also* fathers/fathering; male breadwinner system; masculinity; stay-at-home dads (SAHDs)
mental illness, 23
Merleau-Ponty, Maurice, 168n9
Merrigan, Philip, 139
methodology: fathers and care work, 117-19, 129nn2-3; reduced-rate childcare, 141-42, 143n9; WALL Lifelong Learning Study, 86-88, 96n5, 96nn8-9, 97n11
mid-life care work/caregiving, 35-39, 41, 46
middle-class: constructions of home and family, 3, 4, 152, 156, 196-97; family violence, 20; impact of new economy, 107-8; paid/unpaid work, 4. *See also* nuclear family
migration, 15, 31, 35
Milan, Anne, 24
Milligan, Kevin, 133, 139
minimum wage, 143n4
Ministère de la Famille et des Aînés (Quebec), 136
Mink, Gwendolyn, 204
minorities, 14-15, 19, 23, 34-35, 37-38
Mitchell, B.A., 38
Mohawks/Mohawk language, 67, 80n3
mommy wars, 25
Montpetit Commission (Quebec), 132
Morel, Sylvie, 143
Morgan, George, 112
Morton, Ted, 17
motherhood. *See* mothers/mothering

Mothers Are Women (MAW), 87, 88, 95
mothers/mothering, 194-205; activist mothering, 78; approaches to, 19, 69-72; background, 194-95; devaluation of, 166; feminist views, 204; gendered dimensions, 34; ideology, 153, 159, 160; Indigenous perspectives, 67-80; intergenerational, 30-46; manufactured, 34; maternal emotion, 147; mommy wars, 25; motherhood penalty, 50; mothers' allowance, 195-99, 205n5; motherwork, 119; neo-liberal perspectives, 2, 11, 152, 168n3, 199-204; othermothering, 78; postcolonial discourse, 35; postmodernist discourse, 32-34; as primary wage earners, 5, 32, 33; social constructs, 168n12; social mothering, 26; traditional concept, 32-33, 34, 45-46, 127-28, 209; transnational, 16, 29n5; veneration of, 21, 127-28. *See also* maternal employment; maternalism; single mothers
Mulroney, Brian, 168n6
multi-generational families. *See* extended families
Multilateral Framework on Early Learning and Child Care, 137-38
Mutari, Ellen, 174, 192n9

nannies, 34, 107
Naples, Nancy, 78
National Child Benefit (NCB), 136, 203
National Childcare Program, 204, 209-10
National Children's Agenda (NCA), 137-38
National Study of the Changing Workforce, The, 113n7
National Survey of the Work and Health of Nurses, 105-6
nationalism, 133
Native Peoples. *See* Aboriginal families; First Nations; Indigenous families
Neamtam, Nancy, 135
Nelson, M.K., 28
neo-conservatism, 16-17, 24, 148
neo-liberalism: assumptions about work and family, 2, 152, 168n3, 199-204, 211, 213, 215-16, 216; children-based social policy, 203; citizenship regimes, 214-15; definition, 113n2, 199; gender neutral policy, 199-200, 202; governance, 106; male breadwinner system, 199-200; pro-corporate agenda and organized labour, 100; social policy, 203; views on mothers/mothering, 11, 199-204, 206; views on poverty, 203-4; welfare policies, 6, 194, 200-203; welfare-to-work programs,

53, 61, 62, 200-203, 214

Netherlands, 190

New Brunswick, 198, 205n5

New Brunswick Works (NB Works), 200-201

New Democratic Party, 200

new economy: alienation of workers, 134; downsizing, 101, 104-5, 111; earnings instability, 108, 114n12; employment intensification and diversification, 45, 96n8, 103-5, 113n6, 134, 142, 181-82; fringe banking, 114n10; future of, 111-13; good jobs/bad jobs, 49, 99, 100-103, 113n3; impact on families, 98-114, 142; service sector work, 16, 48-49, 102, 103, 105-6, 142; socio-historical background, 99-106; urbanization, 104, 106, 113n6

New Zealand: child payments and allowances, 59, 59t, 63n8; childcare provisions, 56, 56t, 57-58, 63n9; employment and poverty rates, 53t; family wage, 48, 50; gender wage gap, 52; maternal employment, 50-61; maternity leave, 54, 63n6; parental benefits, 55, 55t; part-time work, 51t; social spending, 57-60, 59t, 63n5; Working for Families program, 57-58

Newfoundland, 60, 205n5

night work, 192n11

no-strike agreements, 113n5

non-standard families, 11, 18-20, 23, 28, 157

non-standard work, 5, 15-16, 100-102, 104, 113n4, 181-82

Nordic countries, 51, 59, 62, 210. *See also* specific countries

Norway, 50-60, 51t, 55, 55t, 56t, 59t, 166

Nova Scotia, 198, 205n5

nuclear family, 11-29; changing trends, 16-17; Family Coalition Party platform, 17; family violence, 20; gendered roles, 22, 70-71; "Golden Age," 20-24; Haudenosaunee Confederacy, 76; ideal of, 4, 11-12, 20, 24-27, 106, 155-56, 165, 198; mothers' allowances, 198; and non-standard families, 18-20; privileging of, 3, 17-20, 21, 70; state income support, 52-55; status of women, 21, 22-23; television portrayals, 22-23. *See also* public policy

occupation segregation, 184

occupational exclusions, 6, 190

one-parent households. *See* single-parent families

Ontario: childcare, 56-57; Conservative governance, 143n2; Douglas Creek Estates protest, 67, 76, 77, 80n3; Family Coalition Party platform, 16-17; Kanesatake-Oka protest, 76, 77, 80n3; male caregivers, 40; mothers' allowance, 198, 205n5; Six Nations Reclamation protests, 77; stress levels survey, 110-11; Supports to Employment Program (STEP), 200-201; workfare programs, 201-2

Ontario Superior Court, 14

opt-out policies, 181-82, 190, 193n26

Organisation for Economic Co-Operation and Development (OECD), 172, 179, 183

other mothers (othermothering), 19, 31, 32, 35, 78

Out of School Care (New Zealand), 58

overtime work: expectation of, 5; increased use of, 177, 186-87; regulating, 6, 170-71, 174-76, 187, 189-90; unpaid, 105, 176, 185, 192n14; and working-time regimes, 181, 183, 184

Overwaitea, 103

Owram, Doug, 21-22

paid/unpaid work: assumptions about, 2, 5, 60, 81-82, 129, 156; background, 82-86; care work–paid work relationships, 7, 25-28, 40, 43-44, 85-86, 130-43, 168nn10-11, 206-18; choice or necessity, 3, 24-26, 142, 154, 194-95, 201, 207-10, 213-14; domestic work, 197, 198; equitable distribution of, 6, 189; European model, 68; gendered patterns, 4, 70-71, 171, 216; hours of, 176-79; learning through unpaid work, 81-97; middle class, 4, 157; shifting time structure, 104-5; social provisioning, 206-9, 213, 216-18; teenagers, 110, 114n13; WALL Lifelong Learning Study, 82, 86-94, 90t, 96n5, 96n8; women's share, 5, 140, 178, 212-13. *See also* employment; overtime work

parental benefits. *See* benefits

Parental Wage Assistance Program, 133

parenting: approaches to becoming, 14, 157, 204n1; changing nature of, 117, 168n3; as collaboration, 32-33; gay fathers, 150; gendered constructions, 125-28, 147-50; impact of new economy, 106, 108, 112, 114n17; lesbians/lesbian parents, 17, 28, 153, 162, 210-11; marital status, 26, 29n6; parent-child relationship survey, 111, 114n15; parental rights, 166; parenting resource centers,

128-29; parents as care receivers, 43; pivot generation, 36; sandwich generation, 39-41; social constructions of, 26, 159-60, 162; stress levels, 110-11; work and family balance, 212. *See also* benefits; children; social networks

Parsons, Talcott, 22

part-time work: access to benefits, 179, 184, 190, 193n29; averaging work hours, 192n19; Commission of Inquiry (1983), 193n29; cross-national comparisons, 51t, 190; by gender, 51t, 178-79; growth of, 15, 61, 101, 103, 173, 178-79, 181-82; maternal employment, 48-49, 194; regulation, 6, 188-89; single mothers, 196-97; welfare-to-work programs, 202; women's share, 25, 81, 178-79, 184, 196-97. *See also* flexible work schedules

Parti Québécois, 132

paternal leave, 137, 143n5, 150

paternalism, 132, 133, 150, 160, 161, 214

payday loans, 114n10

Penning, Margaret J., 42

personal communities, 19

personal service workers. *See* domestic service

phallocentrism, 160, 161

pivot generation, 36

playgroups/play dates, 87, 118, 122, 123, 125, 127

Popovic, Andrija, 39-40

Porteous, Jenny, 42

post-secondary education, 108-9, 110, 198

post-structuralism, 149-50, 154-55, 215

postcolonialism, 35, 46

postmodernism, 32-34, 206-7, 210-11, 215

poverty/poverty rates: anti-poverty programs, 133, 140-41; and employment, 45, 49, 53t; gender divide, 6-7, 168n12; marginalization of, 23; marriage as solution, 207-8; neo-liberal views, 203-4; one-parent households, 52-53, 53t, 157-58; racialization of, 44-45

power relationships: corporate power, 99-100, 106; family, 20, 21, 153-54; redistribution of, 165-66; social power, 217

presenteeism, 104

Preston, Valerie, 112

Prince Edward Island, 205n5

private/public space, 11-12, 27

production workers, 177

productivity, 71, 80n1, 183, 188

professionals, 177, 185-86, 187, 190, 192n14, 193n26

provisioning, 217-18, 218

public policy: care work/caregiving, 43-45, 47-63, 130-43, 167-68; child support allowances, 133-34, 136; childcare, 47-63, 164-65, 196, 204, 210, 212-13; family-oriented, 3-5, 11-12, 16-17, 132-41, 166-67, 168n7, 184, 214-16; flexible work options, 44, 46, 181-82, 183; gender equality, 155, 160, 163-67, 183-84; immigration and nuclear families, 19, 29n3; Indigenous self-determination, 76-78; integration of work and family, 25-26, 28; life course theoretical models, 45; maternal employment, 47-63; mothers' allowances, 195-99, 205n5; National Childcare Program, 204, 209-10; nuclear family as basis, 11-12, 19; regulation of working time, 172-76, 179-83, 188-91, 191n3, 191n5; state income support, 52-55; welfare policy, 6, 168n6, 195-99, 205n5; welfare-to-work programs, 53, 61, 62, 200-202; work-time regulation, 7, 172-84, 187-91, 191n3, 191n5, 192nn11-12, 192n25. *See also* benefits; neo-liberalism; social spending; tax policy

public transit, 104

pulp-and-paper workers, 112

Pupo, Norene, 98-114, 209, 212

Putman, Robert, 98, 113n1

Quebec, 130-43; Act Respecting Child Day Care, 136; anti-poverty programs, 133, 140-41; Campaign 2000, 140-41; Catholic Church, 130, 131, 132, 143n3; *centres de la petite enfance* (CPEs), 138-39, 143n8; changing economy, 134-35; child allowance policy, 133-34, 136, 210; childcare, 130, 136, 137-39, 141-43, 143nn6-7, 209-10; Conservative Party, 138; demographics, 13, 25, 130-34; family-oriented policies, 3, 5, 132-37, 139-41, 143, 210; historical overview, 130-32, 143; Liberal Party, 138; minimum wage, 143n4; Ministère de la Famille et des Aînés, 136; Montpetit Commission, 132; patriarchal traditions, 131-32, 143; progressivism, 133, 143; pronatalist policies, 130, 133, 143; Quiet Revolution, 130, 132-33; Summit on the Economy and Employment, 135; Union Nationale, 132; welfare system, 60, 132, 201; women in labour force, 207, 210; women's status, 130, 132, 133, 140. *See also* benefits

Quebec Longitudinal Study of Child Development (QLSCD), 137, 139

Québécois identity, 131
Quist, Dave, 16

race/racism: discrimination against minorities, 23; government policies, 29n3, 75-76; income gap, 44-45; mothers' allowances, 196; racialized care work, 31, 32, 34-35
railway sector, 192n20
Rake, Katherine, 52
Ray, R.O., 83
Recreation Subsidy (New Zealand), 58
reproductive technologies, 14, 17
residential schools, 18, 29n3, 69, 74
resistance, 67-80, 213
resource extraction jobs, 101, 131
retail sector, 103, 181
Reyes, Angela, 35
risk-management plans, 181
robotization, 101
Roseneil, Sasha, 26
Rosie the Riveter, 23
Roy, Laurent, 133, 140
Rubery, Jill, 174, 192nn8-9
Rubin, Beth, 112-13
Ruddick, Sara, 157
Ruderman, Marian N., 86

Salazar Parreñas, Rhacel, 29n4
same-sex couples, 14, 16, 17, 29n2, 150, 161-62
sandwich generation, 35-41, 39-41
Sarkisian, Natalia, 28
Saskatchewan, 111, 198, 202, 205n5
Schild, Veronica, 217
Schooler, Carmi, 81
"second shift," 81-82, 212
self-determination and resistance, 69, 72, 75, 76-80, 213
self-employment, 15, 101, 191n2
self-sufficiency projects, 200-203
Sempruch, Justyna, 1-7, 147-69, 207, 208, 209, 210, 211, 215
Sennett, Richard, 112
service sector: expansion of, 16, 48-49, 102, 103, 105-6; hours worked, 177; twenty-four hour service, 173, 211; types of occupations, 100, 141
servicing work. See domestic service
Sevenhuijsen, Selma, 118
severance pay, 192n12
sexual citizenship, 161-62, 167
sexual harassment, 163
sexuality: access to social benefits, 150; libidinal economy, 153-56, 162; non-standard forms, 159; reproductive

choices, 14; social constructions, 12, 27, 150-53, 162
Siltanen, Janet, 15
Simonen, Leila, 26
single mothers: children's illness, 58; by choice, 13, 194, 204n1; "doing family," 28; economic status, 50, 157-58; employment of, 203-4; mothers' allowance, 195-99, 205n5; neo-liberal policies, 199-204; self-sufficiency project, 200-203; welfare policies, 6, 133-34, 143n2, 168n6, 194-95; welfare-to-work programs, 200-203. See also part-time work
single-parent families: childcare costs, 56, 56t; debt load, 108; employment, 61, 192n15, 203-4; family-in-decline arguments, 16; family violence, 20; growth in, 181; impact of new economy, 106, 109-11; marginalization, 22; poverty rates, 53t
Six Nations Reclamation protests, 77
Sixties Scoop, 18, 29n3, 69, 75
skip-generation households, 19, 37
Slotsve, George, 176
Smart, Carol, 31
Smith, Mark, 174, 192n8, 192n9
social activism, 70, 71-72, 213
social citizenship, 7, 152, 156-58, 164, 167, 206-7, 208, 214
social constructions: body, 168n2; maternal absence, 152; sexuality, 12, 27, 150-53, 162; stay-at-home dads, 115, 123-27, 150
social economy, 135
social institutions, 214. See also community/community responsibility
social mothering, 26
social networks, 117-27; children as basis for, 120-21; cross-gender, 122-23; and domestic responsibilities, 117-19; gendered nature of, 119-20, 122, 123-27; institutional arenas, 118; involvement by fathers, 119-27; men's friendships, 120-23; playgroups/play dates, 87, 118, 122, 123, 125, 127; and stay-at-home dads, 123-27, 150
social policies, patriarchal dominance, 132, 133, 160, 161, 214
social provisioning, 206-9, 213, 216-18
social reproduction, 134-35, 143
Social Sciences and Humanities Research Council (SSHRC), 96n5, 129n4
social spending: child payments and allowances, 59-61, 59t, 133-34, 136, 158, 210; childcare programs, 47-48, 49, 53-58, 56t, 59t, 136-39, 204, 209-10; cross-

national comparisons, 53-60, 55t, 56t, 59t; neo-liberalism, 199; Nordic countries, 51, 59, 62; nuclear family basis for, 11-12; public policy, 61, 133, 200, 203; reduction in, 113n2; self-sufficiency project, 200-203; state income support, 52-55. *See also* benefits
socio-cultural citizenship, 167
socio-economic factors: class divisions, 107-8; socio-economic citizenship, 167; wage/income gap, 44-45, 50, 52, 60, 63n4, 178, 192n9. *See also* household income
sperm banks, 14
Spitze, Glenna, 35, 43
sports, 112, 126, 128
spousal care, 40-41, 43
Stacey, Judith, 26-27
standard working time, 191n7
Statistics Canada, 28n1, 108-9, 129n1, 140
stay-at-home dads (SAHDs): community judgments of, 115, 123-27, 150; cross-gender friendships, 122-23; increasing numbers, 5, 115, 129n1, 157; and infants, 125-26; male friendships, 120-23; methodology, 117, 129nn2-3; parenting resource centers, 128-29; self-reliance/looking inferior, 121-22; social acceptance, 126-27; social networking, 115, 119-27. *See also* fathers/fathering
Stobert, Susan, 39-40
stress/stress management: burdens of caregiving, 41-43, 46; health care providers, 105-6; impact of new economy, 104, 105, 109-11; increased working hours, 185; increasing levels of, 181; stress levels survey, 110-11
student loans, 110
subject autonomy, 154
substance abuse, 23
suburbanites, 77
Summit on the Economy and Employment (Quebec), 135
Supports to Employment Program (STEP), 200-201
surrogate parenting, 14
Survey of Labour and Income Dynamics, 140
Sweden, 50-60, 51t, 53t, 55t, 56t, 59t, 166, 169n13

tax policy: Canada Child Tax Benefit (CCBT), 136, 158; family-related, 16-17, 43, 53, 55-57, 59t, 136, 158; income tax, 51, 136, 140, 158

technology impact, 99, 100, 101, 103, 104-5, 113n7, 173, 211
teenagers, 106, 110, 114nn13-14, 114n16
telecommuting, 5
temporary work, 15, 101
Thurer, Shari L., 23
time, control over, 170-72, 179, 180, 181, 187, 215-16
Toronto, 104
trade unions, 48-49, 100, 101, 113n5, 170, 172, 175
traditional family. *See* nuclear family
transnationalism, 14, 15-16, 29nn4-5
transportation sector, 175, 193n26
transracial adoption, 14
transsexuals, 17
Treaty of Amsterdam (1998), 163
Tremblay, Richard E., 139
Turcotte, Martin, 13
twenty-four hour service economy, 173

UAW (United Auto Workers), 113n5
unemployment, 192n8, 197, 199, 201, 203
Unemployment Insurance, 197, 198. *See also* Employment Insurance (EI)
United Kingdom: childcare costs, 56, 56t; employment and poverty rates, 53t; house work skill transfer, 83-84; maternal employment, 50-61; multi-generational families, 38; parental benefits, 55, 55t; part-time work, 51t, 190; regulation of working time, 191n5; social spending, 59-60, 59t
United Nations, 58
United States: childcare costs, 56t; employment and poverty rates, 53t; Fair Labor Standards Act, 187, 192n25; family-based ideology, 205n8; income support payments, 60, 61; maternal employment, 50-61; multi-generational families, 38; organized labour, 113n5; parental benefits, 54-55, 55t; part-time work, 51t; social spending, 59t; universal family allowances, 63n2; work-time regulation, 187-88
Universal Child Care Benefit, 138
universal childcare, 26, 139
universalism, 11-29
upper-class families, 107-8
urbanization, 104, 106, 113n6, 113n8, 131

Valverde, Mariana, 155
Vancouver, BC, 15, 38
Vincent, Clark E., 16

Vuorela, Ulla, 29n4

wages/wage labour: background, 71, 74-75, 213; European model, 68, 213; gender constructs, 4, 15, 22, 52, 156; gendered wage gap, 44-45, 50, 52, 60, 63n4, 178, 192n9; living-wage concept, 101, 151; maternal employment, 61-62; primary wage earners, 33-34; role in work-family debate, 1, 70-71; wage-labour paradigm, 77-78; wage-supplement programs, 133, 201; weekly earnings, 102. *See also* family wage model; paid/unpaid work
Wagner, Sally Roesch, 73
Walker, Alexis J., 42
Walker, Janet., 16
WALL Lifelong Learning Study, 82, 86-94, 90t, 96n5, 96nn8-9
Wallace, Joan, 193n29
Walmartization, 113n5
Walters, Vivienne, 41
Walzer, Susan, 116
Waters, Johanna L., 15
wedfare, 208
Weis, Lois, 112
welfare state, 48-49, 59, 142, 158, 198-99
welfare system: access to benefits, 132, 150, 158, 165, 214; history, 148, 195-99, 200; maternal employment, 202, 213; mothers' allowance, 195-99, 205n5; public policies, 6, 60, 132, 168n6, 194, 195-99, 200-203, 213; single mothers, 6, 133-34, 143n2, 168n6, 194-95; social spending, 59-60, 59t; welfare diamond/welfare triangle, 129; welfare-to-work programs, 53, 61, 62, 200-203, 214
West, Candace, 161
Westinghouse, 101
white-collar workers, 193n26
Williams, Cara, 41
Williams, J., 12, 28
Wilson, Susan, 30-46, 215
women: axioms on work and family, 216; colonization and women's roles, 4, 67-69, 72-76, 143n1, 213; "dependency" concept, 21, 48-50, 195, 208; essentialist rationalizations, 12; European working-hours study, 174; exploitation of, 31; full-time employment, 100-103, 215; impact of new economy, 109-11; increased employment opportunities, 45, 49, 165; nuclear family status, 21, 22-23; postmodernist views, 206-7; as primary wage earners, 5, 32, 33-34, 186; as secondary citizens, 132; as secondary work-

ers, 212, 213; social networks, 119-20, 122; traditional roles, 197, 213-15; types of work, 5, 15-16, 103; working-time standards, 170-71. *See also* Haudenosaunee Confederacy; labour/labour markets; work and family discourse
women's suffrage, 73
work: approaches to, 69-72; care work versus paid work, 2, 40, 43, 130-43, 176-79; choice versus necessity, 207-10, 213-14; culture of, 103-5, 186-87, 190, 216; feminist perspectives, 27-28, 213-15; gendered patterns, 15-16, 22, 44-45, 49, 50-53, 102-3, 111-12, 151; good jobs/bad jobs, 49, 99, 100-103, 113n3, 134; Indigenous perspectives, 67-80; job satisfaction, 102; male-incentive structure, 166; neo-liberal views, 2, 11, 152, 168n3, 199-204; productivity levels, 71, 80n1, 183; racialized patterns, 44-45; role overload, 185-86; self-sufficiency projects, 200-203; socio-historical background, 99-106; socio-political topography, 165; time bind, 215-16; work-rich/work-poor dichotomy, 212; workplace restructuring, 134. *See also* households/housework; paid/unpaid work; wages/wage labour; working-time regimes
work and family discourse: background, 1-7; as choice, 24-26, 206, 213-14; as conflict, 3, 28, 107, 166, 176, 192n23, 213-14; control over time, 170-72, 179, 184-85, 187, 216; direct linkage between, 85, 216; feminist perspectives, 206-18; gender constructs, 2, 22, 70-71, 186, 197, 216; *Horizons* report, 206; and job types, 172-74, 185-86; reconciliation policies, 2, 3, 184; work-life balance, 11-12, 24-28, 77-78, 107-8, 116, 182-87, 206-7, 211-16. *See also* male breadwinner system; working-time regimes
workday standards, 174-77, 184-85, 189-90, 191n7, 193n30, 211
worker displacement, 134
workfare programs, 113n2, 201-2
working-class families, 20, 23, 107-8, 112
Working for Families program (New Zealand), 57-58
working-time regimes, 170-93; absenteeism, 104, 192n13, 192n21; background, 170-72; collective bargaining and agreements, 170, 172, 175; components and types, 172-74, 181-82; derogations, 181-82, 190; European "social" market model, 188-89; exemptions and flexibility, 6,

46, 174-75, 179, 180-82, 183; Fair Labor
Standards Act, 187, 192n25; federal
working-time regimes, 174-76; gender
equality, 155, 174, 183-84, 187-91;
hours of paid and unpaid work, 176-79;
hours-of-work rules, 174-77, 184-85,
189-90, 191n7, 193n30, 211; intensification and diversification, 45, 96n8, 103-
5, 113n6, 134, 142, 181-82; job
insecurity, 111; labour standards, 170-
71, 192n17; leave policies, 192n22; leisure time concept, 172; market model,
187-88; regulation of working time, 7,
172-84, 187-91, 191n3, 191n5,
192nn11-12; restructuring, 192n8; time
bind, 216; working-time obligation,
104-5; working while ill/presenteeism,
104; workplace culture, 186-87. *See also*
flexible work schedules; overtime work
workweek, 174-77, 184-85, 186, 187,
188-89

young adults, 43
young families, 108, 109-11, 113n9,
114n10
Young, Iris, 168n9
Young, Sherri, 75
Yuval-Davis, Nira, 164

Zeytinoglu, Isik Urla, 193n29
Zimmerman, Don, 161
Zimmerman, Mary, 25, 26